A Guide to EARLY YEARS & PRIMARY TEACHING

Edited by
DOMINIC WYSE & SUE ROGERS

Los Angeles | London | New Delhi
Singapore | Washington DC | Melbourne

Los Angeles | London | New Delhi
Singapore | Washington DC | Melbourne

SAGE Publications Ltd
1 Oliver's Yard
55 City Road
London EC1Y 1SP

SAGE Publications Inc.
2455 Teller Road
Thousand Oaks, California 91320

SAGE Publications India Pvt Ltd
B 1/I 1 Mohan Cooperative Industrial Area
Mathura Road
New Delhi 110 044

SAGE Publications Asia-Pacific Pte Ltd
3 Church Street
#10-04 Samsung Hub
Singapore 049483

Editor: Jude Bowen
Development editor: Sarah Turpie
Assistant editor: George Knowles
Production editor: Nicola Marshall
Copyeditor: Sharon Cawood
Proofreader: Kate Campbell
Indexer: Silvia Benvenuto
Marketing manager: Lorna Patkai
Cover design: Wendy Scott
Typeset by: C&M Digitals (P) Ltd, Chennai, India
Printed and bound by CPI Group (UK) Ltd,
Croydon, CR0 4YY

First published 2016

Library of Congress Control Number: 2015955045

British Library Cataloguing in Publication data

A catalogue record for this book is available from the British Library

ISBN 978-1-4739-0693-8
ISBN 978-1-4739-0694-5 (pbk)

A Guide to EARLY YEARS & PRIMARY TEACHING

CONTENTS

EDITOR BIOGRAPHIES

Dominic Wyse is Professor of Early Childhood and Primary Education at the UCL Institute of Education, UK, and Head of the Department of Learning and Leadership. The main focus of his research is curriculum and pedagogy. Key areas of his work are the teaching of English language, literacy and creativity. Dominic has led or been a participant in more than 20 funded research projects. He is the author of more than 40 research articles and chapters, and 20 books. These include major international research volumes for which he is the lead editor (including on curriculum, and on research methodology), and best-selling books for teachers and educators that are now in their third edition. Dominic has been an editor, and on the editorial board, of internationally recognised research journals. He is currently an editor of the *Curriculum Journal*, one of the journals of the British Educational Research Association (BERA); he is also an elected member of the BERA Council. He has been consulted by major international companies in relation to the development of packages and approaches that support learning in schools.

Sue Rogers PhD is Professor of Early Years Education at the UCL Institute of Education, UK. Her research explores the relationship between play, curriculum and pedagogy in early childhood, including young children's perspectives and the nature of child–adult interactions in educational settings. Recent work has focused on the use of research evidence in educational practice as a way of improving expertise in the early childhood workforce. Alongside leading several funded projects concerned with both early years pedagogy and professional learning, she has published widely in the field of early childhood education, including three books: *Inside Role Play in Early Childhood Education: Researching Children's Perspectives* (Routledge, 2008, with Julie Evans); an edited collection on play pedagogy entitled *Rethinking Play and Pedagogy: Concepts, Contexts and Cultures* (Routledge, 2011); and *Adult Roles in the Early Years* (Open University Press, 2012, with Janet Rose). Sue is a visiting scholar at the City College, City University New York, developing joint projects on professional learning in highly diverse early childhood urban communities.

CONTRIBUTOR BIOGRAPHIES

Vivienne Marie Baumfield is co-leader of the Centre for Research in Professional Learning at the University of Exeter. Her research focuses on the role of inquiry in teachers' learning and promotes collaborative school–university research partnerships. She taught for 12 years in inner-city schools in the North East of England before taking up her first post in a university.

Gary Beauchamp is Professor of Education and Associate Dean (Research) in the School of Education at Cardiff Metropolitan University. He worked for many years as a primary school teacher, before moving into higher education where he has led undergraduate and postgraduate courses in education. His research interests focus on ICT in education, particularly the use of interactive technologies in learning and teaching. He has published widely in academic journals, books and research reports. In addition, he is Additional Inspector for Estyn, Chair of Governor in a primary school and has served as external examiner for many universities.

Holly Bowman is currently the head teacher at Emneth Nursery School and Children's Centre, Wisbech, Norfolk, and has been working within the early years sector for over 20 years. She started her early career as a nursery nurse then pursued QTS, teaching both nursery and reception-aged children. Her passion is working with the children and families of the under-5s.

Mark Brundrett taught in secondary, middle and primary schools and was a head teacher for a number of years before entering higher education. He has subsequently held posts as Director of the International MBA in Education at the University of Leicester, Professor of Education at the University of Hull and Senior Research Consultant at Manchester University and he is currently Professor of Education at Liverpool John Moores University. He is executive editor of *Education 3–13: International Journal of Primary, Elementary and Early Years Education.*

Cathy Burnett is Professor of Literacy and Education at the Sheffield Institute of Education, Sheffield Hallam University. She worked as a teacher and teacher educator for many years and has published widely for academic and professional audiences. She has diverse professional interests in pedagogy, teacher development and the role of enquiry, drama, media and talk in learning. Her research currently focuses on relationships between literacy and digital technologies in primary education and she is particularly interested in how children and teachers work and play with digital texts in educational settings. Cathy is Vice President of the United Kingdom Literacy Association.

Karen Daniels is a Senior Lecturer in Primary and Early Years English at Sheffield Hallam University. She leads the development of provision for English across Primary and Early Years initial teacher education courses. Her recent research focuses on children's language and literacy learning throughout their first year of school, with an emphasis on the role of children's cultural agency in language and literacy development. Prior to working at Sheffield Hallam, Karen worked as a Key Stage 1 and Foundation Stage teacher and as an Early Years Outreach teacher/ area SENCO and a Children's Centre Lead Teacher.

Corinne Davis has worked in education for 32 years as a mainstream primary classroom teacher, in early years provision and across SEN in a pre-school home visiting service and primary support service. She has been a SENCO for approximately 20 years and is currently working with two mainstream culturally diverse primary schools in the London Borough of Barking and Dagenham.

Chandrika Devarakonda is a senior lecturer in the Faculty of Education and Children's services at the University of Chester. Her research interests include inclusion, diversity, international perspectives of early childhood, and children's rights.

Pamela Di Nardo is currently the head teacher of one large non-denominational, multicultural school and nursery class within North Lanarkshire Council. During session 2014–15, she was the shared head teacher of two non-denominational, multicultural schools and nursery classes operating across two separate associated school groups and catchment campuses. Pamela is currently a member of Education Scotland's Numeracy and Mathematics action forum and has previously worked as a National Development Officer in assessment with Education Scotland and as a Probationer Teacher Support Officer with Falkirk Council.

Pete Dudley is an education leader, writer and researcher. Currently responsible for education in Camden, London, Pete was a primary and secondary teacher and for four years led Labour's Primary National Strategy. He introduced Lesson Study into the UK and has overseen its development since 2001. It is the subject of his book, *Lesson Study: Professional Learning for our Time*, (2015, Routledge). He owns LessonStudy.co.uk, Europe's most popular source of free Lesson Study materials.

Bernadette Duffy is Head of the Thomas Coram Centre in Camden, London which has been identified as a particularly successful school by Ofsted. She has been a member of a number of Department of Education advisory committees and contributed to the development of the *Early Years Foundation Stage Framework*. Bernadette is the author of *Supporting Creativity and Imagination in the Early Years* and co-editor with Dame Gillian Pugh of *Contemporary Issues in the Early Years*.

Rachel Edmondson has been a primary and early years teacher in inner-city London for over 20 years. She has a background in supporting mathematics teaching and learning in schools, including working as a local authority mathematics consultant. She has been involved in various academic research projects and has completed her own doctoral research in collaborative group work.

Steven Ford QC practises exclusively in the field of personal injury and is a specialist in child abuse and other psychiatric injury claims. He represents local authorities and private social care, health and education providers, charities and religious bodies in claims concerning assault, abuse and neglect, and social care, health care and educational negligence. He appears before disciplinary tribunals and at inquests and other enquiries. He advises public sector and corporate bodies on compliance issues associated with his areas of practice.

Josh Franks is a primary school teacher working in the London borough of Islington and a tutor/lecturer working on the Primary PGCE at UCL Institute of Education. His role involves developing partnership in ITE. His research interests include intrinsic motivation in the teaching and learning of writing.

Charles Hale is a specialist family QC of the Bar of England and Wales. He is a family advocate with particular expertise in all aspects of matrimonial finance and Schedule 1 (financial remedies in non-married cases) and private law proceedings. He has extensive experience of Public Law proceedings and the interface between the state and family life. Chambers and Partners recognise Charles as one of only five English family Barristers listed in their *Top 100 Barristers* list. He is a Fellow of the International Association of Matrimonial Lawyers and regularly lectures and writes on international family law and justice.

Louise Hayward was originally a teacher who taught in some of the most challenging schools in Scotland. Now Professor of Educational Assessment and Innovation (University of Glasgow) her research interests lie in assessment, curriculum and pedagogy, social justice and educational change – topics on which she has written extensively. She was a member of the internationally renowned Assessment Reform Group. Throughout her career Louise has worked with policy makers and practitioners nationally and internationally seeking to bring research, policy and practice into closer alignment. She is an editor of the Curriculum Journal of the British Educational Research Association (BERA).

Sharon Hayward is Headteacher of Blairdardie Primary School in Glasgow. She is committed to research informed practice and has a particular interest in approaches to assessment where decisions taken are holistic, based on teachers' professional judgement. As a Headteacher she has worked with teachers, learners and parents to build assessment practices that are of the highest quality. Sharon chairs the Assessment Strategy Group for the City of Glasgow and has recently been appointed to an exciting new post where she will become an Attainment Advisor to support the Scottish Attainment Challenge, a programme designed to promote a first class education for every child in Scotland.

Steve Higgins is Professor of Education in the School of Education at Durham University. After working as a primary school teacher, he moved into higher education where his research interests focus on the use of digital technologies for learning and the use of evidence in professional practice.

Sacha Humphries graduated from St Andrew's University in 1994 with an MA (Hons) in Modern Foreign Languages. She started her career working in risk and compliance in the financial services industry for Equitable Life and Schroders before retraining to become a teacher in 2005. She has subsequently worked across a number of Cheshire schools as a Class Teacher, Assistant Head and a Deputy Headteacher. In her role as Deputy Headteacher, she was seconded to a school requiring Special Measures, which subsequently achieved a 'good' judgement from Ofsted within 12 months. She is currently the Headteacher of Saint Mary's in Congleton, Cheshire.

Amanda Ince is a lecturer in education at UCL Institute of Education. She works across Primary PGCE, MA and doctoral programmes. Her role includes working with schools and early years settings to develop partnerships in ITE, R&D and professional learning. Her research interests are cognitive dissonance and professional learning.

Lucy Jamison has been teaching for seven years in a four-form entry infant school in a culturally and socially diverse area of South London. She currently teaches Year 2, runs Forest School and leads on phonics and provision for more able pupils.

Raymond Kutscher Viola currently works full-time as a P5/6 teacher at Strathblane Primary School in Stirling. He is also currently supporting the development of literacy at the school, based on his previous dissertation findings and research. He particularly enjoys applying and adapting theories of learning and takes pride in the learning experiences he has facilitated to create positive attitudes to reading. Raymond has a Bachelor of Education (honours) degree and will soon be graduating with a Masters in Education at the University of Glasgow.

Gillian Lister has worked for many years as an educator specializing in early childhood. Since 2003 Gillian has worked at the Thomas Coram Centre in Camden, London supporting children from six months to five years. Her particular interests are in child development and person, social and emotion well-being. Gillian retired in summer 2015.

Kay Livingston is Professor of Educational Research, Policy and Practice in the School of Education at the University of Glasgow. Her research interests include the professional development of teachers, including peer mentoring and the inter-relationship of curriculum, assessment and pedagogy. She is a member of the Council of the Association for Teacher Education in Europe (ATEE) and Chair of ATEE's Research and Development Community on the Professional Development of Teachers. She is editor of the *European Journal of Teacher Education* and co-editor of the *Curriculum Journal*.

Sean MacBlain is currently Reader in Child Development and Disability at the University of St Mark & St John, Plymouth. Prior to working as an academic, Sean worked as a teacher in primary and secondary schools and later as an educational psychologist and continues in this field in his own private practice.

Ian Menter is Emeritus Professor of Teacher Education at the University of Oxford. From 2013–15 he was President of the British Educational Research Association and from 2007–09 he was President of the Scottish Educational Research Association. In the 1970s and 80s he taught in primary schools in central Bristol.

Rachel Miller trained to be a teacher through the Teach First graduate programme and after two years of teaching Year 3 pupils in Newham, East London, she is now enjoying a second teaching role within a Year 5/6 class in an outstanding school in Bristol. After graduating with BSc Psychology at the University of Liverpool, MSc in Occupational Psychology at the University of Nottingham and working in strategy for the Ministry of Justice, Rachel followed the footsteps of both her parents and her grandfather and entered the teaching profession with a PGCE from the

Institute of Education, University of London. With a passion for Humanities, particularly History, Rachel is currently enjoying exploring the management of a subject area as well as delivering a rich curriculum within her classroom.

Christine Parker has taught in primary, first and nursery schools in Sheffield, Leeds, Bradford and Peterborough for over 30 years. She has also worked in Karachi, Pakistan as an advisory teacher, supporting teachers in a wide range of settings to provide opportunities for active learning. Christine's research interests have included parental engagement in curriculum matters, children's mark making and meeting the developmental and learning needs of emergent multilingual children. Christine's more recent doctoral studies have focused on how a primary school team has developed a systemic approach to school leadership including themes of collaborative and responsive inquiry and social justice.

Liz Powlay is currently joint owner of Dandelions Day Nursery near Chester, a visiting lecturer for University of Chester and an established author. She has been working in Early Years in schools, for the LEA and the private and voluntary sector for over 25 years.

Neil Purcell was born in Cardiff in 1975 and completed an economics degree in Manchester before returning to Cardiff to train to be a teacher. He worked in three mainstream primary schools before specialising in working with students with SEBD. In 2008 Neil was awarded Special Needs Teacher of the year in Wales (part of the National Teaching Awards), having been nominated by a parent who had seen her son's life transformed while he was in Neil's class. Neil currently works in a SRB in Barry and loves the challenging but rewarding job. He continues to find ways to be the best and get the best he can for the students in his care.

Anne Robertson is a lecturer in primary education at the UCL Institute of Education. She has been a primary teacher for 40 years. She has worked in developing teaching and learning in several curriculum areas including science and mathematics. She has completed her doctorate in listening to children learning through a cognitive development programme in order to understand more fully how teachers can increase the impact on children's attainment. Her current research interests include supporting PGCE students to develop their understanding of how children best learn.

Janet Rose is a Reader in Education, Programme and Award Leader in Education Studies at Bath Spa University. She has over 20 years' experience of working in schools and early years settings and as a specialist early years teacher for several local authorities. She is currently the Academic lead for the Attachment Aware School project, which is a comprehensive programme of support for children affected by early attachment difficulties, trauma and neglect. Her most recent publication is *Health and Well-Being in Early Childhood* (Sage, 2015).

Sue Roffey is an educational psychologist, academic, author, activist and consultant. She is currently Associate Professor (adjunct) at Western Sydney University, Founder of Wellbeing Australia and Director of Growing Great Schools. She is based in London April to December and can be contacted via www.sueroffey.com

Vicky Sawka is lead artist on the Imaginary Communities project at Chol Theatre based in Huddersfield, West Yorkshire. She completed her MA in Applied Theatre at the Royal Central School of Speech and Drama in 2008 and has worked extensively with teachers and children in mainstream education since then. Vicky is currently undertaking a professional Doctorate in Applied Theatre at the University of Manchester questioning the relationship between Chol's Imaginary Communities approach and reflective practice in the classroom.

James Siddle is head teacher of St Margaret's CE Primary School in Lincolnshire. He is also the research lead for the Kyra Teaching School Alliance. James' work on digital feedback was part of the National College 'Closing the Gap' project and featured one of the first school-led randomised control trials.

Margaret Walker was a primary curriculum support teacher before becoming the headteacher of two primary schools, one rural and one in central Bristol. She then worked as an adviser for Bristol City Council and as an Ofsted inspector. She also taught at the University of the West of England. She now writes fiction for children between the ages of 8 and 13, including reading books and novels tackling social and emotional issues.

Joanne Waterhouse is a Senior Lecturer in Educational Leadership at the UCL Institute of Education. Her research interests are focused on leadership studies, particularly distributed leadership and leadership in context. She has also researched collaborative action research processes, and has published articles on the Third Space. Her methodological influences are narrative and dialogic interviewing processes. Joanne is currently involved in an international project on school autonomy and curriculum innovation and is in the process of formulating a conceptualization of contemporary curriculum leadership. Joanne worked for over 20 years in the primary sector and has had experience in a variety of roles, including headteacher, local authority advisor, Ofsted inspector and network facilitator with NCSL.

Felicia Wood has worked in education for 15 years as an English and Music teacher in secondary and primary practice. She has recently gained her MSc in Neuroscience and Education. Felicia also works part time in a research capacity, exploring the relationship between current neuroscience and effective educational practice, particularly for vulnerable learners.

ACKNOWLEDGEMENTS

Editor Acknowledgements

Our warmest thanks and appreciation go to all our authors who have risen to the challenges of this ambitious project to bring the best of research and the best of professional practice together.

This project would not have happened at all without the vision of Jude Bowen – it is always such a rewarding experience to work with Jude. Sarah Turpie has worked tirelessly in so many ways for the project. Nicola Marshall on book production; George Knowles' work on the manuscript; Lorna Patkai on marketing; and Amy Jarrold in the early commissioning are just a few of the many people at SAGE who have made this book and its online resources possible and such a pleasure to work on.

Dominic would like to dedicate this book to Olly who has just started his educational journey at university, and to Esther who has started the next phase of her life-long learning, in the world of paid work!

Sue would like to acknowledge the generosity of the many teachers who have shared their practice and wisdom with her over the years, and without whom this book would not have been possible.

Publisher Acknowledgements

The publishers would like to extend their warmest thanks to the following individuals for their time, help and feedback, which has helped shape this book.

Alexandra Troletti, Hillview School for Girls, Tonbridge, Kent
Diane Boyd, Liverpool John Moores University
Eleanor Cockerton, University of East Anglia
Helen Bradford, UCL Institute of Education
Helen Lewis, University of Wales Trinity Saint David
Jenny Carpenter, York St John University
Jonathan Glazzard, University of Huddersfield
Kate Reynolds, James Dixon Primary School
Mark Betteney, University of Greenwich
Peter Raymond, York St John University

GUIDED TOUR

HOW TO USE YOUR BOOK

LEARNING AIMS

This chapter will enable you to:

- reflect on your own and other people's
- consider different views about what m
- develop an understanding of the infl school, particularly your mentor.

Learning Aims
Detail what you will learn in each chapter

...at becoming a teach...
...to learn from some of the chal...
...d reflect on how differences in views a...
...gnised as opportunities to learn.

spotlight on practice

Dealing with different expectations and values

Matt is a student teacher in a primary school workin
his placement, he had a clear image of the kind of t
stand his pupils as individual learners and create i
where all his pupils could succeed. He wanted
as from him and from other people in th
opportunities where he and his p
constructivist approach

Spotlight on Practice
Short descriptions of practice that enable you to think more deeply about teaching and learning

developed t...
...ividual subjects or areas o...
...grapple with some quite complex is...
...the requirements for breadth and depth...
...erent, so that each learning experience builds...

putting it into practice

Planning together

Try planning with a colleague or colleagues as well...
...ow much can be learned from someone who has...
...meone with a 'fresh eye' can often contribut...
...t been thought of before. When doing...

...a of the key info...

Putting it into Practice
Suggestions for how to implement requirements and ideas for teaching and learning

Reflection Points
Help you to reflect either on what you have just read or your own practice or values

...e opportunities for dia...
...g accepted as static, standards s...
...rs and their mentors to discuss and de...
...at makes for a good teacher through peer dial...

reflection point

Reflect on your own experiences of learning and t...
makes for a 'good teacher'.

Reflect on whether you think professional sta...
describing a good teacher.

List the values you think are essential for a t...

for example, transnational organisati...
been encouraging the introduction of l...
argument to that referred to earlier, that p...
greater commitment and therefore to better...

Web Link

An interesting article in The Guardian ...
accessed through this web link, available...
global-development/2015/sep/16/futur...
early-childhood-development-sdg

Web Links
Direct you to relevant resources selected by the chapter author to help deepen your understanding of chapter topics

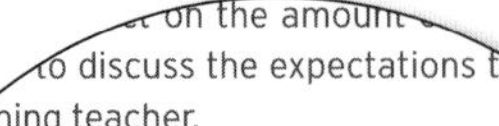

Summaries
Summarise the main points from the chapter to help you 'join the dots'

SUMMARY

The aim of this chapter was to stimulate your th
expectations of beginning teachers. In particular, yo
awareness of other people's different expectations o
ent opinions about what being a good teacher mea
serve as frameworks to stimulate discussion with
eaching means. In interpreting the standards, it i
t underpin people's views. Knowing that pe
will help you to feel more prepared if
discuss and learn from differe
mptions you hold i

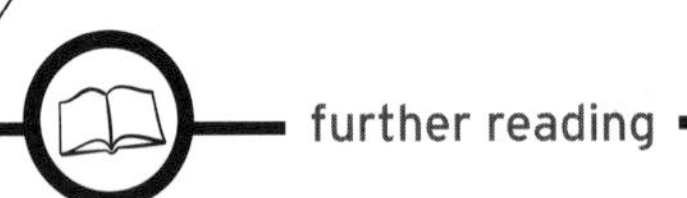

Bowell, P. & Heap, B. (2013). Distilling the principles
Process Drama: Enriching teaching and learning.
non-specialist on planning for drama.

Connected Learning: http://connectedlearning.tv/
and committed to developing pedagogies for t
principles with lots of links to resources.

els, K. (2013). Supporting the develo
research study into the i

Annotated Further Reading
Directs you to other sources of relevant advice and information, including SAGE journal content

Companion Website
A wealth of online resources tailored to each chapter can be found at **https://study.sagepub.com/wyseandrogers**, including classroom activities for you to use in your own teaching, author podcasts including top tips for employability, free access to SAGE journal articles and external website links.

pose of assessment, to s
untability data (Mansell et al., 20
purposes and the tensions that can aris
ance in your school and in your classroom. By

companion website

To access additional online resources please visit: h

Here you will find a classroom activity, free access
sources.

HOW TO USE THE COMPANION WEBSITE

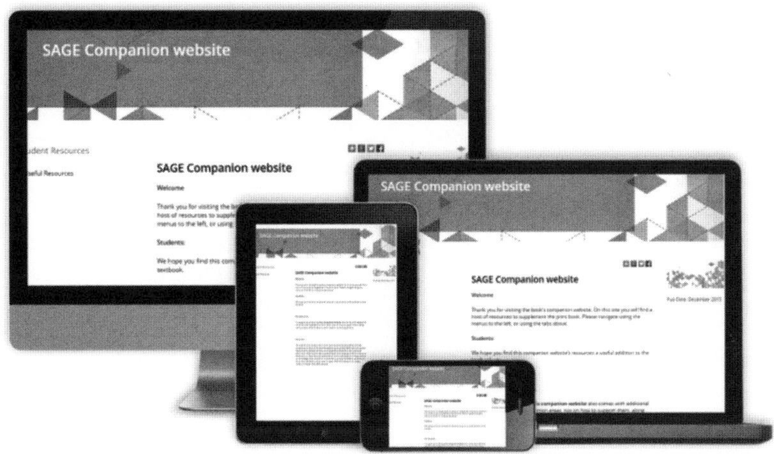

A Guide to Early Years and Primary Teaching is supported by a wealth of online resources for students to aid study, which are available at **https://study.sagepub.com/wyseandrogers**

- **Classroom activities** supply fun and engaging ideas to use in your own teaching.
- A series of **podcasts** from the chapter authors discussing key concepts offer an alternative learning style and provide you with even more insight into early years and primary teaching.
- **Web links** direct you to relevant resources to expand your knowledge and are an ideal starting place for assignments.
- **Selected journal articles** with free access are chosen for each chapter to expand your knowledge and reinforce your learning of key topics.

INTRODUCTION

Dominic Wyse and Sue Rogers

One of the most important things that we have learned from research on effective education is that teachers, and the quality of teaching, really matter. But how do people become effective teachers?

One important way is through their education and training, and for this there are three major aspects:

(a) high quality theory and research
(b) high quality experience of teaching
(c) thoughtful reflection about the connections between theory and practice.

Books and other sources about teaching are a vital part of the picture. There are some books about teaching that give very good accounts of theory and research. There are also popular books that provide readers with a sense of what high quality teaching is like. But there are perhaps no books to date, about early years and primary teaching, that systematically bring together theory and research with the knowledge and wisdom of practitioners in the way that has been done in this book. Our aim has been to publish a state-of-the-art, forward-looking account of early years and primary teaching. The book is written for (1) trainee teachers of both the early years and primary phases; and (2) their tutors/lecturers and mentors. It is intended to be suitable for anyone aiming to achieve Qualified Teacher Status (QTS) or equivalencies regardless of route. The main practical purpose of the book and the accompanying digital resources is to support trainees in their quest to become excellent teachers.

Our project began with serious market research into what key people in the field wanted from a new text about teaching. People working in all the different teacher education and training routes contributed their ideas. These ideas directly shaped the content of the book. We then sought out the people with the ideal knowledge and expertise to write the chapters. Most important of all was our requirement that each chapter should combine the most up-to-date theory *and* practice. The best way to achieve this was, in our view, to have at least two authors per chapter: one author, who had strong expertise that was mainly research based, collaborating with another author whose expertise was mainly based on their experience and practice as a teacher.

Although the idea of evidence-informed practice is familiar, it is still a challenge to relate theoretical knowledge and research studies meaningfully to practice. In order to ensure that rigorous research and theory is the backdrop to all chapters, the authors made careful selections of theory and research to be cited and then synthesized this work in order to maximize the relevance to the work of teachers. Scale of research was one factor in selection, for example the significance of large-scale quantitative work, prolonged qualitative work, longitudinal work and mixed methods designs. A significant aspect of evidence-informed practice includes randomised control trial evidence about 'what works'. Work such as that funded by the Education Endowment Foundation, in addition to the traditional research councils, was taken into account. As a result of this careful selection and synthesis, we have been able to keep the number of citations at a level that we hope will suit our readers' needs. The further reading suggestions enable readers to go into greater depth on specific topics, including more theory and research, as they wish.

Another innovation, compared with many texts in recent years, was to deliberately address early years *and* primary education together, whilst also taking account of their unique features. In one sense, this approach builds on the classic idea of teaching based on children's development. One of the great successes of early years research has been to consolidate its importance as a vital first phase of education. For example, the idea of early intervention has become a powerful international trend. However, the age at which the early years phase officially begins and ends differs according to the country that children are educated in, and in Europe in particular there is wide variation in the length of the early years phase and the start of formal schooling. Children's thinking continues to develop in very significant ways throughout their primary/elementary education and beyond. Primary education as a term is somewhat unique to the UK: in other countries of the world, 'elementary education' is more common (although the phrase 'elementary education' does have historical origins in England at the start of schooling in the 19th century). The international significance of primary education can also be seen, for example, in the continuing global emphasis on the *Sustainable Development Goals* that aim not only for universal primary education for all children, but also for this education to be of high quality (United Nations, 2014). For all these reasons and others, it makes sense to think about children's learning developmentally rather than in rigid educational phase boundaries.

Whilst we pragmatically recognize that this text and the accompanying digital resources are particularly appropriate for teachers in England, the content also explicitly takes account of work in the wider UK and other countries internationally (indeed, our authors include those from other UK countries and further afield such as Australia). At a time when England has an unusual combination of great potential for innovation in some schools, but also conservatism in some areas of policy, in our view it is important to link a clear focus on teacher education and training in England with an outward facing view of teaching in the 21st century that draws on research and practice in England and in other countries.

KEY DEVELOPMENTS IN EARLY YEARS AND PRIMARY TEACHING

Currently, educational provision for children under compulsory school age (the prescribed day following their fifth birthday – see below) in all countries of the UK is offered within a range of settings including: nursery classes; private and voluntary sector nurseries; children's centres; and primary schools. Since 1997, we have seen an unprecedented period of investment, development and change in early years education and care by successive governments, with the express aim to improve the fragmented nature of early years provision, reduce child poverty and disadvantage, and encourage more lone parents (and in particular mothers) back to work. The drive both to increase the quantity, and improve the quality, of early years provision in England led to the development of the *Early Years Foundation Stage* (EYFS; 2012), a framework for children from birth to compulsory school age. Compulsory school age is somewhat complicated in England. In 2014 the regulations were clarified as follows:

> Compulsory school age is set out in section 8 of the Education Act 1996 and the Education (Start of Compulsory School Age) Order 1998. A child reaches compulsory school age on the prescribed day following his or her fifth birthday (or on his or her fifth birthday if it falls on a prescribed day). The prescribed days are 31 December, 31 March and 31 August.

However, following a change to the admissions policy in 2011, in practice most children in England enter school when they are 4 years old. According to section 2.16:

> Admission authorities **must** provide for the admission of all children in the September following their fourth birthday. The authority **must** make it clear in their arrangements that, where they have offered a child a place at a school:

> (a) that child is entitled to a full-time place in the September following their fourth birthday
> (b) the child's parents can defer the date their child is admitted to the school until later in the school year but not beyond the point at which they reach compulsory school age and not beyond the beginning of the final term of the school year for which it was made
> (c) where the parents wish, children may attend part-time until later in the school year but not beyond the point at which they reach compulsory school age. (Department for Education, 2014: 24, emphasis in original)

The admission of young 4-year-olds into primary schools (rather than 'rising 5s' as was previously the case) means that it is essential for the range of educators including teachers to have a clear understanding of the EYFS. The EYFS is based on the following aims:

- setting the standards for children's learning, development and care from birth to compulsory school
- improving quality and consistency in the early years sector
- laying a secure foundation for future learning through individual learning and development planned around the individual needs and interests of the child
- providing equality of opportunity
- creating the framework for partnership working.

The EYFS sets out clear developmental goals for this age group. In turn, these are informed by the three Characteristics of Effective Learning (CoEL), which provide guidance for the types of teaching and learning approaches most suited to young children. These are:

- playing and exploring
- active learning
- creating and thinking critically.

The CoEL reflect a shift from 'what' children learn to 'how' children learn – a point of particular significance to adults working with young children. The EYFS includes references to 'enabling environments', both indoors and outdoors, that support such modes of learning. But it is possible to go further to think in terms of an 'enabling pedagogy', which also includes critically reflective adults who support children in ways which help them to acquire skills but are respectful of children's ideas, particularly in their playful activities (Rogers, 2014).

At the same time, there has been an explicit policy move towards an early years curriculum and pedagogy that ensure 'school readiness'. The increasing 'schoolification' of early years provision is also observed in countries such as Norway and France (Van Laere et al., 2012), New Zealand (Alcock and Haggarty, 2013) and the USA (Brown, 2013). In England, educational intervention in the lives of children from the age of 2 has been introduced for the most disadvantaged children. Many of these children will be located in primary schools due to the lack of available places in nurseries and childcare settings, thus placing further pressure on the sector to provide suitably qualified staff. Some of the tensions between child-centred and government approaches to raising standards in schools feature in several of the chapters in this book. However, professional dialogue and the development of shared understanding between early years and primary colleagues, informed by research and practice (an explicit feature of this book), can help to ensure a smooth transition for children as they progress in their education.

Perhaps the most significant changes to primary education have been seen in the shifting relationships between teacher professionalism, research and educational policy. In England, prior to the enactment of the Education Reform Act (ERA) 1988, teachers and schools had high levels of professional autonomy. Teachers planned the learning of their pupils in ways they saw fit based on their professional knowledge, in collaboration with colleagues, and informed by local education authority guidelines. Some teachers also actively engaged with research, for example through the emerging methodologies of practitioner research or through projects funded by the Schools' Council, in addition to study for Master's degrees and doctorates. The monitoring of standards was carried out through rigorous research, based on sampling the population of pupils (for example, the Assessment of Performance Unit: APU) not on national testing. Her Majesty's Inspectorate was regarded more as a group of external colleagues with sharp insight, who acted in a less punitive role than inspectors in what became Ofsted.

The enactment of the ERA 1988 provided the government with much greater control of teachers and schools, and introduced ideas such as 'market forces' into education. From that point onwards, schools were to demonstrate their standards through high test scores of their pupils, in part so that parents could choose the best schools, according to the market forces ideology. The ERA also brought the requirement that the Secretary of State for Education should establish a national curriculum and associated national testing system, hence bringing direct control of curriculum and assessment (and ultimately aspects of pedagogy) into the hands of government (this is not the case in Scotland, Wales and Northern Ireland as the first book-length analysis of national curricula in these countries showed (Wyse et al., 2013)).

Similar to the way in which governments have assumed more control over education, the place of research and its relationship to policy have also been subject to some tensions. One project that particularly exemplified these tensions was the Cambridge Primary Review (CPR). In part, this aimed to revisit the field of primary education in the way that the Plowden Report had done 40 years before. One significant part of the CPR was its research surveys (Alexander et al., 2010), which reveal the wealth of research that could have been used to underpin primary education policy. The findings of the CPR's own empirical work were reported in the book that summarized the outcomes of the CPR (Alexander, 2010). The CPR was accompanied by significant media attention, and hence reaction from the New Labour government of the day. In spite of this, ultimately the influence of research like the CPR on government policy seems to have been limited. A lack of influence of research can also be seen in the development of the current national curriculum (that was implemented after the CPR and Sir Jim Rose's government-commissioned review of the national curriculum in England), as can clearly be seen in the account by one of the expert group who advised the Conservative–Liberal Democrat coalition government of the day (see www.bera.ac.uk/promoting-educational-research/issues/background-to-michael-goves-response-to-the-report-of-the-expert-panel-for-the-national-curriculum-review-in-england).

At present, many primary teachers and schools maintain their professional identity through their passion to innovate in ways that are informed by their professional experience, and ideas that they encounter through their networks that include research networks. There is some government support for schools to innovate, but this is complicated by the fact that academies and free schools have more capacity for this than other schools. It is also complicated by national testing arrangements and by the national curriculum. The most significant shifts in the relationship between teacher professionalism, research and education policy have come as a result of the increasing amount of assessments, which in England begin with statutory assessment in the early years, then proceed towards the phonics screening check, and later statutory assessments and tests, for example when children are in Year 6 (ages 10 to 11). However, in spite of the context for educational policy (in England particularly), there is considerable opportunity for teachers and schools to collaborate in order to use their professional autonomy to explore new ways of helping children's learning. This guide exemplifies this kind of exploration by featuring innovative teaching closely linked to rigorous theory and research.

STRUCTURE OF THE BOOK

The innovations that are part of the book not only come from its rationale and content but also from its structural features. Each chapter of the book is oriented around a set of aims for students'/trainees' learning stimulated by the market research for the book, and by the authors' interpretation of the key learning required. The main body of the chapter addresses essential practical and professional areas of knowledge and their relation to theory and research. To support the aims of the chapter, and to further exemplify practice, there are several unique features. The *Spotlight on Practice* sections are vignettes that describe examples of practice in more specific detail and encourage critical reflections. The *Putting it into Practice* sections are shorter and give more direct recommendations for implementation in practice. Following succinct *Summaries* of the chapters as a whole, *Further Readings* are recommended. These further readings include recommendations that mainly focus on professional and practical learning but also on research and theory. There are also digital resources on a *Companion Website* for the book to support each chapter; these include *classroom activities* to use in your own teaching; *author podcasts* including top tips for employability; free access to SAGE *journal articles* and *book chapters* and *links* to external websites selected by the authors.

We hope you enjoy the book, that it supports your learning and teaching, and that we will have the chance to engage with you on the issues that it raises.

REFERENCES

Alcock, S. and Haggarty, M. (2013) 'Recent policy developments and the "schoolification" of early childhood care and education in Aotearoa New Zealand', *Early Childhood Folio*, 17(2): 21–6.

Alexander, R. (ed.) (2010) *Children, their World, their Education: Final Report and Recommendations of the Cambridge Primary Review*. London: Routledge.

Alexander, R., Doddington, C., Gray, J., Hargreaves, L. and Kershner, R. (eds) (2010) *The Cambridge Primary Review Research Surveys*. London: Routledge.

Brown, C. P. (2013) 'Reforming preschool to ready children for academic achievement: A case study of the impact of pre-k reform on the issue of school readiness', *Early Education and Development*, 24: 554–73.

Department for Education (DfE) (2014) *School Admissions Code*. London: DfE.

Rogers, S. (2014) 'Enabling Pedagogy', in J. Moyles, J. Payler and J. Georgeson (eds) *Early Years Foundations: Meeting the Challenge*. Maidenhead: Open University Press.

United Nations (2014) *The Millennium Development Goals Report 2014*. New York: United Nations.

Van Laere, K., Peeters, J. and Vandebroeck, M. (2012) 'The Education and Care Divide: the role of the early childhood workforce in 15 European countries', *European Journal of Education*, 47(4): 527–41.

Wyse, D., Baumfield, V., Egan, D., Gallagher, C., Hayward, L., Hulme, M., et al. (2013) *Creating the Curriculum*. London: Routledge.

1

BECOMING A TEACHER

Kay Livingston and Pamela Di Nardo

LEARNING AIMS

This chapter will enable you to:

- reflect on your own and other people's expectations of a beginning teacher
- consider different views about what makes for a 'good' teacher
- develop an understanding of the influence of those who support you in school, particularly your mentor.

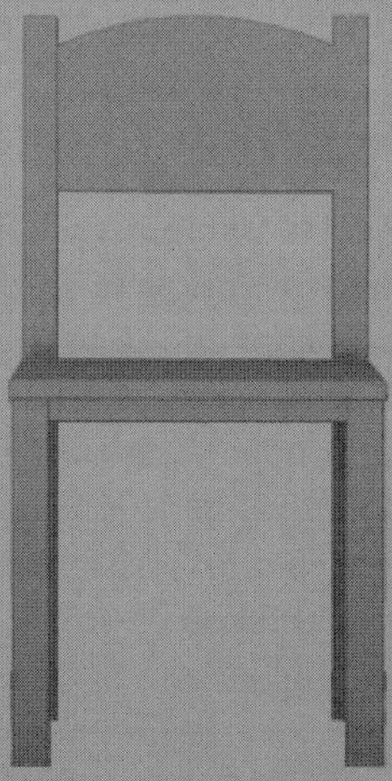

In the countries of the UK and beyond, there is a variety of routes into becoming a teacher, including university-led, school-led and a combination of school and university or other providers working in partnership or consortia arrangements. Different routes into becoming a teacher mean that the experiences for individuals differ, and diverse institutional and provider arrangements mean that within the main pathways into teaching there are also differences. In addition, teachers have their own personal and professional identities, and between schools and within schools their work is highly differentiated. However, results from the *Becoming a Teacher Project* conducted in England (Hobson et al., 2009) indicate that whilst statistically there are significant variations in beginning teachers' experiences of initial teacher education, these variations are largely 'washed out' by subsequent experiences of teaching in school. This does not imply that all teachers have the same experiences once they are in school but no matter their route into teaching they teach within the realities of school, and many teachers' experiences are influenced by similar factors – for example, relationships with pupils, parents and colleagues in school; curriculum and assessment policies; and quality assurance and accountability measures including teaching 'standards'.

The different pathways into teaching mean that for some beginning teachers their teacher training is mainly school-based whilst for others (who follow the university-led route) their first experiences in school as a teacher will be on a practice placement. Consequently, some beginning teachers may be more acutely aware of the differences in people's expectations and views when they are a student teacher, whilst for others it may not be until they are in their first year of teaching. The early phase of becoming a teacher considered in this chapter includes student teachers and those in their first year of teaching who are working towards qualified teacher status.

As a beginning teacher, you have to relate to and interact with others in your context on a daily basis. In the first section of the chapter, beginning teachers' own expectations and those of others in school are explored. The implications of contrasting views about models of teacher education, professional knowledge, values and learning and teaching are discussed. The impact of different expectations and views on the formation and re-formation of beginning teachers' identities will be considered. In the final section, those who support beginning teachers' professional development in school are discussed, particularly mentors.

DIFFERENT EXPECTATIONS OF A BEGINNING TEACHER

Beginning teachers generally look forward to taking up their first school placement with excitement and anxiety in equal measure. In a study with student teachers, Anspal et al. (2012) highlighted their mixed feelings of anxiety, joy, concern and doubts about becoming a teacher. There are many reasons why people decide to become a teacher but often a beginning teacher's decision stems from a belief that teaching provides opportunities to make a difference to children's lives, to inspire them and help them to grow and develop. This belief may underpin feelings of excitement you have when you meet and work with your first class. At the same time, feelings of anxiety may stem from realising the responsibility for children's learning, and for establishing, developing and maintaining the learning environment and culture in your classroom, including the norms for behaviour, relationships, communication and classroom organisation.

reflection point

What were your reasons for wanting to become a teacher?

What are your feelings about becoming a teacher?

The amount of autonomy you have for the decisions you take, and your learning and teaching choices in the classroom as a beginning teacher, are very context-specific depending on local and national circumstances. Schools, local authorities and/or national guidelines or prescribed policies will to a greater or lesser extent shape your and other's views about your role as a beginning teacher and your relationship with your teacher education provider. Schools and their policies sit within larger contexts and they are shaped by different purposes and values. As Conway et al. (2009) point out, as with all teachers, your work is embedded in historical, cultural and political contexts. Whilst you have expectations about your role and responsibilities in becoming a teacher, others also have expectations of you. People's expectations about what beginning teachers should know, care about and be able to do may align or contrast with your own. In a series of studies of mentors working with beginning teachers, Livingston and Shiach (2013, 2014) consistently found that the mentors reported differences in people's expectations about beginning teachers, their roles and responsibilities and how they should act in the classroom and school. These differences served as a source of learning and development and/or as a source of emotional angst for the beginning teachers (examples of some of the different expectations are explored below).

spotlight on practice

Different expectations of a beginning teacher

Sam has just begun a placement in a primary 3 class but she will also have opportunities to observe classes in other stages of the school. Different people in school have expressed their views about the expectations they have of Sam as a beginning teacher.

The school leader's expectations

As children, our pupils are our most precious members of society. It should therefore be considered a privilege to teach them and to support parents/carers with the nurturing and educational development of their children in the early years and primary school stages. The role of the teacher requires a proactive mindset, regardless of the stage being taught. I expect Sam to evaluate herself, her learning about the context of the school, the primary stage and, most importantly, the pupils she is working with. I expect that the learning experiences of her class

(Continued)

(Continued)

are appropriately paced and delivered. It is important that she makes effective use of class planning to support her with the organisation and management of classroom learning and teaching. It is also essential that her daily preparation and organisation support effective learning and teaching and promote pupil independence. In the early years and primary school stages, it is particularly important that she demonstrates that she is able to work in partnership with the parents/carers to get it right for each child and ensure that responsive and appropriate teaching and learning are taking place. I am also expecting her to develop links with colleagues across the school and learn about the policies and procedures within the school.

The expectations of Sam's mentor

I still remember the feelings I had as a beginning teacher: looking forward on the one hand to having a class to teach but on the other hand wanting to make sure that I understood what the school and the parents expected of me. It is a bit of a balancing act. Beginning teachers have to demonstrate that they are capable teachers and understand what being a professional means but they also need to show they are open to learning from others' experiences. I expect Sam to have her own views and ideas about what she is doing but, at the same time, be willing to find out how we function as a school and learn from working with colleagues. I have high expectations but these are all about caring for the pupils and ensuring they have the best possible start in their learning journey in the best possible learning environment.

The expectations of a parent of a primary 3 pupil

I have some concerns about a beginning teacher taking the class that my child is in. The early years are so important for my child to feel safe and enjoy going to school. It is important that my daughter has strong foundations for her learning. I want her to be happy but I don't want her to fall behind in her work. I am sure the head teacher will keep an eye on what is happening.

reflection point

The case study indicates that different people have different expectations of Sam as a beginning teacher. What expectations do you have of yourself as a beginning teacher?

Reflecting on why others have different expectations is an important step in developing as a reflective practitioner, and in beginning to understand why views differ and conflicts can arise in relationships. There are many possible reasons for differences in people's expectations but they often cluster around different views about:

- what makes for good teaching and learning
- what knowledge matters most

- models of teacher education, and the nature and level of support that beginning teachers should receive
- how ready beginning teachers are to teach when they arrive in school and what they are expected to do at the start of their placement or career.

How aware you are of your own expectations and how much you understand about the expectations others have of your role as a beginning teacher will depend to some extent on your own personal experiences and the support you have to reflect on different expectations in an open and explicit way. Developing an awareness of the expectations and assumptions we have of ourselves as teachers is not an easy task. Brookfield (1995, p. 2) says: 'Becoming aware of the implicit assumptions that frame how we think and act is one of the most challenging intellectual puzzles we face in our lives.'

Contrasting views about what makes for a good teacher

Feiman-Nemser (2001) believes that student-teachers enter teacher education with beliefs that have been shaped by many years of exposure to educational practices as pupils in school and through experiences within families or youth groups in the community. This follows Lortie's (1975) views about a long 'apprenticeship of observation' which creates deeply held images of teachers and teaching. This suggests that, as a beginning teacher, you will have some pre-formed expectations about what makes for a 'good teacher'. However, the spotlight on Sam's placement in school illustrates that your views are likely to interact with a web of other people's views and assumptions about what it means to be a 'good' teacher. For example, individuals have their own beliefs and values about the purpose of education, what knowledge is worthwhile, how children learn and develop and what are the most appropriate or effective learning and teaching approaches. Korthagen (2004) highlights the difficulty of answering the question, 'What makes for a good teacher?' He says it is 'too ambitious to try to introduce any norm describing what a good teacher should look like' (p. 78) because the answer depends on a range of interacting factors. He proposes a model, which he calls the 'onion model', to assist thinking about the various layers of factors influencing what makes for a good teacher – mission, identity, beliefs, competences, behaviour and environment (Korthagen, 2004). Differences in answering the question arise because of the unique nature of teachers' personal biographies and professional identities, and because the multiple social interactions involved mean learning and teaching are complex and unpredictable processes. Knowledge about what and how people learn is continually developing, and more diverse populations of learners with individual personalities and changing learning needs add new challenges for teachers. Teachers are expected to respond to individual learners and take account of their learning in and outside the school – in the family and out in the community. They are also expected to embrace and respond to the social context of the individual school and community in which they work in order to engage effectively and meaningfully with pupils and their parents. In addition, greater emphasis on inter-connected learning communities means that teachers work with a wider number of professionals in their own classrooms and in the education system generally (Livingston and Shiach, 2010).

These complex challenges can bring significant fulfilment to teachers in the early years and primary stages as they see children's learning developing. However, the challenges also mean there is a continuing need for teachers to adapt and develop their knowledge, skills and values about what is to be taught and why as well as how, where and when. There are many decisions to be taken in planning for learning and teaching and whilst in action in the classroom:

> The reality of professional practice is complex and changeable ... practitioners constantly have to face the question: What in the given circumstances is the best way to act, in order to achieve what is important at this moment? (Ponte and Ax, 2009: 325)

The development of an understanding of the complexity of teachers' work and the many influences that shape people's expectations of a teacher require an understanding of the multiple interactions between people, policies and context. The knowledge, skills and dispositions a teacher needs are increasingly being set out in lists of competences or professional standards by a growing number of governments/national agencies. Beginning teachers have to demonstrate their competence in relation to these requirements before they are recognised as qualified teachers. The standards or competences could have a significant influence on shaping their understanding of becoming a teacher and influence those who support them in the early phase of their career. In general, the documents include competences concerning professional knowledge, skills, values and dispositions. For example, the Standard for Registration as a Teacher in Scotland (GTCS, 2012) includes:

- values (for example, integrity, trust, respect, social justice)
- professional knowledge and understanding (including knowledge and understanding of the curriculum, education systems and professional responsibilities)
- professional skills and abilities (including planning coherent, progressive and stimulating teaching and assessment programmes which match learners' needs and abilities, communicating effectively, organising and managing the classroom, employing a range of teaching strategies and resources to meet the needs and abilities of learners, building relationships with colleagues and other professionals, pupils, their parents and members of the wider school community)
- self-evaluation, self-reflection and continuous professional development.

The Teachers' Standards for use in schools in England (DfE, 2011) include a brief preamble which summarises the values and behaviours that are expected of teachers, a set of standards which concern teaching and a set of standards which concern personal and professional conduct. All accredited Initial Teacher Training providers in England must ensure that the content, structure, delivery and assessment of their programmes are designed to enable trainee teachers to meet all the standards for qualified teacher status (QTS) across the age range of training (ages 5–11 in the case of primary teachers), and ensure that trainee teachers are not recommended for the award of QTS until they have met all of the required standards.

reflection point

Explore some of the differences in the standards for teachers in at least two different countries:

www.gov.uk/government/uploads/system/uploads/attachment_data/file/301107/Teachers_Standards.pdf (Teachers' Standards in England, Guidance for school leaders, school staff and governing bodies, updated 2013)

www.gov.uk/government/uploads/system/uploads/attachment_data/file/283567/Teachers_standards_how_should_they_be_used.pdf (Teachers' Standards (England) How they should be used, updated 2014)

www.gov.uk/government/uploads/system/uploads/attachment_data/file/283566/Teachers_standard_information.pdf (one-page summary of Teachers' Standards in England)

www.gov.uk/government/uploads/system/uploads/attachment_data/file/211646/Early_Years_Teachers_Standards.pdf (Early Years Teachers' Standards in England, 2013)

www.gtcs.org.uk/web/FILES/the-standards/standards-for-registration-1212.pdf (The Standards for Registration: Mandatory Requirements for Registration with the General Teaching Council for Scotland, 2012)

www.teacherscouncil.govt.nz/content/graduating-teacher-standards-english-rtf-38kb (Graduating Teacher Standards, Aotearoa, New Zealand)

Standard documents can be helpful if they are recognised as a framework to stimulate discussion with others in your school about expectations of beginning teachers' roles and responsibilities and how you are progressing in your development as a teacher. They can assist your own reflection and the identification of your personal strengths and next steps in professional development. However, not everyone agrees about the helpfulness of standards in describing what makes for a good teacher. Doubts have been raised not only about the validity and reliability of lists of competences as indicators of what makes for a competent teacher but also about whether 'good' teaching can be reduced to a number of discrete standards. The imposition of teacher standards may have a positive or negative effect on shaping teachers' professionalism. Sachs (2012) suggests that the different ways that the standards are interpreted and understood depends on the values, principles and assumptions that underpin them. Differences in values and assumptions have the potential to result in divergent interpretations and differences in the values that are attached to standards nationally and between teachers in schools. The guidance for school leaders, school staff and governing bodies in England states: 'The standards need to be applied as appropriate to the role and context within which the trainee or teacher is practising' (DfE, 2011: 6). However, interpretations of what is appropriate to the role and context of the trainee or teacher vary. For example, the mentors in Livingston and Shiach's (2013) study in Scotland reported that they found differences in opinion arose concerning interpretations of what specific standards mean in practice and how well beginning teachers should be able to meet them.

Whilst some people see the standards as an attempt to provide a framework that describes the requirements of a competent teacher, others view the standards as an attempt to increase teacher accountability. The extent to which people agree that the standards are open to discussion and negotiation could depend on whether they view standards as regulatory and fixed or as developmental and serving as a framework for self-evaluation and professional learning. The way they are interpreted and the value attached to them also depend on the context in which they are implemented and the opportunities for dialogue and negotiation of what they mean in practice. Rather than being accepted as static, standards should be recognised as an opportunity for beginning teachers and their mentors to discuss and develop a shared understanding of their views about what makes for a good teacher through peer dialogue.

Reflect on your own experiences of learning and teaching and write down what you believe makes for a 'good teacher'.

Reflect on whether you think professional standards for teachers help or hinder you in describing a good teacher.

List the values you think are essential for a teacher to have.

Evaluate and reflect on teachers' values

The Preamble of the Teachers' Standards in England (DfE, 2011: 10) summarises the values and behaviours that all teachers must demonstrate throughout their career. For example, it emphasises that teachers act with honesty and integrity and forge professional relationships.

Write down examples of a teacher acting:

- with honesty and integrity
- in a professional way.

Discuss the examples with your mentor, a stage partner or another student teacher or trainee. Consider together how your views are similar or different and why.

The General Teaching Council for Scotland's (GTCS) website has a helpful Values Wheel to assist your self-evaluation and reflection on how to put values into action and to help you consider who you are as a professional: www.gtcs.org.uk/standards/Self-evaluation/self-evaluation-values.aspx

Contrasting views about teacher education and about learning and teaching

It is important to be aware of your views and assumptions about pupils' ability to learn, what knowledge is important and what it means to be a teacher. Taking time to reflect on your views and assumptions will help you acknowledge how your values and beliefs impact on your behaviour and attitudes to teaching and to new experiences whilst working with other colleagues in school. Hargreaves (1998, cited in Pollard, 2014: 10) 'reminds us that it is not only the values we go into teaching with that matter but how we feel able to put these into practice'. Your values may align with those prevailing in school but this may not always be the case. Some staff members may have differing views from you based on their own personal values. Understanding some of the possible reasons for differences in views and recognising them as opportunities to reflect on different interpretations may reduce the tensions that can arise when you or they do something that seems different from what is expected.

The different routes into teaching are underpinned by differences in views about how best to 'train' or 'educate' teachers and definitions of good teaching and learning. Conflicting views can arise concerning whether greater emphasis should be placed on the craft of teaching and the development of skills through observation and advice from an experienced teacher or on the development of reflective, enquiring professionals. Views of teachers as technicians (who acquire a set of competences to deliver the curriculum and implement local and national policies) contrast sharply with views of adaptive responsive teachers (who understand the complexity of learning and teaching and develop professional knowledge and values which enable them to question policies and their own practice through ongoing reflection and enquiry). The current debate concerning models of teacher education often focuses on conflicting theories of learning, different approaches to supporting and challenging the development of teachers' professional learning, and different views concerning what professional knowledge is and what knowledge is important for effective learning and teaching. For example, beliefs about the relative importance of formal and practical knowledge can underpin differences in views about the role of teachers and approaches to teacher education. Fenstermacher (1994) describes formal knowledge as a type of knowledge developed through conventional research, and practical knowledge as that developed by teachers based on their experiences of classroom teaching.

Behaviourist or social-constructivist theories often underpin contrasting conceptions of learning and teaching. Teachers whose main focus is the delivery of subject knowledge to their pupils may hold beliefs about learning and teaching associated with behaviourist theories (for example, as proposed by Skinner). They may believe that engaging in knowledge transmission is the most effective way to teach – the teacher as the knowledgeable expert delivers the curriculum content that has to be covered to the pupils, correcting their mistakes and reinforcing positive learning outcomes. In contrast, teachers whose views align more closely to social-constructivist theory (for example, as proposed by Vygotsky) may believe that knowledge is created from and by social interaction between pupils, or between pupils and the teacher. These views may underpin beliefs about a teacher's role in addressing the individual learning needs of the pupils, supporting them to engage in their own learning and construct meaning of the curriculum for themselves. From both these perspectives, learning and teaching decisions may also be influenced differently according to what a teacher thinks the expectations and requirements of policy makers, school leaders, parents and/or pupils are, or they may be influenced by beliefs about pupils' ability to learn, how they learn and/or what makes for effective teaching (Livingston, 2015).

Contrasting views can be confusing and unsettling for beginning teachers striving to develop their professional identity. The results of the *Becoming a Teacher Project* (Hobson et al., 2009) demonstrate that becoming a teacher can be an 'affectively charged experience'. It is therefore important to learn from some of the challenging experiences that some beginning teachers have had and reflect on how differences in views and misinterpretations of actions can be avoided or recognised as opportunities to learn.

spotlight on practice

Dealing with different expectations and values

Matt is a student teacher in a primary school working with pupils aged 11 years. Before he began his placement, he had a clear image of the kind of teacher he wanted to be. He wanted to understand his pupils as individual learners and create interesting and exciting learning environments where all his pupils could succeed. He wanted them to be able to learn from one another as well as from him and from other people in the local community and beyond. He also wanted to explore opportunities where he and his pupils could learn new things together. He had learned about social-constructivist approaches on his teacher education course and felt his views about learning and teaching aligned with learning through social interaction, collaborative approaches and ongoing reflection and enquiry. However, on his first meeting with his mentor in school (an experienced primary teacher, who had been teaching for 19 years), he immediately felt uneasy. Her expectations were that he would observe her in order to understand the learning and teaching approaches already in place in the school and adopt the practices already established in the classroom. Matt felt constrained and distressed by these expectations because in his view there were limited opportunities for him to experiment and try out his own ideas. He found it difficult to conform to his mentor's expectations because he felt uncomfortable with her very structured approaches and routines in the classroom and didn't fully understand how to go about putting them into practice. It seemed to him that it wasn't possible to develop his own professional identity in a context which appeared to collide with his values and beliefs about learning and teaching. He felt anxious and upset because he was caught between wanting to hold firm to his own beliefs and values and his desire to feel a sense of belonging to the school culture.

Sinner (2012) narrates a similar story of a student teacher who experiences tensions and strong emotions during her school placement when beliefs and values differ about the most effective approaches for learning and teaching, the level of involvement of the pupils in developing their own learning, and the best way to support beginning teachers' development. According to Sinner, the student teacher believed that the tensions around differences in her and her mentor's views were underpinned by conflicting beliefs about the apprenticeship model and the enquiry model of teacher education. Similar to Matt, she was distressed by the tensions that arose and found it difficult to negotiate her roles as a learner and a teacher.

FORMING AND RE-FORMING PROFESSIONAL IDENTITY

Undoubtedly, it is challenging to learn *about* teaching and learn *to* teach, whilst trying to make sense of your identities as a learner and a teacher. It is important to recognise that as teachers we are learners ourselves and that in becoming a teacher there are multiple opportunities to embrace learning 'in the role' of a teacher whilst supporting the learning of others. This means acknowledging that being a learner is part of and not separate from your identity as a teacher. This is not easy when, as a beginning teacher, you may feel caught between trying to demonstrate your teaching competence and credibility to pupils, colleagues and parents and wanting to seek support for your own learning and development. This situation can be exacerbated when some school leaders and colleagues expect you to take on responsibilities similar to experienced teachers from the outset of your school placement.

Describing what 'professional identity' means is difficult, and, as with other concepts discussed in this chapter, people have different views. Contested views are evident in the research literature with differing definitions offered from psychological, sociological and philosophical perspectives (see Day et al., 2006). However, Pillen and colleagues (2013) suggest that researchers who study teachers' professional identity generally agree that professional identity is not a stable entity, rather it is dynamic and continually changing and developing over time. This means that whilst your professional identity will be shaped by your unique characteristics, you should also be open to potential changes over time as your identity is influenced by different contexts, people and experiences. Pollard (2014) reminds us that in school settings, the influence of other colleagues on the school staff is often considerable. They represent 'significant others' providing feedback in relation to your professional identity. Part of the process of becoming a teacher is being aware of and reflecting on the way your professional identity is formed and re-formed through your interactions with others and a variety of experiences. As in Matt's case, this can be emotionally challenging. How you manage conflicting emotions depends, in part, on the context and culture of your learning and working environment, the support you receive to reflect on and manage your own and other's emotional responses and your ability to develop your personal resilience. Pillen et al. (2013) argue that if the personal and the professional aspects of becoming a teacher are not in balance, what is found relevant to the profession may conflict with a teacher's personal beliefs and expectations. They remind us that becoming a teacher means, among other things, deciding how to express yourself in the classroom and learning when and how to adapt your personal understandings and ideals to institutional demands without compromising your core values and beliefs:

> Professional identity development is seen as the process of integrating one's personal knowledge, beliefs, attitudes, norms and values, on the one hand, and professional demands from teacher education institutes and schools, including broadly accepted values and standards about teaching, on the other. (Pillen et al., 2013: 243)

In many schools, statements of the school aims and their values are displayed in prominent places and/or in the school handbook and/or website. These statements offer a good starting point for a discussion about professional knowledge and values with your mentor. A thoughtful balance is required between establishing your own ways of working with your class according to your own values and beliefs, and meeting your pupils' specific learning needs within the context of the school and the routines that are already established. Without discussion and transparency of views, beginning teachers' struggles to make sense of conflicting values and beliefs can remain invisible to teacher educators and to their mentor in school. Livingston and Shiach's (2013) research suggests that mentors can misinterpret beginning teachers' actions. For example, beginning teachers' reticence to ask questions for fear of appearing to lack competence can be misinterpreted by their mentor as an inability to self-evaluate or a disinterest in learning to develop as a teacher. Ongoing communication and the development of trusting relationships are necessary to avoid these misconceptions. The roles and responsibilities of those who support you, as a beginning teacher, in establishing trust and enabling discussion of views and expectations are explored in the final section of this chapter but as a developing professional you also share responsibility. Actively seeking multiple contexts for your own learning provides you with opportunities to reflect critically on different views of learning and teaching and assists you in making sense of your own learning and your contribution not just to your own pupils' learning but also to the learning culture of the whole school.

Studies by McNally and Blake (2010) and Hobson et al. (2009) indicate that for beginning teachers establishing good relationships often assumes huge importance. For example, Hobson et al. reported that the beginning teachers in their study consistently mentioned colleagues as a factor in helping them to develop as teachers. This means you should be open to learning opportunities that enable you to reflect on different ways of doing things and different ways of being a teacher.

Discussing values and expectations with others

Make a list of opportunities you could create to discuss expectations that other people have of you as a beginning teacher, find out about what they value in teaching and learning and their expectations about 'good' teaching. Be ready to share your values about learning and teaching and your expectations.

Thinking about *how* you discuss your and others' expectations is just as important as thinking about *when* to ask them. Think about the messages you convey by choice of language, tone of voice and body language.

Whilst your focus is on your own development as a teacher and the development of the pupils you are working with, other people will have a broader picture of the school as a whole. Some of the contrasting views may arise from school leaders', mentor teachers' and parents' views about not wanting to take risks with children's learning and the practical realities of delivering the curriculum within contextual restrictions that are not immediately apparent to you as a beginning teacher.

School leaders have responsibility for the quality of learning and teaching throughout the whole school. Reading school handbooks, school plans, policies and reports and information for parents will give you an insight into the expectations that are held for learning across the school. You may be able to access this information from the school website before you arrive at the school. Throughout your experience in school as a student teacher or as a newly qualified teacher, you should continue to look for opportunities to talk to other teachers, as well as your own mentor or supporter, and to the school leader, at appropriate times, to find out what is expected of all pupils and teachers in the school and what is expected of you as a beginning teacher.

Parents want the best start for their children. Conway et al. (2009: 44) emphasise that one of the distinctive features of contemporary teaching is the increase in interaction with parents/carers required of teachers. They highlight the way that relationships with parents have changed significantly over the last two decades. According to them, this is due first to a new appreciation of the role of parents and the home in enhancing children's learning, and second, to new reporting and communication practices between home and school, driven by increasing attention to issues of accountability. Seeking opportunities, as appropriate, to develop strong and trusting relationships with parents/carers and to demonstrate your ability through the learning experiences that their children receive in your class are important aspects of becoming a teacher. Find out how other teachers build relationships with parents and discuss the different opportunities that are open to you to talk to parents.

INFLUENCES AND CHALLENGES OF THOSE WHO SUPPORT YOU AS A BEGINNING TEACHER

Fewer teachers today find themselves working in isolation. For many teachers, team or stage planning is now the norm. As more schools seek to include all children with diverse learning needs, more staff members (for example, teachers and additional support assistants) work together in one classroom. In early years settings and primary schools, there are often greater expectations that teachers will plan and work together. This can generate rich collaborative learning experiences for those working as part of a team. However, teachers working together in enquiry and reflection need to be nurtured and supported. School leaders have a key role in developing supportive collegiate cultures and enabling ongoing opportunities to share views, including views about beginning teachers' roles and responsibilities, professional knowledge and values, and learning and teaching approaches. Effective mentoring is also being advocated in more countries. The importance of supporting and challenging beginning teachers is widely recognised but the roles that a mentor has and what they do in practice differ greatly depending on the country context, teacher education provider regulations, partnership agreements with schools and the mentor's own characteristics and understanding of mentoring. In some countries, the allocation of mentors to beginning teachers is mandatory whilst in other countries informal mentoring from experienced colleagues is still the norm. The ethos in the school for collaboration and the value and time school leaders attach to mentoring can impact significantly on the quality of mentoring, no matter whether it is mandatory or informal. In Matt's case, his relationship was poor but many beginning teachers have a good relationship with their mentor. In Hobson et al.'s study (2009), 65% of the beginning teachers rated their relationship with their mentor as 'very good' and 29% said it was 'good'. However, there are different understandings of what it means to be a 'good mentor'.

Being a mentor is an important and challenging responsibility and it needs to be recognised that teachers in schools who work with beginning teachers are being asked to take up the role of a 'teacher educator'. It cannot be assumed that the knowledge and skills teachers have, which enable them to work effectively with young learners, are the same as the knowledge and skills required when working with beginning teachers, who are adult learners. Many teachers in the education system today have not had a mentor themselves. They may have been in the position of having to 'sink or swim' at the start of their career and may not think deeply enough or be sufficiently prepared for a mentoring role. Some mentors, often in an effort to give what they perceive as the best support for beginning teachers, focus on providing advice drawn from what they do themselves in the classroom and share resources that work for them. This puts the emphasis on socialising beginning teachers into existing cultures and ways of working in the mentor's classroom or in the school (usually with insufficient explanation of how they developed the expertise and the underpinning relationships and classroom cultures required). In Matt's experience, his mentor expected him to adjust and conform to existing practice but she may have believed that this was the best way to support him because of her different beliefs about what makes for a good teacher or because of her concern not to interrupt the pupils' learning and the plan of work that was expected of them. Other mentors, again often with good intentions, put the emphasis on providing social and emotional support. They are ready with words of comfort when things go wrong or a pat on the back when things go well, but words of comfort are not enough to support the development of reflection on and understanding of how to avoid or build on experiences for the future. Given the traditional definition of a mentor as someone who educates, supports and guides a novice, it is not surprising that many teachers' understanding of the role is as described above. However, the complexity of learning to teach is increasingly recognised as an enquiry process and beginning teachers are expected to engage in ongoing reflection and self-evaluation to identify pupil learning needs, the strengths of their own practice and further development needs for learning and teaching. In this context, beginning teachers require more from their mentors than advice and emotional support.

Mentors need a complex range of knowledge, skills and dispositions to support and critique the development of reflective and enquiring teachers. Yet, many mentors have little or no training to support them in understanding the conditions required for effective mentoring. This may be because many school leaders and teachers themselves assume that teachers already have sufficient skills to support beginning teachers in learning to teach. Undoubtedly, there are significant differences in the nature and amount of mentoring support that is provided for beginning teachers and in the quality and amount of training available to mentors. Some specific requirements for mentoring may be set out by national policies and/or the provider of your beginning teacher training, which state you must have a mentor, but there is less clarity about *how* the mentor engages with you in the mentoring role or about how they, as learners themselves, are supported in the role.

Effective mentoring, in an environment of collegiate support, should start with recognition of you as an individual learner, supporting you to uncover and explore the impact of your prior experiences, beliefs and values on the development of your own professional identity. This process should enable you and your mentor to share your views about learners and learning and the relationship with curriculum and teaching approaches. At this stage, you are both learners trying to understand each other's views and experiences and build a trusting relationship. A planned mentoring programme should be agreed including: observation of your practice; pre- and post-focused mentoring conversations involving carefully structured dialogue which supports and challenges your analysis of your pupils' learning, identifies strengths in your practice, as well as the challenges to be addressed and the next steps in your teaching to improve your pupils' learning; opportunities for your mentor to model practice through collaboration, joint planning and teaching; and regular professional reviews of your progress as a teacher (against the standards where relevant). For many school leaders and teachers, this will require a re-conceptualisation of the role of a mentor to take account of the more complex contexts, demands and expectations of beginning teachers as reflective, enquiring professionals.

reflection point

Make a list of your expectations of the amount and type of support you will receive from your mentor. Reflect on the amount of time a mentor has available to support you. Identify opportunities to discuss the expectations that you and your mentor have about support for you as a beginning teacher.

SUMMARY

The aim of this chapter was to stimulate your thinking about your own and other people's expectations of beginning teachers. In particular, you have had the opportunity to develop your awareness of other people's different expectations of your role as a beginning teacher and different opinions about what being a good teacher means. Standard documents have the potential to serve as frameworks to stimulate discussion with your mentor and colleagues about what good teaching means. In interpreting the standards, it is important to be aware of the values and beliefs that underpin people's views. Knowing that people may interpret what you do in very different ways will help you to feel more prepared if tensions arise and encourage you to seek opportunities to discuss and learn from different approaches. Thinking more deeply about the values, beliefs and assumptions you hold is challenging but it will help you to reflect on how your preconceived images and beliefs influence what you do and your openness and willingness to learn from alternative approaches.

As a beginning teacher, you may have a sense of who you want to be as a teacher. However, your professional identity will be formed and re-formed as you develop as a teacher. For many beginning teachers, this is emotionally challenging. Being aware of the complexity of the development of your own identity and being prepared to see challenges as opportunities to reflect critically and learn contributes to your development as a resilient and reflective teacher. It is not easy to do this alone. School leaders and your mentor have a key role in supporting your development. However, the support provided for them in developing the necessary knowledge and skills in mentoring is variable. A better understanding of the value of mentoring processes is needed and of the importance of quality training as the role of mentor expands from giving advice and emotional support to scaffolding, supporting and critiquing your development as a reflective enquiring professional who is equipped to adapt and respond to the complex and changing learning and teaching contexts of the 21st century.

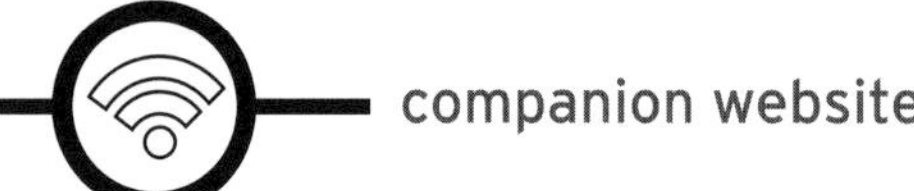

To access additional online resources please visit: **https://study.sagepub.com/wyseandrogers**

Here you will find an activity for new teachers, author podcasts including Kay Livingston's top tips for employability, free access to SAGE journal articles and links to external sources.

Avraamidou, L. (2014) 'Tracing a Beginning Elementary Teacher's Development of Identity for Science Teaching', *Journal of Teacher Education*, 65(3), 223-40. This article explores the development of a primary teacher's identity from a number of different perspectives. For the purpose of the article, the context is science teaching but the discussion of identity development is relevant to all areas of the curriculum.

Warren, A. (2014) 'Relationships for Me are the Key for Everything: Early Childhood Teachers' Subjectivities as Relational Professionals', *Contemporary Issues in Early Childhood*, 15(3), 262-71. This article provides a further example of two becoming teachers who experience conflicting beliefs and values about learning and teaching and tensions in relations with colleagues in school. It explores how the differences impacted on their development as teachers.

www.teacherscouncil.govt.nz/sites/default/files/Guidelines%20for%20Induction%20and%20Mentoring%20and%20Mentor%20Teachers%202011%20english.pdf - the Learning to Teach (2007-08) research project in New Zealand identifies the distinction between limited mentoring, geared around advice and emotional support, and intensive, pedagogically oriented mentoring, often referred to as 'educative mentoring'.

REFERENCES

Anspal, T., Eisenschmidt, E. and Löfström, E. (2012) 'Finding Myself as a Teacher: Exploring the Shaping of Teacher Identities through Student Teachers' Narratives', *Teachers and Teaching: Theory and Practice*, 18(2), 197–216.

Brookfield, S. (1995) *Becoming a Critically Reflective Teacher*. San Francisco: Jossey-Bass.

Conway, P., Murphy, R., Rath A. and Hall, K. (2009) *Learning to Teach: A Nine Country Cross National Study*. Maynooth, Ireland: The Teaching Council.

Day, C., Kington, A., Stobart, G. and Sammons, P. (2006) 'The Personal and Professional Selves of Teachers: Stable and Unstable Identities', *British Educational Research Journal*, 32(4), 601–16.

Department of Education (DfE) (2011) *Teachers' Standards*. Introduction updated June 2013. Available from: www.gov.uk/government/uploads/system/uploads/attachment_data/file/301107/Teachers__Standards.pdf (accessed 8 May 2014).

Feiman-Nemser, S. (2001) 'From Preparation to Practice: Designing a Continuum to Strengthen and Sustain Teaching', *Teachers College Record*, 103(6), 1013–55.

Fenstermacher, G.D. (1994) 'The Knower and the Known: The Nature of Knowledge in Research on Teaching', in L. Darling-Hammond (ed.) *Review of Research in Education* (p. 356). Washington, DC: American Educational Research Association.

General Teaching Council for Scotland (GTCS) (2012) *The Standards for Registration: Mandatory Requirements for Registration with the General Teaching Council for Scotland*. Available from: www.gtcs.org.uk/web/FILES/the-standards/standards-for-registration-1212.pdf (accessed 4 December 2014).

Hargreaves, A. (1998) 'The Emotional Practice of Teaching', *Teaching and Teacher Education*, 14(8), 835–54. [Also in A. Pollard (2014) *Reflective Teaching in Schools*, 4th edition. London: Bloomsbury.]

Hobson, A.J., Malderez, A., Tracey, L., Homer, M., Ashby, P., Mitchell, N., et al. (2009) *Becoming a Teacher: Final Report*, Research Report No. DCSF-RR115. Available from: www.dcsf.gov.uk/research/data/uploadfiles/DCSF-RR115.pdf (accessed 2 March 2015).

Korthagen, F.J. (2004) 'In Search of the Essence of a Good Teacher: Towards a More Holistic Approach in Teacher Education', *Teaching and Teacher Education*, 20, 77–97.

Livingston, K. (2015) 'Pedagogy and Curriculum: Teachers as Learners', in D. Wyse, L. Hayward and J. Pandya (eds) *The Sage Handbook of Curriculum, Pedagogy and Assessment*. London: Sage.

Livingston, K. and Shiach, L. (2010) 'A New Model of Teacher Education', in A. Campbell and S. Groundwater-Smith (eds) *Connecting Inquiry and Professional Learning*. London: Routledge.

Livingston, K. and Shiach, L. (2013) *Teaching Scotland's Future: Mentoring Pilot Partnership Project – Final Report*, November, Education Scotland. Available from: www.educationscotland.gov.uk/Images/GUAUMentorPilotProjectNov13_tcm4 825825.pdf

Livingston, K. and Shiach, L. (2014) *Teaching Scotland's Future: Further Developing and Sustaining a Strengthened Model of Professional Learning through Mentoring Processes in the Context of Career-long Professional Learning – Final Report*, Education Scotland. Available from: www.educationscotland.gov.uk/Images/GUAUMentorPilotProjectFinalReportDec201tcm4-845885.pdf

Lortie, D. (1975) *Schoolteacher: A Sociological Study*. Chicago: University of Chicago Press.

McNally, J. and Blake, A. (eds) (2010) *Improving Learning in a Professional Context: The New Teacher at School*. London: TLRP.

Pillen, M., Beijaard, D. and den Brok, P. (2013) 'Tensions in Beginning Teachers' Professional Identity Development, Accompanying Feelings and Coping Strategies', *European Journal of Teacher Education*, 36(3), 240–60.

Pollard, A. (2014) *Reflective Teaching in Schools*, 4th edition. London: Bloomsbury.

Ponte, P. and Ax, J. (2009) 'Pedagogy as a Method', in S.E. Noffke and B. Somekh (eds) *The SAGE Handbook of Educational Action Research*. London: Sage.

Sachs, J. (2012) *Teacher Professionalism: Why are We still Talking about it?* Keynote address presented at the Association of Teacher Education in Europe annual conference, Anadalou University, Turkey, 29 August.

Sinner, A. (2012) 'Transitioning to Teacher: Uncertainty as a Game of Dramatic Hats', *Teachers and Teaching: Theory and Practice*, 18(5), 601–13.

2

SCHOOL AND SOCIETY

Ian Menter and Margaret Walker

LEARNING AIMS

This chapter will enable you to:

- better understand the experience of a young child entering an early years setting or primary school for the first time
- develop an understanding of the relationships between early years and primary education institutions and the community - locally, regionally, nationally and internationally
- begin to recognise the importance of society, including history, culture and tradition, in relation to early years and primary schooling
- reflect on the role and responsibilities of the teacher in relation to the child and his/her family.

When a child goes to their first nursery or early years centre or primary school, this is a hugely significant step for him or her. In almost all cases, this will be the first institutional setting the child will experience. Whilst he or she may have attended health clinics, dentists or even hospital, any of these is likely to be a brief and temporary visit. For the great majority, the educational setting will be the first time the child will experience a transition from complete immersion in the family setting into a separate and detached institution where they will be just one of many children being cared for by paid employees. The most common exception to this might be where children have been with a childminder during their parents' working day, but even if this is the case they are likely to have been with just a small number of other children.

Most nurseries and schools go to considerable lengths to make this transition from home to school (or equivalent) as smooth and harmonious a process as possible, but it is clearly a hugely important symbolic experience and can also for some children be a very disruptive one. This is effectively the very first step the child will take towards being an independent citizen within society. The school or nursery they are entering will certainly have some educational function but it can easily be argued that of equal importance is the social function the institution is providing, taking the child out of the intimacy of the home and family into a wider social context for the first time.

reflection point

What are your own recollections of starting at school or at nursery?

What was exciting? What was scary?

Who do you remember from your first days there?

This chapter examines the implications, for early years settings, primary schools and those who work in them, of the relationship between the child, the family and the educational institution. In the chapter, we move from the very local implications of the relationship between the school and its immediate community, though a consideration of wider relations in the regional community, through to thinking of national and even international ramifications. As the child's horizons steadily grow during their early years, so too can we consider how there may be wider implications for early years and primary education. We consider how these implications may change as the child him- or herself develops from birth through to the age of about 11.

In general terms, the early years or primary educational setting may have three purposes so far as the child is concerned. The first is perhaps the most obvious one – that of equipping the child with the skills, knowledge and understanding that will help them to develop as an educated human being – this we can call the intellectual purpose, or what most people might simply call the educational function of the primary school. But integration into society also involves developing social skills and understanding which are about relationships and interaction with others. This can be called the social function of schooling. The third purpose or function the primary school fulfils, as part of the longer-term educational journey for the child, is what we may call the economic function. In most countries of the world, primary school is seen as preparation for a subsequent phase of education, namely secondary schooling, and for many young people there will also be a subsequent tertiary phase; the primary phase is thus not preparing the child for direct entry into the workforce (in many low-income countries, very few children move to secondary schooling because their families need them to work). Nevertheless, primary school will be providing the initial basis for subsequent gainful employment (hopefully) and hence the preparation of the child for engagement in the wider economy. Therefore, it is not unreasonable to suggest that this economic function is an important one, even at this early stage, as we shall see.

Writing about primary education as long ago as 1965, the sociologist W.A.L. Blyth suggested that primary education in England had developed from three quite distinctive traditions, what he called: the preparatory, the elementary and the developmental traditions (Blyth, 1967). Each of these can be seen to relate in some way to the three functions we have mentioned above. The preparatory tradition strongly emphasises the preparation of the child for the 'real' learning that should take place in secondary school. Indeed, the word 'preparatory' was strongly associated with the independent or private sector of schooling, in which many children were not only leaving the home on a daily basis, but were actually living away from their homes. The boarding tradition is strongly associated with private schooling in the UK, and the whole trajectory for young people in this sector was designed to prepare them to enter the elite occupations. It was in effect a tradition based on elitism. Nevertheless, Blyth argues, it did influence the shape of primary education for all.

The second tradition, the elementary, was directly associated with mass state schooling. The elementary schools, which had emerged out of the industrial revolution, were designed to ensure that there was a literate and numerate (and obedient) workforce that could play its part in industry, commerce and business. This then was also associated with the economic function but not with the elite parts of the economy, rather with what might be seen as working-class and middle-class occupations.

The developmental tradition started with the idea of the child as a being with potential – the emphasis here was on creating the conditions for the child to flourish and develop in ways that might not be predictable but could lead to the development of talent and creativity.

reflection point

Thinking back to your own primary school days, can you identify which of these traditions was most dominant - preparatory, elementary or developmental? And what is your evidence for this judgement?

As we proceed through the chapter, we will see how these traditions have played a part and have interacted in different ways at different times to create what we now understand as primary education. So, we turn first to consider the early years or primary school setting and its immediate or local community.

THE SCHOOL AND ITS LOCAL COMMUNITY

During the nineteenth century, both in rural and in urban areas, the school was commonly a focal point for the local community. The notion of the village school has certainly endured until now but started many years ago. The village school was usually provided by the church. The school master (almost always a master rather than a mistress) was seen as a pillar of the community and was expected to set a clear example of moral and religious values and behaviour. As urban settlements grew, and schooling for the industrial communities of the large cities also developed (initially under the auspices of churches), schools played a similar part in the local community. The vicar or priest was usually a frequent visitor to the school and would seek to ensure that the children were provided with appropriate religious education, usually in the form of bible studies.

The close association between faith and education was very significant for the children and there was a deep assumption that children should be brought up as Christians who would be 'God-fearing' and law-abiding (echoing aspects of the social function mentioned above). As the secular state became increasingly involved in the provision of education in the late nineteenth and early twentieth centuries, this association began to vary much more. Whilst religious education did become one of the few mandatory elements of the school curriculum (until the introduction of the National Curriculum in 1988, when many other subjects also became compulsory), not all schools were directly governed by the church. Indeed, local school boards and then local authorities became major providers of early years and primary education.

Primary education as a separate phase really emerged strongly in England as early as 1931 when the Consultative Committee of the Board of Education published a report entitled *The Primary School*. The report argues:

> we should deprecate very strongly ... any tendency to make the improvement of the schools attended by the older children an excuse for offering inferior accommodation to children under the age of eleven ... The primary school is on the way to becoming what it should be, the common school of the whole population, so excellent and so generally esteemed that all parents will desire their children to attend it. The root of the matter is, after all, simple. What a wise and good parent would desire for his [*sic*] own children, that a nation must desire for all children. (Maclure, 1986: 191)

Then a 'Primary Memorandum' was published in Scotland (Scottish Education Department, 1965; see Cassidy, 2013), followed by a major enquiry into primary education in England and Wales commissioned by a government body and carried out by a committee chaired by Lady Plowden. The Plowden Report was published in 1967 (Central Advisory Council for Education, 1967) and became a defining document, especially in England and Wales but also had significant influence across the rest of the UK and indeed beyond, with many overseas visitors coming to observe English primary school practice.

The Plowden Report was called *Children and their Primary Schools* and started with the famous sentence 'At the heart of the educational process lies the child', thus apparently prioritising Blyth's developmental tradition, which sees child development as the guiding influence on primary education, as the Scottish memorandum had also done. The report was a sustained and serious attempt to engage with primary education, to consider what was important in teaching and learning for young children and to establish the key elements of the primary school curriculum. Indeed, there was a very strong focus on literacy and numeracy. However, the report was also deeply significant in recognising how critical the relationships between home and school were, and how important a school is within its community. The Committee commissioned one of the first major sociological studies on the association between home background and educational achievement. The seminal book *The Home and the School*, by J.W.B. Douglas (1967), was the outcome. This major study revealed a close association between social background and educational achievement in the primary school. Whilst state education was increasingly being seen as a route to social advancement in the optimistic days of the 'post-war social democratic settlement', which of course included the creation of the National Health Service and the significant development of social welfare schemes, Douglas' study suggested that there was not an even playing field for educational success. Children from poor backgrounds were far less likely to do well at school than children from more prosperous backgrounds. Indeed, the Plowden Report expressed deep concerns about educational deprivation in many (especially urban) areas and led to what have become known as schemes of 'positive discrimination' designed to try to ensure that educational inequalities are challenged and indeed neutralised.

Thus in England, in the wake of the Plowden Report, we saw the creation of Educational Priority Areas (EPAs); we also saw teachers receiving an additional allowance for working in these schools, which were seen to be more demanding than schools elsewhere. It was not long before, in the wake of EPAs, the idea of community education started to take hold with the introduction of bold schemes, not only to increase the funding of schools in such disadvantaged areas, but to bring a wider range of activities into the school setting, with community work, social work and provision for enhanced medical care all being seen as part of the school-based provision. One of the leading architects of these approaches was Eric Midwinter who wrote a series of publications outlining 'Priority Education' (1972).

During the 1970s therefore, there was much optimism in primary education. Not only was English primary school teaching and learning seen as among the best in the world, with many international visitors coming to see what was happening, there was also a great determination to raise the achievement of disadvantaged young children and to provide them with a strong start to secondary education. It was also increasingly recognised that positive initiatives need to catch the child whilst still young – it was never too early to ensure the best conditions for children and so there was also a huge expansion in nursery education. Indeed, the 1972 White Paper on education, produced when Margaret Thatcher was Secretary of State for Education, was called *A Framework for Expansion* (DES, 1972) and included a plan to greatly increase early years education, mainly through much wider provision of nursery education for 3–5-year-olds, primary education having become increasingly clearly defined as provision for the age range 5–11.

Early years pedagogy developed enormously during this period and we saw the increasing influence of many European early educators such as Johann Pestalozzi, Maria Montessori and Friedrich Froebel. Many colleges of education – which had also been expanding during this time – were actively pursuing and promoting child-centred approaches to the education of the young. Throughout all of these developments, the importance of the relationship between home and school was emphasised.

Another development happening during this period was the recognition of the increasingly multicultural and multilingual nature of primary school populations and their related communities. Especially in the major cities, following waves of economically driven migration, there were increasing numbers of children from what would now be called minority ethnic backgrounds, but were usually referred to then as immigrants. It was very often the parents rather than the children themselves who were immigrants. There were families from Caribbean countries settling in many cities and also growing numbers of families from the Indian sub-continent. The increasing diversity of children in primary schools was often seen as a problem rather than as a benefit and certainly many teachers found it challenging to connect with children from such a variety of backgrounds. It did become clear that, for many black children, schooling was a negative experience and eventually, by the end of the 1970s, the government had set up a number of enquiries to examine the nature of the problem, including committees chaired by Anthony Rampton (1981) and Lord Swann (1985).

The challenges were indeed complex and primary schools in England were often found to fall short in their ability to provide equally effective education for all children. Interest in variations in achievement by ethnicity have continued through to the present time, with complex patterns emerging and important 'intersectional' aspects arising in relation to gender and social class in particular (Gillborn and Mirza, 2000).

Given that Plowden had strongly argued for the fundamental importance of language education within primary schools, it should have come as no surprise that linguistic diversity in the community should create new challenges for primary schools. The importance of bilingual support for young children, as well as the potential for enriching the whole curriculum through building on linguistic diversity, is still not always recognised.

During the second half of the 1970s and then into the 1980s, the agenda for primary education began to shift significantly. There was growing concern about the alleged negative influence of 'progressive ideologies' on the achievement of children, and this was sometimes specifically associated with the achievement of children from working-class and minority ethnic backgrounds. In particular, there were concerns about levels of literacy and suggestions that there were too many children transferring to secondary education whose literacy was very poor. Some empirical studies of primary education practice were said to demonstrate how ineffective progressive practices were (e.g. Bennett, 1984), although others seemed to show that the best progressive practice was actually more effective than other approaches (Galton et al., 1980). The political effect of such debates however was to lead to a re-emphasis on curriculum and to suggest that children should have a strengthened subject knowledge and a much increased focus on literacy and numeracy. So it was that a report by the inspectorate as early as 1978 suggested that the curriculum rather than the child should be seen at the centre of the primary school (HMI, 1978). By the early 1990s, another report commissioned by government, and written by three senior educationists who became dubbed 'The Three Wise Men', drew attention to classroom organisation and curriculum structure and suggested that subject-based teaching should be emphasised in the upper stages of primary school (Alexander et al., 1992).

During this period of debate however, we had seen the introduction of the National Curriculum and Assessment, from 1988 onwards (Wyse et al. (2013) includes an account of this and, over time, of increasingly different approaches in Northern Ireland, Scotland and Wales). All of these developments, which emphasised the curriculum, tended to lead to the downplaying of the community element of primary education. It was not that parents were being ignored – indeed, in terms of choosing which school to send their children to, they were very much brought to the centre (see below). However, in terms of the school as a positive focus for local community, this was generally being downplayed in many ways.

An example of an effective home-school relationship

When Adam began nursery at 3 years old, he had already been diagnosed as autistic. Initially, he found it difficult to settle into the routines of the school morning even though his mother had been encouraged to stay with him for the first hour or so. His support worker and the other EY practitioners then suggested that Adam's mother brought him to school before the official start time to give him an opportunity to adjust to the classroom setting without the distraction of other children. His mother, however, believed that this would only serve to make Adam continue to feel different. Her belief was that he should start the day at the same time and in the same way as the other children, i.e. she would no longer accompany him but leave him to go into class independently. The nursery staff agreed to trial this. Adam responded very positively to being treated in the same way as the other children. Without his mother there to guide him, he took his lead from his peers, watching what they did and adapting his own behaviour.

This is an example of an effective home-school relationship where the nursery practitioners were able to acknowledge that, at that time, Adam's mother may well have had a clearer understanding of the particular needs of her son than they did.

As the 1990s proceeded, the concern that pupils in disadvantaged communities were being poorly served re-emerged and this gave rise, especially under the Labour Government that came to power in 1997, to some new community and family-focused policies, such as Educational Action Zones and ideas of 'wraparound' and 'extended' schooling, which sought to increase support for state provision for children from working families as well as from poor families. These initiatives were complemented by even further attention to literacy and numeracy, for it was this government that launched the National Literacy and Numeracy Strategies. In relation to early years provision, there was again enormous emphasis on this during this period with the government setting up Sure Start Centres for integrated children's services and also developing the 'Every Child Matters' strategy. The Social and Emotional Aspects of Learning (SEAL) programme was also introduced into 90% of primary schools. Approaches such as these, since then abandoned, had a very strong focus on parental engagement and community involvement (Dyson et al., 2009). More recently, we have seen the introduction of additional funding, known as the Pupil Premium, given to schools in proportion to the number of children entitled to Free School Meals and intended to be spent on supporting those particular children.

Web Link

More information on the SEAL programme can be accessed through this web link, available on the companion website: www.gov.uk/government/uploads/system/uploads/attachment_data/file/181718/DFE-RR049.pdf

---

The whole idea of multi-professional working had been present in these debates and the idea of schools becoming a focus for multi-agency support for children and families sometimes worked extremely well. For example, one can see in the case of Sheffield Children's Centre, described by Broadhead et al. (2007), how powerful such approaches could be in providing support and focused development for families under severe economic pressures.

Thinking of a primary school or early years centre that you know, identify examples of effective 'multi-professional' working and how they benefit children.

More recent major initiatives on primary education in England consist of two reports, one of which was commissioned by government from one of the trio of authors of the earlier 'Three Wise Men' report; the other was independent, funded by a charity, but also led by another of the trio. The first, the Rose Report, published in 2009, was a review of the national curriculum (Rose, 2009). The second, the *Cambridge Primary Review*, led by Robin Alexander (2010), was a very wide-ranging investigation and review that attempted to recreate the scale of the Plowden Report from more than 30 years earlier. Whilst the Rose Report was being picked up by the Labour Government before it left office in 2010, the *Cambridge Primary Review* had more of an uneven influence on government because of its strong criticisms of significant elements of government policy, including the 'marketisation' of primary education that had taken place under successive governments of both major persuasions. This we will discuss in more detail in the next section.

THE PRIMARY SCHOOL AND THE WIDER COMMUNITY

One key element of the policy shifts which were launched in the 1988 Education Reform Act was what became known as the 'marketisation' of education. Whilst initially much of the emphasis here was on performance and choice in the secondary school sector, the whole trend has increasingly had an influence on primary early years and school provision (Vincent and Ball, 2006) and arguably has fundamentally shifted the relationship between primary schools and their communities both at local and regional levels.

Choice and Diversity was the name of a White Paper in 1992 (DfE, 1992) and signalled this marketisation quite clearly. The national assessment procedures that had been introduced in 1988, with national statutory tests (commonly known as SATs) for all children at the ages of 7, 11 and 13, were one element that enabled the government to produce school 'league tables' that would be published with a view to helping parents to decide which school they wished to send their children to. Another element though was the new approach to the inspection of schools under the auspices of the Office for Standards in Education (Ofsted) which was created in 1992 and again led to very public reporting on Ofsted's judgements about the quality of schools. This approach has continued into the twenty-first century, with schools each being allocated to a particular category ranging (now) from 'Outstanding' through to 'Inadequate'.

Web Link

A White Paper on 'Choice and Diversity' can be accessed through this web link, available on the companion website: www.educationengland.org.uk/documents/wp1992/choice-and-diversity.html

These changes were designed to bring in a competitive element between schools in the belief that competition would lead to improvement, and that schools which did not improve would have to either close or be taken over by new leadership. Indeed, 'school leadership' was the other element in this new competitive orientation. In the 1988 Act, the phrase used was Local Management of Schools (LMS) and again this was but the beginning of a move towards greater 'independence' for schools.

From the middle of the twentieth century onwards, the local education authorities (LEAs) had taken a major role in the management of schools. Not only were they responsible for ensuring that there was a sufficient level of provision in communities for all children to be able to attend schools in reasonable proximity to their homes, the LEAs were also responsible for the recruitment and employment of teachers and for providing appropriate professional support to head teachers and governing bodies. Each school did have its own governing body but these were supported and in some cases administered by the LEA. From 1988 onwards, this local authority influence and responsibility for school management progressively reduced, so that by the first part of the new century LEAs typically held only residual powers, indeed being required to step in in cases where the school was judged to be inadequate in some way or to ensure that the children with the most severe special educational needs were being provided for.

From the late 1990s onwards, radically new approaches to the governance of schools were being introduced, which saw many of them becoming completely detached from the LEA. Under the Labour Government from 1997, it became possible for schools to become 'academies' which were run independently of the LEA. Labour tended to focus on the 'poorest performing' schools in their academisation plans, picking up failing schools by putting new head teachers in and creating independent governance structures. When the Conservative–Liberal Democrat Coalition was in power in 2010, with education policy under the leadership of Michael Gove as Secretary of State for Education, there was a rapid expansion of the academy programme so that in some areas of England (because the policy is not followed in other parts of the UK) all schools had become academies. Many of them were members of 'Multi-Academy Trusts' or MATs, which were networks managed by an overarching Board of Directors, much like a commercial chain of companies. However, in addition to the expansion of the academies programme, the Coalition Government started on another track of creating what it called 'free schools'. Apparently building on models derived from Scandinavia, Sweden in particular, local groups were encouraged to apply to the

Department for Education to create entirely independent schools. These could be 'conversions' from existing schools but could also be brand new start-ups.

More or less any group could establish itself and apply to create such a school. It would be expected to provide a rationale for the creation of the school which would, usually, consist of an argument about a distinctive approach to education or to providing a centre of excellence in an area where it was claimed there was a lack of high quality provision. There was considerable political controversy around the government's claim that the establishment of these schools as new players in the market would lead to greater competition and hence to the improvement of all provision. Opponents pointed out a number of aspects to counter this. One was that there was not a level playing field – the new free schools could set their own admission policies and therefore admit only those children capable of contributing to successful results for the school, creating a sense of 'sink schools' elsewhere in the local educational community. Furthermore, given that there was not required to be any demonstrable shortage of school places within a community in order for a new free school to be established, the new provision could seriously undermine the local planning for provision of school places, creating considerable volatility in pupil rolls and making existing schools unviable. The government also made it possible for teachers without a recognised teaching qualification to be employed in these schools. In spite of such opposition, the government was determined to pursue this approach and when re-elected as a Conservative Party government in 2015, announced its continuing commitment to these approaches.

The Conservative Government argued that self-managing and locally led developments were creating more democratic approaches because they were giving 'power' to local communities in shaping local educational provision. The fact that there were no local electoral processes feeding into these arrangements was not seen as a problem in this marketised view of how education should be managed. A wide range of organisations, including charitable trusts, private companies and religious organisations have been among those who have taken the opportunities created by these policies to engage in the provision of schooling, including primary schooling, at a local level. Some of these organisations, however, operate regionally or at a national level and are creating a new kind of educational management infrastructure which has sidelined local government and, in the name of local self-management, has actually created what some critics see as a heavily centralised power base for the Secretary of State (Ball, 2013). Funding for these schools comes directly from central government and it is the Secretary of State who has the power to determine whether new schools should be created and what their status and admissions policy should be. For critics, a major worry is that we will see an increasingly differentiated schooling system with strong and vibrant schools in areas where parents have the social and cultural capital to ensure that standards are high, whilst local authorities are left to protect and defend the residual provision in hard-pressed and disadvantaged areas where there are high levels of poverty and unemployment.

Research has shown how middle-class parents have adapted their behaviour in response to the education marketplace, with families moving home, especially in metropolitan areas, so that they can stake a claim for their children to attend the better schools (Vincent and Ball, 2006). Denominational schools tend to favour families who can prove a commitment to their particular church and so that has also sometimes played a part in families' behaviour. Rather than having a universal commitment to state provision of high quality for all schools, the current approach is one based on a view that increased diversity and specialisation will create a better education service. Although the funding continues to be provided centrally through the taxes raised by the Treasury, the funds are disbursed to foster different provision in different locations. It is a fractured localised system which is centrally funded, locally administered but not by democratically elected bodies. So it is that the relationship between schools and the wider society has been fundamentally changed.

reflection point

What kinds of early years settings and schools are there in your local area? Examine the extent to which they are controlled and run as commercial enterprises rather than as state provision.

All of this in England is in very stark contrast to what has been happening elsewhere in the UK, most particularly in Scotland, where local authorities continue not only to plan provision but also to employ teachers and support schools. There is a much more uniform approach to primary school provision north of the border. There are some differences between schools – for example, a significant minority of primary schools are associated with the Roman Catholic church – but there is a universalism that prevails that is in very strong contrast with the approach now being taken in England (Cassidy, 2013).

spotlight on practice

Using SEAL (Social and Emotional Aspects of Learning) materials to encourage inclusion

Belle moved schools in Y4. Most of the children in the class she joined had been together since beginning school and had formed strong relationships. They made very little attempt to include Belle in their already well-established groups. In spite of the teacher's interventions and support, Belle felt more and more isolated and became increasingly withdrawn. The teacher introduced some of the SEAL materials for Y3/4 on relationships to the class. In circle time, she used ideas of 'lost' and 'lonely', encouraging each child to say 'I felt lost when...' and 'I felt lonely when...' Most of the children contributed. Belle did not. The teacher discussed ideas of responsibility with the children: that we all need to take responsibility for what we choose to do and its consequences; that our behaviour may hurt others or it may help them. Then she introduced the idea of conscience. The children were asked to imagine one character sitting on either shoulder: one character is 'conscience' who will tell them what a wise, fair or kind choice might be; the other will tell them the opposite. Through working with these materials, the children gradually realised that their behaviour may have contributed to Belle's isolation and that they had some responsibility for her loneliness. It took a long time but, with a lot of help from her newly-aware friends, Belle eventually settled into the class.

NATIONAL AND INTERNATIONAL CONTEXTS FOR EARLY YEARS AND PRIMARY EDUCATION

In this section, we stand back and consider how the developments in primary education in the UK, especially England, relate to equivalent provision elsewhere in the world. Much earlier on, we mentioned how practices in some European countries had been very influential in the development of primary education in the UK, and indeed how much of the 'child-centredness' that typified early years and primary education in the 1960s and 1970s had its origins elsewhere.

One of the most striking differences between UK primary education and provision elsewhere nowadays is the heavy emphasis in the UK on early literacy. It is an expectation that is dominant here that children will be able to read by the age of 7 at the latest. In other words, in England when they transfer from KS1 to KS2, they are expected to be competent readers. However, in many other European countries children are not formally introduced to reading until the age of 6 or 7 years. There also tends now to be a much greater emphasis elsewhere on learning through play in the early years of schooling, rather than through formal instruction.

In a seminal study carried out across five countries (England, France, India, Russia and the USA), Robin Alexander explored the connections between national cultures and primary school pedagogy (Alexander, 2000). In a fascinating analysis, Alexander finds strong connections between how children are understood and valued within a society and the ways in which they are taught. He criticises the extent to which central government has intervened in many aspects of primary schooling:

> England, for long bracketed with the United States as an emblem of decentralisation and professional autonomy, became within the space of a decade the most centralised and ruthlessly policed of all our five systems of primary education. At the same time, like the others, it displays powerful historical continuities that counter government claims of 'modernization'. Most prominent are the twin legacies of elementary minimalism and progressive idealism [Blyth's elementary and developmental traditions, as referred to above], the one still shaping school structures and classroom practice, the other continuing to influence professional consciousness and classroom practice. (Alexander, 2000: 532)

The extent to which 'progressive idealism' is still influencing teachers may have reduced since Alexander carried out his study, such has been the disempowering effect of many policy changes in the recent past.

It is also worth considering whether these insights from five nations have anything to tell us about the comparisons between approaches within the four jurisdictions of the UK. Such comparative study has rarely been undertaken here but could be very fruitful. At a superficial level, there would appear to be a growing consistency between the approaches in Scotland, Wales and Northern Ireland, with the English approach being increasingly distinctive or divergent from the rest. Whether this English trajectory can be related to fundamental cultural differences between that part of the UK and the rest is somewhat doubtful. It seems much more likely that the explanation lies more centrally within political ideologies and discourses. However, as the *Cambridge Primary Review* demonstrates very clearly, we do see a divergent pattern that is really quite surprising.

One of the factors that has been suggested as causing some of these different developments is the growing influence of international league tables of educational attainment. We mentioned earlier how league tables have played an increasingly significant role within provision in England, but politicians and policy makers have become increasingly preoccupied with performance at a national level in surveys such as the Programme for International Student Assessment (PISA). PISA offers international comparisons in attainment in many aspects, including reading, mathematics, science and in more social areas such as happiness at school. When the results of the international surveys are published every few years, politicians become very sensitive to their own nation's performance and sometimes take rather drastic action. This was the case, for example, in Wales when, a few years after dropping national statutory assessment through SATs, their standards were found to have dropped; they immediately reintroduced a national assessment system.

Web Link

More information about PISA can be accessed through this web link, available on the companion website: www.oecd.org/pisa/aboutpisa/

It would generally be true to say that in the UK we have seen increasing direct political intervention into educational policy in a way that was not apparent through most of the twentieth century. Education, including primary education, has become a highly politicised aspect of social provision during this period. It seems quite ironic that in some societies that have actually performed relatively well in the PISA surveys over many years, there has been far less political intervention and the professionals – that is, the teachers and administrators – have been left very much to take responsibility for the development of policy and practice. The prime example of this is Finland, another northern European country, perhaps more similar in scale to Scotland than to England, where test results have been consistently high and teaching, including primary teaching, is seen as a very highly rated profession, with far more applicants for training places than can be made available (Sahlberg, 2011).

reflection point

Can you recall any recent stories in the media (press, TV, radio, Twitter) and statements by politicians about how they would improve primary education provision, that draw attention to international comparisons in primary education?

Elsewhere in the world, primary education provision is a key plank in development strategies for many poorer countries. The adoption of 'Universal Primary Education' in several African countries, for example, has been a key element in their economic development plans. Even in such settings, however, there have been tensions around the nature of provision. In parts of India, for example, transnational organisations, including 'for profit' companies such as Pearson, have been encouraging the introduction of low-cost private provision (Ball, 2012), again in a similar argument to that referred to earlier, that personal investment in children's education will lead to greater commitment and therefore to better standards of provision.

Web Link

An interesting article in The Guardian Online about universal primary education can be accessed through this web link, available on the companion website: www.theguardian.com/global-development/2015/sep/16/future-perfect-investing-child-wellbeing-brings-big-payoff-early-childhood-development-sdg

putting it into practice

Helping children understand the world

Children can be encouraged to explore similarities and differences in relation to places, objects, materials and living things by talking about the features of their own immediate environment and how these environments might vary from one another.

Teachers can try this as a classroom activity by splitting children into small groups supplied with large pieces of paper and coloured pens. The teacher then explains that some places (environments) are different from others, for instance, in many ways the school environment is different from home. At home, you might have a bedroom but you do not have a bedroom at nursery. In the nursery, there might be lots of chairs; at home, there may be only five or six chairs. In turn, each of the children describes something which belongs in their home, e.g. a red sofa. You can record this on one of the pieces of paper. Then the children describe something in the nursery which is different from home. Record this on the other piece of paper.

The outcome of this activity is that the children will have extended their understanding of differences in relation to place.

SUMMARY

In this chapter, we have considered the relationship between primary school and the wider community. We have considered this at several levels: the local, the regional, the national and the international. The child starting in an early years setting, or going to primary school for the first time, is likely only to be aware of the people he or she meets in the setting or school – the other children, the staff. As they adjust to the new social context, they may get a sense of how their home life and school life connect with each other. However, young children are not aware that the educational institution they experience is part of a much wider structure that has connections with the wider community and society. But that, in a way, is the very purpose of the primary school – to provide an introduction to wider social structures, including knowledge structures, that go beyond the family and the household. Yes, the primary school is there to support children's learning, to broaden their understanding and develop their skills, but it is also there to ensure that as they grow and develop, children become aware of, and indeed become part of, a wider social setting. The primary school has important connections with the wider society and the ways in which it is governed, and the ways in which local, regional and national enterprises relate to it, whether commercial, industrial, cultural or educational, are ultimately of great significance.

reflection point

Consider some of the implications of school's place in society for teachers and other educators who are preparing to work in the primary and early years sector:

- What is it that the children themselves bring into school from their home and family? For example, their language and/or languages; their knowledge of the wider world; their knowledge of the local community and its resources?
- How can the teacher help the child to adjust to this very different context in a way that is conducive to good emotional health and to developing the child's disposition towards learning?

companion website

To access additional online resources please visit: **https://study.sagepub.com/wyseandrogers**

Here you will find a classroom activity, author podcasts including Ian Menter and Margaret Walker's top tips for employability, free access to SAGE journal articles and links to external sources.

further reading

The Plowden Report (Central Advisory Council for Education, 1967) and the *Cambridge Primary Review* (Alexander, 2010) are two reports that offer a full sense of the connections between primary schools and society.

(Continued)

(Continued)

Cunningham, P. (2012) *Politics and the Primary Teacher.* London: Routledge. Chapter 8 is called 'Local accountability: school, community and local democracy' and provides more detail on some of these issues. The book also reminds us of how politics is a central consideration for all in education.

Wyse, D., Hayward, L. and Pandya, J. (eds) (2015) *SAGE Handbook of Curriculum, Pedagogy and Assessment*. London: Sage. Several contributors to these international research volumes examine the influence of international league tables on curriculum, pedagogy and assessment - see, especially, the chapter by one of the main architects of PISA, Andreas Schleicher.

REFERENCES

Alexander, R. (2000) *Culture and Pedagogy*. Oxford: Blackwell.

Alexander, R. (ed.) (2010) *Children, their World, their Education: Final Report and Recommendations of the Cambridge Primary Review*. London: Routledge.

Alexander, R., Rose, J. and Woodhead, C. (1992) *Curriculum Organisation and Classroom Practice in Primary Schools: A Discussion Paper*. London: DES.

Ball, S. (2012) *Global Education Inc.: New Policy Networks and the Neoliberal Imaginary.* London: Routledge.

Ball, S. (2013) *The Education Debate* (2nd edn). Bristol: Policy Press.

Bennett, N. (1984) *Teaching Styles and Pupil Progress*. London: Open Books

Blyth, W. (1965) *English Primary Education: A Sociological Description*. London: Routledge & Kegan Paul.

Broadhead, P., Meleady, C. and Delgado, M. (2007) *Children, Families and Communities: Creating and Sustaining Integrated Services*. Maidenhead: Open University Press.

Cassidy, C. (2013) 'Scottish primary education: philosophy and practice', in Bryce, T., Humes, W., Gillies, D. and Kennedy, A. (eds) *Scottish Education* (4th edn). Edinburgh: University Press. pp. 39–49.

Central Advisory Council for Education (CACE) (England) (1967) *Children and their Primary Schools* (The Plowden Report). London: HMSO.

Consultative Committee of the Board of Education (1931) *The Primary School* (The Hadow Report). London: HMSO.

Department for Education (DfE) (1992) *Choice and Diversity.* London: HMSO.

Department of Education and Science (DES) (1972) *A Framework for Expansion (White Paper).* London: HMSO.

Douglas, J. (1967) *The Home and the School.* London: Panther Books.

Dyson, A., Farrell, P., Kerr, K. and Mearns, N. (2009) '"Swing, swing together": multi-agency work in the new children's services', in Chapman, C. and Gunter, H. (eds) *Radical Reforms*. London: Routledge.

Galton, M., Simon, B. and Croll, P. (1980) *Inside the Primary Classroom*. London: Routledge & Kegan Paul.

Gillborn, D. and Mirza, H. (2000) *Education Inequality: Mapping 'Race', Class and Gender – a Synthesis of Research Evidence*. London: Ofsted.

Her Majesty's Inspectorate of Schools (HMI) (1978) *Primary Education in England: A Survey by Her Majesty's Inspectorate of Schools*. London: HMSO.

Maclure, S. (1986) *Educational Documents – England and Wales 1816 to the Present Day* (5th edn). London: Methuen.

Midwinter, E. (1972) *Priority Education*. Harmondsworth: Penguin.

Rampton, A. (1981) *West Indian Children in our Schools*. London: HMSO.

Rose, J. (2009) *Independent Review of the Primary Curriculum*. London: DCSF.

Sahlberg, P. (2011) *Finnish Lessons*. New York: Teachers' College.

Scottish Education Department (1965) *Primary Education in Scotland*. Edinburgh: HMSO.

Swann, Lord (1985) *Education for All*. London: HMSO.

Vincent, C. and Ball, S. (2006) *Childcare, Choice and Class Practices: Middle-class Parents and their Children*. London: Routledge.

Wyse, D., Baumfield, V., Egan, D., Gallagher, C., Hayward, L., Hulme, M., et al. (2013) *Creating the Curriculum*. London: Routledge.

3

CURRENT DEVELOPMENTS IN EDUCATION

Gary Beauchamp with Neil Purcell

LEARNING AIMS

This chapter will enable you to:

- develop an understanding of current developments in early years and primary education in the countries of the UK
- consider current developments in their historical context
- understand better how education and politics are linked
- think about future ways of working in view of the impact of social media on the lives of children and teachers.

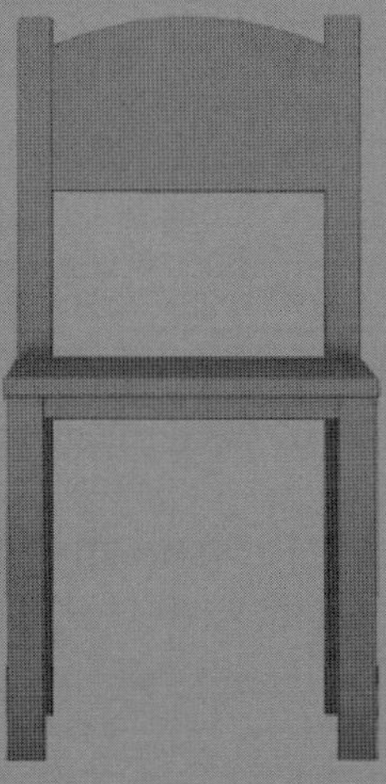

When W.E. Forster introduced the Elementary Education Act of 1870 in the House of Commons, it aimed to 'provide a truly national system of education' which would 'penetrate the length and breadth of the land, and as quickly as possible bring within the reach of every child in England and Wales the means of learning reading, writing, and arithmetic' (HL DEB, 1870). Although rather late compared to the rest of Europe, this Act not only began the process of making primary education compulsory for all children, but also moved control of education away from the early dominance of the established church and firmly into the hands of politicians. We will return to the influence of politicians on primary education in the UK below, but one of the most pressing issues in primary education for politicians around the world today is that, despite arriving in the UK in 1870, Universal Primary Education (UPE) is still not available to all children around the world.

UNIVERSAL PRIMARY EDUCATION (UPE)

At the turn of the century, world leaders at the United Nations (UN) agreed a Millennium Declaration and outlined eight Millennium Development Goals (MDGs) to be met by 2015. Alongside aims such as to 'Eradicate extreme poverty and hunger', the second of these goals was to 'Achieve Universal Primary Education', including ensuring 'that, by 2015, children everywhere, boys and girls alike, will be able to complete a full course of primary schooling' (UN, 2014: 16). By 2014, 'Despite impressive strides forward at the start of the decade, progress in reducing the number of children out of school has slackened considerably' (UN, 2014: 16). In the final review of 2015, despite the headline 'The number of out-of-school children has been cut almost in half since 2000' (UN, 2015: 25), an estimated 57 million children of primary school age remained out of school worldwide, with particular challenges in sub-Saharan Africa. As such, the aspiration for universal primary education remains a very current issue, particularly in view of increasing global migration, and one that should help us to contextualise some current issues in the UK.

POLITICS AND THE CURRICULUM ACROSS THE UK: HOW WE GOT TO WHERE WE ARE NOW

The altruistic aims of the UN would no doubt be echoed by contemporary politicians in the UK, but we should be in no doubt that 'education is essentially a political activity' (Kelly, 2009: 187), reflected in the 'colonisation, by the government of the primary school curriculum, with regard to its aims, nature, assessment and delivery' (Campbell, 2001: 31). In fact, Alexander (2010: 1) asserts that 'From the early 1990s... primary education was a problem to be fixed, and the fixes were not to be teachers or local authorities, for they had had their chance and blown it, but central government'. As long as politicians maintain control over the curriculum and the examination system, the cyclical nature of elections and the potential for the education system to form part of a minister's legacy (Beauchamp and Jephcote, 2016) mean that longer-term planning and the implementation of effective policy, beyond the life cycle of a parliament, are unlikely. In fact, many of the current developments in primary education we will discuss below may even have changed by the time you read this!

Within the UK, an added complication is the ongoing impact of the devolution of educational powers to Scotland, Wales and Northern Ireland. In the latter, Leitch (2009) notes the unique impact of a prolonged period of civil conflict and political instability. Even prior to these devolved powers, however, despite political rhetoric to the contrary, Britain was 'not homogenous but is, and always has been, plural, fragmented and differentiated' (Grosvenor, 2005: 285). Since control of education has been devolved, amongst other powers, it is perhaps inevitable that these differences will become more evident and reflect the national identity of each individual country. For primary teachers (and indeed for primary pupils), this has potentially far-reaching consequences in terms of mobility between the nations and the 'portability' of qualifications and knowledge of the curriculum for each country.

As in many aspects of education, England is increasingly becoming an outlier both in the actual content of the curriculum and in how it is organised across the primary school and beyond (Beauchamp et al., 2015). Indeed, it is becoming increasingly difficult to think about a 'primary curriculum' in isolation from the rest of a child's education. In terms of the content of the curriculum, differences began to emerge even with the introduction of a National Curriculum in the Education Reform Act of 1988. For instance, even though educational policy in Wales was in reality controlled by the English government at the time, separate curriculum orders were developed to reflect Welsh history, geography and music, and an additional subject of Welsh (as a second language) was added.

Given the historical context of each individual *nation*, even the concept of a 'national curriculum' itself was questioned both when it was introduced and since. Even leaving aside concerns about how the curriculum reflected emerging national identities, the 1988 national curriculum was heavily criticised at the time because of its 'almost exclusive reliance on traditional subject disciplines' (Chitty, 2014: 154). Quite how traditional the subjects were is shown by Aldrich's (1988, cited in Chitty, 2014) comparison with the secondary curriculum introduced in 1904. Table 3.1 (developed from Chitty, 2014) outlines current developments in the curricula of countries in the UK. I will leave you to make your own judgements about how far the curriculum in each country has evolved since this time.

Table 3.1 shows a growing divergence in what is taught in the early years, and in primary schools in England compared to the rest of the UK. (For a more detailed consideration of the curriculum in England, see Chapter 8.) The English curriculum retains a focus on individual subjects (having explicitly rejected the more integrated approach to the curriculum proposed by Rose in 2009), whilst the rest of the UK has already moved, or is in the process of moving, to a broader focus on areas of learning, explicitly integrated with each other. In his review of the curriculum in Wales, Donaldson (2015) reports that this is part of an international trend and, in addition to Scotland and Northern Ireland above, he cites similar examples in Australia, New Zealand (eight

Table 3.1 Current and proposed curricula in the UK

1904 First introduction of subject-based secondary curriculum	**1988 Introduction of National Curriculum**	**2014 England *National Curriculum***	**2014 Scotland[1] *Curriculum for Excellence***	**2014 Proposed new curriculum Wales[2]**	**2014 Northern Ireland[3] *The Northern Ireland Curriculum Primary***
	Introduced 1988	Revised 2014	Introduced 2010	Proposed and accepted 2015	Introduced 2007
		Early Years Foundation Stage: pre-school, nursery and Reception	Curriculum 3-18	Curriculum 3-16	The Foundation Stage: Years 1 and 2
		Key Stage 1: 5-7 years Key Stage 2: 7-11 years		The Board of Education requirements specified nine subjects for the new secondary schools	Key Stage 1: Years 3 and 4 Key Stage 2: Years 5, 6 and 7
	The statutory national curriculum had **10 subjects** that should be taught to all pupils.	The statutory national curriculum has **11 subjects** that should be taught to all pupils.	The curriculum **3-18** is organised into **eight curriculum areas.**	The curriculum **3-16** should be organised into **six Areas of Learning and Experience** with three cross-curriculum responsibilities: literacy; numeracy; and digital competence.	The curriculum applies to all 12 years of compulsory education. In primary school made up of **six Areas of Learning.**

1904 First introduction of subject-based secondary curriculum	1988 Introduction of National Curriculum	2014 England *National Curriculum*	2014 Scotland[1] *Curriculum for Excellence*	2014 Proposed new curriculum Wales[2]	2014 Northern Ireland[3] *The Northern Ireland Curriculum Primary*
English	English	English	Mathematics	Languages, Literacy and Communication	Language and Literacy
Mathematics	Mathematics	Mathematics	Sciences	Mathematics and Numeracy	Mathematics and Numeracy
Science	Science	Science	Religious and Moral Education	Science and Technology	The World Around Us
History	History	History	Expressive Arts	Expressive Arts	The Arts
Geography	Geography	Geography	Health and Well-being	Health and Well-being	Personal Development and Mutual Understanding
Foreign Language	Modern Foreign Language	Foreign Language (KS2 only)	Languages	Humanities	Physical Education
Drawing	Art	Art and Design	Social Sciences		
Physical Exercise	Physical Education	Physical Education	Technologies		
Manual work/ Housewifery	Technology	Design and Technology			
	Music	Music			
		Computing			

Notes:

1. The curriculum areas and subjects are only part of the curriculum – see www.educationscotland.gov.uk/learningandteaching/thecurriculum/whatiscurriculumforexcellence/understandingthecurriculumasawhole/index.asp
2. Currently Foundation Phase (3–7 years) with seven Areas of Learning and Key Stage 2 with 11 subjects (English, Welsh, mathematics, science, design and technology, information and communication technology, history, geography, art and design, music, and physical education).
3. www.nicurriculum.org.uk/docs/key_stages_1_and_2/northern_ireland_curriculum_primary.pdf

areas of learning) and the Netherlands (six broad areas). There are also suggestions that Finland may also be following this lead in the near future.

The key feature of the debate in England appears to be a focus on *knowledge*, compartmentalised into discrete subjects. The statutory guidance for the national curriculum in England states that 'the national curriculum provides pupils with an introduction to the essential knowledge they need to be educated citizens'.

This belief in the need for 'essential knowledge' seems unlikely to change under the current government as Nicky Morgan, the Secretary of State for Education, recently asserted in a speech: 'At the heart of our reforms has been a determination to place knowledge back at the core of what pupils learn in school. For too long our education system prized the development of skills above core knowledge.'

We arrive here back almost where we started in 1870 with a discussion of who decides what should be taught in primary school and, perhaps an even wider issue, what the purpose of primary education is. In considering the most recent review in England, it is interesting to note here an extract from a House of Commons briefing intended to provide information 'to Members of Parliament in support of their parliamentary duties'. It contends:

Web Link

An interesting article about the Finnish education system can be accessed through this web link, available on the companion website: www.independent.co.uk/news/world/europe/finland-schools-subjects-are-out-and-topics-are-in-as-country-reforms-its-education-system-10123911.html

More information about the national curriculum in England can be accessed through this web link, available on the companion website: www.gov.uk/government/publications/national-curriculum-in-england-framework-for-key-stages-1-to-4/the-national-curriculum-in-england-framework-for-key-stages-1-to-4

Nicky Morgan's speech in full can be accessed through this web link, available on the companion website: www.gov.uk/government/speeches/nicky-morgan-why-knowledge-matters

> There has been widespread support for the review's aims and some support for changes that have been made to the 'content' of individual national curriculum subjects. The Government argues that the proposals have been developed giving 'due regard' to the views of subject experts and teachers and to the findings of international best-practice comparisons.

> However, many commentators have raised concerns about both the review process, and its outcomes. They have queried the level of involvement of specialists in determining the subject content, the degree of prescription in terms of what should be taught, and to what extent the new curriculum is likely to meet the Government's stated aims. (Roberts, 2014: 1)

The writing style is typical of some government documents as it is impossible both to identify who the 'many commentators' are and what the writer considers to be 'many', making it hard for objective judgements to be made. What is clearer, however, is the view of some of the 'specialists'. For instance, during the consultation process for the revision of the National Curriculum in England, 100 senior education academics signed a letter published in *The Independent* on 20 March 2013 attacking the narrowness of the curriculum and the implied distrust of teachers and expert advice.

Web Link

The letter in full, entitled 'Gove will bury pupils in facts and rules', can be accessed through this web link, available on the companion website: www.independent.co.uk/voices/letters/letters-gove-will-bury-pupils-in-facts-and-rules-8540741.html

Despite such views, the curriculum in England was reviewed in line with government policy and 'policy in England appears to be diverging from that elsewhere in the UK' (Beauchamp et al., 2013: 9). It is impossible to predict the longer-term implications of this, for teachers and pupils, but it remains a very real issue for many in primary education.

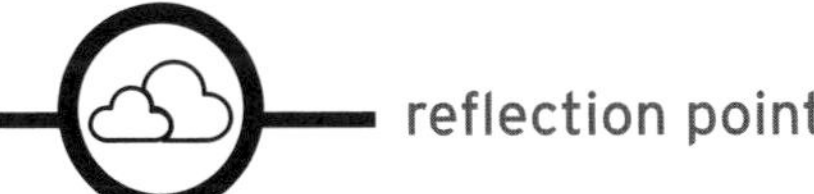

reflection point

What are the strengths and weaknesses of this divergence in educational policy across the UK and what are the implications for primary education?

ICT AND COMPUTING: A CASE STUDY IN CURRICULUM CONTENT

Another anomaly in Table 3.1 above is the inclusion of 'computing' in the national curriculum for England in place of Information and Communication Technology (ICT), which has been a compulsory subject since the NC was introduced in 1988. In fact, the disappearance of ICT is a common theme across the UK (although it currently retains a place in Key Stage 2 in Wales), but England is the only country where ICT has been explicitly replaced by computing alone. Again, it could be suggested that this change was ideologically driven, particularly by Michael Gove, the Secretary of State for Education at the time, although support was provided by other organisations such as the Royal Society (RS). In 2012, the RS produced a report entitled 'Shut down or restart? The way forward for computing in UK schools', which concluded:

> The current delivery of Computing education in many UK schools is highly unsatisfactory. Although existing curricula for Information and Communication Technology (ICT) are broad and allow scope for teachers to inspire pupils and help them develop interests in Computing, many pupils are not inspired by what they are taught and gain nothing beyond basic digital literacy skills such as how to use a word-processor or a database.

This is mainly because:

> 1.1 The current national curriculum in ICT can be very broadly interpreted and may be reduced to the lowest level where non-specialist teachers have to deliver it;
>
> 1.2 There is a shortage of teachers who are able to teach beyond basic digital literacy ... (Royal Society, 2012: 5)

It is interesting to compare this with Ofsted's (2011: 4) findings about ICT in the primary school from a year earlier:

> The teaching of ICT was good or outstanding in nearly two thirds of the primary schools visited, with many teachers and teaching assistants increasingly confident and able to support pupils effectively. There were weaknesses in the teaching of more demanding topics such as data handling or control, but in many of the schools this gap had been identified and was being addressed.

From this, it would appear that 'non-specialist teachers' are well able to move beyond the 'lowest level'. Indeed, as the primary curriculum required teachers to teach ICT, it is perhaps hardly surprising that some would conclude that computing is not being well taught. In reality, however, such views were seized on by the government in England who used its prevailing rhetoric regarding the need for 'rigour' to justify a move to computing as a subject in the national curriculum. Speaking in January 2014 (about a curriculum to be introduced in September that year), Gove asserted, without providing evidence to support his claims, that the existing 'unambitious, demotivating and dull' ICT curriculum 'had to go' (to be replaced by a new computing curriculum – notably drawn up by 'industry experts', rather than education experts).

Web Link

Michael Gove's speech about computing and education technology can be accessed through this web link, available on the companion website: www.gov.uk/government/speeches/michael-gove-speaks-about-computing-and-education-technology

It is hardly surprising that this move was welcomed by organisations such as Computing at School (CAS), but even their own guidance to primary schools acknowledges that the introduction of computing 'represents continuity and change, challenge and opportunity ... [and that] ... the focus of the new programme of study undeniably moves towards programming and other aspects of computer science' (CAS, 2013: 4).

In Northern Ireland, we have already seen that ICT was no longer a discrete subject, but is instead a cross-curricular skill. In Scotland, as part of the 'Technologies' curriculum area, *computing* science is only one part of six 'organisers':

- technological developments in society
- ICT to enhance learning
- business
- computing science
- food and textiles
- craft, design, engineering and graphics.

It is also worth noting that the Scottish *Principles and Practice* document for Technologies reminds teachers:

> Technologies are connected strongly with all other areas of the curriculum, through extending and applying the specialist knowledge and understanding developed in the sciences, through the creative use of technology in the expressive arts, through interdisciplinary learning, for example linking mathematics, science and technologies in an engineering context, and through the use of technologies to enhance learning. (www.educationscotland.gov.uk/Images/technologies_principles_practice_tcm4-540109.pdf, p. 4)

As such, not only does this specifically acknowledge the wider role of ICT in enhancing learning in the primary school, it also indicates that computing science is only one facet of the use of technology, rather than an individual subject.

In Wales, the very recently published review of the curriculum[1] (accepted in full by the Minister for Education and Skills in July 2015) 'recommends that literacy, numeracy and digital competence should be Cross-curriculum Responsibilities for all teachers and people who work with children and young people' (Donaldson, 2015: 40). In addition, like Scotland, the review 'proposes the introduction of computer science – spanning, for example, the kinds of thinking skills used in computation (including analysis, use of algorithms and problem solving), design and modelling, and developing, implementing and testing digital solutions – as a specific component within the Science and Technology Area of Learning and Experience' (Donaldson, 2015: 51). Again, we see computer science as part of a more rounded view of technology, rather than as an individual subject.

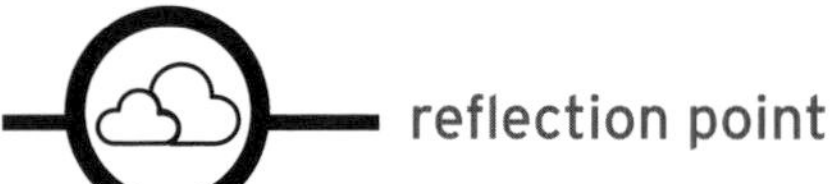

Consider what practical and pedagogic skills you need to develop in whatever country you work in - not only immediately but also ongoing and in the future.

ITT OR ITE: WHAT DIFFERENCE DOES IT MAKE?

All that we have seen above will inevitably impact on the initial preparation of teachers to teach in the primary classroom and this is currently the focus of much debate within the UK. We have seen that devolved educational powers have resulted in different curricula across the UK. As these become more unique, it is perhaps inevitable that preparation to teach them also becomes more distinctive, reflected in nomenclature employed in official documentation and, as a result, within institutions which prepare teachers for the primary classroom.

Furlong (2015: 5) pointedly titles a report published in 2015 in Wales 'Teaching Tomorrow's Teachers: Options for the future of initial teacher education in Wales'. He does acknowledge at the outset, however, that:

> There is a range of different ways in which the initial professional preparation of teachers is described in policy documents within the UK.
>
> In England, and indeed in Wales until now, there has been an insistence on the term - 'training' - hence 'initial teacher training' or 'ITT'. In this report the term 'initial teacher education' or 'ITE' is used instead. This is because the word 'education' is being used as an inclusive term.
>
> It is fully accepted that ITE courses necessarily include within them important elements of both 'education' and 'training'.

In this chapter, we will accept Furlong's logic and use the acronym ITE. In doing so, we will also accept that the term 'trainee' implies a rather narrow conception of what is involved in the initial professional development of teachers, so we will use the term student (teacher) instead.

The end result of political devolution is that the possibilities for cross-national divergences in educational policy have increased (Raffe, 2005). Beauchamp et al. (2015) note that reviews of teacher education have taken place in Northern Ireland (2013), Scotland (2011), Wales (2013 and 2015) and multiple times in England. In addition, revised initial teacher standards/competencies have also been introduced in England (2013), Scotland (2012), Wales (2011) and Northern Ireland (2007). In this context, it is hardly surprising that student teachers are faced with growing challenges in moving between the nations. Not only do they face teaching a different curriculum, there is also a growing potential for potential employers to question the relevance of the initial teacher education they have received. At present, officially this is not an issue within the UK[2], but any student (or indeed serving) teacher preparing for an interview in another country will inevitably have to consider how to answer questions about how well their ITE has prepared them to teach the relevant curriculum. It is also becoming increasingly easy to make mistakes in interviews for a first job or in applying for an ITE place. For instance, I have seen both students and teachers in interviews in Wales confuse the Foundation Stage in England with the Foundation Phase in Wales, which refer to different age groups, teaching philosophies and curriculum content.

SUSTAINABILITY OF ITE WITHIN HIGHER EDUCATION (HE)

Another consequence of the differing policies in each country, and also a reflection on politicians' beliefs about where ITE should take place, is a growing concern about the sustainability of ITE within many higher education institutions (HEIs). In England in particular, government policy has shown a deliberate move away from HEI providers towards increased training provided by schools.

This situation is, however, changing with the growth in England of initiatives such as School Direct, reflecting a government emphasis on moving training into schools. These changes in delivery model are creating instability in the sector as ITT student numbers in universities are decreased with a 23% cut in directly allocated places between 2012–13 and 2015–16. Such cuts have inevitably led to concerns about the long-term viability of delivering ITT courses in some universities, with some even questioning the impact of the potential cuts on the overall supply of teachers in England; a particular concern in primary school where pupil numbers are predicted to rise in the coming years. Universities UK (2014) also raise concerns about the potential reduction in diversity of training options, leaving students with less choice about where and how they train, and also about the negative impact on schools seeking partners to deliver School Direct training programmes.

At present, in Scotland, Wales and Northern Ireland, universities maintain a significant presence as providers of ITE. As Beauchamp et al. (2015: 2) report:

> ITE in Northern Ireland is currently provided through five higher education institutions (HEIs), two local universities and two university colleges, plus the Open University. There are no school-based routes into teacher education. From 2001 teacher education in Scotland has been provided through universities. There are currently eight university providers and no school-centred (SCITT) or employment-based (EBITT) routes. In Wales teacher training is provided by three regional 'centres', each made up of collaborating HEIs and, since 2013, Teach First Cymru. Each regional centre ... managing and delivering an allocated number of employment-based training routes under the Graduate Teacher Programme (GTP) on behalf of the Welsh Government.

In England, the situation is much more complex and diverse, and further complicated by the introduction of the School Direct route. In Scotland, Wales and Northern Ireland, there are currently only 21 providers in total. By contrast, Smithers, Robinson and Coughlin (2013) report that in 2011/12 in England there were 348 providers for approximately 35,790 ITE students. Although this can be partially explained by the much higher number of ITE students in England, this is only part of the problem. We are therefore faced with a situation where ITE students have an ever-increasing range of providers, but, as a result, there may be potentially an ever-decreasing number of universities providing ITE. Whilst ITE faces challenge across the UK, perhaps the most direct current threat therefore is to its viability within higher education in England.

THE ROLE OF RESEARCH IN ITE

Another potential consequence of moving ITE to schools is the potential to dilute the role of research. A recent large-scale enquiry by the British Education Research Association (BERA) and the RSA considered the role that research could make:

> to the development of teachers' professional identity and practice, to the quality of teaching, to the broader project of school improvement and transformation, and, critically, to the outcomes for learners: children, young people and adults, especially those for whom the education system does not currently 'deliver'. (BERA/RSA, 2014: 3)

The inquiry commission took advice from an expert panel, commissioned seven academic papers from international experts and collected evidence from a wide range of stakeholders. It concluded: 'The evidence gathered by the Inquiry is clear about the positive impact that a research literate and research engaged profession is likely to have on learner outcomes' (BERA/RSA, 2014: 6). (For the full report, see web links at the end of the chapter.)

If concerns about the provision of ITE within universities in England were to translate into fewer university providers, this would further complicate the provision of research-rich cultures for student teachers in that country. This is not to suggest that similar challenges do not exist in other countries in the UK, as some face their own challenges, such as the need to rebuild educational research capacity in Wales (Furlong, 2015). Nevertheless, the withdrawal of universities from ITE provision in England would present a considerable problem, given the number of students who train there.

EARLY YEARS TRAINING AND PROVISION

Another challenge facing all ITE providers is the growing divergence in early years pedagogy and practice across the UK. Early childhood education and care in the UK has experienced significant changes in both organisation and quality in the last 20 years (Faulkner and Coates, 2013) and is also increasingly the focus of public policy around the world (Oberhuemer, 2005). This policy has been informed by a growing body of research, in particular the large-scale, longitudinal Effective Pre-School, Primary and Secondary Education (EPPSE) research project. This has resulted, for instance, in recognition of the need to improve the qualifications and skills of the early years workforce in general and in the recent emergence in England of specialist qualification routes leading to early years teacher status.

Across the countries of the UK, however, policy and practice have taken different forms and happened at different speeds. Palaiologou et al. (2016) provide a useful summary of these developments and note that a key theme is the emphasis on play and play-based activities. We will briefly consider two examples of this to explore current developments in this area.

The introduction of the Early Years Foundation Stage (EYFS) in England in 2008 for children aged 0–5 years recognised the particular demands of working with children in this age phase. The most recent version states:

> Each area of learning and development must be implemented through planned, purposeful play and through a mix of adult-led and child-initiated activity ... As children grow older, and as their

> development allows, it is expected that the balance will gradually shift towards more activities led by adults, to help children prepare for more formal learning, ready for Year 1. (DfE, 2014: 9)

One could debate at length the distinctions between 'planned' play versus 'child-initiated activity', but what is clear is that the planned curriculum of Key Stage 1 in England means that control is handed over to the teacher to the detriment of child-initiated activity. What is less clear, however, is whether this is what teachers actually want. Indeed, in a small-scale study in England, Roberts-Holmes (2012: 30) noted a 'pedagogic tension' in reception classes 'between the child-led play-based EYFS approach and the knowledge-led National Curriculum', resulting in primary head teachers suggesting that EYFS should be extended into Key Stage 1. Such a move is perhaps less likely with an increased emphasis on 'school readiness' and findings by Ofsted (2014: 4) that 'Too many children start school without the range of skills they need', although it was noted that there were many different definitions of 'school readiness' in settings – in itself a cause for concern.

Similar pedagogic tensions have resulted from the introduction of the Foundation Phase (FP) in Wales, which was introduced in the same year (but building on a pilot phase from 2004/05 and fully implemented by 2010). The FP provides a 'Framework for Children's Learning' for children aged 3–7 years and has replaced Key Stage 1. Like the EYFS it is predicated on a central tenet that 'Children learn through first-hand experiential activities with the serious business of "play" providing the vehicle' (DCELLS, 2008: 4). What is interesting, however, is that this has now led to current concerns about the transition in Wales from the FP to Key Stage 2, which currently has a subject-based curriculum. Indeed, a Welsh Government (2014) evaluation found that 'Year 3 teachers have mixed feelings regarding Foundation Phase to Key Stage 2 transition, and transition strategies put in place vary considerably' (p. 1), 'Many children find the dramatic reduction in the use of Foundation Phase pedagogies across the year groups difficult' (p. 2) and 'Some practitioners and head teachers are explicitly trying to extend Foundation Phase pedagogies into Key Stage 2 in an attempt to ensure children continue to enjoy learning' (p. 3). It will be interesting to see if the new curriculum outlined earlier in this chapter will eventually address these concerns.

As we have already seen, this is potentially being addressed in Wales with a move to a curriculum which does away with key stages completely and focuses on a 3 to 16 curriculum. But, until such time as it is implemented, this transition will remain an issue not only in Wales but for any move from a play-based and child-led pedagogy to a more formal subject-based pedagogy.

OUTDOOR LEARNING AND RISK

Learning outside of the classroom is central to effective early years education and indeed across the primary school. It has been an essential feature of education in many countries for many years and is now becoming increasingly important within the UK. It is explicitly required in the Foundation Phase in Wales which states:

> Indoor and outdoor environments that are fun, exciting, stimulating and safe promote children's development and natural curiosity to explore and learn through first-hand experiences. The Foundation Phase environment should promote discovery and independence and a greater emphasis on using the outdoor environment as a resource for children's learning. (DCELLS, 2008: 4)

The benefits of such an approach are recognised by Estyn (2011: 1), the Welsh inspectorate, who report that for children under 5:

> Most schools and settings are making at least adequate use of the outdoors and children's learning generally benefits from this. In most cases, children's enjoyment, wellbeing, behaviour, knowledge and understanding of the world, and their physical development improve as a result of using the outdoors.

In Scotland, the *Curriculum for Excellence through Outdoor Learning* requires that 'The journey through education for any child in Scotland must include opportunities for a series of planned, quality outdoor learning experiences' (Learning and Teaching Scotland, 2010: 5); whilst in Northern Ireland, *Learning Outdoors in the Early Years* (Bratton et al., 2005: 11) states that 'Outdoors is an equal player to indoors and should receive planning, management, evaluation, resourcing, staffing and adult interaction on a par with indoors'.

Guidance on learning outdoors in Scotland and Northern Ireland

Early years provision is different in Scotland and Northern Ireland (NI). Both provide specific guidance on learning outdoors.

In Scotland, there is the *Curriculum for Excellence through Outdoor Learning* (www.educationscotland.gov.uk/Images/cfeOutdoorLearningfinal_tcm4-596061.pdf). This publication provides the vision and rationale for outdoor learning but also considers a range of topics including working with partners, parent and carer involvement and residential experiences. This publication is supported by downloadable files covering different arenas of the curriculum (expressive arts, health and well-being, literacy and English, modern languages, numeracy and maths, religious and moral education, science, social studies and technologies) (www.educationscotland.gov.uk/learningandteaching/approaches/outdoorlearning/about/experiencesandoutcomes.asp). Each file uses a code to show how well suited each part of the curriculum is to different ages for outdoor learning.

The Scottish documents, however, do not give specific examples of activities. By contrast, in NI, *Learning Outdoors in the Early Years: A resource book* (www.nicurriculum.org.uk/docs/foundation_stage/learning_outdoors.pdf) not only provides an early years outdoor curriculum, but also gives many examples of how to use what they call 'learning bays'. These include lists of resources for an imaginative area, creative area, snack area, quiet area, small-equipment area and wheel-vehicle area, amongst others. These range from suggestions for plants and flowers (for instance, those that can be grown in tubs, ground dwellers or fast growers) to materials and resources for a digging area, to ideas for boundaries and screens for quiet areas.

Although the curriculum may be different from where you work, these resources provide many ideas that can be adapted for early years teaching and indeed throughout the primary school.

An element of risk is both explicit and implicit in all outdoor activities, but, although 'a positive and necessary aspect of children's physical, emotional and social development' (Waters and Maynard, 2010: 475), unfortunately, 'in response to litigation concerns over managing "risk", some schools are limiting out-of-school activities, therefore eliminating potentially rich learning experiences for children' (Malone, 2008: 5). Stan and Humberstone (2011) suggest that whilst primary teachers need to find a balance between providing appropriate risk-taking opportunities and ensuring safety, there is a danger that this fear of risk means teachers manage or avoid risk to suit their own concerns, but potentially at the expense of children's learning.

Best practice for safeguarding in schools

All teachers are responsible for safeguarding children and young people in school. This is clearly stated in the statutory guidance 'Keeping Children Safe in Education 2015' (www.gov.uk/government/publications/keeping-children-safe-in-education-2) and 'Working Together to Safeguard Children 2015' (www.gov.uk/government/publications/working-together-to-safeguard-children-2). (See Chapter 16: Legal Issues.)

Schools must have a Designated Safeguarding Lead (DSL) who delivers training to school staff and to whom concerns must be reported. The DSL also liaises with other agencies regarding safeguarding issues. It is the school's duty to ensure that the safeguarding policy and procedure for reporting concerns is part of the new staff induction process.

Task

Identify the DSL in your school and ensure you are aware of policy and procedures.

Agree to work with friends in other schools to discuss similarities, differences and good practice.

Remember, *you have a responsibility to take action* if you have any concerns regarding the welfare of the children in your school.

SOCIAL MEDIA AND PROFESSIONAL LEARNING NETWORKS: SHARING AND LEARNING AS CPD

One of the reasons for teachers' concerns in contemporary society may be the immediacy with which any incidents become available to potentially worldwide audiences through the use of social media. In April 2015, the teaching union NASUWT's annual survey of teachers suggested that more than a fifth of respondents (21%) 'had adverse comments posted about them on social media sites and of those, 64% were from pupils, 27% were from parents and 9% by both pupils and parents'.

Web Link

The NASUWT's press release on the abuse of social media in schools can be accessed through this web link, available on the companion website: www.nasuwt.org.uk/Whatsnew/NASUWTNews/PressReleases/AbuseOfSocialMediaRifeInSchools

Unfortunately, as the union did not report how many respondents there were in the survey, it is impossible to assess the true scale of these claims, but it did note that the overwhelming majority of comments were posted by secondary pupils. Nevertheless, given the rise in the use of social media at all ages, particularly by parents, this situation is unlikely to reassure primary teachers considering taking risks with their pupils. It is also a potential concern for primary teachers within the classroom and one which is unlikely to become less so with the growing digital competence of primary school pupils.

Consider your own social media profile and that of your colleagues and friends or the setting where you work. Reflect on, and discuss with others, whether all the different forms of social media you and the setting use (and it may be more than one - do not forget that your 'digital footprint' lasts even if you have not visited a site for a long time) portray the image you want to give as a professional teacher or learning environment.

This development should not mean, however, that primary teachers avoid the use of social media to showcase the work they do, as a potential learning tool or, increasingly, as a source of continuing professional development (CPD). To support this, many organisations (such as ITTE) now give advice to teachers on the use of social media, particularly Twitter, and this also increasingly features in ITE programmes. We will consider here, however, the growing potential for social media to provide CPD to primary teachers.

In addition to the use of social media, 'many teachers are joining online communities of like-minded individuals and are subscribing to various blogs and websites to continue learning and improve their professional practice' (Trust, 2012: 133). These online professional, or personal, learning networks 'support teachers to cooperate across regions and countries, without the need for physical travel. As such, they provide opportunities for cooperation that may not exist locally or may be inhibited by institutional barriers' (Holmes, 2013: 107). These communities are also often linked with, and enhanced by, the use of social media which has resulted in a growth of peer-to-peer teacher CPD operating beyond the traditional provision supplied by schools and local authorities.

Effective use of social media in schools

Primary schools are increasingly making use of Twitter to highlight and promote what is going on in the school or even in a class. Despite the 140-character limit of each message, or 'Tweet', the ability to include hyperlinks, pictures and short videos means that primary schools can communicate with both a local and a global audience, both on computers and, more importantly, on mobile devices such as phones and iPads.

Gorsey Bank Primary School in Wilmslow (http://gorseybank.net/page/twitter/10787) lists many uses of Twitter. They say:

> The uses of Twitter in schools are endless but some examples include the following:
>
> 1. Celebrating achievement - of individuals, teams and the school as a whole
> 2. Collaborating with pupils and teachers in other schools
> 3. Updating you about school events and news (including links to new posts on gorseybank.net)
> 4. Engaging our pupils by connecting with people all over the world including industry experts, scientists, sports people, musicians...
> 5. Engaging the whole school community in discussion about what matters in our school
> 6. Giving our pupils an insight into, and stimulating conversation about, events and issues around the world that matter to them.
>
> Reprint courtesy of Joe Maguire, Gorsey Bank Primary School

Because tweets can be uploaded using a mobile phone or other tablet device, they are also increasingly popular in keeping parents up to date with children who are away on school trips or residential visits.

It is important to note that it is necessary to both develop new school policies and adapt existing ones, before setting up a school Twitter account (or other social media). For instance, the school may not have a specific social media policy and one will be needed - including the ability for parents to opt out. In addition, existing policies on taking photographs and videos may need to be adjusted and any existing e-safety policies may need updating. One very important factor relates to child protection and all primary school Twitter feeds are very careful not to identify children by name or give any information that will lead to a child being identified. Furthermore, the Twitter site is only really effective if it is up to date but this means that someone within the school will have to ensure that regular updates are provided and decisions made about who to 'follow' - with potential workload implications. Primary schools may even wish to consider if pupils are allowed to contribute to tweets. Finally, it is important that the purpose and benefits of the school Twitter site are communicated well to parents and that they are clear about how to interact with the site.

This type of online peer-to-peer support has many advantages for teachers, especially the fact that they can personalise not only the content of their professional development, but also who provides it and when and where to take part in development activities. Duncan-Howell (2010) suggests that this latter feature is attractive to teachers who have to juggle work and personal commitments. Like all uses of technology, there are some new skills to learn, but this support can also be provided by online communities. McCulloch, McIntosh and Barrett (2011: 4) propose that by 'using emerging technologies and social media tools, teachers are beginning to take control of their own professional development, finding new ways to learn from each other, to reflect on their own practice, and to develop learning and support networks of like-minded professionals all over the world'. They conclude (p. 18) that the key benefits for teachers in using social media to support professional development include:

- keeping up to date with current debates in a way and at a time that suits them
- drawing on ideas from around the world, challenging their own perspectives and inspiring new ways of thinking
- encouraging them to reflect on their own practice and to shape ideas through discussion of this practice
- connecting with others in similar positions in order to share plans and approaches, and for support and reassurance.

This latter point is particularly important, as it allows teachers and student teachers to pose open-ended questions and gain a variety of responses from people outside of an individual primary school community. The potential for gaining support is enormous, particularly in online forums. These can be very large, for instance Times Educational Supplement (TES) Connect (https://community.tes.co.uk/) claims '3.6 million registered online users in 279 countries and territories'. In reality, however, this also means it is very difficult to moderate posts and replies, meaning that, however useful they may be, teachers still need to exercise professional judgement to use them effectively.

SUMMARY

In this chapter, we have considered some of the current developments in education both in the UK and beyond. Inevitably, the selection of topics covered has been selective and we can be sure that new issues will continually arise. We have highlighted the impact of government policy on education in the primary school and identified emerging differences in educational policy in the primary school across the UK. We have also considered how current policies may adversely affect the continued provision of ITE within universities and how this may limit access to research-rich ITE environments. In this analysis, England has consistently emerged as an outlier in the UK.

Perhaps the one thing we can be sure of is that anyone embarking on a career in primary school teaching today will witness a continually evolving education system, influenced both by politics and other factors such as developments in technology. It is clear that primary schools will need flexible and responsive teachers, able to adapt quickly to change. In addition, those training to be teachers in one country in the UK are increasingly less prepared in terms of the curriculum to teach in other countries. Reassuringly, however, despite all the potential changes we have discussed above, a good primary teacher remains a good primary teacher wherever they are working and whatever they are teaching.

To access additional online resources please visit: **https://study.sagepub.com/wyseandrogers**

Here you will find author podcasts including Gary Beauchamp's top tips for employability, free access to SAGE journal articles and links to external sources.

Aussie Ed: http://aussieed.com - an example of how teachers in Australia use ICT for professional development. There is a regular Ed-chat each Sunday on Twitter at #aussieED and the site also has links to other resources such as a blog and an archive of past chats. Although Australia has a different education system, much of the discussion is relevant to the UK and may also provide new ideas from other systems.

Beauchamp, G., Clarke, L., Hulme, M. and Murray, J. (2013) *Policy and Practice within the UK (Research and Teacher Education: the BERA-RSA Inquiry)*. London: BERA. (Available at: http://tinyurl.com/BERA-res-ITT.) This text examines policy and practice in initial teacher education across the four jurisdictions of the UK (England, Northern Ireland, Scotland and Wales). The paper identifies past and present areas of similarity in ITE across the four jurisdictions, but it also argues that there is now some marked divergence, with England emerging as the exception or outlier.

BERA/RSA report into research and teacher education: www.bera.ac.uk/project/research-and-teacher-education - this link takes you to the final report of the BERA/RSA enquiry into research and teacher education, as well as the seven background papers commissioned by the Inquiry - including reviews of UK and international policy and practice.

Effective Pre-School, Primary and Secondary Education (EPPSE) research project: www.ioe.ac.uk/research/153.html - the EPPSE project is the first major study in the UK to focus specifically on the effectiveness of early years education. The project is a large-scale (3,000 children) longitudinal study of the progress and development of children. It follows children from pre-school to post-compulsory education.

Fitzgerald, D. and Kay, J. (2016) *Understanding Early Years Policy*, 4th edition. London: Sage.

Furlong, J. (2015) *Teaching Tomorrow's Teachers: Options for the future of initial teacher education in Wales*. Oxford: Oxford University.

NOTES

1. This was led by Professor Donaldson, who also oversaw the review of the curriculum in Scotland, resulting in the Curriculum for Excellence.

2. The situation is much more complicated for those from outside of the UK, even if they have been granted QTS by an institution within the UK. For instance, the education workforce council in Wales refers to 'school teachers who trained in Australia, Canada, New Zealand and the USA and who have been awarded QTS by the National College for Teaching & Leadership (NCTL) in England. This recognition is NOT recognised under Welsh regulations' (www.ewc.wales/site/index.php/en/registration-information-for-school-teachers/applying-for-registration-as-a-school-teacher).

REFERENCES

Alexander, R. (ed.) (2010) *Children, Their World, Their Education: Final report and recommendations of the Cambridge Primary Review*. London: Routledge.

Beauchamp, G. and Jephcote, M. (2016) 'Initial teacher education in Wales: a question of legacy?' in Beauchamp, G., Clarke, L., Hulme, M., Jephcote, M., Kennedy, A., Magennis, G., Menter, I., Murray, J., Mutton, T., O'Doherty, T. and Peiser, G. *Teacher Education in Times of Change*. Bristol: Policy Press. pp.109–24.

Beauchamp, G., Clarke, L., Hulme, M. and Murray, J. (2013) *Policy and Practice within the UK (Research and Teacher Education: the BERA-RSA Inquiry)*. London: BERA.

Beauchamp, G., Clarke, L., Hulme, M. and Murray, J. (2015) 'Teacher education in the United Kingdom post devolution: convergences and divergences', *Oxford Review of Education*, 41, 2, pp. 154–70.

Beauchamp, G. and Jephcote, M. (2015) 'Initial teacher education in Wales: a question of legacy?' in Beauchamp, G., Clarke, L., Hulme, M., Jephcote, M., Kennedy, A., Magennis, G., Menter, I., Murray, J., Mutton, T., O'Doherty, T., Peiser P. (2015) *Teacher Education In Times Of Change*. Bristol: Policy Press.

BERA-RSA (2014). *Research and the teaching profession. Building the capacity for a self-improving education system. Final report of the BERA-RSA Inquiry into the role of research in teacher education*. Available at www.bera.ac.uk/wp-content/uploads/2013/12/BERA-RSA-Research-Teaching-Profession-FULL-REPORT-for-web.pdf Accessed 30.11.15

Bratton, C., Crossey, U., Crosby, D. and McKeown, W. (2005) *Learning Outdoors in the Early Years*. Available at http://ccea.org.uk/sites/default/files/docs/curriculum/area_of_learning/fs_learning_outdoors_resource_book.pdf Accessed 30.11.15

Campbell, J. (2001) 'The colonisation of the primary curriculum', in Phillips, R. and Furlong, J. (eds) *Education, Reform and the State: Twenty-five years of politics, policy and practice*. London: Routledge. pp. 31–44.

Chitty, C. (2014) *Education Policy in Britain*, 3rd edition. Basingstoke: Palgrave Macmillan.

CAS [Computing At School] (2013) *Computing in the national curriculum. A guide for primary teachers*. Available at http://www.computingatschool.org.uk/data/uploads/CASPrimaryComputing.pdf Accessed 30.11.15

DCELLS (2008) *Foundation Phase: Framework for children's learning for 3- to 7-year-olds in Wales*. Cardiff: WAG.

Department for Education (DfE) (2014) *Statutory Framework for the Early Years Foundation Stage: Setting the standards for learning, development and care for children from birth to five*. London: DfE.

Donaldson, G. (2015) *Successful Futures: Independent review of curriculum and assessment arrangements in Wales*. Welsh Government: Crown Copyright. Available at https://hwbplus.wales.gov.uk/schools/6714052/Documents/Donaldson%20Report.pdf Accessed 30.03.16

Duncan-Howell, J. (2010) 'Teachers making connections: online communities as a source of professional learning', *British Journal of Educational Technology*, 41, pp. 324–40.

Estyn (2011) *Outdoor Learning: An evaluation of learning in the outdoors for children under five in the foundation phase*. Cardiff: Estyn.

Faulkner, D. and Coates, E. (2013) 'Early childhood policy and practice in England: twenty years of change', *International Journal of Early Years Education*, 21, 2/3, pp. 244–63.

Furlong, J. (2015) *Teaching Tomorrow's Teachers: Options for the future of initial teacher education in Wales*. Oxford: Oxford University Press.

Grosvenor, I. (2005) 'There's no place like home: Education and the making of national identity' in McCulloch, G. (2005) *The RoutledgeFalmer Reader in History of Education*. pp. 273–89.

HL DEB (1870) 25 July 1870 vol 203 cc821–65.

Holmes, B. (2013) 'School teachers' continuous professional development in an online learning community: lessons from a case study of an eTwinning learning event', *European Journal of Education*, 48, 1, pp. 97–112.

Kelly, A.V. (2009) *The Curriculum: Theory and practice*, 6th edition. London: Sage.

Learning and Teaching Scotland (2010) *Curriculum for Excellence through outdoor learning*. Available at https://www.educationscotland.gov.uk/Images/cfeoutdoorlearningfinal_tcm4-596061.pdf Accessed 30.11.15

Leitch, R. (2009) 'Harnessing the slipstream: building educational research capacity in Northern Ireland – Size matters', *Journal of Education for Teaching: International Research and Pedagogy*, 35, 4, pp. 355–71.

Malone, K. (2008) *Every Experience Matters: An evidence based research report on the role of learning outside the classroom for children's whole development from birth to eighteen years*. Available from: www.face-online.org.uk/face-news/every-experience-matters Accessed 5.4.15.

McCulloch, J., McIntosh, E. and Barrett, T. (2011) *Tweeting for Teachers: How can social media support teacher professional development?* Available at www.itte.org.uk/sites/default/files/Tweetingforteachers.pdf Accessed 29.03.16

Oberhuemer, P. (2005) 'International perspectives on early childhood curricula', *International Journal of Early Childhood*, 37, 1, pp. 27–37.

Ofsted (2011) *ICT in Schools: An evaluation of information and communication technology education in schools in England 2008–2011*. London: Ofsted. Available at www.ofsted.gov.uk/resources/110134 Accessed 29.03.16

Ofsted (2014) *Are You Ready? Good practice in school readiness*. London: Ofsted.

Palaiologou, I. (ed.) (2016) *The Early Years Foundation Stage: Theory and practice*, 3rd edition. London: SAGE.

Raffe, D. (2005) 'Devolution and divergence in education policy'. In *Devolution in Practice: Public policy differences within the UK*. Newcastle: IPPR North. pp. 52–69.

Roberts, N. (2014) *National Curriculum Review. Standard note SN 06798*. Available at www.parliament.uk/briefing-papers/SN06798.pdf Accessed 30.11.15

Roberts-Holmes, G. (2012) '"It's the bread and butter of our practice": experiencing the Early Years Foundation Stage', *International Journal of Early Years Education*, 20, 1, pp. 30–42.

Rose, J. (2009) *Independent Review of the Primary Curriculum: Final report*. London: DCSF.

Royal Society (2012) *Shut down or restart? January 2012 The way forward for computing in UK schools*. Available at https://royalsociety.org/~/media/education/computing-in-schools/2012-01-12-computing-in-schools.pdf Accessed 30.11.15

Smithers, A., Robinson, P. and Coughlan, M.D. (2013) *The Good Teaching Guide*. Centre for Education and Employment Research: University of Buckingham.

Stan, I. and Humberstone, B. (2011) 'An ethnography of the outdoor classroom: how teachers manage risk in the outdoors', *Ethnography & Education*, 6, 2, pp. 213–28.

Trust, T. (2012) 'Professional learning networks designed for teacher learning', *Journal of Digital Learning in Teacher Education (International Society for Technology in Education)*, 28, 4, pp. 133–8.

United Nations (UN) (2014) *The Millennium Development Goals Report 2014*. New York: United Nations.

United Nations (UN) (2015) *The Millennium Development Goals Report 2015*. New York: United Nations.

Universities UK (2014) *The Funding Environment for Universities 2014: The impact of initial teacher training reforms on English higher education institutions*. London: Universities UK.

Waters, J. and Maynard, T. (2010) 'What's so interesting outside? A study of child-initiated interaction with teachers in the natural outdoor environment', *European Early Childhood Education Research Journal*, 18, 4, December 2010, pp. 473–83.

Welsh Government (2014) *Evaluating the Foundation Phase Key Findings on Transitions and Assessment*, Research Summary No. 74/2014. Cardiff: WAG.

4

TEACHING AND LEARNING

Sean MacBlain and Holly Bowman

LEARNING AIMS

This chapter will:

- introduce readers to the complexity of teaching and learning and the importance of adapting practice for children in the 21st century
- discuss the contributions made by a number of key thinkers, in particular John Hattie, Robert Marzano, Jerome Bruner, Lev Semyonovich Vygotsky and Reuven Feuerstein
- explore child- and teacher-centred models of teaching as well as reasons and ways to develop evidence-based teaching strategies
- offer a number of case studies to assist readers in gaining insights into what makes for effective and purposeful teaching and learning.

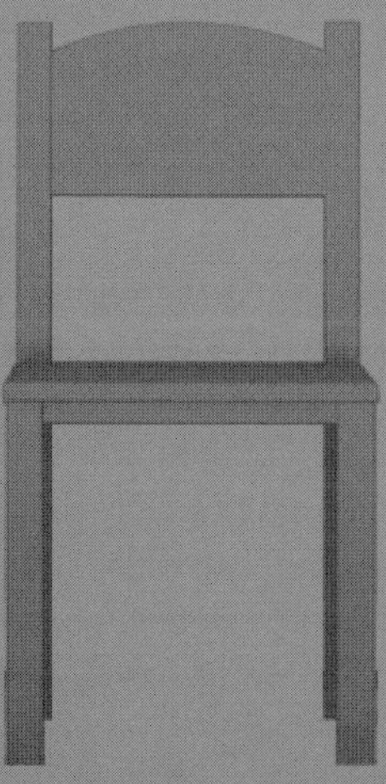

Childhood is changing and for many children in the 21st century the realities of modern living can be extremely complex and challenging. Schools are now more diverse than ever before, as are the life experiences of many young children. Recently, Cowie (2012: 2) commented as follows:

> Today's young people seem to face severe stresses that were unknown a generation ago... There are disturbing statistics on the number of children and young people who run away from home or care... These amount to around 100,000 episodes each year in the UK, with... one in ten running away before the age of ten.

Cowie went on to comment on how in 2012 the National Society for the Prevention of Cruelty to Children (NSPCC) was dealing with 30,000 cases, amounting to some 0.25 per cent of the population. Such statistics are, indeed, very worrying and present a view that challenges many of the conceptions held by some regarding childhood in the 21st century. These statistics clearly suggest that teachers today need to adapt their teaching to the changing nature of childhood and to take greater account of how they might manage the learning of their pupils. This is not, however, as easy as it might first seem given the often highly controversial debates, which permeate our understanding of what constitutes 'good' teaching and learning.

The lack of agreement on what constitutes good teaching and learning can be seen in the following two quotations offered by the British philosopher Richard Pring (2007) in relation to the highly influential but controversial educationalist John Dewey (1859–1952):

> when I came to Oxford in 1989, I was seated at dinner next to Lord Keith Joseph, who had been Secretary of State for Education under Prime Minister Margaret Thatcher. He accused me of being responsible for all the problems in our schools – because I had introduced teachers to John Dewey. (p. 3)

Pring also cites the American philosopher Nel Noddings (2005), as follows:

> not only has he [Dewey]: been hailed as the savior of American education by those who welcome greater involvement of students in their own planning and activity [but also] he has been called 'worse than Hitler' by some who felt that he infected schools with epistemological and moral relativism and substituted socialization for true education. (Pring, 2007: 3)

More recently, the extent of tensions in early education reached the popular press in February 2012 when Graeme Paton, education editor for the national online UK newspaper *The Telegraph*, reported that in a letter to the paper a number of authors and academics had expressed concerns that controversial reforms were 'robbing' children under 5 years of age of important opportunities for play, which was, they claimed, leading to 'schoolification' in the early years (Paton, 2012). These experts went on to claim in their letter that the system was too inflexible when it came to meeting the developmental needs of a widely diverse population of young children.

It is with these tensions in mind that we now turn to exploring the nature of teaching and learning and what these two terms mean in practice.

Web Link

The article by Graeme Paton can be found on The Telegraph Online entitled, 'New style "nappy curriculum" will damage childhood', and can be accessed through this web link, available on the companion website: www.telegraph.co.uk/education/educationnews/9064870/New-style-nappy-curriculum-will-damage-childhood.html

THE NATURE OF TEACHING AND LEARNING

Conceptualising teaching: what do we mean by teaching?

In an attempt to gain a better understanding of teaching and learning in schools and its impact on children, Hattie (2008) examined and synthesised the findings of over a decade of research involving thousands of students. This represented one of the biggest collections of evidence-based research outputs ever taken in the field of education. Hattie examined six key areas that play a part in learning, namely: (1) the children themselves, (2) their homes and (3) the teachers, (4) schools and (5) curricula they experience, and (6) the teaching and learning approaches that take place within the children's schools. Whilst he proposed that the key to making real differences in children's learning lies in the need to make teaching and learning 'visible' (i.e. where teachers come to evaluate their own teaching and view the learning through the eyes of their pupils – Hattie, 2012; Hattie and Yates, 2014), he also offered a rather disconcerting reference point for examining what has been happening in schools to date:

> It is the case that we reinvent schooling every year. Despite any successes we may have had with this year's cohort of students, teachers have to start again next year with a new cohort. The greatest change that most students experience is the level of competence of the teacher... It is surely easy to see how it is tempting for teachers to re-do the successes of the previous year, to judge students in terms of last year's cohort, and to insist on orderly progression through that which has worked before.
>
> (Hattie, 2008: 1)

reflection point

View the following excellent and informative YouTube video entitled, *Why are so many of our teachers and schools so successful? John Hattie at TEDxNorrkoping* (www.youtube.com/watch?v=rzwJXUieDOU), in which Hattie poses a number of questions as to what makes for good teaching. Then, reflect on your own experiences of teachers who motivated and inspired you. What qualities made these teachers successful?

Further insights into the nature and effectiveness of teaching and learning approaches in the classroom can be found in the work of Marzano (Marzano, 2005, 2007; Marzano and Kendall, 2006).

Marzano has proposed that 'good' teachers, which would include early years practitioners, set goals and offer feedback, provide their pupils with simulations and competition that are of a 'low stake', support pupils in interacting with new knowledge and learning, have clear classroom rules that are observed and followed, maintain positive relationships with their pupils and communicate high expectations to them. Importantly, Marzano proposed a 'New Taxonomy', perhaps in response to the more widely acknowledged Bloom's Taxonomy, which has three systems: the *Self-System*, the *Metacognitive System* and the *Cognitive System*, as well as a Knowledge Domain, which are all central to effective thinking and learning.

When a child is asked to begin a new activity or task, their *Self-System* engages in a process whereby they make a decision to engage with the new activity or just carry on with what they were doing at the time. The *Metacognitive System* then sets goals once the activity or task is engaged with and monitors the progress of these. Finally, the *Cognitive System* engages in processing all of the already existing information with the new information, whilst the *Knowledge Domain* furnishes the content. Interestingly, Marzano also identified three sub-sets of knowledge, which he conceptualized as: *information*, and *mental* and *physical* procedures. The first of these refers to the organization of ideas and principles, such as where the child generalizes about phenomena using vocabulary. This is important because it allows the child to store greater amounts of information by allocating ideas and new concepts to categories. Take the example of a child who is told by one of his friends about a new present he has received from his parents, which is a 'bugle'. When he asks his friend what a 'bugle' is, his friend replies that it is a musical instrument. The child can then know that he already has existing knowledge about this new item as he already knows a great deal about musical instruments. The second sub-set proposed by Marzano, that of *mental* procedures, might include such complicated processes as solving complex mathematical computations or writing an essay, or more simple processes such as following simple directions and instructions in a children's game. With the third, that of *physical* procedures, the extent to which these appear within learning situations varies enormously and of course it depends greatly on the nature of the material being learned or the relevant subject matter.

View the following YouTube video clip, entitled *The Art & Science of Teaching: Dr Robert Marzano*, which offers an excellent introduction to Marzano's thinking in regard to teaching and learning in the classroom and what are the most effective means of achieving impact with children: www.youtube.com/watch?v=YhB_R_FT9y4. Now, consider some of your own experiences when working with children and what verbal strategies such as questioning you use to gain the greatest impact on the children's learning.

What is learning and how do we recognise it?

All too often, we hear others making such statements about children as, 'He doesn't seem to be able to learn his times tables'; 'She has finally learned how to do fractions'; 'He's learning to read but he is struggling with it'; 'She learns her spellings every week but forgets them the next'. Such statements, however, offer little in the way of explanation as to what exactly is happening within the child. They are what psychologists often refer to as 'fuzzy statements' and provide little, if any, information to others that is accurate or meaningful. Would it not be more accurate to suggest, for example, that children failing to learn their spellings do so because of underlying processing problems that affect short-term auditory processing or because of perceptual difficulties that affect the manner in which they 'see' words and shapes? Being overly simplistic or 'fuzzy' when communicating statements about a child's learning can, at best, lead to misinterpretation and, at worst, to a characterization of the child's abilities and skills that come to define the child as a learner of limited potential.

Only a decade ago, Jarvis (2005: 2–3) commented as follows:

> When we pause and try to define learning in depth, we cannot help but be struck by the awesome breadth and complexity of the concept... Does learning take place within an individual or is it an interpersonal process? Should we think of it as a set of cognitive mechanisms or rather as an emotional, social and motivational experience?

One key theorist who has contributed much to our understanding of learning is Reuven Feuerstein. Key to Feuerstein's approach is the important fact that it is not the teacher who originates and structures children's responses; rather, the teacher applies him/herself to developing and extending those processes whereby their pupils problem-solve and manage their own thinking through to completion of a task. In this way, teachers are acting as *mediators* and engaging their pupils in a process which develops thinking at a much deeper and more critical level.

Feuerstein proposed that the belief systems we hold about learning need to view human potential as having almost no limits, whilst also acknowledging the existence of artificial barriers that inhibit positive change. Feuerstein further proposed that all children, no matter what their degree of difficulty, can, with the appropriate support, become effective learners. Through adopting such belief systems, he believed that teachers can be freed from the type of constrained thinking that limits their vision of what is possible. When this happens, a number of consequences occur within children's thinking, the most notable of which Feuerstein termed *structural cognitive modifiability*. This refers to the idea that the cognitive structure of children's brains can be altered through an enabling process at the centre of which is the notion of learners learning how to learn. In practice, learning becomes cumulative and then impacts positively on children's performance throughout their life (Burden, 1987). In effect, the approach becomes directed at changing the structural nature of cognitive development. It should be noted that Feuerstein saw structural change as a child's manner of 'acting on' sources of information and then responding to them. He suggested that the central feature involved in learning how to learn is what he termed Mediated Learning Experience (MLE) and it is this that lies at the very core of Feuerstein's Social Interactionist theory of learning. Feuerstein et al. (1980: 16) referred to MLE as:

> the way in which stimuli emitted by the environment are transferred by a 'mediating' agent, usually a parent, sibling or other caregiver. This mediated agent, guided by his intentions, culture, and emotional investment, selects and organises the world of stimuli for the child... Through this process of mediation, the cognitive structure of the child is affected.

The central features of MLE are that the teacher or *mediator* should be aware of, make known and ensure that the child has understood what is intended (intentionality and reciprocity), that the mediator should explain why they are going to work at a task (investment of meaning) and that the act should be viewed as having value over and above the here and now (transcendence) (Burden, 1987).

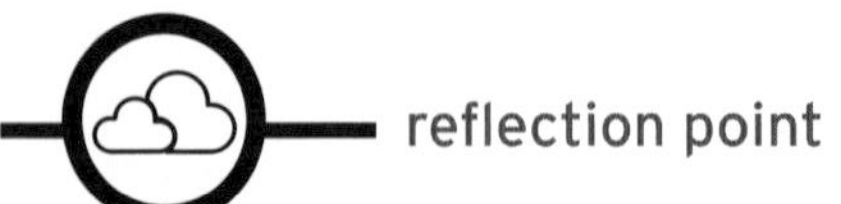

reflection point

Take time to view the following two YouTube video clips, entitled *Feuerstein Method* (www.youtube.com/watch?v=dSGEMrOKHVI) and *Down Syndrome Film: 'Looking Up On Down' (Glow Films/Feuerstein Institute film by David Goodwin)* (www.youtube.com/watch?v=lqSQI6VJgLk), and then consider the following spotlight on practice in terms of how children's thinking is being extended in the way that Feuerstein proposed.

spotlight on practice

Meeting the needs of individual children

Michael is 10 years of age and was recently assessed by an educational psychologist following a referral from his teacher who was concerned by Michael's limited progress in literacy and his growing lack of self-confidence. The educational psychologist reported as follows:

> *Michael presented as an articulate, pleasant and cooperative child... In conversation with Michael I learned that whilst he was generally positive about his school he has, at times, been very unhappy. Michael told me that on most days he felt very alone and isolated from his friends. He indicated that this was most often the case when his peers were engaged in group work and left to get on with it by their teacher. He commented, 'I don't think they want me in their group 'cause I'm not very good at things'. My assessment of Michael's current level of intellectual functioning (Table 4.1) and aspects of his literacy (Table 4.2) offered the following:*

Table 4.1 Current level of intellectual functioning

Aspect of intellectual functioning being assessed	Centile
Verbal comprehension	92
Perceptual reasoning	90
Working memory	12
Processing speed	08

Table 4.2 Literacy

Area of literacy being assessed	Centile	Age equivalent
Word reading	4	7 years 0 months
Reading comprehension	19	9 years 0 months
Spelling	7	7 years 6 months

Two thirds of children are considered to function within the average range of ability and this range is represented between the 16th and 84th centiles ... The 85th centile upwards represents increasingly higher ability with the 99th centile representing the top 1% of ability and the 1st centile representing the lowest 1% of ability.

The above example represents the experience of many children in the primary stage of schooling who, after considerable input from teachers and early years practitioners, find themselves struggling with aspects of their learning (Ofsted, 2005, 2010). Why, then, do so many children fail to respond to the teaching and learning they have experienced on a daily basis for many years? The answer of course is not a simple one. Whilst social and economic factors can, for example, impact on children's learning, so too can the teaching and learning they receive. For too many children, the experience of learning can be overly 'teacher-centred' and fail to meet their individual learning needs or, as Hattie would have it, their learning needs are invisible to their teachers. In Michael's case, it is clear that he is a highly intelligent child, as evidenced by his scores on the Verbal Comprehension and Perceptual Reasoning Index tests (Table 4.1), but he is presenting with problems relating to Working Memory and the speed at which he processes information (see MacBlain, 2014, Chapter 8, pp. 193–4 for an explanation of Working Memory and how it affects children's learning). It is likely to be the case that the reason for Michael's failure does not only lie in 'within-child' factors, such as his weaknesses in Working Memory and Processing Speed, but perhaps more worryingly in the way he has been taught.

The following 'spotlight on practice' is an example of how it is possible to meet the needs of individual children through child-centred practice underpinned by important principles of learning and children's intellectual, social and emotional development. It presents an example of practice in a nursery setting in the UK, which will be referred to as 'Edenvale,' and begins by focusing on the importance of play. In this nursery children are viewed as competent, powerful learners and practice is organised around children's key characteristics of learning as outlined in the Early Years Foundation Stage.

spotlight on practice

I am an explorer: Meeting children's individual needs through child-centred practice

Routines are flexible and our timetable allows for over two and a half hours of uninterrupted play. Children have freedom to be active and to explore both the indoor and outdoor

(Continued)

(Continued)

environment. Children are encouraged to persevere with tasks and activities even when they are challenging and staff make time to model problem-solving skills. A key aim is to develop the children's 'scientific minds' during their explorations of tasks and their environment through, for example, making suggestions, investigating, testing and problem solving. Children are actively encouraged to take managed risks within their day-to-day experiences.

I am confident and independent...

Children are encouraged to make informed choices about their play ... The curriculum is carefully planned and organised with the children's interests being central to all that the staff do. Activities are revisited in order to give the children that important time and cognitive-temporal space in which they can develop new skills and, importantly, establish consolidations and connections within their learning.

I can collaborate and build relationships...

When settling into the nursery, children are given adequate time in which they can build relationships and manage being part of a larger social group. A Key Person approach ensures that all children have one special adult who will care for and understand them at a deeper emotional level. Most importantly, the children are openly encouraged to share their feelings appropriately and grow to understand that they are valued, loved and cared for by the nursery team.

Adults and children take time to listen to one another and it is central to the ethos of the nursery that all children have a right to have their voices heard... Children are encouraged to demonstrate empathy and are supported in developing their understanding of the key fact that everyone has strengths. Staff encourage the children to work collaboratively and understand the consequences of their behaviours on other children, the environment and animal life.

I can have my thinking challenged...

Communication is key... It is a central tenet to the work of all staff at the nursery that learning requires not only 'knowing' but also perseverance with finding out and resilience when things go wrong.

Through their experiences children are encouraged to raise questions about what they observe, to investigate and then to draw conclusions from what they see, hear and touch. Together with adults as co-learners the children's thinking is challenged and they develop skills which enable them to respond to challenges, think logically and experiment and play with ideas.

I am a good communicator...

Children use verbal and non-verbal communication including Makaton to express their needs and feelings, with practice in signing and the use of gesture being encouraged as everyday activities... Most importantly, children are given reasons to communicate and share their thoughts and feelings whilst adults act as rich role models for language acquisition.

I can make decisions...

Children are encouraged to take responsibility for their bodies and to make decisions about when they need a snack and are thirsty. Sleep routines are flexible and children take responsibility for how they feel and when rest is needed. They take responsibility for caring for resources and putting them away at sorting time... ideas and thinking are challenged and they are inspired to find new ways of doing things and make decisions about how to solve simple problems linked to everyday experiences.

I have a strong sense of self...

Family plays a vital role in the learning process and communication between home and nursery allows for children's learning journey to be planned. Children engage in meaningful experiences based on staff observations and discussions with the children, promoting a sense of belonging and self-worth... Learning is seen as a journey and one that values the processes as opposed to the end product and children are proud of their achievements.

I am creative and use my imagination...

Opportunities for children to engage in music, role play and dance allow children to represent their own experiences and creativity. Children use a range of tools and materials for 2D and 3D work... they are encouraged to plan their work and share feelings about their intentions, being resourceful when representing their ideas... Children use instruments to explore sounds and build up a range of songs and rhymes... express themselves through movement when listening to music at a level which feels comfortable for them... Time on their own is respected and staff acknowledge children's choosing to have 'me' time. Children have their own ideas and adults are led by this as a starting point for learning, with the adult skilfully recognising when to intervene in play to scaffold and challenge next steps.

These examples reflect the views expressed by Piaget, that knowledge and meaning are actively constructed by children through interacting with their environments and of the work of Vygotsky, who, as MacBlain (2014: 49) has commented, 'viewed play as "self-education" – not as an activity that children merely repeat but as an active process often characterized by mimicking those around them'.

Readers may also be drawn to more recent views proposed by Bruner in regard to learning, at the centre of which lies three key elements: acquiring new information, which might also involve the reworking of already stored information; the transformation and manipulation of knowledge; and, finally, the checking of what Bruner called the 'pertinence' and 'adequacy' of knowledge. The purpose to which Bruner applied himself was eloquently expressed some three decades ago by one of the author's professors (Brown, 1977: 74):

> Bruner's thesis was that the study of children in problem-solving situations had concentrated too much on the nature of the tasks and the stimuli presented to the child, and too little on the dynamic qualities the child brought to the tasks in order to solve them.

Members of the nursery staff are dealing with risk as an important element in the development of their pupils. The importance of risk has been identified by the notable psychologist Erik Erickson,

Table 4.3 Erickson's psychosocial stages: Stages 1 to 4 (of 8)

Stage		Approximate age
1	Trust versus mistrust	0 to 18 months
2	Autonomy versus shame and doubt	18 months to 3 yrs
3	Initiative versus guilt	3 to 5 yrs
4	Industry versus inferiority	5 to 12 yrs

who, in his theory of psychosocial development, identified eight stages (see Table 4.3 for the first four) through which individuals move as they grow from birth to adulthood.

At Stage 2, children's physical development is rapid and they are becoming increasingly mobile. They are beginning to be more assertive, especially in terms of their independence. They are increasingly walking and moving away from their mother or primary caregiver and can be observed to enjoy choosing items to play with and asserting their wish to have certain foods, wear favourite clothes and play with particular peers. They are increasingly internalising their understanding in regard to their own skills and abilities and acquiring a sense of autonomy and independence. They are also, however, learning about their own limits and, with support from adults (in this case the nursery staff) around them, will explore these limits and in doing so prepare themselves for later stages of development when they will be acquiring a much stronger sense of identity. It is essential, therefore, that adults support children at this stage to explore limits and thereby develop their confidence, their independence and autonomy and their self-efficacy. Parents and adults working with children need to achieve a balance between doing things for their children and encouraging them to do things for themselves. When children are encouraged and supported at this stage, as with the children at Edenvale Nursery, they develop in confidence and ultimately their self-esteem and self-efficacy will grow. If not, they can, as Erikson proposes, develop feelings of inadequacy and come to doubt themselves and what they believe they can achieve.

At Stage 3, children are increasingly engaging in planning and cooperating with others and initiating activities and actions. If supported, they will feel secure in taking the initiative and making decisions. If, however, they are overly protected and smothered or censored through, for example, criticism or over-control, as is all too frequently the case in teacher-centred learning situations, then they will, according to Erickson, be prone to developing feelings of guilt, as they may perceive themselves as being a nuisance to those around them. The result will be that they will typically refrain from taking initiative. At this stage, children are also asking many questions as their desire to understand the world around them grows and they seek greater knowledge. If adults deal with children's questions in a manner that makes them trivial or annoying, then children may again develop feelings of guilt and even shame. Excessive feelings of guilt at this stage can mean that the child will be inhibited when dealing with others and may find their creativity being diminished. At this stage, children with the right type of support will develop a strong sense of purpose.

The nursery staff actively promote an ethos where adults and children learn together and where trial and error and persistence are viewed as key to future successes. The above examples reflect several key theories of teaching and learning. Erikson and Feuerstein, for example argue that individual children's thinking needs to be supported and challenged. Ideas come from the children and are supported and extended by adults, This way of working supports children's problem-solving and helps them to become confident, critical and creative learners. We see evidence of Feuerstein's notion of *structural cognitive modifiability*, whereby attempts are being made to influence children's cognitive structure through an enabling process at the centre of which lies that most crucial of ideas – learning how to learn. In practice, the nursery aims for the children's learning to be cumulative so that it impacts positively on their performance in primary school and throughout their lives (Burden, 1987). As with the ideas of Feuerstein and other notable theorists, most notably Vygotsky and Bruner (Gray and MacBlain, 2015), the fundamental importance of communication in its broader sense and how this underpins almost every aspect of learning is fully acknowledged, and acted on, by staff. The importance that the staff at Edenvale Nursery place on emotional development as a central component of learning and the wider impact of emotional intelligence (MacBlain et al., 2015) is also evident here.

The chapter now turns to how staff might put ideas into practice through implementing the above key principles for young children.

putting it into practice

Classroom ideas to aid teaching and learning in early years settings

On a frosty day, take the children (early years) outside and encourage them to touch and run their gloved fingers across a frosted surface. As they do so, they will begin to make patterns and marks. This can be further encouraged as they search outdoors for other frosted areas and make more patterns, write names and continue to explore this white substance they now know is called 'frost'. Encourage the children to increase their vocabulary using words like 'cold', 'springy', 'fluffy', 'sparkles', 'shiny' as their senses engage with the frost and they observe the visual patterns of their own mark making. Encourage the children to discover tools independently such as spoons, paintbrushes and sticks to make further imprints and patterns, thus developing their hand-eye coordination, fine motor and writing skills. The hunt for frost might continue whilst the children are encouraged to sing 'We're going on a frost hunt, we're going to find some freezing frost, and we're not cold'. Children can be encouraged to work collaboratively as they locate pockets of frost together supervised by an adult who can then mediate in the experience to facilitate discussion with the children about what they see.

Provocations are also important and staff, after observing that the weather is going to drop below freezing later in the evening, can leave water around outside in a range of containers for children to find the following day. As puddles become frozen, the children begin to understand at first-hand about slippery surfaces. They can then be supported in managing their own sense of risk whilst at the same time allowing the activity to continue. Staff can draw the children's attention to how ice changes over a period of time and mediate the learning experience by exploring with them, through the use of language, the concept of melting and freezing. In doing so, staff can also become excited and thereby indirectly motivate the children to develop their curiosity about what they see around them. Staff will model thinking skills, again using more sophisticated language structures such as, 'What if...?', 'I wonder what might happen if...', 'Why do you think...?', and so on. In this way, they are extending hypothetico-deductive reasoning (Burden,

(Continued)

(Continued)

1987; Feuerstein et al., 1980; MacBlain, 2014) in the children who are then being encouraged to problem-solve and to apply logic, which is much higher-order thinking.

As children also enjoy exploring a range of learning experiences on a small scale, staff can set up an area inside with jar lids, ice cubes, food dye and pipettes. Children can place a single ice cube on the jar lid and then very carefully use the pipettes to drop different coloured dyes onto the cube. They can observe how the colours combine to make new colours, thus revisiting and reinforcing work done previously on colour mixing. This is in addition to observing and recording how water begins to form in the jar lid as the ice cube melts because of temperature change. Children's vocabulary can again be extended to include words such a 'melt', 'dripping', 'wet', 'runny', 'swirly', and so on, to describe what they are seeing and, perhaps more importantly, to use when they are explaining to others what they are seeing and doing. The children are, in effect, being encouraged to investigate, problem-solve, conceptualise and recall, as well as formulating new questions and articulating verbal responses to some quite complex scientific questions.

Later, a sensory tray can be set up indoors to mimic snow and ice outside, using ice cubes, fake snow and arctic animals. This could be developed alongside the use of such relevant stories as *Iris and Isaac* (2011) by Catherine Rayner, a story of two polar bears and friendships. Props can also be provided for the children to re-tell the story and to explore the value of friends, friendship and working together as they did outdoors. Photographs and non-fiction books about snow and ice can also be made available to the children, in order to deepen their understanding and consolidate new as well as prior learning even further.

REASONS AND WAYS TO DEVELOP A REPERTOIRE OF EVIDENCE-BASED TEACHING STRATEGIES

The next spotlight on practice offers insights into the formation of a strong belief system by the senior manager at Edenvale Nursery. The study highlights the tensions that exist for many practitioners working within early years settings in regard to the curriculum, their sense of ownership of what they teach and how they teach, and their perceptions of external influence on their own practice.

Understanding the wider learning experiences of children

I can remember it vividly, the moment where the light bulb went off in my head. I was in a room of 200 people listening to Margaret Edgington, an early years consultant speaking at the 2012 Early Excellence conference in Huddersfield. The conference was held on the back of the Tickell Review and the ongoing debate around terms such as child-initiated and adult-directed learning and that appalling and depressing term 'school readiness' which sees every passionate early years teacher sink low into their chair. Margaret Edgington spoke about developing curricula and environments that support but most importantly inspire young children, curricula that develop life skills, not just to prepare them for school but more importantly for their life-long journey! It was clear when networking that all of the changes we had seen as early years teachers were resulting in us losing our way and what we all knew as sound pedagogical principles and practices, such as sustained shared thinking, outstanding learning environments, relationships and attachment theory, as well as many other key ideas, things that had previously excited us, were being forgotten and lost. On return I embarked on a research project and held consultations with the staff. The team at Edenvale Nursery are inspirational and passionate and were fully behind proposed curriculum changes. We spent time thinking about what we truly wanted for our children and overwhelmingly agreed that nurturing dispositions in children was going to bring us all back to our pedagogical beliefs. We recognised the importance of curriculum areas such as mathematics and literacy but felt that the environment and resources would ensure that children still developed their knowledge and that our priority was to give children the character to cope with higher-order thinking and knowledge. My research focused on two curricula in the main: Te Whāriki in New Zealand and Reggio Emilia in Italy... What was crucial about both of these curriculums was the significant impact they were having on outcomes for children, and still today the UK fails to build an early years curriculum using these outstanding examples of good practice. The opening statement in Te Whāriki really resonated with me: 'to grow up as confident learners and communicators, healthy in mind, spirit, secure in their sense of belonging and in the knowledge that they make a valued contribution to society.' The emphasis on the child being unique as a learner, with a strong set of skills and knowledge was not new, but having this central to our EYFS curriculum was, as demonstrated in the flawed Development Matters document, uninspiring, with a compartmentalised learning that fails to enable teachers and practitioners to look at the child holistically. What does it mean to be 22–36 months in maths? Te Whāriki really cemented our agreement to focus on dispositions through its emphasis on the critical role adults play in supporting learning with vocabulary such as collaboration, guided participation, observation, exploration and reflection. It was about now that the structure of our curriculum was forming in my head! Although New Zealand was instrumental in our emerging curriculum, Reggio Emilia's approach ran parallel, echoing that children are not empty vessels waiting to be filled but with unlimited potential, eager to interact with and contribute to the world. Reggio Emilia believe children are driven by curiosity and imagination, are able to be responsible for their own learning and deserve to be listened to and valued, echoed by our team. It is very important to us at that we challenge ideals and ask questions and reflect on what is best for our children. Early years education is seen as a springboard to later stages of formal education, as opposed to a distinct developmental phase. Sadly this continues throughout children's lives with preparation for tests, Key Stage 1, Key Stage 2, SATs and secondary schooling. Teaching in this way is going to lead to a breakdown in childhood, where children are frightened to have a go and make mistakes, as well as lead to significant mental health issues for our children... The introduction of our curriculum placed emphasis on eight key principles... Our principles are:

- Exploration (curiosity, investigation, persevering, hands-on, testing);
- Independence (ownership, choices, responsibility, focus, concentration, interest, autonomy);
- Collaboration and relationships (working together, turn taking, sharing, friendship, boundaries, key person, home-school links);
- Creativity and imagination (fooling about, supposing, wonder, new ideas, inventiveness, risk taking, discovery);
- Challenging thinking (clarifying, suggesting, speculating, reciprocating, modelling, open ended);

(Continued)

(Continued)

- Communication (initiating, sharing thoughts, responding, understanding, interaction, focus and attention, listening to each other);
- Decision making (learning, planning, actively involved, interested, choices, having a voice);
- Strong sense of self and belonging (family, attachments, respect, uniqueness, loved, happiness, valued, well-being, respected).

Although the principles of EYFS run through our curriculum, this holistic view has enabled us to understand our children and families more deeply and children have become active in this process with practitioners and teachers focusing foremost on each individual child's set of skills, knowledge and interests ... The main difference is this move away from segregated curriculum areas and allowing practitioners time to play and interact with children more freely without pressure to record, thus really getting to know individual children better and noticeably improving outcomes for our children.

The above spotlight on practice offers a fascinating insight not only into how the practice at Edenvale Nursery evolved but also how the practitioners' understanding of the wider learning experiences of children and their families and environment informed what they did with the children. We now turn to look at the importance of children's needs in relation to teaching and learning.

IDENTIFYING CHILDREN'S NEEDS

> I frequently have teachers say to me that a child needs a full-time classroom assistant or so many hours with a classroom assistant. I say to them that the child doesn't need a classroom assistant - what the child needs is a different approach to teaching. What most children primarily need are different strategies that work for them, not an extra adult in the classroom. All too often, teachers confuse their own needs for adult support in the classroom with those of the child's - it's a real problem. After all, whose needs are we aiming to meet?

The above extract from an interview with an educational psychologist offers an important insight into why teachers should be more focused on identifying the individual and underlying cognitive and emotional needs of their pupils and on employing appropriate interventions such as teaching new strategies and problem-solving approaches, as opposed to all too readily accepting that the needs of their pupils can be met primarily in terms of additional resources such as a classroom assistant. More crucially, perhaps, it is now commonly accepted that children need to be given a greater voice (Cox, 2011; Lundy, 2007; Rudduck and Flutter, 2000) and to be afforded a voice in decisions directly impacting on their education and learning.

In a recent study, *Children Decide*, which explored decision making amongst children and how they might be empowered to make decisions by their teachers, Cox (2011: 124) found the following:

> These children were crossing the boundaries between the domain beyond the school and the domain of the school itself. In coming to see, metacognitively, how their teacher holds power and how that might be challenged, on the basis of what they have learned from their relations in other social settings, and seeing the possibility of a different relationship with their teacher, the children open up the possibility of taking action in the classroom community in ways that can change it.

Even more recently, the new *Special Educational Needs and Disability Code of Practice – 0 to 25* (DfE and DoH, 2014: 20, Section 1.6) in England, introduced in September 2014, proposed that:

> Children have a right to receive and impart information, to express an opinion and to have that opinion taken into account in any matters affecting them from the early years. Their views should be given due weight according to their age, maturity and capability (Articles 12 and 13 of the United Nations Convention on the Rights of the Child).

This view clearly represents a considerable step forward in providing *all* children with a much greater voice in regard to their learning and how they are taught.

reflection point

Take time to view the following YouTube video link, entitled '*Question 3: Involving children, parents and young people in decision making*': www.youtube.com/watch?v=TURUPRHmRE4. Then consider how early years practitioners might work in partnership with parents and other professionals to meet the needs of all the children they work with.

TEACHING STYLES LINKED TO 21ST-CENTURY STUDENTS

Everywhere one looks one sees children, even very young children using mobile phones and other digital devices. For many children, the time they spend each day on social activity sites is significant, often amounting in some instances to hours. All too frequently, many children fail to have the time they spend on these sites and the material they access monitored by adults. Recently, Dunn (2015), cited in MacBlain, Long and Dunn (2015: 217), drew attention to the growing use of tablet technology amongst children:

> Recent data gathered in Europe suggests that 50% of Swedish children aged between 3 and 4 use tablet computers; 23% of children in Norway from 0 to 6 years old have access to touch-screens at home; and 17% of families in Germany with children aged 3 to 7 have touchscreen tablets. In the UK the use of tablet computers by children has increased from 2% to 11% between 2011 and 2012 and the current rate of uptake is likely to be considerably higher than this (Holloway et al., 2013).

The growth in digital technologies has been substantial with young children and young people forming a significant percentage of the market for these. One commonly hears such terms as *technoliteracy*, *digital literacy* (Merchant, 2006, 2009, 2015) and *multiliteracies* (MacBlain et al., 2015), with new terms emerging almost daily as digital technology becomes more sophisticated and accessible to children (see Chapter 14, 'New Technology', by Steve Higgins and James Siddle).

SUMMARY

Learning is a complex affair and requires practitioners working with children to not only acknowledge its complexity but also to develop their understanding of what exactly is happening when they believe that children are learning and how their teaching impacts on the children's experience. To this extent, it is fundamental that teachers engage in evidence-based practice and take time to reflect and critically engage with others about what they consider to be sound evidence of learning in their pupils. To do so offers the teacher and the early years practitioner much deeper insights into the learning of their pupils and, perhaps as importantly, the underlying cognitive processes employed by their pupils (MacBlain, 2014; Gray and MacBlain, 2015). Recent attempts by researchers and theorists working in the field have identified key areas that contribute to effective teaching and learning, perhaps most notably the importance of making teaching and learning more visible and encouraging teachers and early years practitioners to evaluate their own teaching and view the learning taking place in their classroom or setting through the eyes of the pupils. This is now more important than ever before, given the rapidly changing nature of childhood and the exponential growth in digital technology.

To access additional online resources please visit: **https://study.sagepub.com/wyseandrogers**

Here you will find a classroom activity, author podcasts including Sean MacBlain's top tips for employability, free access to SAGE journal articles and links to external sources.

Cox, S. (2011) *New Perspectives in Primary Education: Meaning and Purpose in Learning and Teaching*. Maidenhead: Open University Press – Chapter 8, 'Making sense of learning: assessment in context'. A most interesting and insightful approach in regard to examining learning through assessment within modern contexts.

Crafter, S. and Maunder, R. (2012) 'Understanding transitions using a sociocultural framework', *Educational and Child Psychology*, 29(1): 10–17. An excellent and highly relevant article focusing on the complex nature of transitions with an emphasis on the importance of culture.

Fabian, H. and Mould, C. (2009) *Development and Learning for Very Young Children*. London: Sage. An excellent text offering clear and relevant insights into the complex nature of learning and development in young children.

Kennedy, E., Cameron, R.J. and Greene, J. (2012) 'Transitions in the early years: educational and child psychologists working to reduce the impact of school culture shock', *Educational & Child Psychology*, 29(1): 19–30. A highly relevant and interesting article focusing on the complex nature of transitions and how educational and child psychologists can work to support children and practitioners in this area.

Miller, L. and Pound, L. (2011) *Theories and Approaches to Learning in the Early Years*. London: Sage – Chapter 9, 'Forest schools in the early years'. An excellent account of the impact and importance of forest schools for children in the early years.

Nutbrown, C. (2006) *Threads of Thinking: Young Children Learning and the Role of Early Education*. London: Sage. A classic text, which offers a comprehensive account of learning in the early years.

The following YouTube video, entitled 'Jerome Bruner: How does teaching influence learning?', at www.youtube.com/watch?v=aljvAuXqhds, offers an excellent interview with Jerome Bruner only a week after his 99th birthday.

The following two YouTube videos: 'Scaffolding Language Development' at www.youtube.com/watch?v=gLXxcspCeK8, and 'Teaching Matters: Scaffolding' at www.youtube.com/watch?v=9gNjGD_W3dM, offer excellent insights into, and examples of, scaffolding in different situations.

REFERENCES

Brown, G. (1977) *Child Development*. Shepton Mallet: Open Books.

Burden, R.L. (1987) 'Feuerstein's instrumental enrichment programme: important issues in research and evaluation', *European Journal of Psychology of Education*, 2(1), 3–16.

Cowie, H. (2012) *From Birth to Sixteen: Children's Health, Social, Emotional and Linguistic Development*. London: Routledge.

Cox, S. (2011) *Children Decide: Power, Participation and Purpose in the Primary Classroom*. University of East Anglia: CfBT Education Trust. Available at: http://cdn.cfbt.com/~/media/cfbtcorporate/files/research/2007/r-children-decide-2007.pdf (accessed 31 March 2016).

Department of Education (DfE) and Department of Health (DoH) (2014) *Special Educational Needs and Disability Code of Practice*. London: DfE/DoH.

Feuerstein, R., Rand, Y., Hoffman, M. and Miller, R. (1980) *Instrumental Enrichment*. Baltimore, MD: University Park Press.

Gray, C. and MacBlain, S.F. (2015) *Learning Theories in Childhood*. (2nd edn). London: Sage.

Hattie, J. (2008) *Visible Learning: A Synthesis of Over 800 Meta-Analyses Relating to Achievement*. London: Routledge.

Hattie, J. (2012) *Visible Learning for Teachers: Maximising Impact on Learning*. London: Routledge.

Hattie, J. and Yates, G.C.R. (2014) *Visible Learning and the Science of How We Learn*. London: Sage.

Holloway, D., Green, L. and Livingstone, S. (2013) *Zero to Eight: Young Children and Their Internet Use*. LSE London: EU Kids Online Network.

Jarvis, M. (2005) *The Psychology of Effective Learning and Teaching*. Cheltenham: Nelson Thornes.

Lundy, L. (2007) 'Voice is not enough: conceptualising Article 12 of the United Nations Convention on the Rights of the Child', *British Educational Research Journal*, 33(6): 927–42.

MacBlain, S.F. (2014) *How Children Learn*. London: Sage.

MacBlain, S.F., Long, L. and Dunn, J. (2015) *Dyslexia, Literacy and Inclusion: Child-centred Perspectives*. London: Sage.

Marzano, R. (2005) *School Leadership that Works: From Research to Results*. Alexandria, VA: ASCD.

Marzano, R. (2007) *The Art and Science of Teaching: A Comprehensive Framework for Effective Instruction*. Alexandria, VA: ASCD.

Marzano, R. and Kendall, J.S. (2006) *The New Taxonomy of Educational Objectives* (2nd edn). Thousand Oaks, CA/London: Sage.

Merchant, G. (2006) 'A Sign of the Times: Looking Critically at Popular Digital Writing', in J. Marsh and E. Millard (eds), *Popular Literacies, Childhood and Schooling* (pp. 93–108). London: Routledge.

Merchant, G. (2009) 'Literacy in Virtual Worlds', *Journal of Research in Reading*, 32(1): 38–56.

Merchant, G. (2015) 'Keep Taking the Tablets: iPads, Story Apps and Early Literacy', *Australian Journal of Language and Literacy*, February Issue.

Office for Standards in Education (Ofsted) (2005) *English 2000–2005: A Review of Inspection Evidence*. London: The Stationery Office.

Office for Standards in Education (Ofsted) (2010) *The Special Educational Needs and Disability Review*. London: Ofsted.

Paton, G. (2012) 'New-style "nappy curriculum" will damage childhood', *The Telegraph*, 6 February. Available at: www.telegraph.co.uk/education/educationnews/9064870/New-style-nappy-curriculum-will-damage-childhood.html (accessed 28 January 2015).

Pring, R. (2007) *John Dewey: A Philosopher of Education for Our Time?* London: Continuum.

Rayner, C. (2011) *Iris and Isaac*. London: Little Tiger Press.

Rudduck, J. and Flutter, J. (2000) 'Pupil participation and pupil perspective: carving a new order of experience', *Cambridge Journal of Education*, 30(1): 75–89.

5

CHILD DEVELOPMENT

Janet Rose and Felicia Wood

LEARNING AIMS

This chapter will enable you to understand:

- research and theory from developmental psychology and neuroscience that can help us better understand children's development and its implications for teaching
- how our relationships with children affect their learning and learning environment
- key theories of learning to help explain how children build their knowledge and understanding
- the importance of adopting a holistic model of children's development to inform your practice and support children's learning.

This chapter outlines some key insights drawn from research and theory that have attempted to understand children's development. Such an understanding is important for teachers so that you take this into consideration when creating an appropriate and optimal learning environment for children in your classroom. The study of children's development has drawn largely from the field of psychology, but increasingly this is being complemented by relatively new research from the neurosciences. Traditional theories about child development have arisen largely from studies of observable behaviour with subsequent surmising about how such behaviour might be being driven from our mind via cognitive processes – from the outside in. In contrast, neuroscientific research focuses attention on the biological and physiological mechanisms of brain functioning and then infers how this translates into thinking and behaviour – from the inside out.

A FRAMEWORK FOR UNDERSTANDING CHILDREN'S DEVELOPMENT

In your own education, you may have come across debates about the 'nature–nurture' model of child development – the debate on whether development is a product of genetic inheritance (nature) or the product of environmental experiences (nurture). To some extent, this debate remains unresolved. However, researchers and theorists from different fields are increasingly adopting a more *consilience* approach to understanding children's development. A consilience approach takes into account multidisciplinary perspectives. This chapter therefore frames children's development within a *biopsychosocial systems model* to provide a more holistic and contextualised explanation for thinking and behaviour. This model of development acknowledges the physiological, psychological, sociological and neurobiological dimensions of development, affirming the 'dynamic interchange of biological dispositions and environmental provisions' in the creation and functioning of the psychological mind (Feldman and Eidelman, 2009: 194). In other words, genes (biology) and experiences (environment) are indivisible, interrelated and interdependent, with each affecting and enabling the expression and growth of the other (McCrory et al., 2010). In adopting a consilience approach, this chapter shows how children's learning is a holistic and multi-layered process affected by shifting and interacting multiple layers of influence (Rutten et al., 2013; Sroufe and Siegel, 2011). These 'layers of influence' are articulated in the *ecological systems model* of human development originated by Bronfenbrenner (2005).

Bronfenbrenner considered that a child's development occurs via the interpersonal and indirect relationships that a child encounters within different (and increasingly complex) environments or influences. The first interpersonal 'system' a child experiences is the caregiving environment, which gradually extends beyond the home into the local community, such as the school they attend. Over time, a child will be affected by a wider range of social environments or indirect influences that will hinge on their development, such as circumstances regarding parental employment, which might affect the quality of life the child experiences, government policy such as the national curriculum and broader cultural values and norms which may affect a child's belief system, for example their religious upbringing. A less distinct impact might be socio-historical circumstances or events that continue to operate as a pervading force, such as the advent of equal opportunities. This model emphasises the importance of relationships in promoting children's development and learning.

THE DEVELOPING BRAIN

Although we need to be cautious about how we interpret the emerging findings from the field of neuroscience (Rose and Abi-Rached, 2013), it is important that teachers have an understanding of brain development and function. Given that the brain is the major organ integral and universal to learning and teaching, knowledge of its functioning can better support effective educational experiences for the next generation of children in schools.

Children's thinking and behaviour are products of the mind and are essentially reliant on electrical and chemical activity, involving nerve cells known as neurons passing 'messages' to each other in the brain (Matlin, 1998). The brain consists of billions of neurons, most of which are created early on in prenatal development (neurogenesis) (Twardosz, 2012). There is a huge proliferation in neuronal synapses (synaptogenesis), the connections between the neurons, after birth. Neuronal synapses connect neurons, creating neuronal circuits or networks within and between different areas of the brain. Collectively, these neuronal networks are known as our 'connectome' (Seung, 2012).

Different areas of the brain create neuronal synapses at different times, with some development driven by human maturation following a predictable pattern (for example, the visual and auditory cortices). But the majority of brain development hinges on the child's accumulating experiences within and from the surrounding environment and context. For example, at birth, a baby does not have the neuronal capacity or necessity to learn to read but the journey begins via synaptic connections within the visual cortex which focuses on creating the efficient connections necessary to support survival. In time, particular experiences help to create a web of complex connections between different parts of the brain that are necessary to enable a child to read. The brain has the capacity to grow and learn throughout our lifetime but is most responsive during childhood, particularly in the early years, with connection density peaking just before puberty and not reaching adult levels until a youngster is in their 20s. Although it can take on average 25 years for the brain to reach maturity, the neuronal networks do not stop growing and changing, albeit with less flexibility. The ability to adapt, respond to and learn from the environment (thereby increasing neuronal capacity) is known as *neuroplasticity* (Twardosz, 2012).

As the neurons mature, they become covered in a fatty white sheath (myelination), which further improves the conductivity between neurons. The more the synapses are used, the stronger and quicker they become, and the brain develops 'superhighways' of information-processing circuits. These connect many neurons in different parts of the brain, allowing information to be shared quickly. One such super highway is the Corpus Callosum, which joins the two brain hemispheres (sides), letting information pass easily between the left and the right sides of the brain (Ward, 2010).

Learning about the brain

This is a suggested lesson plan for helping Key Stage 2 pupils learn about the brain.

Starter questions - what do you know about the brain, why is it important?

Watch this YouTube clip called 'The learning brain': www.youtube.com/watch?v=cgLYkV689s4

Tell the pupils they need to remember some facts about what they're watching.

After watching the clips:

- Pupils write down everything they can remember from the clip on their white boards.
- Pupils share with a friend one thing they have learnt about how their brain works and one thing it does to help them to learn.
- In groups, make a poster to show how the brain helps you to learn.

Plenary - Groups share their posters.

Because building our connectome requires enormous amounts of energy, any unused, damaged or degraded neurones are 'pruned away' (apoptosis) to enhance neuronal network capacity (Howard-Jones, 2010). For example, if we think about how we learn to read 'CAT', initially C, A and T may be sounded separately. This is practised until the word can be recognised and we can reject the step-by-step nature of reading, relying instead on a faster recognition circuit. The old step-by-step circuit may still be used for new words, but as word recognition increases, so the brain circuits change in complexity to meet new challenges.

MULTISENSORY LEARNING

When we think, patterns of electrical activity move around our brains using the neuronal networks we have previously made through learning. However, maturation of brain function is not uniform. The prefrontal cortex is primarily responsible for core 'executive' functions, such as working memory, attention control, planning and self-regulation. These are essential skills to support effective learning but they take the longest to mature (Howard-Jones, 2010). It is the interplay of physiological maturation and the extending and strengthening of neuronal networks that supports more sophisticated cognitive thinking, such as that around abstract mathematical concepts. Maturing neural circuits rely to an increasing extent on external experiences to create and maintain robust interconnected networks, and neuroscientific evidence implies that teaching which stimulates a variety of our senses fosters stronger learning, as Goswami and Bryant highlight:

> Learning depends on the development of multi-sensory networks of neurons distributed across the entire brain. For example, a concept in science may depend on neurons being simultaneously active in visual, spatial, memory, deductive and kinaesthetic regions, in both brain hemispheres. (2007: 1)

Therefore, practitioners need to create diverse learning contexts that stimulate many areas of the brain and body, given that 'learning is strengthened not only in relation to how many neurons fire in a neural network, but also by how they are distributed across different domains, such as the motor and sensory cortices' (Alexander, 2010: 96). The aphorism 'neurons that fire together, wire together; neurons that fire apart, wire apart', and the familiar adage 'use it or lose it', remind us that personal experience creates neuronal connections and repetition strengthens these neuronal connections and the efficiency of the connectome.

Web Link

An excellent summary of neuroscientific educational interventions and approaches can be accessed through this web link, available on the companion website: https://educationendowmentfoundation.org.uk/uploads/pdf/NSED_LitReview_Final.pdf

NEUROMYTHS

Neuromyths are ideas that have developed about brain-based learning strategies that are based on limited scientific evidence from neuroscience. Neuromyths have sometimes had a profound and long-lasting effect on pedagogy, despite a lack of rigorous authority from an appropriate evidential base. An example of this is Visual, Auditory and Kinaesthetic (VAK) learning.

VAK represents a method of categorising individual learning styles through personal, preferred sensory experiences. The assumption of VAK is that as the senses are processed in different brain regions, individual differences in the efficiency of these locations justify teaching a child in a learning style that supports their particular strength. However, if one considers the complexity of the brain's connections, we experience the world (and our learning) from a cross-modal and multisensory perspective. We automatically use all our senses at the same time and, although we may have personal preferences and strengths, the best teaching is delivered using multisensory methods where feasible. This variety is what keeps learners motivated and interested (Goswami and Bryant, 2007).

reflection point

Think about a recent lesson you have observed or delivered - how might it have engaged the children's brain via different sensory stimulation?

THE DEVELOPMENT OF EXECUTIVE FUNCTION FOR LEARNING

There appear to be two neurophysiological systems – the stress regulation system and the social engagement system – which are fundamental to learning as they help to establish and regulate working memory, attention control, planning and self-regulation skills (Porges, 2011). Collectively, these skills are known as *executive function skills* and are largely associated with the prefrontal cortex of the brain. They enable children to 'behave in a contextually appropriate and goal-driven manner' (Buss and Spencer, 2014: 1) and filter distractions, control impulses, focus and re-direct attention, hold and manipulate information, prioritise tasks, set, achieve and adapt goals. Thus, they support cognitive self-regulation and the ability to learn. In other words, they regulate emotions, thinking and behaviour by helping a child to manage the stresses of life, feelings, social engagements and the effort of learning. Imagine what life in the classroom might be like if children were unable to stay focused on a task or could not remember simple instructions. Teachers rely on children having reasonably effective executive function skills in order to teach, and this reliance increases as children's minds mature. Executive function skills support the 'how' of learning in order to enable the mastering of the 'what', and become life-long learning skills (NSCDC, 2011). Not surprisingly, children with stronger executive skills have a better capacity to regulate behaviour, better attentional skills and a stronger working memory, and thus do better academically (NSCDC, 2011).

Web Link

Useful resources on executive function skills can be accessed through this web link, available on the companion website: http://developingchild.harvard.edu/key_concepts/executive_function/ (Center on the Developing Child: Harvard University website).

Like many aspects of children's development, executive function skills appear to evolve through the transaction between genes and environment and appear to be particularly sensitive to the caregiving environment the child experiences. Indeed, brain regions and circuits associated with executive functioning have extensive 'interconnections with deeper brain structures that control the developing child's responses to stress' (NSCDC, 2011: 4). Some children in the classroom may have impaired executive functioning through reduced capacity in their working memory and reduced ability to inhibit impulsive behaviour (Music, 2014). Impairments in executive functioning are also strongly associated with children with diagnosed learning difficulties such as ADHD and ASD (Dovis et al., 2015). Adverse social factors such as harsh parenting, experience of conflict and family stress can also damage executive skill function (Hackman et al., 2010).

This is not to state that all children who find school difficult are suffering from a problem of brain development, but teachers need to be mindful of the experiences a child might bring to school on a daily basis. Given the evidence from neuroscience that supportive relationships help to moderate the stress response and have been shown to have positive significance for the development of brain functioning (Rappolt-Schlictmann et al., 2009), teachers' relationships with their pupils have important implications for their learning. Brains require nurturing, socially and emotionally, to work at their optimum and allow for healthy growth and development. Like a muscle, brains can be worked and changed with time and practice, but they suffer if lonely, isolated, overly stressed or lacking in exercise (NSCDC, 2014).

putting it into practice

Developing executive function skills

The following are some suggested activities that can help to improve executive function skills such as memory, reasoning and problem solving for all key stages.

Foundation Stage (memory)

Sing the children's favourite nursery rhymes (chosen by the pupils). Conduct a fun nursery rhyme quiz afterwards - for instance, when does the mouse run down the clock? What are some of the colours in the rainbow song? How did Jack get down the hill? (Ask questions with different openers.)

Key Stage 1 (reasoning)

Take a key character from a familiar story, e.g. Cinderella. The teacher takes on the role of the character. The class is given a list of different openers: 'what', 'when', 'how', where', 'who' and 'why' questions. In pairs, they have to think of questions that begin with the different openers to ask the character, for example, 'where do you live?' or 'what did the glass slippers feel like?'

Key Stage 2 (problem solving)

Put pupils in groups of four. Give each group an everyday item such as a paper clip or cup. Ask them: could this item be used for anything else? Groups brainstorm ideas and share with the class - representation of the idea could be communicated in multimodal ways, such as in role play or a picture.

RECEPTIVE LEARNING THROUGH AFFECTIVE TEACHING

The traditional separation of cognition from emotions has been superseded by evidence showing how thinking and reasoning and emotional processing are fundamentally integrated in the brain at multiple levels. In order to generate successful learning, educators must also engage in the *affective* dimensions of pupils' minds. Immordino-Yang and Damasio have pointed out how neuroscience has identified the integral connections between emotions, social functioning and decision making, so much so that 'the aspects of cognition that we recruit most heavily in schools, namely learning, attention, memory, decision making, and social functioning, are both profoundly affected by and subsumed within the processes of emotion' (2007: 3).

Indeed, all rational decision making (executive functioning) is impossible without emotional processing or 'emotional thought'. So-called 'higher-level' cognitive skills, such as reading and mathematics, do not operate as 'rational, disembodied systems detached from emotion' but are instead grounded in emotional functions (Goswami, 2011: 28). Therefore, because emotions and relationships influence motivation and give meaning to our knowledge formation, the how and what we learn are, in part, controlled and mediated by our emotional capacity to engage with our physical and social world. The following illustrates this point:

> Why does a high school student solve a math problem, for example? The reasons range from the intrinsic reward of having found the solution, to getting a good grade, to avoiding punishment, to helping tutor a friend, to getting into a good college, to pleasing his/her parents or the teacher. All of these reasons have a powerful emotional component and relate both to pleasurable sensations and to survival within our culture. (Immordino-Yang and Damasio, 2007: 4)

Cuevas et al. (2014) have identified that adults who employ sensitive interactions, take notice of what might be happening in a child's mind, provide appropriate stimulation and scaffolding, and gently encourage children's decisions and goals appear to generate more effective executive function skills in children. Hence, 'what it means to be a "good" teacher is not only a mix of professional knowledge and skills, but also an ability to empathise and build relationships with the learner' (McNess et al., 2003: 244). With neuroscientific research confirming the links between education and learning and relationships (Cozolino, 2013), schools need to consider the way in which pupils *attach* to their teachers.

ATTACHMENT THEORY AND INTERNAL WORKING MODELS

Attachment theory has important implications for teachers as it highlights how children's receptivity to learning is affected by their early relationships and how close, positive relationships in school can foster more effective learning (Kennedy and Kennedy, 2004). The theory of attachment was first proposed by the psychiatrist John Bowlby (1969), who believed children developed either secure or insecure attachments with their main caregiver as a result of the quality of their early experiences. Secure attachments develop from nurturing relationships and support mental processes that enable the child to regulate emotions, reduce fear, attune to others, have self-understanding and insight, empathy for others and appropriate moral reasoning (Sroufe and Siegel, 2011). Insecure attachments can develop if early interactions are more negative, insensitive, unresponsive, inappropriate and/or unpredictable, and can have long-term deleterious consequences. If a child cannot rely on an adult to respond to their needs in times of stress, they are unable to learn how to self-soothe, manage their emotions or engage in reciprocal relationships later on (Sroufe and Siegel, 2011). A child's natural, initial dependence on others provides the experiences and skills to learn how to cope with frustrations, develop self-confidence and pro-social relationships with others and eventually act independently (self-regulate). External experience is absorbed and transformed into an internal mental state known as 'symbolic representation' which informs behavioural responses and has a recursive action. According to Bowlby, early experiences are symbolically represented in the form of an *internal working model*. This internal working model appears to primarily be regulated by the brain and body's stress response system and the social engagement system, laying the foundations for the executive function skills discussed earlier (NSCDC, 2012; Porges, 2011).

Research has inextricably linked secure attachment relationships and positive internal working models to school readiness and school success (Commodari, 2013; Geddes, 2006). Indeed,

Riley (2009) and Kennedy and Kennedy (2004) identify that children can and will form 'bonds' with significant adults such as teachers, who become 'attachment figures' to pupils. Bergin and Bergin concur, noting how 'secure teacher–student relationships predict greater knowledge, higher test scores, greater academic motivation, and fewer retentions or special education referrals than insecure teacher–student relationships' (2009: 154). They suggest a need to acknowledge and forge – within the realms of professional boundaries – 'attachment-like' relationships between pupil and educator. Indeed, close and supportive relationships with teachers have demonstrated the potential to mitigate the risk of negative outcomes for children who may otherwise have difficulty succeeding in school (Verscheuren and Koonen, 2012). This is an important message for teachers who can play an important role in helping to alleviate some of the difficulties children may have as a result of trauma. Some preliminary studies suggest that being an 'attachment-aware school' and implementing attachment-based strategies can improve behaviour, attendance and academic outcomes (Parker et al., 2016).

Web Link

Useful resources for developing attachment-aware schools can be accessed through this web link, available on the companion website: http://attachmentawareschools.com/

spotlight on practice

Supporting children with attachment difficulties

One of the ways in which attachment difficulties might be seen in the classroom is with children who try to maintain close proximity to their teachers. Jane was in year one and followed her teacher round the classroom at every opportunity. She found it very difficult to stay focused on any activity without the presence of her teacher and she found many excuses to ask questions and have physical contact like holding hands. Jane needed reassurance that her teacher could be on the other side of the room and still be aware of her.

Rather than insisting that Jane worked by herself, the teacher began to ensure that Jane was able to sit next to her whenever possible. For example, when the class met on the carpet, Jane was able to sit next to the teacher. Jane was also given opportunities to complete tasks that brought her into close proximity such as turning the pages of the class reading book. When working more independently, the teacher began to catch Jane's eye and used facial expressions to let her know that she had been noticed. This allowed her to 'check in' with Jane without always having to be physically close.

Over the next few days and weeks, Jane's teacher slowly reduced the amount of proximity with Jane and ensured that the space closest to the adult became shared with other children. However, the teacher showed she was still connected to Jane by increasing her use of eye contact and facial expressions when they were further apart. Jane learned that a connection could be maintained with her teacher at a physical distance and gradually felt more confident to work more independently.

From an educational perspective, a key message is that the brain's attachment system takes priority over the brain's exploratory system – feeling safe and secure is more important than learning (Sroufe and Siegel, 2011). Smith (2006) looks at the wider school community and notes how 'attachment to school' also affects the degree of commitment to and engagement with schooling felt by pupils. Strong or secure attachments reflect a sense of value and purpose in school, whilst weak or insecure attachment to school reflects scepticism, indifference and/or hostility towards school. If cognitive skills are grounded in emotional functions, then attachment is the basis on which the best learning can take place. Thus, to be an effective teacher you need to be an *affective* teacher (Rose et al., 2012). Nonetheless, although a nurturing environment may be necessary for optimal learning, a teacher still needs to provide a context which stimulates cognitive growth and the rest of this chapter turns its attention to some of the theories that have attempted to explain children's cognitive development.

reflection point

Think about your own relationships with teachers from your own schooling. Which teachers did you feel more secure with and why?

When on school placement, think about the experiences of children who might not feel secure around adults. What might you do to help them feel more secure and help their brains to feel safe, relaxed and ready to learn?

THEORIES OF SYMBOLIC REPRESENTATION

Neuroscience has shown that learning is incremental (Goswami, 2011) but how exactly a child's continuous multisensory experiences of life become the neurochemical and physiological phenomenon of the connectome and are then ultimately transformed into mental and physical behaviours, remains a mystery. However, we do have hypothetical constructs to explain the bridge between physiological activity in neurons and how this translates into thinking and, in turn, behaviour. Some early attempts to explain these processes led to somewhat rudimentary information-processing theories (Sternberg, 1985). However, the field of developmental psychology has provided the most influential theories about children's cognitive development, notably the work of Piaget, Vygotsky and Bruner. Their theories of *symbolic representation* provide helpful insights into the ways in which children make sense of external reality by representing such experiences internally.

According to theories of symbolic representation, children's experiences are internalised via a variety of sensory information and are actively organised and stored as mental or cognitive structures commonly known as 'schemas'. 'Schema' is a term developed by a leading theorist of developmental psychology, Jean Piaget, and Rumelhart (1980) referred to schemas as the building blocks of cognition. Therefore, since the brain is the chief vehicle for learning we now believe that schemas are literally the neural connections within our brain, which offers guidance on how we can support children's thinking (Goswami, 2011).

PIAGET'S THEORY OF CONSTRUCTIVISM

Piaget stated that children are intrinsically motivated to learn and actively construct their own meaning, hence the term 'constructivism'. Indeed, the importance of active learning has been endorsed by neuroscientific research which indicates that active engagement is a prerequisite for changes in the brain circuitry for learning (Winer and Schreiner, 2011). According to Piaget, external actions/events/objects are turned into schemas which may take the form of images or symbols that enable us to represent the world and make sense of it. Schemas develop through learning experiences and are dynamic structures or 'working theories' that are constantly changing as the child actively engages with and adapts to the world. They are based on patterns that connect different experiences. In this respect, Piaget's theories again resonate with the neuroscientific research which shows how neural pathways connect in response to stimuli within the environment. When a state of 'cognitive conflict' or 'disequilibrium' arises, such as when a child encounters new experiences that cannot be assimilated to an existing schema, to restore cognitive harmony or 'equilibrium' the child adapts existing schemas to accommodate the new experience. As Sutherland describes it, 'assimilation involves transforming experience within the mind, whereas accommodation involves adjusting the mind to new experience' (1992: 26). Thought is essentially 'internalised action' and children make sense of new experiences by assimilating them and fitting them into existing schemas of thought, or adapting their schemas and devising new working theories. Thus, the complementary processes of assimilation and accommodation, and the drive to achieve equilibrium, enable children's learning.

Piaget believed children's thinking develops in a linear manner through four, distinctive, pre-ordained phases of increasing complexity. Although associated with particular ages, he acknowledged that stages might vary in their duration for different children and could overlap. The first, sensori-motor, stage is when babies begin to actively construct schemes through sensory and physical activities. During the pre-operational stage between 2 and 7 years, toddlers and young children are able to mentally represent the world as images or concepts and are less reliant on the concrete physical world to manipulate their own thinking. The concrete and formal operational stages occur from age 7 to the mid-teens and mental representation becomes more complex with development shifting away from concrete to more abstract thought processes. Images in the mind build on and extend the earliest 'action' representations and culminate in more logical and cultural classifications, notably language, with thought and symbolic representation becoming increasingly logical and systematic and gradually assuming priority over action.

VYGOTSKY'S SOCIAL CONSTRUCTIVIST THEORY

A serious challenge to Piaget's work was his relative neglect of the socio-cultural context of learning. We now know that all learning is socially mediated and arises from the 'intrinsically social and communicative nature of human life' (Mercer and Littleton, 2007, cited in Alexander, 2010: 91). Research on the impact of the environment on our brains endorses the significance of the socio-cultural context in promoting neural growth, such that brains are viewed as a 'social organ' (Cozolino, 2013). More emphasis is now given to the impact of the socio-cultural milieu on children's learning, as originally proposed by Vygotsky (1978) and Bruner (1963). Vygotsky's ideas helped focus attention on the social and cultural dimensions of cognitive development. He shares Piaget's constructivist views of children's learning, but emphasises the importance of social interactions, and the way in which children's experiences are embedded in the socio-cultural context, hence the term *social constructivism* is applied to his work.

For Vygotsky, 'human learning presupposes a specific social nature and a process by which children grow into the intellectual life of those around them' (1978: 88). The emphasis shifts from individual discovery to social interaction and from biological control to cultural transmission. Vygotsky's model identifies two dimensions to learning – the interpersonal and the intrapersonal. He believed children internalise experiences via a series of transformations such that an external, interpersonal activity is reconstructed as an intrapersonal, internal mental state. He saw this transformational process as a prolonged 'series of developmental events' in which 'higher mental processes' evolve and a child's cognition becomes increasingly more abstract or symbolic (1978: 56).

In addition to the cultural and social context of learning, one of the most significant aspects for teachers is the focus on cognitive abilities that are 'not yet matured but are in the process of maturation, functions that will mature tomorrow but are currently in the embryonic state' (1978: 86). Vygotsky defined this as the 'zone of proximal development' (ZPD), the distance between the actual developmental level as determined by independent problem solving and the level of potential development as determined through problem solving under adult guidance or in collaboration with more capable peers. Vygotsky's theory accommodates variation between children and acknowledges that children's potential development could vary independently of their actual development. He maintained that differences in ability lay in the children having different 'developmental dynamics', so they had 'wider' or 'narrower' ZPDs. As such, like Piaget, he acknowledged that 'learning should be matched in some manner with the child's developmental level' (1978: 85), but felt that the extent of the ZPD is variable over time and in different contexts. The American psychologist Bruner extended the work of Vygotsky.

BRUNER'S MODAL THEORY

Bruner's (1990) theory of child development, also known as 'modal' theory, moves away from a maturational, stage-dependent perception of cognitive development but retains roots in the constructionist perspective and could be considered as a synthesis of both Vygotsky and Piaget. Like Piaget, Bruner placed emphasis on a child-centred context that enables active, discovery learning to occur. However, as an educationalist, he found Piaget's ideas 'too passive and deterministic for teaching purposes' (Sutherland, 1992: 2) and drew on Vygotsky's emphasis on culture and social instruction.

Bruner was also interested in how children made sense of the world. Like Piaget, he believed that children develop from using concrete to abstract ways of interacting with their environment but that the process is not strictly sequential. He considered that children develop their thinking via a process of skill acquisition and learn to represent aspects of their experience in three different modes – enactive, iconic and symbolic. He argued that knowledge is stored primarily in the form of sensorimotor responses which he called the *enactive mode*. In this mode, knowledge can only be understood or expressed through physical actions. We can also represent meaning primarily in the form of visual images which he called the *iconic mode* – here, images or pictures are needed to understand or express knowledge. Finally, in the *symbolic mode*, we are able to represent the world in a more abstract way, or symbolically, so that we are free from the immediate context. In this mode, knowledge is stored primarily as words, mathematical symbols or via other symbol systems, so we can understand or express our knowledge without relying on actions or images. We might equate these different modes with Piaget's stages of development, but Bruner believed that modal representation is not necessarily wholly maturational since we may continue to represent meaning in the various modes throughout our lives. However, whilst children may move between these forms of representation, it is likely they begin to operate in the enactive mode, moving towards the iconic mode and increasingly operate within the more abstract, symbolic mode.

Bruner also envisaged the process of representation as a 'spiral' in which 'learning is both recursive that is, repeated in different contexts, and incremental, embodying developing expertise' (Robson, 2006: 32). In effect, children learn progressively and at increasingly sophisticated levels by teachers 'intuitively' operating within a child's capability and then supporting them to master more complex learning by 'circling' back, reinforcing, if necessary, and building on their learning (Bruner, 1996). Thus, whilst a child might not grasp an idea or a concept as would an adult, Bruner felt that even young children could understand some aspects, and the adult's role is to intervene at the appropriate level within the child's spiral learning process until the child achieves independent mastery or self-regulation. Bruner, with others, developed Vygotsky's ZPD, suggesting the notion of *scaffolding* to describe the 'interactive, instructional relationship' between teacher and pupil (Wood et al., 1976).

Multimodal representation

Kress (2010) has researched the *multimodality* of children's meaning-making practices and identified a range of modes within which children make meaning. Although today's world requires children to be familiar with technology and visual or graphic means of expression, school learning is still dominated by the need for children to use 'traditional' pencil and paper methods to record and represent their understanding. Kress suggests that multimodality is a 'domain of enquiry' which recognises the representation of meaning in different modes as distinct, rather than merely as a replication or illustration of what is said verbally or in writing. This demonstrates the importance of acknowledging the meaning, for example, of a child's drawing, role play or model-making, as fully representative of their thinking.

In order to create a multimodal classroom, resources and materials need to be accessible and readily to hand so that children can make choices and decisions about how to represent and communicate their thinking. Resources might include opportunities for role play, collage and model-making artefacts, art and natural materials and digital media.

Hattingh's (2014) research with young children reveals the multimodal ways children can represent their thinking. For example, a 5-year-old playing chose to explore his discovery of bees

(Continued)

(Continued)

in his garden by making a bee mask out of string and card to re-tell the story of the beekeeper who came to remove them. His 6-year-old sister used natural objects to create a house out of grass, little stones, conkers and twigs, which was used to support a story she had made up, whilst another child used straws and card to make puppets at school to re-tell the story of Snow White with her friends. In a Year 1 classroom, straw, paper and sellotape were used to create a treasure map for friends in the playground. Blended phonics learned in a phonics lesson were written spontaneously during play, with arrows drawn to represent the directions needed to take to find the treasure. One 5-year-old in a reception class drew a picture of the school's slide to represent his feelings about some children who had blocked the entrance and prevented other children from taking turns. He made the drawing and talked about the event, which appeared to aid him in dealing with the incident. Hattingh (2014) cites these examples to show how children's imaginative use of materials which are around them enables them to create, problem-solve and extend their literacy skills.

A multimodal approach to learning allows children to continually adjust their ideas according to the way in which they interpret their world, links coherently to the ideas on multisensory learning and may help children to move from concrete to more abstract thinking.

A CAUTIONARY NOTE: CHALLENGES TO RESEARCH AND THEORY ON CHILDREN'S DEVELOPMENT

Before considering the implications for your role as a teacher, it is worth noting some of the controversies and critique of the theory and research presented in this chapter. Given that children's development arises from a vast and complex range of processes, events and contexts, it is important that we adopt a critical approach to researchers and theorists who claim to have unearthed how children develop. A consilience approach attempts to draw together different perspectives so that we have a more holistic outlook, but we need to ensure that we continue to question the claims being made, particularly given the rate at which neuroscience is revealing new insights into the developing brain.

We have already highlighted some of the concerns being raised about findings from the neurosciences which indicate some of the issues around such research, including the gap between experimental, jargon-ridden scientific papers and the practical translation of these findings into classroom applications (Hruby, 2012). We need to tread carefully in applying new neuroscientific findings since much of the more recent research rests largely on identifying 'what lights up' in the brain via neuroimaging techniques, but this may not necessarily satisfactorily explain the complexity of children's thinking or how this translates into behaviour. In time, broader theoretical explanations are likely to emerge, particularly when we combine neuroscientific findings with traditional theories of child development. But what has become apparent from the bulk of psychological research and theory on children's development, is how critical questioning can reveal flaws in grand theories and help to establish more clarity and a more comprehensive understanding of children's development.

For example, in relation to Piagetian theory, new research and theory have led to less emphasis being placed on a linear model of child development demarcated by specific stages and more to an acceptance that children's maturational development is less uniform and more complex than

Piaget suggested. It is now broadly agreed that 'differences between age groups may be ones of degree rather than kind' (Siegler, 1998: 22) and that 'development proceeds in a web of multiple strands, with different children following different pathways' (Evangelou et al., 2009: 4). Indeed, Siegler notes that 'learning tends to follow irregular paths involving regressions as well as progress, short lived transitional approaches, inconsistent patterns of generalization, and other complexities' (2005: 770). Much of Vygotsky's work is speculative rather than grounded in research and his early death has meant a reliance on interpretations of intent. For example, Vygotsky's ZPD is somewhat abstract and provides only a vague definition of the so-called 'zone', making it difficult to specify the ZPD (Edwards and Rose, 1994). Most criticism of Bruner's work refers to the belief that children's learning can always be accelerated through appropriate intervention (Sutherland, 1992).

Nonetheless, the bulk of neuroscientific and psychological research and theory have provided some valuable insights into children's development, which can help us to support children's learning in the classroom.

reflection point

Role-modelling

Another learning theory that is worth noting is Bandura's Social Learning Theory (1977), the key message of which is that children learn through observation and imitate others' behaviour. This correlates with a neuroscientific discovery of specialised neurons called *mirror* neurons (Lepage and Theoret, 2007). Mirror neurons are activated both when a person performs an action and when they observe someone else performing it, and appear to provide a neural mechanism for children to internally represent other people's actions. Observational learning is significant for teachers given that all their actions and interactions in the classroom are a potential source of pupils' learning.

Think about the idea of the teacher as a role-model - what might the pupils in your classroom learn from their observations of you?

LEARNING IN THE CLASSROOM: CARING AND DARING TEACHING PRACTICES

A key issue for a teacher is how insights into children's development can and should affect their role in supporting learning and guiding teaching approaches. Sometimes this can create a challenge, when theory appears to provide conflicting arguments about what this role should entail. For example, Piaget's maturational theories about children's 'readiness' to learn raises questions about how proactive the adult role ought to be. With his emphasis on children as individual learners, defined by biological developmental phases and independently exploring their environment through a process of self-discovery, the implication is that the adult role is largely to provide a suitable context for exploration, allowing the child to develop at their own natural pace. However, a Piagetian approach neglects the importance of negotiation and collaboration in learning. The work of Bruner, Vygosky and from cognitive neuroscience emphasises the social and cultural context as being intrinsic to learning and gives the adult a more pivotal and proactive role in determining the advancement of children's learning. The role of the adult in scaffolding learning may range from helping to engage a child's interest to maintaining a child's motivation to perform a task, or may entail simplifying an activity to suit a learner's capability with appropriate demonstration and assistance (Wood et al., 1976). Wood and Wood (1996) refer to this support as *contingent instruction*, since it involves constant assessment of the child's performance with accompanying changes in the level of assistance offered. However, others warn that such intervention may stifle a child who is creatively pursuing a solution independently (Robson, 2006). Additional research draws attention to the complexities of interactions between adult and child, such as the ways in which teachers talk to children, which can influence their learning, memory, understanding and motivation to learn (Goswami and Bryant, 2007). This is supported by work on attachment which emphasises the relational qualities between pupil and teacher (Bergin and Bergin, 2009).

Responsive and critically reflective practitioners will reflect on all this research and theory and select what seems 'fit for purpose' as they accompany their pupils along their learning journey – sometimes reinforcing, sometimes pointing out new ideas, sometimes setting a challenge, sometimes gently guiding and sometimes leaving them to discover new learning alone. In essence, the classroom environment and teaching activity rely on a teacher's sensitive integration of theoretical considerations on how best to facilitate learning – whether to *care* or whether to *dare*.

This chapter has highlighted that foundational to supporting children's development and learning is the creation and maintenance of active, concrete, multisensory and multimodal environments and sensitive, scaffolded relationships that balance nurture with challenge. This is described as *caring* and *daring* practice (Kohlrieser et al., 2012). Much of a teacher's day might be spent in ascertaining when a child needs more caring – reinforcing, scaffolding, supporting, nurturing – and when they are ready to be more daring – acquire new learning, tackle something independently. Daring practice promotes taking risks to learn and provides a source of inspiration and energy for exploration and challenge. A stimulation activity aims to 'up-regulate' a child's arousal system – that is, to increase their interest and engagement by stimulating the sensory and nervous systems responsible for progressing learning – whereas a soothing and supporting activity is designed to 'down-regulate' a child's arousal, to calm and enable the sensory and nervous systems to restore balance (cognitive and emotional equilibrium) in the brain, making them more receptive to the next stimulating learning experiences (Shore, 2014). It is a *safety/risk* paradox not dissimilar to the one posed by Alexander (2010: 95) when he asks if we should 'develop a child' or 'watch a child develop'. The teacher needs to be able to recognise and adjust the classroom environment, their relationship with the child and the nature of their interactions to sustain a 'golden' balance to optimise every child's learning.

putting it into practice

Caring, daring and differentiation

Caring and daring practices essentially translate into creating lessons which will accommodate all children's needs and capabilities - in other words, *differentiation*. This is not just about catering for a range of academic abilities, but also about consideration of the spectrum of social and emotional needs within a typical class. For example, in creating a Mother's Day card, some children will be able to be left to create their own cards independently. Other children may need more sensitive support, such as those who may not have a mother or who have experienced a traumatic caregiving experience. Another example might be introducing a new mathematical concept - some children will be receptive to the challenge and easily grasp the new ideas, whilst others will require more scaffolding to clarify the concept and/or encouragement to increase their confidence before working independently. There may also be some pupils who are not yet in a position to 'dare' and need a lot more 'caring' emotionally and intellectually to help move them forwards.

SUMMARY

Children's development is not a case of following a linear pattern of learning. It should be viewed holistically and can be framed by a biopsychosocial model and ecological systems model, where there is interaction between genetic predispositions and key environmental influences. Importantly, these are based on social relationships. Children's brains develop via neural connections in response to the socio-cultural environment as they symbolically represent the world with increasing complexity. The best learning takes place at the early stages through cooperative relationships and develops on a cumulative basis. Affective teaching enables pupils' exploratory system to take precedence over the attachment system; they feel safe and secure within the environment so can take risks, be curious and learn effectively. An effective learning environment therefore comprises active, multimodal and multisensory learning opportunities, supported by contingent scaffolding to meet individual needs and abilities. The skills of the teacher are to identify the particular needs of the individual children and to support their learning, whilst offering appropriate challenges. Teachers need to both nurture and challenge, providing a caring and daring classroom to optimise learning.

companion website

To access additional online resources please visit: **https://study.sagepub.com/wyseandrogers**

Here you will find a classroom activity, author podcasts including Janet Rose's top tips for employability, free access to SAGE journal articles and links to external sources.

further reading

Goswami, U. (2006) Neuroscience and education: from research to practice? *Nature Reviews Neuroscience*, 7, 406-413. This article provides a helpful review of neuroscientific research and its implications for educational practice.

(Continued)

(Continued)

Gray, C. and MacBlain, S. (2012) *Learning Theories in Childhood*. London: Sage. This book offers a comprehensive overview of the key learning theories related to children's development.

Parker, R., Rose, J. and Gilbert, L. (2016) Attachment aware schools: an alternative to the behaviourist paradigm. In Noddings, N. and Lees, H. (eds) *The International Handbook of Alternative Education*. London: Palgrave. This chapter outlines attachment theory and some of the research regarding its relevance to teachers and pupils.

Rose, J., Gilbert, L. and Richards, V. (2016) *Health and Wellbeing in Early Childhood*. London: Sage. This book provides a useful insight into the development of children's stress response system and social engagement system and the implications for learning.

REFERENCES

Alexander, R. (Ed) (2010) *Children: their World, their Education*. London: Routledge.

Bandura, A. (1977) *Social Learning Theory*. Englewood Cliffs, NJ: Prentice-Hall.

Bergin, C. and Bergin, D. (2009) Attachment in the Classroom, *Education Psychology Review*, 21.2, 141–170.

Bruner, J. S. (1963) *The Process of Education*. London: Random House.

Bruner, J. S. (1990) *Acts of Meaning*. Cambridge, MA: Harvard University Press.

Bruner,]. S. (1996) *The Culture of Education*. Cambridge, MA: Harvard University Press.

Bowlby (1969) *Attachment and Loss: Attachment*, Vol 1, New York, Basic Books.

Bergin and Bergin (2009) Attachment in the Classroom, *Education Psychology Review*, 21.2, 141–170.

Bronfenbrenner, U. (2005) *Making human beings human: Bioecological perspectives on human development*. Thousand Oaks, CA: Sage.

Buss A. and Spencer, J. (2014) The emergent executive: a dynamic field theory of the development executive function. *Monographs Of The Society For Research In Child Development*, 79.2, 1–103.

Commodari, E. (2013) Preschool teacher attachment, school readiness and risk of learning difficulties. *Early Childhood Research Quarterly*, 28, 123–133.

Cozolino, L. (2013) *The Social Neuroscience of Education: Optimizing attachment and learning in the classroom*. London: Norton & Co.

Cuevas, K., Deater-Deckard, K., Kim-Spoon, J., Watson, A., Morasch, K. and Bell, M. (2014) What's mom got to do with it? Contributions of maternal executive function and caregiving to the development of executive function across early childhood. *Developmental Science*, 17.2, 224–238.

Dovis S., Van der Oord S, Wiers R. and Prins P. (2015) Improving Executive Functioning in Children with ADHD: Training Multiple Executive Functions within the Context of a Computer Game. A Randomized Double-Blind Placebo Controlled Trial. *PLoS ONE*, 10.4, 1–30.

Edwards, G. and Rose, J. (1994) Promoting a quality curriculum in the early years through action research: a case study, *Early Years*, 15.1, 42–47.

Evangelou, M., Sylva, K., Kyriacou, M., Wild, M. and Glenny, G. (2009) *Early Years Learning and Development: Literature Riview*. Research Report DCSF-RR176. Oxford: Oxford University.

Feldman, R. and Eidelman, A.I. (2009) Biological and environmental initial conditions shape the trajectories of cognitive and socio-emotional development across the first years of life. *Developmental Science*. 12.1, 194–200.

Geddes, H. (2006) *Attachment in the Classroom. The links between children's early emotional wellbeing and performance in school*. London: Worth.

Goswami, U. (2011) Cognitive neuroscience and learning and development. In Moyles, J., Georgeson, J. and Payler, J. (eds.) *Beginning Teaching Beginning Learning in Early Years and Primary Education*. Maidenhead: Open UP.

Goswami, U. and Bryant, P. (2007) *Children's Cognitive Development and Learning: The Primary Review Research Survey 2/1a*. Cambridge: University of Cambridge.

Hackman D. A., Farah M. J. and Meaney M. J. (2010) Socioeconomic status and the brain: mechanistic insights from human and animal research. *Nature Reviews Neuroscience*, 11, 651–659.

Hattingh, L. (2014) *Literacy on the edge: three to eight year olds make meaning*. Unpublished doctoral dissertation. Bath: Bath Spa University.

Howard-Jones, P. (2010) *Introducing Neuroeducational Research: Neuroscience, education and the brain from contexts to practice*. London: Routledge.

Hruby, G. (2012) Three requirements for justifying an educational neuroscience. *British Journal of Educational Psychology*, 82, 1–23.

Immordino-Yang, M. and Damasio, A. (2007) We feel, therefore we learn: The relevance of affective and social neuroscience to education. *Mind, Brain and Education Journal*, 1.1, 3–10.

Kennedy, J.H. and Kennedy, C.E. (2004) Attachment Theory: Implications for school psychology. *Psychology in the Schools*, 41.2, 247–259.

Kress, G. (2010) *Multimodality: A social semiotic approach to contemporary communication*. London: Routledge.

Kohlrieser, G., Goldsworthy, S. and Coombe, D. (2012) *Care to Dare: Unleashing Astonishing Potential Through Secure Base Leadership*. San Francisco: John Wiley & Sons.

Lepage, J-F and Theoret, H. (2007) 'The mirror neuron system: grasping others' actions from birth?'. *Developmental Science*, 10:5, 513–529.

Matlin, M.W. (1998) *Cognition*. Fort Worth: Harcourt Brace College.

McCrory, De Brito and Viding (2010) Research Review, the neurobiology and genetics of maltreatment and adversity. *Journal of Child Psychology and Psychiatry*, 51.10, 1079–1095.

McNess, E., Broadfoot, P. and Osborn, M. (2003) Is the effective compromising the affective? *British Educational Research Journal*, 29.2, 243–257.

Music, G. (2014) 'Top down and bottom up: trauma, executive functioning, emotional regulation, the brain and child psychotherapy', *Journal of Child Psychotherapy*, 40.1, 3–19.

NSCDC (2011) *Building the Brain's 'Air Traffic Control' System*, Working Paper 11. Harvard: CDC.

NSCDC (2012) *The Science of neglect: The persistence absence of responsive care disrupts the developing brain*, Working Paper 12. Harvard: CDC.

NSCDC (2014). *Excessive Stress Disrupts the Architecture of the Developing Brain:* Working Paper 3. Harvard: CDC.

Parker, R., Rose, J. and Gilbert, L. (2016) Attachment Aware Schools – an alternative to the behaviourist paradigm. In Noddings, N. and Lees, H. *The International Handbook of Alternative Education*. London: Palgrave.

Porges, S. W. (2011) *The Polyvagal Theory: Neurophysiological Foundations of Emotions, Attachment, Communication, and Self-regulation (Norton Series on Interpersonal Neurobiology)*. New York: Norton & Company.

Rappolt-Schlichtmann, G., Willet, J., Ayoub, C., Lindsley, R., Hulette, A. and Fischer, K. (2009) Poverty, relationship conflict and the regulation of cortisol in small and large group contexts at child care. *Mind, Brain and Education*, 3.3, 131–141.

Riley, P. (2009) An adult attachment perspective on the student-teacher relationship and classroom management difficulties. *Teaching and Teacher Education*, 25, 626–635.

Robson, S. (2006) *Developing Thinking and Understanding in Young Children: An introduction for students*. London: Routledge.

Rose, J., Gilbert, L. and Smith, H. (2012) Affective teaching and the affective dimensions of learning. In Ward, S. (ed) *A Student's Guide to Education Studies*. London: Routledge.

Rose, N. and Abi-Rached, J. (2013) *The New Brain Sciences and the Management of the Mind*. Princeton: Princeton UP.

Rumelhart, D.E. (1980) 'Schemata: the building blocks of cognition'. In R.J. Spiro, B.C. Bruce and W.F. Brewer (eds) *Theoretical Issues in Reading Comprehension: Perspectives from cognitive psychology, linguistics, artificial intelligence and education*. Hillsdale: Erlbaum.

Rutten, B., Hammels, C., Geschwind, N., Menne-Lothmann, C., Pishva, E., Scchuers, K., Van Den Hove, D., Kenis, G., Van Os, J. and Wichers, M. (2013) Resilience in mental health: linking psychological and neurobiological perspectives. *Acta Psychiatricia Scandinavia*, 128, 3–20.

Seung, S. (2012) *Connectome – how the brain's wiring makes us who we are*. London: Allen Lane.

Shore, A.N. (2014) Early interpersonal neurobiological assessment of attachment and autistic spectrum disorders. *Frontiers in Psychology*, 5.1049, 1–13.

Siegler, R.S. (1998) *Children's Thinking*. Upper Saddle Ridge, NJ: Prentice Hall.

Siegler, R.S. (2005) Children's learning. *American Psychologist*, 60, 769–778.

Smith, D. (2006) *School experience and delinquency at ages 13 to 16*. Edinburgh: Centre for Law and Society, Edinburgh University.

Sroufe, A. and Siegel, D. (2011) *The Verdict Is In: The case for Attachment theory*. Psychological Networker [online]. Available at: http://www.drdansiegel.com/uploads/1271-the-verdict-is-in.pdf [accessed 26.12.14].

Sternberg, R. (1985) *Beyond IQ: A triarchic theory of human intelligence*. Cambridge: Cambridge UP.

Sutherland, P. (1992) *Cognitive Development Today: Piaget and his critics*. London: Paul Chapman.

Twardosz, S. (2012) The Effects of Experience on the Brain: The Role of Neuroscience in early development and education, *Early Education and Development* 23, 96–119.

Verschueren, K. and Koomen, H. M.Y. (2012) Teacher-child relationships from an attachment perspective. *Attachment and Human Development*, 14.3, 205–211.

Vygotsky, L. S. (1978) *Mind in Society*. London: Harvard University Press.

Ward, J. (2010) *The Student's Guide to Cognitive Neuroscience* (2nd Ed). Psychology Press.

Winer, J. and Schreiner, C (Eds) (2011) *The Auditory Cortex*. New York: Springer.

Wood, D., Bruner, J.S. and Ross, G. (1976) The role of tutoring in problem-solving, *Journal of Child Psychology and Psychiatry*, 17, 89–100.

Wood, D. and Wood, H. (1996) Vygotsky, Tutoring and Learning, *Oxford Review of Education*, 22(1), 5–16.

6

PLANNING

Mark Brundrett and Sacha Humphries

LEARNING AIMS

This chapter will:

- enable you to gain a greater understanding of the importance of planning learning in both the medium and the long term
- provide you with a clear knowledge of research and practice about the organization of the physical arrangement of classrooms
- help you to understand how different approaches to teaching and learning relate to methods of classroom organization
- give you a clear overview of the best ways to support group work.

THE DEVELOPMENT OF IDEAS ABOUT CURRICULUM PLANNING AND CLASSROOM ORGANIZATION

Attitudes to planning and organizing classrooms changed significantly during the course of the 20th century. Gillard (2009) points out five influences that brought about change in primary classrooms, including:

- the kindergarten movement, based on Froebel's theory and practice from the 1890s onward, with its focus on natural development and spontaneity in learning
- the work of Maria Montessori in the early 1900s, with its emphasis on structured learning, sense training and individualization
- Margaret and Rachel McMillan and their emphasis on improving hygienic conditions, overcoming children's physical defects and providing an appropriate 'environment' for young children
- *What is and What Might Be*, published by the former Chief Inspector of Elementary Schools, Edmund Holmes, in 1911. This was 'the first manifesto of progressives education in its condemnation of the arid drill methods of the contemporary elementary school' (Galton et al., 1980: 34)
- Susan Isaacs' two books of 1930 and 1933 on the intellectual and social development of children.

This vision of a new approach to learning and teaching gained its greatest impetus in the late 1960s with the publication of the Plowden Report (CACE, 1967), the central message of which was summed up in a phrase that was to become famous: 'At the heart of the educational process lies the child' (1967: 7). The report went on to state that: 'One of the main educational tasks of the primary school is to build on and strengthen children's intrinsic interest in learning and lead them to learn for themselves rather than from fear of disapproval or desire for praise' (1967: 196).

The Plowden recommendations were never welcomed universally but they have had a lasting influence on debate about the ways learning should be structured in primary schools, both in England and internationally. It has been argued that in large areas of the country many schools and local authorities embraced the implications of the report and the methodology of 'class teaching' was rapidly discarded (Galton et al., 1980: 39), but more recent analysis has suggested that there was comparatively little evidence of a widespread move to more child-centred approaches to teaching and learning (Wyse et al., 2010). However, it is clear that new ideas about the ways in which classrooms should be arranged in order to facilitate enriched approaches to the curriculum and teaching did at least begin to emerge which have impacted on methods of classroom planning and organization in primary schools ever since. Nonetheless, such approaches have remained open to challenge and Kelly (2014) argues that 'direct teaching' dominated much of basic skills education in primary schools in England in the 1990s and 2000s as a result of the many government frameworks and strategies.

THE IMPORTANCE OF TEACHERS MAKING PROFESSIONAL DECISIONS ABOUT PLANNING

Despite the various government initiatives and directives of recent years, teachers in schools today need to make professional decisions about the approaches to teaching and learning that they employ based on the needs of both children and the material being taught. Research has shown that group-based approaches to learning have many advantages, both in terms of social development and learning achievement. Indeed, learning itself can be defined as a change in participation in a set of collective practices (Lave and Wenger, 1991), and this change comes about through adaptation or adoption of a community's way of speaking, acting and interacting (Esmonde, 2009: 1011; Rogoff, 2003).

In their most expansive form, these ideas are seen as part of a 'social ecology' of learning within which all the cultural forms available to teachers are brought together, including histories of practice, the local context and social structures in the wider environment (Esmonde, 2009: 1012). These ideas underpin some of the most influential work on learning theory of recent decades, such as those by Bronfenbrenner (1979) and Erickson (2004). It is for these reasons that teachers need to bear in mind that when planning activities children need opportunities to exercise autonomy and to make choices about their learning. Put simply, when children cooperate they learn to listen to others, to give and receive help, and share ideas, and in so doing they construct new understandings (Gillies, 2008; Johnson and Johnson, 2003). Planning processes thus need to take account of this complex ecology of learning and classrooms need to be organized in ways in which such an ecology can be fostered.

PLANNING LEARNING FOR BOTH THE MEDIUM AND THE LONG TERM

Good planning is essential in order to ensure that the complex environment of the classroom, discussed above, is managed and developed appropriately, but it is also essential to make sure that the learning that takes place addresses the needs of all children and meets the requirements of the school community and wider frameworks such as the National Curriculum in England. The school will also want to ensure that meaningful links are made between different subjects and that the curriculum meets broader societal expectations, such as promoting the spiritual, moral, cultural, mental and physical development of pupils so that they can take a full and active part in society. Indeed, teachers will need to address quite deep philosophical questions about what primary education is for (Alexander, 2010: 174) and the answers that they come up with may vary greatly according to the needs of a particular community, personal beliefs, and the religious denomination of the school, if any. In this sense, the planning process will reflect choices made by the teacher and other staff that are based on their beliefs and values, and teachers need to work together to think very carefully about what the school is trying to achieve before curriculum planning begins (Ashcroft and Palacio, 1997: 21).

Web Link

The website for the Cambridge Primary Review Trust is very useful and can be accessed through this web link, available on the companion website: http://cprtrust.org.uk

It is important that planning should not become burdensome and those in the school community should remember that most national accountability frameworks, including that operated by the Office for Standards in Education (Ofsted), do not require schools to provide individual lesson plans and do not specify how planning should be set out, the length of time it should take or the amount of detail it should contain, since inspectors are interested in the effectiveness of planning rather than the form it takes.

Web Link

You can find more information about Ofsted in the Ofsted School Inspection Handbook, which can be accessed through this web link, available on the companion website: www.ofsted.gov.uk/resources/school-inspection-handbook

For this reason, planning should be focused on meeting the needs of staff and children in order to ensure the best outcomes. Any curriculum plan will be based on certain principles (Ashcroft and Palacio, 1997: 18) and it will:

- outline the selection of content for the curriculum in terms of what is to be learned and what is to be taught
- state or at least imply the teaching approach or approaches to be used
- provide a clear timeline for what is to be taught and in what sequence it will be taught in order to ensure curriculum continuity
- take account of the needs of different pupils and show how the work takes account of differentiation issues
- show how children's progress is to be evaluated or at least relate to the agreed evaluation strategy for the class, group or school as a whole
- take account of the local context as well as any national requirements for a curriculum.

Planning must also take account of the different timelines that operate in a school. For instance, a teacher will wish to plan the content of individual lessons, whole days and weeks of work for the children in their care. This is short-term planning. In the context of this chapter, we are, however, concerned with longer-term planning, which can itself be subdivided and needs to address:

- the *medium term*, such as each school half-term and term and whole school year
- the *long term*, such as each key stage and the phase of schooling.

These two different types of planning will overlap and it is a matter of judgement whether planning for a whole school year really falls into the medium or the long term. However, there are fairly clear differences between the two in the expectations that are placed on teachers. Medium-term planning will be quite specific about content and will relate to the 'timetable' for that period; it will set out the overall objectives for learning for the children to achieve; it will define the kinds of learning experiences that are expected to take place; and it will address any issues relating to progression in learning. In constructing such plans, the teacher will want to take account of the key knowledge, concepts and skills that are to be acquired and the attainment targets that are set for the children involved (either 'officially' in the National Curriculum or locally by the school) (Medwell, 2014: 153).

Long-term plans need to address the wider context of how the whole of the curriculum is to be taught and so relate to the overall learning experiences that a child might be expected to have (Dean, 2009: 110). In other words, such planning relates to the overall experiences that a child will have had whilst in a particular phase of schooling. Such plans will involve the school as a whole and so they must be developed through whole-staff discussion with the input of curriculum specialists for individual subjects or areas of learning. When devising these plans, the school will be forced to grapple with some quite complex issues, including whether the curriculum being offered meets the requirements for breadth and depth in learning, and whether what is being offered is coherent, so that each learning experience builds on the past learning that children have had.

putting it into practice

Planning together

Try planning with a colleague or colleagues as well as developing your own plans. It is amazing how much can be learned from someone who has taught a topic before, but it is equally true that someone with a 'fresh eye' can often contribute something new and suggest an approach that has not been thought of before. When doing joint planning, try to:

- get a clear idea of the key information and skills that you are trying to convey or develop with the children so that your aims and the required learning outcomes are known from the start
- audit the resources that are available so that you make the best use of what the school, parents, children and the wider community have to offer
- brainstorm the lessons and think of what has worked in the past but also what new approaches you might take.

Think about the needs of the subject matter in terms of what you have to convey but also the needs of the children, and try to develop activities accordingly. Remember to respect each other's ideas and try to draw on as much extra expertise as you can; so try consulting the subject leader or key stage leader for their advice. Why not try consulting the children and their parents too!

putting it into practice

Planning for different teaching and learning approaches

Keep in mind that lessons can be taught in a variety of different ways and that teaching approaches can, and should, be adjusted to take account of the needs of the children and the resources available. Try planning to teach lessons on a particular topic in different ways in order to see which approach is more appealing and successful in terms of the children's learning. Make sure that

(Continued)

(Continued)

you evaluate the lessons in some way - either formally through an examination of the pupil outcomes and suchlike, or simply by spending some time reflecting on what worked and what didn't. Adjust future planning accordingly but remember that what works on one day with one group of children may not work on another day (even with the same children), and it is sometimes worth persevering with a particular approach even if you do not meet with immediate success.

PLANNING FOR THE DIFFERENT PHASES OF PRIMARY EDUCATION

Different nations take contrasting approaches to planning. For instance, in Denmark, a great deal of emphasis is placed on considering the views of the children, parents and community; in New Zealand, the curriculum is based on fundamental 'Directions for Learning' composed of vision, values, key competencies and learning areas, which lead to the key principles for the curriculum (see Chapter 8); and Scotland has developed a 'Curriculum for Excellence', which emphasizes the need for a coherent, flexible and enriched curriculum right through from 3 to 18. The curriculum requirements for primary schools in England address the various phases or stages of education, including:

- the Early Years Foundation Stage (EYFS), which relates to children of 5 years and under and sets out six key areas of learning around which activities should be based
- Key Stage 1, which relates to children aged 5–7
- Key Stage 2, which addresses the needs of children from 7 to 11.

Within the national curriculum, the programmes of study give detail of what children should be taught, know and do, but it is important to note that these requirements do not apply to schools that have taken up academy status.

Web Link

Further information about curriculum requirements, which will help you plan for the different phases of primary education, can be accessed through the following web links, available on the companion website:

The Curriculum in Scotland: www.educationscotland.gov.uk/learningandteaching/thecurriculum/

The Curriculum in England: www.gov.uk/government/publications/national-curriculum-in-england-framework-for-key-stages-1-to-4

The ways that children are taught to read has increasingly come to be the subject of central control but it is crucial for our purposes here to note that, in general, in most subject areas, the EYFS and national curriculum documents do not set out how children should be taught the knowledge and skills that they are expected to achieve, and it is here that the professional knowledge and experience of the teacher and the school come into play in terms of the way that learning is planned. Nonetheless, certain key issues will need to be addressed in planning that are common to all schools and these are outlined in the Putting it into Practice 'Key issues' box below.

Web Link

When creating a policy for planning or when planning work in the long or the short terms, including individual lessons, it is well worth remembering to check the websites of the relevant subject associations, many of which provide free advice or planning materials for primary education. The relevant websites can be accessed through these web links, available on the companion website:

Association for Science Education - www.ase.org.uk/home/

Geographical Association - www.geography.org.uk

Historical Association - www.history.org.uk/resources/primary.html

Mathematics Association - www.m-a.org.uk/jsp/index.jsp

National Society for Education on Art and Design (NSEAD) - www.nsead.org/home/index.aspx

UK Literacy Association (UKLA) - www.ukla.org/publications/view/primary_english_teaching/

putting it into practice

Key issues in developing a curriculum planning policy

Mission, beliefs and values

The curriculum planning policy should relate to the overall mission or vision of the school which will be specific to the school community and reflect the values and beliefs of all those involved. This is the case for all schools and may reflect such factors as issues related to the school catchment area and the religious affiliation of the school (if any).

Aims

The policy should:

- set clear and achievable aims and objectives
- ensure work will enable the pupils to make good progress

(Continued)

(Continued)

- challenge all pupils appropriately and seek to extend their knowledge and understanding
- ensure that work is matched to the pupils' abilities, experience and interests
- ensure that there is progression, continuity and subject coverage throughout the school
- relate closely to the assessment procedures used in the school
- make provision for evaluation of the teaching and learning and use this to inform future planning
- ensure that the activities undertaken employ the appropriate teaching and learning strategy for the needs of the children and the subject, including individual work, group work and whole-class teaching, as well as encouraging children to research, investigate and work independently.

The policy should also take into consideration:

- national curriculum requirements
- programmes of study, schemes of work, rolling programmes and curriculum mapping
- attainment targets and teacher- and pupil-defined learning targets
- cross-curricular links, where appropriate
- the need to provide differentiated activities that meet the needs of all children
- the resource implications of the curriculum that has been planned.

The planning policy should also:

- identify how support staff will be deployed so they can effectively support learning during the lesson
- be consistent throughout the school and ensure that all staff work to an agreed format for planning
- include differentiation or 'personalized learning' approaches for groups of pupils, including the more able, SEN, high achievers, middle achievers and low achievers
- involve all staff in a key stage working together to ensure coherence and curriculum continuity
- promote a broad and balanced curriculum which promotes creativity, excellence and enjoyment
- show how outcomes will be audited as part of rigorous monitoring and evaluation processes by teachers, subject leaders and the school management team.

In the Spotlight on Practice, on p.113, the planning for progress in literacy shows several of the key characteristics of a really good lesson. The teacher commences by identifying a clear and well-defined learning aim, an audio-visual aid is employed in the form of a video and some role play is used, and it is only after this input that some writing takes place. Additional challenge is added towards the end of the lesson and there is a focus throughout on making progress.

Planning for outstanding progress in literacy

Holly is an experienced Year 2 teacher. In an observed English lesson, she has been asked to plan shared writing and demonstrate pupil progress in all parts of the lesson. The lesson starts with Holly addressing misconceptions identified from the children's work; namely that many of them are spelling 'with' incorrectly and are using a lower-case letter when writing the personal pronoun 'I'. Following a video and some role plays, which are used as stimuli for writing, she teaches the children about comparative adjectives and the spelling rules for adding 'er' to the root word, whilst also reminding them about adding punctuation and recapping on the use of a capital letter for 'I'. Holly then carries out shared writing with the children where, yet again, she makes the most of every single teaching opportunity. In the space of two sentences, she teaches the children about the length of ascenders, complex sentences, use of a comma prior to the main clause, doubling consonants prior to adding 'ing' and homophones (through). Later, Holly provides yet more challenge to the more able by introducing 'personification', which they also incorporate successfully into their writing. Holly gives the children a time challenge before reviewing their work using a visualizer. At this point, she leads the children to identify that a full stop was missing between two clauses and they correctly identify that they need to add the conjunction 'and' to correct the error. Holly's planned teaching of new content and continual recapping ensures that the children make outstanding progress, as evidenced by the quality of writing produced by the end of the lesson.

The Spotlight on Practice below shows the value of teachers working together to develop plans. The school operates a clear planning cycle and both long- and short-term planning is evident.

Impact on SPAG tests and the planning of English

The school decides that there is a need to change the way in which it plans for the teaching of English following the introduction of the Spelling, Punctuation and Grammar (SPAG) tests in 2013. The approach to planning is discussed at a staff meeting, which includes teachers, teaching assistants and members of the senior leadership team. In medium-term planning, staff are asked to incorporate a word-level objective from 'Support for Spelling' and a sentence-level

(Continued)

(Continued)

objective from 'Grammar for Writing' or 'Developing Early Writing' relevant to the text type being taught. From this starting point, there is a discussion as to what the planning cycle might look like. Staff members feel that the fortnightly planning cycle should include a number of features such as the discrete teaching of grammar, planned opportunities for children to apply new knowledge in their writing and a weekly lesson during which children are expected to redraft and improve their work. The English subject leader drafts a short-term planning format to reflect the agreed cycle. At a subsequent staff meeting, teachers and teaching assistants meet in key stage groups to jointly plan a series of lessons based around the new planning cycle for one of the year groups. All staff report that they enjoy working collaboratively and feel their lesson planning is more creative as a result. Teachers report that the lessons have been delivered successfully and pupils make good progress as a result. Following the implementation of the revised planning cycle, end of Key Stage 2 attainment in writing and SPAG improves from 2013 to 2014 (the percentage of pupils achieving Level 4 increased by 5% and 6% in writing and SPAG respectively).

The final Spotlight on Practice, below, shows that there is value in purchasing high quality schemes of work, but that these need to be used flexibly and be supplemented by input based on the knowledge and skills of staff.

The effect of schemes of work on teachers' professional decisions about planning

The school takes the decision to purchase a scheme of work for the teaching of mathematics in order to ensure that the content of the new National Primary Curriculum is covered, there is progression through topics from one year group to the next and to reduce the planning workload for staff. Throughout the year, progress in mathematics unexpectedly slows across a number of year groups, yet observations of teaching and initial book scrutiny provide evidence of good teaching and confirmation that the learning objectives are appropriate for the ability of the children. To identify the reason for the slowing progress, the mathematics subject leader subsequently reviews the planning and identifies that certain areas of shape, space and measure are only taught briefly, often as a one-off lesson. The class teachers agree that certain areas are not taught in sufficient depth, but explain they feel compelled to move at the pace of the scheme of work rather than use their professional judgement about planning. The teachers are now using the planning from the scheme of work more flexibly and spending longer teaching certain topics to ensure pupils achieve confidence and competence or 'mastery'.

What are the key issues that have to be taken into account in planning in your own school?

Is planning clear and consistent across the school?

How are outcomes monitored and changes to planning made in order to improve practice?

CLASSROOM ORGANIZATION AND THE NEED FOR BALANCE IN LEARNING AND TEACHING APPROACHES

It is widely agreed that *classroom organization* has a specific meaning in educational discourse. That meaning focuses on the physical environment of the classroom and relates to the way that furniture, learning resources, displays and other physical factors in the 'landscape' of the classroom are set out. Effective teachers organize a safe classroom environment and they place furniture, learning centres and materials strategically in order to optimize student learning and reduce distractions (Stronge et al., 2004: 54). In this way, classroom organization is allied to, but separate from, *classroom management*, which relates to the ways in which teachers control and direct pupil behaviour in order to ensure the smooth running of the classroom (Wang et al., 1993).

The physical layout of classrooms also has a further meaning in that the layout of furniture and resources communicates a set of messages to children about the ways in which they are expected to learn and reveals the way in which the teacher expects to teach. In many primary schools, current approaches to classroom organization are characterized by desks or tables in small groups, with books and other materials, including ICT resources, easily accessible. This approach communicates to pupils the notions that appropriate talk and discussion are encouraged and that learning is meant to be active. For these reasons, colleagues, parents and, most importantly, children will infer a great deal about what teachers value from the way the room is set out, the ways in which furniture is grouped and from what is displayed and how it is presented (Kelly, 2014: 168).

It is important to note, however, that the skilled teacher will wish to use the approach which seems appropriate for what is being taught and the children that are doing the learning. This is important since there will be times when the focus should be on the teacher, such as during initial explanation and instruction giving and lesson summation, but there will be other times when the children may need to interact or move around the classroom. The *Statutory Framework for the Early Years and Foundation Stage* in England places a strong emphasis on play and active learning but notes that adults will take an increasing part in guiding learning as children develop:

> Children learn by leading their own play, and by taking part in play which is guided by adults. There is an ongoing judgement to be made by practitioners about the balance between activities led by children, and activities led or guided by adults. Practitioners must respond to each child's emerging needs and interests, guiding their development through warm, positive interaction. As

> children grow older, and as their development allows, it is expected that the balance will gradually shift towards more activities led by adults, to help children prepare for more formal learning, ready for Year 1. (DfE, 2014: 9)

This guidance gives excellent advice for teachers of pupils of all ages in that the emphasis is on making good professional judgements about which approach is suitable for the children, the stage of learning and the topic under scrutiny. This means that classroom organization needs to reflect the needs of the children and must also be flexible enough to allow for different approaches within and between different lessons. This concept has a close relationship to notions of reflective teaching which views teaching as a complex and highly skilled activity, which, above all, requires classroom teachers to exercise judgement in deciding how to act, and high quality teaching, and thus pupil learning, is dependent on the existence of such professional expertise (see, for instance, Pollard et al., 2014).

ORGANIZING CLASSROOMS TO SUPPORT LEARNING THROUGH GROUP APPROACHES

Although we have noted that there are many occasions when the teacher will wish the class to focus on direct instruction, there is considerable evidence that the provision of group work based on the individual learning of all group members can motivate children to greater learning (Slavin, 2014). Huss argues that group work must be challenging and rigorous and should contain five main and essential components:

1. positive independence - whereby all members of the group feel that they can only succeed in the task if they all work together
2. face-to-face interaction - in which pupils should discuss and impart knowledge to others as a community of learners
3. individual and group accountability - where all children are required to contribute
4. interpersonal skills - which require that pupils develop trust in others, gain leadership skills, make decisions and resolve problems
5. group processing - which requires that pupils discuss how well they are doing and analyse their own effectiveness individually and as a group. (Huss, 2006: 21-2)

The size of groups also has a significant implication for the ways in which classrooms are set out. Gillies points out that research has revealed that the ideal size of a group of children is probably four individuals (2003: 44), but Blatchford et al. note that in an average class of 30 or more children this would mean that the teacher would have to interact with and supervise up to eight groups of children (Blatchford et al., 2003: 164) and so decisions on group size will need to be taken, at least in part on a pragmatic basis but also based on the age of the children, the purpose of the work and any classroom contextual features (2003: 164).

A number of studies have shown that where a group-work approach is used, groups of children at a similar stage of learning are more successful than differentiated groups where 'tracking' is employed which organizes children based on ability, ethnicity or gender (Hattie, 2003). When children of different abilities are trained to work together in groups, they are consistently more cooperative and more helpful with their peers than untrained groups and they attain higher learning outcomes, but if cooperative learning is to be successful it needs to be relevant to the pupils' needs (Gillies and Ashman, 2000: 19). This, however, needs careful management since gifted children can feel 'exploited', whilst middle- and low-ability learners may begin to see their perceptions of themselves as competent learners begin to suffer when cooperative learning is predominant and groups are made up of learners at different stages of development. For this reason, there is an argument that the use of such approaches should be reserved for challenging, creative and open-ended tasks, whilst more direct approaches of instruction are employed for learning basic information or rudimentary skills (Huss, 2006: 19–20).

This body of contemporary research reinforces the fact that the physical design of the classroom needs to cater for a variety of teaching and learning approaches and the layout of the classroom itself needs careful planning and serious thought.

reflection points

How does the way that your classroom is organized enable children to cooperate in their learning?

How could the physical layout of the room be changed to help children and adults interact better?

What is the balance between 'direct instruction' and group work in your teaching?

DEVELOPING A POLICY FOR CLASSROOM ORGANIZATION

The implications of recent developments in learning theory make it imperative that schools develop an agreed policy for classroom organization in order that approaches to learning and assessment can be made common across the school and expectations can be communicated to staff and to children. The General Teaching Council (GTC) for Scotland offers the following fairly simple and sensible guidance to student teachers, probationers and those in the early phase of their career.

putting it into practice

Scottish GTC guidance on classroom organization

Manage resources and save time

Managing your resources saves you time, keeps you organized and, most of all, calm. If you know where everything is, how to get it and what you need, life will be so much easier. It allows you time to teach the lesson and not ponder what colour of folder your worksheets were last placed in.

(Continued)

(Continued)

The classroom is not a storeroom

Don't allow pupils to use your classroom as a storeroom. Lunch boxes, pieces of artwork and rucksacks can turn your room into a junkyard. Pupils have a great capacity for denying all knowledge of abandoned items so take control and keep your classroom empty of left luggage!

Don't allow graffiti

Keep jotters and folders clean of graffiti. Entire conversations can be conducted on the paper in your classroom so don't let it happen. Also, it can be hurtful to a pupil to find a comment on their jotter or folder so protect your pupils and keep the room smart.

Give pupils responsibility

Make your pupils responsible in class and get them to issue and collect jotters, folders and books. They should learn early on that classroom organization is partly their responsibility. Failing to do this lets them know that you fetch and carry - not a good early message.

Set a good example

Always try to set your class a good example by being organized. Pupils get to know quickly if they can waste time at the start of a lesson whilst you rummage in your desk or try to remember where you left their folders and books.

(GTC Scotland, 2014, www.gtcs.org.uk/home/home.aspx)

The relevant educational authorities in other nations sometimes provide very detailed guidance about ways of organizing the learning environment for specific subjects, such as reading. For instance, the Australian Government Department of Education, Science and Training gives excellent advice on the ways the classroom should be organized to facilitate the teaching of reading, which includes suggestions about small group work, cooperative learning strategies, learning roles, and the roles of parents and carers in the classroom (DEST, 2014). Where such guidance is not available from a government agency, or even when it is, many schools have developed clear aims for classroom organization. Overall, the main aims of classroom organization should be to:

- facilitate a variety of approaches to learning and encourage pupils to have pride and confidence in their work and achievements by demonstrating that the school values their learning
- create a learning environment that stimulates interest and promotes discussion and social interaction to challenge children's knowledge and understanding of the world
- encourage respect for the school and wider environment and ensure that it is a fulfilling, safe and interesting place to work and learn

- influence children positively in their behaviour, their organization of learning and their personal organization
- 'publish' work, celebrate achievement and raise self-esteem for all learners and thus impact positively on learning, and display the activities being undertaken by children to staff, parents and other visitors.

School policies can then go on to include very detailed expectations for each classroom or can allow individual teachers, phases or departments some latitude to develop their own policy. Some general advice about these issues, collated from various sources (see, for instance, Promethean Planet, 2014; TES Connect, 2014), is given in the Putting it into Practice box below.

Key issues in classroom organization

1. Seating arrangements

The arrangement of pupils' seating is one of the most crucial decisions that has to be made about classroom organization. Bearing in mind what was said earlier in the chapter about the need to arrange the classroom in order to facilitate different learning and teaching approaches, seating can be arranged in different ways, such as:

- desks in rows to encourage more independent study
- desks in small groups to encourage group work and pupil interaction
- desks in a U-shape to facilitate whole-group or whole-class discussion.

Keeping a seating chart of who sits where is especially useful at the start of term or for temporary or new teachers, or in very large schools where teachers may teach a number of different class groups.

2. Learning resources and workstations

Learning resources need to be placed in such a way that they are functional for their purpose and minimize unnecessary disruption:

- learning resources such as books that are used for reference need to be easily accessible to all pupils
- supplies, such as pencil sharpeners and waste bins, should be placed in the perimeter of the room to encourage flow and minimize distraction
- workstations should be set out in a logical way, taking account of key resources and accessibility (for instance, art materials usually need to be near a sink; reading areas may require some carpet or individual seating as well as being next to book boxes or shelves; and science areas may need access to power or specific supplies).

(Continued)

(Continued)

3. Classroom technology and ICT resources

The positioning of all classroom technology and ICT resources needs to be considered carefully if the items are to be put to maximum use with minimum problems:

- interactive whiteboards and other teaching-related resources need to be placed at a point where they can easily be seen by all pupils
- some schools provide all pupils with laptops or tablets and these will need to be to hand; where this is not the case, most classrooms will have ICT workstations that must be accessible but should not dominate the classroom
- peripherals such as add-ons and printers need to be to hand, along with the relevant supplies to support them.

4. Storage

Storage can be one of the most problematic issues in classrooms and both teachers and pupils need to know where everything is, how it can be accessed and what the expectations are for keeping things in order. To do this, make sure that:

- suitable receptacles are provided for each child such as drawers or storage boxes
- large collections of materials such as books are placed in special shelving or storage systems
- delicate or potentially hazardous materials are kept in a safe place where access can be monitored.

5. Display

The way that pupils' work and other displays are treated will say a very great deal about the teacher in charge of the room and will communicate attitudes of approbation or disapproval. Displays should:

- be designed and organized well in order to show material or work to their best effect
- be grouped in different areas for different types of work such as by subject, theme or role (for instance, providing classroom instructions where necessary)
- always show respect for pupils and should ensure equality in the way that children are treated, regardless of their level of achievement.

6. Labelling and coding

Most successful teachers like to keep a classroom very tidy and one of the simplest ways of accomplishing this is to establish a clear but simple nomenclature for all resources, which is labelled in a way that is understood by everyone who visits the room. In order to achieve this, it is worth remembering that:

- colour coding can be a very good way of keeping things organized and can work especially well for children with learning difficulties or those whose reading skills have not yet matured

sufficiently to allow them to understand labels - one colour can be allocated to each subject, to each type of learning resource or to each area of the classroom
- where written labels are used, they should be legible and should ideally represent the expectations that are made of pupils in terms of their own presentation skills
- particular collections of items such as reading resources may need a special system of labelling or coding according to the level or type of material - this might be colour coding, numeric coding or a more sophisticated nomenclature such as the Dewey Decimal system for older children.

putting it into practice

Organizing your classroom

Think carefully about how you organize your own classroom. Consider things like:

- Is the classroom tidy and well ordered?
- Do staff and children know where things are and do they have easy access to the resources they may need?
- Is the classroom set out in a way that allows the teacher and key learning resources to be seen by the children?
- Does the way the furniture is arranged allow for a variety of learning approaches, including whole-class teaching, group work and individualized learning?

Remember that the goals are to allow the teacher to be confident about managing the class but also to encourage children to take some ownership of their learning. Children's work should be displayed in a way that celebrates what they have achieved and shows respect for their efforts. Also remember that classrooms need to be safe environments so things should be ordered in such a way as to prevent accidents!

reflection points

What is the policy for classroom organization in your school and could it be improved?

Does your classroom make the best use of space and of the resources available?

What policies are in place for display and for organizing and labelling materials and resources, and are they applied consistently?

https://study.sagepub.com/wyseandrogers

SUMMARY

Attitudes to classroom learning and teaching have undergone a series of major shifts from teacher-centred approaches to more eclectic and targeted strategies that allow children to work as individuals, in groups and as part of a whole class of children. For this reason, planning documents for both the medium and the long term need to be constructed in such a way as to allow a variety of approaches to learning that include positive social interaction. Outcomes will be enhanced if the physical organization of the classroom is thought out carefully in ways that enable children to have easy access to resources and to discuss their learning, when appropriate, but also to focus on the teacher or other adults in the classroom when necessary. The talented, confident and well-informed teacher will plan the right strategy for learning and link this to the correct organizational approach to ensure that all those within the social network of the classroom are busy, occupied and achievement focused.

companion website

To access additional online resources please visit: **https://study.sagepub.com/wyseandrogers**

Here you will find a classroom activity, author podcasts including Mark Brundrett's top tips for employability, free access to SAGE journal articles and links to external sources.

further reading

Barnes, J. (2015) What does cross-curricular practice look like? in *Cross-Curricular Learning 3-14*, London: Sage, Chapter 3. This chapter shows clearly what cross-curricular learning is in practice and gives sound advice on planning.

Barnes, S. (2015) An introduction to cross curricular learning, in P. Driscoll, A. Lambirth and J. Roden (eds) *The Primary Curriculum: A Creative Approach*, London: Sage, Chapter 13. An accessible introduction to creative approaches to the primary curriculum that shows just how important it is to plan and structure lessons well when using a creative approach.

Fawson, S. (2014) Early years, in P. Smith and L. Dawes (eds) *Subject Teaching in the Primary School*, London: Sage, Chapter 1. A good general introduction to teaching in the early years that emphasizes the importance of planning and preparing well.

National Curriculum in England: Complete Framework for Key Stages 1-4, www.gov.uk/government/publications/national-curriculum-in-england-framework-for-key-stages-1-to-4. The full National Curriculum documents.

REFERENCES

Alexander, R. (2010) *Children, Their World, Their Education*, London: Routledge.

Ashcroft, K. and Palacio, D. (eds) (1997) *Implementing the Curriculum: A Teacher's Guide*, London: Falmer Press.

Blatchford, P., Kutnick, P., Baines, E. and Galton, M. (2003) Toward a social pedagogy of classroom group work, *International Journal of Educational Research*, 39: 153–72.

Bronfenbrenner, U. (1979) *The Ecology of Human Development: Experiments by Nature and Design*, Cambridge, MA: Harvard University Press.

Central Advisory Council for Education (CACE) (England) (1967) *Children and their Primary Schools* (The Plowden Report). London: HMSO.

Dean, J. (2009) *Organising Learning in the Primary Classroom*, 4th edition, London: Routledge.

DEST (2014) *MyRead: Strategies for Teaching Reading in the Middle Years*. Available at: www.myread.org/organisation.htm (accessed 13 August 2014).

DfE (2014) *Statutory Framework for the Early Years and Foundation Stage*, London: DfE.

Erickson, F. (2004) *Talk and Social Theory: Ecologies of Speaking and Listening in Everyday Life*, Malden, MA: Polity Press.

Esmonde, I. (2009) Ideas and identities: supporting equity in cooperative Mathematics learning, *Review of Educational Research*, 79, 2: 1008–43.

Galton, M., Simon, B. and Croll, P. (1980) *Inside the Primary Classroom (The ORACLE Report)*. London: Routledge & Kegan Paul.

Gillard, D. (2009) Short and fraught: the history of primary education in England, *Forum*, 5, 1: 143–63.

Gillies, R. M. (2003) Structuring cooperative group work in classrooms, *International Journal of Educational Research*, 39: 35–49.

Gillies, R. M. (2008) The effects of cooperative learning on junior high school students' behaviours, discourse and learning during science-based learning activity, *School Psychology International*, 29, 3: 328–47.

Gillies, R. M. and Ashman, A. F. (2000) The effects of cooperative learning on students with learning difficulties in the lower elementary school, *The Journal of Special Education*, 34, 1: 19–27.

GTC Scotland (2014) *Classroom Organisation*. Available at: www.in2teaching.org.uk/hints-and-tips/View/946.aspx (accessed 13 August 2014).

Hattie, J. (2003) Classroom composition and peer effects, *International Journal of Educational Research*, 37: 229–81.

Huss, J. A. (2006) *Gifted Child Today*, 29, 4: 19–2.

Isaacs, S. (1930) *Behaviour of Young Children*, London: Routledge & Sons.

Isaacs, S. (1933) *The Social Development of Young Children: A Study of Beginnings*, London: Routledge and Kegan Paul.

Johnson, D. W. and Johnson, F. P. (2003) *Joining Together: Group Theory and Group Skills*, 8th edition, Boston, MA: Allyn & Bacon.

Kelly, P. (2014) 'Organising your classroom for learning', in T. Cremin and J. Arthur (eds) *Learning to Teach in the Primary School*, London: Routledge.

Lave, L. and Wenger, E. (1991) *Situated Learning: Legitimate Peripheral Participation*, Cambridge: Cambridge University Press.

Medwell, J. (2014) Approaching long and medium term planning, in T. Cremin and J. Arthur (eds) *Learning to Teach in the Primary School*, London: Routledge.

Pollard, A., Black-Hawkins, K., Cliff Hodges, G., Dudley, P., James, M., Linklater, H., et al. (2014) *Reflective Teaching*, 4th edition, London: Bloomsbury.

Promethean Planet (2014) *Classroom Design and Organisation*. Available at: www.prometheanplanet.com/en-gb/professional-development/back-to-school/classroom-design-and-organisation.aspx (accessed 13 August 2014).

Rogoff, B. (2003) *The Cultural Nature of Human Development*, Oxford: Oxford University Press.

Slavin, R. E. (2014) Cooperative learning in elementary schools, *Education 3–13: International Journal of Primary, Elementary and Early Years Education*, 43, 1: 5–14.

Stronge, J. H., Tucker, P. S. and Hindman, J. L. (2004) *Handbook for Qualities of Effective Teachers*, Alexandria, VA: Association for Curriculum Development.

TES Connect (2014) *Classroom Organisation Resources*. Available at: www.tes.co.uk/article.aspx?storyCode=6262570 (accessed 13 August 2014).

Wang, M. C., Haertel, G. D. and Walberg, H. J. (1993) Toward a knowledge base for school learning, *Review of Educational Research*, 63, 3: 249–94.

Wyse, D., McCreery, E. and Torrance, H. (2010) The trajectory and impact of national reform: curriculum and assessment in English primary schools, in R. J. Alexander, with C. Doddington, J. Gray, L. Hargreaves and R. Kershner (eds) *The Cambridge Primary Review Research Surveys*, London: Routledge, Chapter 29.

7

TEACHING STRATEGIES

Cathy Burnett, Karen Daniels and Vicky Sawka

LEARNING AIMS

This chapter will:

- explore a range of teaching strategies including play and drama
- consider both child-led and outcomes-led learning
- examine issues related to the transition between the Foundation Stage and Key Stage 1
- help you reflect on the assumptions underpinning different teaching approaches
- consider new possibilities for teaching and learning generated by digital technologies
- invite critical evaluation of a range of approaches to differentiation.

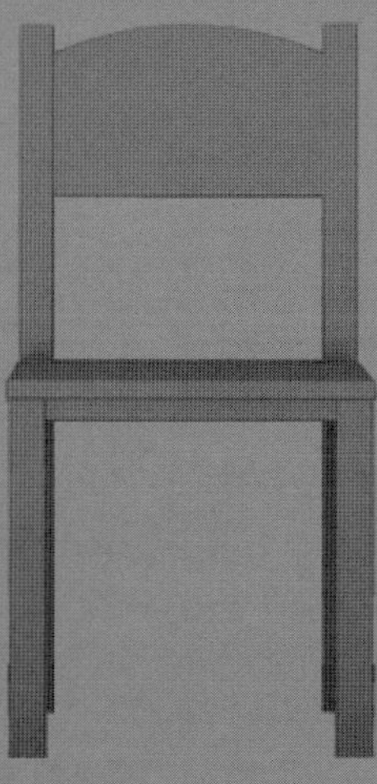

As a teacher, you will add to and review your repertoire of teaching strategies throughout your career. Deciding which strategies are, or are not, effective, however, is not straightforward. Teaching strategies are only effective in so far as they support the learning of children, and what is effective in one context – for one child or group, on one day, for one topic – may not be effective in others. Moreover, different kinds of teaching may support different kinds of learning. The strategies you use to teach children a skill, such as passing a ball, may differ from those needed to develop understanding of an idea or promote creativity and criticality. Importantly, as well as learning a specific skill or concept, children will learn other things from *how* teachers teach: about what is valued, about themselves, about relationships and about the nature of learning itself. The following example illustrates this complexity.

spotlight on practice

The sand tray

In a Year 2 class (for children aged 6–7), one area of the classroom contains a sand-tray set at child height. In the sand tray, the teacher, Dianne, has placed a selection of building materials, including pieces of wood of different sizes, small bricks and stones, and some play figure construction workers. On the bookshelf nearby, there are books about homes in the past. Dianne has attached a large set of building plans to the wall. There is a 'writing box' on the floor containing paper, pencils and other writing materials.

Four children are in the area around the sand tray. Two are chatting and busy, their attention focused on each other and the task they have set themselves. They have built an outline of a house using a few layers of bricks in the sand and are trying to straighten the uneven layers of the walls. James is watching the pair intently. In his hand, he has a small plastic cat, taken earlier from the 'farm' resources drawer. He carefully places the cat onto the wall, smiling at the pair building. Joe meanwhile is standing against the bookshelf. He has drawn lines and crosses on his paper, representing the outer wall of a building, and is now drawing people inside the wall. He has written his house number on the door and is carefully writing his own address on the paper.

putting it into practice

Advice on putting the sand tray activity into practice

Dianne's commentary: *As well as focused lessons and activities linked to different subjects, I give children time to play, to do what they choose. As they play they're learning many things, for example developing and sharing ideas, working together and making links with learning from other activities. In literacy this week we have been writing in the form of a letter, and also writing* *formal and informal emails using iPads, and perhaps this is partly why Joe has taken an interest in writing his address. Through building the house they are learning about the properties of materials and they can use their developing literacy skills by browsing the books or writing. If I think I can extend the learning, I sometimes join in with the children and ask them questions to help them solve problems, for example how they might use the sand to join the bricks together or organise the bricks differently. Sometimes, though, they show more initiative and creativity if I leave them to get on without me. It is good to see them getting on together and sharing their ideas too. James' activity is interesting, isn't it, the way he is getting involved by putting the cat onto the wall, linking his own experiences and interests with the wall building? He seems to be inviting the others to take part in what might be the beginnings of narrative play. This class do like to make up and tell stories as they play. I have noticed that.*

A casual observer might conclude that the teacher plays no active role in supporting the children's learning around the sand tray. However, Dianne's comments demonstrate that she is drawing on a range of strategies, and that the decisions she makes as a teacher are influenced by her beliefs and understandings about the complex and multifaceted ways that children learn. She selects resources and sets up the learning environment, chooses how and when to intervene in children's learning, and decides when to provide time and space to explore their own lines of enquiry and interests. She also identifies how she might intervene to extend their understanding in certain areas; she describes how she might use questioning, for example, to encourage children to solve problems, applying their knowledge about the properties of wet and dry sand (linked to planned learning outcomes in science). The social and emotional 'climate' of the classroom is important to Dianne and she provides opportunities for the children to develop relationships and collaborate.

As this example illustrates, judgements about effective teaching strategies depend on beliefs about the learning process, about what schools are for and about what should be learned. When reflecting on your own or others' teaching, therefore, it is important to consider what *kind* of learning is being supported, how effectively strategies may support the *particular* learning focus and what *else* children might learn in addition to what is intended. In this chapter, we present examples intended to generate questions about what 'effective' teaching strategies might involve and which present teaching as multi-layered. We do not distinguish between different forms of organisation: the strategies presented could be used with whole classes, groups or individuals. They are all, however, in different ways, underpinned by 'sociocultural' theories of learning which, as outlined in Chapter 4, assume that children learn as they interact with people, materials, tools and symbols within their environment (Daniels, 2001), and that they refine their individual understandings through developing understandings with others.

Sociocultural theories assume that interactions with more experienced 'others' can enable learners to move from an existing level of understanding, knowledge or skill to a greater level (Vygotsky, 1978). Teaching from a sociocultural perspective therefore involves exploring understandings with learners, rather than simply telling or teaching by 'transmission' (Barnes, 1976). It involves planning to support or 'scaffold' (Wood et al., 1976) learners to move just beyond what they can already do alone and ensuring there are plenty of opportunities for children to work with their peers.

In summary, the chapter starts from the premises that:

- Teaching is most effective when it takes place in a context in which what is being learned is meaningful to the learner
- Teaching and learning are social processes
- Talk plays an important role in learning
- Teaching needs to start from what a learner already knows.

The strategies we describe relate to both 'child-led' and 'outcomes-led' learning. We consider the role of play and strategies for teaching specific outcomes and raise issues related to the transition between Foundation Stage and Key Stage 1. We use an example of the use of drama to explore how 'playful pedagogies' might be used throughout the primary years, arguing that such pedagogies may be particularly appropriate in equipping learners for their current and future lives. Finally, we discuss approaches to differentiation and consider the kinds of teacher/pupil interactions that most effectively support learning.

PLAY AND LEARNING

Definitions of 'play' differ across cultures and disciplines (Fleer, 1999). Garvey (1977) distinguished play from other activity by describing it as: enjoyable to the learner, spontaneous and voluntary, involving active engagement and having intrinsic goals. Others have highlighted that play is essentially self-directed (Else, 2014). Extensive research has explored the role of play in learning (Wood, 2014). Broadhead (2004), for example, describes how cooperative play with peers can involve high levels of intellectual challenge, and Moyles (1989) draws on Vygotskian theory to explain how children explore ideas through play within self-maintained boundaries when interacting with others and the things around them.

Web Link

An example of one child's explorations can be accessed through this web link, available on the companion website: http://webarchive.nationalarchives.gov.uk/20111202195039/youtube.com/watch?v=fsyaDbq-fFI

In England, a play-based approach to pedagogy is embedded within national policy for the Early Years Foundation Stage (EYFS) (DfE, 2014). Early years guidance, *Development Matters in the Early Years Foundation Stage* (DfE, 2012), encourages practitioners to provide an enabling environment that offers rich learning opportunities through play and playful teaching. Practitioners are advised to provide opportunities for self-initiated activity alongside teacher-led activities. Children's learning in the EYFS is seen as holistic; practitioners are encouraged to observe the areas of learning addressed through children's play and to use their observations to inform decisions about which experiences to offer.

Web Link

More information about the Early Years Foundation Stage can be accessed through these web links, available on the companion website:

www.foundationyears.org.uk/files/2012/03/Development-Matters-FINAL-PRINT-AMENDED.pdf

www.gov.uk/government/uploads/system/uploads/attachment_data/file/335504/EYFS_framework_from_1_September_2014__with_clarification_note.pdf

spotlight on practice

An early years outdoor area

A group of children are playing outdoors. Earlier, the teacher, Adam, drew a road track on the tarmac with the help of two children and chalked on signs including 'Slow' and 'School Crossing'. Adam has asked two children to fill buckets of water and set up a carwash outside. Others climb onto bikes and begin pedalling around the track. Two boys ask a girl on a bike to stop whilst they clean the bike's wheels with sponges. Another takes a tool box, full of metal spanners, and begins to 'fix' the wheels. Another girl, dressed as a road traffic officer, walks into the road holding up a stop sign and raises a hand, signalling 'stop'. The traffic comes to a halt.

putting it into practice

Advice on putting outdoor activities into practice in early years settings

Adam's commentary: *The children enjoy the bikes and they get really excited about them, and riding the bikes supports their balance and physical development. They're having to take turns and ride safely so are developing their understanding of each other's needs and what's fair. They like to bring stories and scenarios into their play, such as, they are late for school or going on holiday or shopping. It lets them bring in their own experiences and they like to share these with each other. When they take on the roles of the road safety officer or the mechanic fixing the bikes, they can try out being someone else. I always let the children design the track with me, as it brings in early literacy as they draw on their experiences of print in their environment. And I think it's also important that the children fill and carry the buckets and help set up the carwash. It supports their self-esteem, confidence and independence.*

Adam explains how he uses the environment to support children's development in many areas of learning, including literacy, communication and language, personal, social and emotional development, and physical development. Adam also encourages the children to use their imagination to make meaning and draw on their personal interests and experiences.

OUTCOMES-LED LEARNING

As explored above, the EYFS Curriculum in England (DfE, 2014), like other early years curricula and approaches, such as Reggio Emilia in Italy and Te Whāriki (1996) in New Zealand (Soler and Miller, 2010), places value on play-led learning and recommends that learning starts from children's interests and concerns. As children move through the primary years in England, however, their learning is likely to be framed by national expectations and more prescriptive programmes of study. Learning is planned to be predominantly 'outcomes-led', with teachers designing activities to support specific learning objectives linked to the curriculum.

Web Link

More information about Reggio Emilia and Te Whāriki can be accessed through these web links, available on the companion website:

www.educate.ece.govt.nz/learning/curriculumandlearning/tewhariki.aspx

www.reggiochildren.it/identita/reggio-emilia-approach/?lang=en

Drawing on an extensive review of research evidence, Hattie (2008) concluded that the teaching most likely to have an impact on student attainment is that which involves: setting challenging learning goals for students which are made explicit; supporting students to know how to reach those goals; and providing feedback on how far, and how, these have been met. These ideas have been very influential and we find that many common practices in primary school are underpinned by such principles. They may however be translated into practice in different ways. You are likely, for example, to see teachers sharing learning objectives and assessment criteria (the WALT – What Are we Learning Today; and WILF – What Am I Looking For), negotiating learning targets with children, discussing how they can meet those targets and giving feedback on what they have attempted. Learning goals may be quite specific (e.g. focused on a particular skill), or relate to a project or task (e.g. making a film), with feedback provided along the way. The latter approach allows teachers to respond to an ongoing assessment of what children need to learn next, and also perhaps to plan more effectively for collaboration. From a very different perspective, Rogoff (1995: 139) explores learning within communities and families, noting how

> children take part in the activities of their community, engaging with other children and with adults in routine and tacit as well as explicit collaboration (both in each others' presence and in

otherwise socially structured activities) and in the process of participation become prepared for later participation in related events.

She describes how learning happens through three planes: *apprenticeship* (at community level) as less experienced individuals interact with more experienced people; *guided participation*, which involves 'side-by-side' or 'distal' joint participation; and *participatory appropriation*, through which individuals change as they engage in new activities and are prepared to engage in them again. Rogoff argues that these planes are inseparable and that we always engage in all three at once. Whilst her ideas challenge some of the assumptions underpinning outcomes-based learning, they can be helpful in thinking about the different roles teachers may play in supporting children's learning. The Reflection Points below explore some possibilities and these are expanded in Table 7.1 and exemplified using Dianne's commentary on 'The sand tray'. Importantly, learning often involves moving backwards and forwards between different levels of support, rather than a rigid progression from teacher modelling to independence.

Table 7.1 Teacher roles

Teacher role	Sample teaching strategy	Description
Teacher as expert	Modelling	Teacher 'models' activity/skill, often talking through the process and exploring the reasons for and impact of any choices made, e.g. Dianne's shared writing of email (see below).
Teacher as coach	Guided individual/group work	Teacher supports children, encouraging them to think through decisions or processes as they do so, e.g. Dianne's proposed intervention when children find wall-building challenging.
Teacher as facilitator	Individual/group activities	Teacher provides resources, observes how effectively child engages in task, supports review, encourages experimentation, provides further challenge as appropriate, e.g. Dianne sets up sand-tray, observes activity and re-visits her decisions about provision.

reflection points

Identify something you have learned recently, e.g. a sporting activity, or use of a device or piece of equipment. Reflect on how others supported your learning.

Perhaps you watched people tackling the task, maybe live or on YouTube. (Online resources, for example, can be powerful in exemplifying aspects of teaching - see, for example, the following guidance on managing a role-play area: http://archive.teachfind.com/ttv/www.teachers.tv/videos/early-years-role-play-managing-and-changing.html)

Consider what was helpful to you as you observed, such as the 'expert' providing commentary on *how* they accomplish the task, talking through the processes involved.

(Continued)

(Continued)

You may have attempted the task with someone else, or perhaps someone guided you, helping you to think through what to do next and how to do it. Maybe they provided feedback about how you were doing and what you needed to do to improve.

At some points, you may have tackled the task alone. What made you feel confident to do so? And did you start to improvise, adapt or personalise the approach in any way? If so, what enabled or encouraged you to do this?

FOUNDATION STAGE/KEY STAGE 1 TRANSITIONS

As children move from the Foundation Stage to Key Stage 1 (KS1), they are required to meet the requirements of the national curriculum (DfE, 2013). Sanders et al. (2005: 142), following consultation with parents and children about EYFS/KS1 transition, identified the differences seen in Table 7.2.

Within the EYFS, planning is holistic and children are encouraged to seek out activities that interest and motivate them. The national curriculum, however, foregrounds the concepts, attitudes, skills and knowledge associated with specific subjects. These changes can bring challenges for children and teachers as the emphasis on play-based approaches becomes difficult to manage against the increasingly structured curricular goals of national policy frameworks (Woods, 2013). However, many primary teachers do succeed in blending child-led and outcomes-led approaches. In our opening example, Dianne values children's self-initiated, play-based learning but also ensures children make progress against statutory goals linked to national curriculum subjects. Commenting further on this activity, she explained:

> My approach with the sand-tray activity is quite different from my approach to teaching a literacy lesson. For example, today in our literacy lesson we looked at an email that was written formally and compared this with one to a friend. The children considered how the email was set out, talked about the use of language, the signature. We then did a shared writing activity where we composed an email together, asking the local historian if she could give us a guided tour of old buildings in the locality as part of our local history project.

Table 7.2 Differences between the Foundation Stage and Key Stage 1

Foundation Stage	Key Stage 1
play-based	work-based
active	static
led by adults or children	directed by adults
thematic	subject based
emphasises a range of skills	emphasises listening and writing

Source: Sanders et al. (2005)

Dianne uses shared writing to model the composition process related to a specific learning objective, but also uses strategies often associated with early years practice. She gives children time to follow their own lines of interest and inquiry, identifies opportunities to extend their learning and then links it back to the statutory curriculum and the properties of materials. Having observed the children's play, Dianne can identify the next steps in learning and consider how to build on her pupils' interests and ideas. Following the sand-tray activity, for example, she suggested they research brickwork arrangements using the iPad and planned an investigation of the properties of wet and dry sand. Dianne's judgements are based on her knowledge of the children, the statutory curriculum and her understanding of how children learn.

PLAYFUL PEDAGOGIES: PEDAGOGIES OF THE FUTURE?

In primary classes with older children, in our experience it is less usual for teachers to teach as flexibly and responsively as Dianne. Increasing curriculum demands mean that teachers often feel they lack the time for an open-ended approach. Many have argued, however, that teacher-led provision can limit opportunities for learning and that approaches that generate opportunities for play, problem solving and improvisation are needed to support the kind of learning students need in their current and future lives (Ito et al., 2013). Jenkins et al. (2006) identified how everyday uses of digital technologies are generating, or at least facilitating, 'participatory' practices that involve new ways of relating to one another and the world around us. For example, they note that digital technologies have made it easier to:

- develop networks and belong to communities that extend beyond our immediate environment (through social networking and online forums)
- make public our own ideas, thoughts and creations (through blogging, wikis, podcasts, videocasts, fanfiction, etc.)
- solve problems and play together (e.g. through alternate reality gaming)
- create and produce digital forms through easy access to a range of tools and through remixing others' creations.

Web Link

More information about participatory practices using digital media can be accessed through this web link, available on the companion website: www.macfound.org/media/article_pdfs/jenkins_white_paper.pdf

These possibilities, Jenkins et al. (2006) argue, have implications not just for what we teach about digital media, but also for the *kinds of learning opportunities* we should provide. As explored in Chapter 14, new technologies are continually changing and we need to critically evaluate the learning opportunities they offer. However, engaging with participatory practices requires not only technical skills, but also skills linked to collaboration, problem solving, flexibility and creativity. Recently, innovative projects have therefore tended to employ what we might call 'playful pedagogies' that draw on the enjoyment, spontaneity, self-direction, intrinsic goals and active engagement associated with play. For example, the international 'Connected Learning' movement (connectedlearning.tv) has established design principles for planning projects that are 'peer-supported', 'interest powered' and 'academically orientated'. Such approaches raise questions about the teacher's role: how can and should teachers support 'playful' activity with older children? When and how should they intervene to ensure learners are challenged to extend understandings, skills and knowledge? The next two sections provide an example of a teacher using drama in ways that involve participating *with* children, and then explore playfulness in digital spaces. We suggest that the strategies described usefully complement those often associated with outcomes-based learning and that such strategies may be particularly appropriate for supporting learning in an age of increased digital participation.

USING DRAMA: IMAGINARY COMMUNITIES

Drama that is used to support learning and that engages children as participants is often known as 'process drama' (O'Neill, 1995). There is not space in this chapter to explore the different manifestations, purposes or possibilities associated with process drama, although we recommend this as an area for further reading (e.g. see O'Neill, 2014). Here, we focus on strategies that engage teachers directly in drama through working collaboratively with children *in role* as characters and *out of role* as 'playwrights and curriculum planners' (O'Toole et al., 2009: 106). To illustrate these strategies, Vicky Sawka shares another example. Vicky directs the Imaginary Communities project for Chol Theatre.

Web Link

More information about the Imaginary Communities project can be accessed through this web link, available on the companion website: www.imaginarycommunities.co.uk/

spotlight on practice

Paradise Island

It is Thursday morning and a class of 8- and 9-year-old children are energetically crowding into their classroom after their morning break. I begin to rearrange the classroom to represent our imaginary island. I have been working with this class and their teacher, Sally, for a few days in setting up an imaginary environment (see the lesson plan on the companion website) and several children come to help. Sally starts the lesson: 'I'm so excited to see our island taking shape again, who can remember what it's called?' Lots of children volunteer to share the name that we agreed at the end of yesterday's literacy lesson; we have created the village of Rolloxbridge, located on Paradise Island. After recapping where the forest, beach, caves and village are in our classroom, the children remind us about the precious jewels that form in the caves underneath the ground.

Sally asks for a volunteer to start us off by taking a frozen position as a character on our island. Sahib stands up first and places himself on the edge of the beach. He leans forward as if pushing something in front of him with his hands. Sally asks the class to share their ideas about who they think Sahib is before he comes to life for a few moments and explains that he is a local fisherman called Nick and is pushing his fishing boat out to sea. After being questioned by the group, we discover that he provides fish for the best restaurants in Rolloxbridge. The next character to join the picture is Bob, the parrot handler. The children ask Bob about his job and he explains that he looks after a rare species of parrot that only live on Paradise Island. They are intelligent, talking parrots and his favourite is called Koko. After more children step into character, I invite Sally to join and she places herself in the village area, one hand over her ear and the other in front of her. She looks relaxed and happy. When questioned she explains that her name is Sarah and she is a local DJ; she loves her job and living on this wonderful island. Finally, after all the children have stepped into character, I too take a position and become Geoffrey, a 14-year-old beach comber.

Next, working out of role, the group discuss a good time of day to bring our island to life and decide to set our scene first thing in the morning. There is a buzz of excitement as we arrange ourselves in new positions in the classroom. I can hear two girls chatting about why their characters would walk through the forest together to their job at the restaurant, and I see the fishermen gathering on the beach near me as I decide to settle down in my favourite spot under the shade of a tree. Sally briefly steps out of her position to indicate that it is time to play: 'I cannot wait to find out what our characters are doing right now on the island. When I count down from 3 we are going to bring our characters to life: 3, 2, 1...'

Sarah, the DJ, swings an imaginary bag over her shoulder and greets the two young women on their way to the restaurant; they chat about how busy they will be today and suggest that Sarah should call in for lunch. They pass Bob and the parrots and I decide to head over to see what he is up to. I shout 'morning' to Nick and the other fishermen as I pass and wish them luck with the first catch of the day. Once I have stepped into the cool shade of the forest I see the parrot handler: 'Hi Bob, how's it going?' He looks concerned and whispers: 'Koko has told me something this morning.' I lean in really close because the island is now getting noisy as everyone wakes up and prepares for the day. Bob continues: 'Koko was out flying this morning and he has seen a pirate ship, he thinks they are after the jewels.' We immediately know we must inform the rest of the island.

putting it into practice

Advice on putting the paradise island activity into practice

In this approach, all participants, including Sally, were free to establish their own characters. Sally did not pre-select or direct the children's roles. This was slightly different from a 'Mantle of the Expert' approach (O'Neill, 2014), in which children are positioned as experts in a particular

(Continued)

(Continued)

context (see www.mantleoftheexpert.com/). Rather than starting with fixed learning outcomes in mind, Vicky, Sally and the children worked together to establish a shared dramatic context and a set of characters to inspire and guide their learning for the next six weeks. Sally initially worked with the children *out of role* to establish the imaginary context, bringing together their ideas, and questioning, challenging and contributing her own ideas and information. Next, working *in role*, she was able to work more collaboratively with the children than her usual 'teacher' position allowed (O'Toole et al., 2009) and she and the children explored life on Paradise Island together. The children's characters directly informed the drama and their interactions opened up new learning opportunities. The precious caves, the rare animals and the threat from pirates all came from the children and generated opportunities for the islanders to arrange meetings, send letters to the pirates, sneak onto the pirate ship, find Captain Blackbeard's diary and send the fisherman to bring him ashore. As the drama unfolded, learning outcomes were associated with:

> *Working with others: The usual group dynamics altered, e.g. those from different friendship groups worked together because it was logical within the dramatic context and given their characters' roles. Children who usually found it difficult to take a leading role were empowered to do so when playing their characters. Bob was played by Charlie who was usually very quiet. He was able to safely create a character alongside his peers and then use his intelligent, talking parrots to lead the drama.*
>
> *Environmental issues: The term's topic for this class was 'environmentalism' and, with this in mind, they created Paradise Island with its rare species of animals and precious jewels in the caves. As the pirate threat grew, the children, through their characters, began to experience why the protection of the environment is more important to some people than money and trade.*

Just as Dianne made decisions about when to intervene in the children's play and when to observe, Sally decided when to be in and out of role and which role to play. Importantly, she participated in the drama *with* the children, stepping into her character as Sarah part-way through the session. She created her character in the moment, responding to the developing plot and guided by personal interest and enjoyment. Sally's genuine enthusiasm and engagement with her own character 'legitimised the play' (Kitson, 1994: 97). Those children who had not immediately stepped into role responded by following suit and committing to the drama. Together, Sally and the children shared the responsibility of being 'playwrights and curriculum planners' (O'Toole et al., 2009: 106) in a playful and enjoyable way. Bob was able to develop the drama through Koko's warnings about the pirates and Sally was able to respond both as Sarah within the drama *and* as a collaborative teacher seeking new directions for learning with her pupils.

Sally also took the role of additional characters to support the drama and extend learning. After sending letters to Blackbeard, Sally and the children decided what Blackbeard would look like, how he would walk and talk, and what temperament he might have. When Sally stepped into role as Blackbeard, she became the character they had just devised together. As Blackbeard, she teased out persuasive techniques as they tried to convince him/her to leave their island alone and responded in role to demonstrate how effective their persuasive attempts had been: 'Well, now you are making me feel guilty, I had never thought of it that way before', but also not making it too easy, 'but I am a pirate and I will wash down my guilt with the rum I will buy when I get my hands on those precious jewels and those stupid talking parrots'. Working in role, Sally could share the learning adventure with her children as Sarah and adopt other roles to challenge the children or create opportunities to practise and develop curriculum-related skills. Later, after reading Blackbeard's diary and realising he was still planning to destroy their island to reach the caves, she and the children reflected on the difference between persuasion and negotiation (addressing further outcomes linked to persuasive language).

PLAYFULNESS IN DIGITAL SPACES

In recent years, some primary teachers have experimented with using digital environments such as virtual worlds, computer games and online forums to create imaginary worlds that support open-ended approaches to learning, similar to those enabled by the Paradise Island project. It may well be that, as Carroll et al. (2006) suggest, process drama strategies will become increasingly common when teaching and learning in digital environments; such approaches provide practical ways to facilitate playful engagement, problem solving and interaction in imagined times and spaces.

reflection point

Consider the following examples. (References to full accounts are provided.) What kinds of learning opportunities might they generate? What has the teacher done/could the teacher do to generate these opportunities? How might the teacher support the children's learning? Which of the teaching strategies described in this chapter might she or he draw on? And how?

- Angela Colvert worked with a Year 6 (10–11-year-olds) class to develop an alternate reality game. Using a class novel as a stimulus, the class generated a mystery scenario and a series of digital clues which they posted on a website (news reports, websites, YouTube videos, etc.). Year 5 children were tasked with piecing together the clues to solve the mystery, using an online forum to pose questions to characters 'played' by the Year 6 game creators (Colvert, 2012).
- Chris Bailey established an optional Minecraft Club at the suggestion of children in his Year 6 class who loved playing Minecraft at home. The class created its own Minecraft community, building places to live as well as leisure facilities (e.g. rollercoaster, hotel, library, theatre). The children played together, sometimes planning and holding events, e.g. staging musicals and holding coffee mornings - and working out how to deal with any conflicts on or off screen (Burnett and Bailey, 2014).

SCAFFOLDING LEARNING THROUGH DIFFERENTIATION

Teaching relies on knowing what children already understand and can do in order to decide how to support and challenge. However, what children know and can do may not be immediately obvious. Thomas (2002) argues that teachers should assume each child brings to school a 'virtual schoolbag' full of knowledge, beliefs and skills they have already. Children are able to 'unpack' these bags if this knowledge, these beliefs, and so on, are aligned with those they encounter in school. Some children's 'bags', however, remain tightly closed, with implications for what they subsequently learn and for their own and their teacher's views of their 'ability'. To avoid this, the teacher's role is to recognise and build on these 'funds of knowledge' (González et al., 2005). Kamler and Comber (2005), for example, worked with teachers to develop 'turn-around pedagogies', which involved learning more about their students' experiences and existing skills and using this knowledge to teach in ways that acknowledged what children already knew and could do. The 'turn-around' was two-fold: a 'turn-around' in children's attainment in literacy at school was enabled by a 'turn-around' by teachers to teach from a different standpoint. As Kamler and Comber (2005: 125) write:

> Turning around... enabled teachers in our project to gain distance on the taken-for-granted practices in their classrooms, so that the problems children encountered were not just attributed to the individual, but seen in relationship to the structure and design of the teacher's curriculum and pedagogy.

Equipped with awareness of children's existing knowledge, attitudes, skills and understanding, teachers can scaffold activities in ways that suit the varied learning needs of their pupils. In Kamler and Comber's project, for example, one teacher drew on her class's extensive knowledge of technology and popular culture to produce animations and then built on this experience to challenge them to develop a range of narratives.

reflection point

You are likely to observe teachers using the following strategies to differentiate learning for children. Teachers may provide different:

(1) learning objectives: with different levels of challenge, e.g. in a mathematics lesson:

- to solve word problems involving addition
- to identify the appropriate operation to solve an addition or subtraction word problem
- to solve addition and subtraction problems, selecting and applying the correct operation.

The teacher allocates different objectives to different groups or asks them to select one to tackle, and perhaps later select another to extend their learning.

(2) outcomes: all children are given the same brief, e.g. write a story, but are expected to produce outcomes of different quality; sometimes different groups are provided with different success criteria, e.g. identifying features they are expected to include; sometimes success criteria are negotiated with children.

(3) tasks: children are given different tasks; some tackle open-ended tasks (e.g. design an experiment to investigate the relative strength of specified materials), whereas others face simpler tasks (e.g. sorting materials according to properties).

(4) adult support: adults work with some children/groups (supporting those having difficulties or extending the learning of those who have already grasped a concept).

(5) resources: children are provided with different resources, e.g. a word bank or writing framework, a table to record findings from an experiment; alternatively, children select the resources they think will be most useful.

(6) grouping: children may be grouped according to ability, but also in mixed ability, self-selected or friendship groups, or with those sharing a language. Note that research has suggested that allocating children to fixed 'ability groups' can be counter-productive (Boaler et al., 2000; Hattie, 2008).

Identify when and how these strategies are used in the classrooms you visit. You may encounter other approaches too. Note that sometimes the teacher specifies the scaffolding to be provided, whilst at other times the child makes these choices. Consider how effective each approach is in scaffolding children's learning. Does the strategy support their learning or does it just enable them to complete a task? What are they learning about themselves as learners or about what is valued in this setting? How else could learning be scaffolded?

LEARNING INTERACTIONS

In this final section, we consider the learning conversations that take place as teachers interact with children in whole classes, groups or one to one. As explored in Chapter 5, talk plays a key role in learning (Mercer and Littleton, 2007) and reviewing the nature and quality of classroom talk is therefore an important part of the teachers's role. Part of this involves reflecting on how best to promote talk between children (Littleton and Mercer, 2013). Here we focus on talk between teachers and children. Concerns about the quality of teacher/pupil dialogue have been raised repeatedly by researchers, particularly in England and the USA (e.g. Flanders, 1970; Wells, 1985). Studies have found that teacher–pupil dialogue tends to be teacher-dominated, includes very little child-initiated talk and is dominated by closed questions that are unlikely to encourage higher-order thinking (e.g. Hardman et al., 2003; Myhill, 2006). Sinclair and Coulthard (1975) identified the most common pattern of teacher/pupil talk as a sequence that involved *Initiation–Response–Feedback* (IRF). The following example, taken from Hardman et al.'s study, illustrates this:

T: OK, now we've been doing a lot of work on non-fiction texts in our shared reading; non-fiction is made up of what, Paul?

P: Facts.

T: It's full of facts, that's right.

T: I wonder who can remember what the piece of non-fiction text we looked at last week was about? Katy, what was our piece of non-fiction text about?

P: It was about smoking.

T: Yes, it was about smoking, well done.

T: And what did the article tell us about smoking, John?

P: How dangerous it was.

T: Right, well done. (Hardman et al., 2003: 211)

In this example, the teacher asks closed questions that require a specific answer – all pupil comments are made to the teacher and there is no pupil/pupil dialogue. The teacher *initiates* the interaction by asking a closed question: 'non-fiction is made up of what, Paul?' The pupil *responds* with an answer, 'facts', and the teacher provides *feedback* in the form of an evaluation: 'it's full of facts, that's right.' The teacher does not engage in discussion with the children or show genuine interest in their opinions but responds to each comment with an evaluation: 'that's right', 'well done'. In sequences like this, teachers remain in charge. Essentially, the interaction works as a 'check' that pupils have taken in what they have been told or taught.

Whilst IRF patterns may sometimes be appropriate, Nystrand et al. (2003) found that teachers who, judged on student attainment, were most effective tended to use more open questions and engage in more cognitively demanding interactions characterised by:

- authentic teacher questions that seek perspectives or points of view rather than testing accurate recall, e.g. What do you think? What do others think? Tell us more about…
- teachers inviting pupils to extend, elaborate on or defend ideas by following up responses, e.g. But what if…? Can you give us an example?
- teachers listening carefully to what students say and responding, e.g. offering another example or personal opinion
- teachers allowing time for discussion.

Guidelines on productive teacher dialogue can be helpful in supporting teachers to review and reflect on their own use of talk. There is however no automatic relationship between certain conversational moves and pupil response. You may find, for example, that children are more or less willing to engage in discussion with different teachers or that different groups engage differently with the same topic. Interaction is complex and is generated not by teachers *or* children but by children and teachers *together* (Nystand et al., 2003). Moreover, communication involves more than language; meanings and understandings are also developed through a combination of modes including gesture, posture and facial expression (Taylor, 2014).

The quality of dialogue is likely to depend on teachers' relationships and ways of working with children over time. Boyd and Markarian (2011), for example, describe a teacher who made frequent use of closed questions but still generated genuine engaged discussion with his pupils. They argue that it is not just what teachers say that matters but also their 'dialogic stance'. Achieving a 'dialogic stance' involves showing genuine interest in what children have to say and being committed to exploring ideas together. It also involves establishing an environment where all feel that their ideas will be respected. Various guidelines and approaches have been developed in recent years which build on these principles and you may encounter these, and others, in school:

- Siraj-Blatchford and Sylva (2004) recommend that adults in the early years engage in 'sustained shared thinking' with children, which involves encouraging children to extend their ideas and elaborate on their thinking, prompting them to make hypotheses and reason (see www.youtube.com/watch?v=SmZsDfVTa8I).
- Drawing on analysis of classroom interactions in five countries, Alexander developed

recommendations for 'dialogic teaching' that promote the use of teacher/pupil dialogue that is collective, reciprocal, supportive, cumulative and purposeful (2006: 28) (see www.robinalexander.org.uk/dialogic-teaching/).

- The 'Communities of Enquiry' approach, often used in Philosophy for Children (Lipman et al., 1980), involves a group 'thinking together' around a stimulus, topic, question or problem. The teacher operates as facilitator, enabling but also working to stimulate and deepen discussion.

putting it into practice

Reflecting on your own teaching strategies

Audio- or video-record yourself interacting with children during a lesson or activity. (Ensure you gain permission from the children, teachers and school and agree what will happen to the recording.) Choose a lesson or activity in which you are exploring a new concept with the children or considering different perspectives, such as an investigation in science or maths, or discussing a picturebook/chapter from a novel:

(1) Listen to the recording. How far did the discussion seem to promote the children's engagement with the topic/issue/idea? What kinds of questions or prompts did you use? What was the relationship between what you said and what the children said? How far do you think this interaction was supportive to the child/children's learning? If working with a group/class, did some children talk more than others? If so, why do you think this happened?

(2) Reflect on how far you managed to achieve a 'dialogic stance' or engage in 'sustained shared thinking'. What seemed to help (or get in the way)? Consider: topic or focus, relationships, use of resources, classroom layout, aspects of communication in addition to language, e.g. gesture, posture, proximity, tone of voice.

SUMMARY

In this chapter, we have considered a range of teaching approaches and emphasised that teaching strategies will reflect certain values and beliefs about education and learning. We have also emphasised that you are always teaching more than knowledge and skills, whether or not you intend to do so. As a teacher, therefore, you will not simply accumulate and apply strategies but adopt and adapt them for different situations. During the course of your teaching career, it is possible that schools – and teaching – may start to look very different, as we become better equipped and more confident in using digital technologies to generate opportunities for learning that are challenging, creative and stimulating. However, it will always be important to continually problematise *how* teaching happens and consider how effectively the approaches you use are suited to the learners you teach.

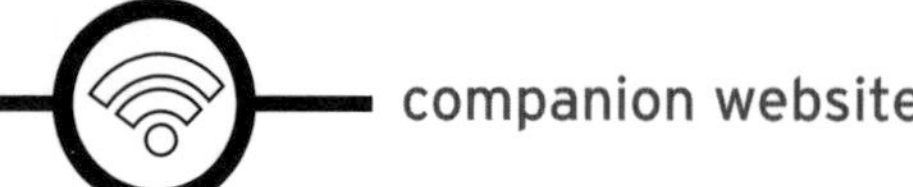

To access additional online resources please visit: **https://study.sagepub.com/wyseandrogers**

Here you will find a classroom activity, author podcasts including Karen Daniel's top tips for employability, free access to SAGE journal articles and links to external sources.

Bowell, P. & Heap, B. (2013). Distilling the principles for planning for process drama. In: *Planning Process Drama: Enriching teaching and learning*. Oxon: Routledge. Useful guidance for the non-specialist on planning for drama.

Connected Learning: http://connectedlearning.tv/ - an international network based in the USA and committed to developing pedagogies for the 21st century. This website establishes clear principles with lots of links to resources.

Daniels, K. (2013). Supporting the development of positive dispositions and learner identities: an action research study into the impact and potential of developing photographic learning stories in the early years. *Education 3-13*, 41(3): 300-15. Explores the author's experiences as an early years teacher implementing and reflecting on the use photographic learning stories with young children. Provides insights into the diverse ways in which children learn and the need to be responsive to these.

Larson, J. & Marsh, J. (2015). Reframing sociocultural theory: identity, agency, power. In: *Making Literacy Real: Theories and practices for learning and teaching*, 2nd edition. London: Sage. Includes an accessible account of sociocultural theory and a case study illustrating how this can be put into practice.

REFERENCES

Alexander, R. (2006). *Towards Dialogic Teaching*. London: Dialogos.

Barnes, D. (1976). *From Communication to Curriculum*. London: Penguin.

Boaler, J., Wiliam, D. and Brown, M. (2000). Students' experiences of ability grouping: disaffection, polarisation and the construction of failure. *British Educational Research Journal*, 26(5): 631–48.

Boyd, M.P. and Markarian, W.C. (2011). Dialogic teaching: talk in service of a dialogic stance. *Language and Education*, 25(6): 515–34.

Broadhead, P. (2004). *Early Years Play and Learning*. London: Routledge.

Burnett, C. and Bailey, C. (2014). Conceptualising collaboration in hybrid sites: playing *Minecraft* together and apart in a primary classroom. In: C. Burnett, J. Davies, G. Merchant & J. Rowsell (eds) *New Literacies around the Globe: Policy and Pedagogy*. Abingdon: Routledge.

Carroll, J., Anderson, M. and Cameron, D. (2006). *Real Players? Drama, technology and education.* Stoke-on-Trent: Trentham Books.

Colvert, A. (2012). 'What is the MFC?' Making and shaping meaning in alternate reality games. In: G. Merchant, J. Gillen, J. Marsh & J. Davies (eds) *Virtual Literacies*. London: Routledge.

Daniels, H. (2001). *Vygotsky and Pedagogy*. London: Routledge.

Department for Education (DfE) (2012). *Development Matters in the Early Years Foundation Stage.* London: Early Education.

Department for Education (DfE) (2013). *National Curriculum in England.* [Online] Available at: www.gov.uk/government/uploads/system/uploads/attachment_data/file/210969/NC_framework_document_-_FINAL.pdf

Department for Education (DfE) (2014). *Statutory Framework for the Early Years Foundation Stage.* [Online] Available at: www.gov.uk/government/uploads/system/uploads/attachment_data/file/335504/EYFS_framework_from_1_September_2014__with_clarification_note.pdf

Else, P. (2014). *Making Sense of Play*. Maidenhead: Open University Press.

Flanders, N. (1970). *Analysing Teacher Behaviour*. Reading, MA: Addison-Wesley.

Fleer, M. (1999). Universal fantasy: the domination of Eastern theories of play. In: E. Dao (ed.) *Child's Play: Revisiting play in early childhood settings*. Sydney: Maclennan and Petty.

Garvey, D. (1977). *Play*. London: Open University Press.

González, N., Moll, L.C. and Amanti, C. (eds) (2005). *Funds of Knowledge*. Mahwah, NJ: Lawrence Erlbaum.

Hardman, F., Smith, F. and Wall, K. (2003). Interactive whole class teaching in the National Literacy Strategy. *Cambridge Journal of Education*, 33(2): 197–215.

Hattie, J. (2008). *Visible Learning*. Abingdon: Routledge.

Ito, M., Gutierrez, K., Livingstone, S., Penuel, B., Rhodes, J., Salen, K., et al. (2013). *Connected learning: an agenda for research and design.* [Online] Available at: http://clrn.dmlhub.net/publications/connected-learning-an-agenda-for-research-and-design

Jenkins, H., Clinton, K., Purushotma, R., Robinson, A.J. and Weigel, M. (2006). *Confronting the Challenges of Participatory Culture: Media education for the 21st century*. Chicago, IL: MacArthur Foundation.

Kamler, C. and Comber, B. (2005). Turn-around pedagogies: improving the education of at-risk students. *Improving Schools*, 8: 121–36.

Kitson, N. (1994). Fantasy play: a case for adult intervention. In J. Moyles (ed.) *The Excellence of Play.* Buckingham: Open University Press.

Lipman, M., Sharp, A. and Oscanyan, F. (1980). *Philosophy in the Classsroom.* Philadelphia, PA: Temple University Press.

Littleton, K. and Mercer, N. (2013). *Interthinking: Putting talk to work.* Abingdon: Routledge.

Mercer, N. and Littleton, K. (2007). *Dialogue and the Development of Children's Thinking: A sociocultural approach.* London: Routledge.

Myhill, M. (2006). Talk, talk, talk: teaching and learning in whole class discourse. *Research Papers in Education*, 21(1): 19–41.

Moyles, J. (1989). *Just Playing*. Buckingham: Open University Press.

Nystrand, M., Wu, L., Gamoran, A., Zeiser, S. and Long, D. (2003). Questions in time: investigating the structure and dynamics of unfolding classroom discourse. *Discourse Processes*, 35(2): 135–98.

O'Neill, C. (1995). *Drama Worlds: A framework for process drama.* Portsmouth: Heinemann.

O'Neill, C. (ed.) (2014). *Dorothy Heathcote on Education and Drama.* London: Routledge.

O'Toole, J., Stinson, J. and Moore, T. (2009). *Drama in the Curriculum: A giant at the door.* Dordrecht: Springer.

Rogoff, B. (1995). Observing sociocultural activity on three planes: participatory appropriation, guided participation, and apprenticeship. In: J. Wertsch, P. del Rio & A. Alvarez (eds) *Sociocultural Studies of Mind*. Cambridge: Cambridge University Press.

Sanders, D., White, G., Burge, B., Sharp, C., Eames, A., McEune, R. and Grayson, H. (2005). *A Study of the Transition from the Foundation Stage to Key Stage 1*. Nottingham: DfES Publications.

Sinclair, J. and Coulthard, M. (1975). *Towards an Analysis of Discourse*. Oxford: Oxford University Press.

Siraj-Blatchford, I. and Sylva, K. (2004). Researching pedagogy in English preschools. *British Research Educational Research Journal*, 30(5): 713–30.

Soler, J. and Miller, L. (2010). The struggle for early childhood curricula: a comparison of the English Foundation Stage curriculum, Te Whāriki and Reggio Emilia. *International Journal of Early Years Education*, 11(1): 57–68.

Smith, F., Hardman F., Wall, K. and Mroz, M. (2004). Interactive whole class teaching in the National Literacy and Numeracy Strategies. *British Educational Research Journal*, 30(3): 395–411.

Taylor, R. (2014). Meaning between, in and around words, gestures and postures: multimodal meaning-making in children's classroom discourse. *Language and Education*, 28(5): 401–20.

Thomas, P. (2002). *Schooling the Rustbelt Kids: Making a difference in changing times*. Crows Nest, NSW: Allen and Unwin.

Vygotsky, L. (1978). *Mind in Society*. London: Harvard University Press.

Wells, G. (1985). *Language, Learning and Education*. Windsor, UK: NFER-Nelson.

Wood, D., Bruner, J.S. and Ross, G. (1976). The role of tutoring in problem solving. *Journal of Child Psychology & Psychiatry & Allied Disciplines*, 17(2): 89–100.

Wood, E. (2014). Free choice and free play in early childhood education: troubling the discourse. *International Journal of Early Years Education*, 22(1): 4–18.

8

THE CURRICULUM

Rachel Edmondson and Anne Robertson

LEARNING AIMS

This chapter will:

- provide you with a description of the term 'curriculum'
- help you reflect on the aims and values that underpin a curriculum
- provide you with details about the statutory curriculum requirements for EYFS and primary education
- enable you to understand decisions that affect curriculum implementation at a school and a classroom level, including approaches that have been shown to make a difference.

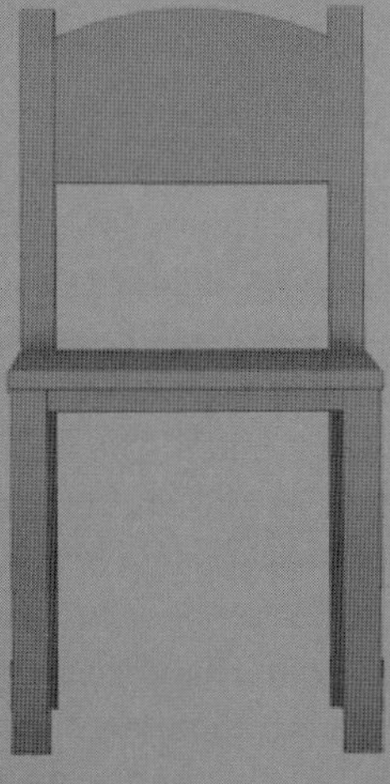

There is broad agreement that there should be clear plans for what teachers should teach and children should learn. However, opinion is often divided about the aims, structure and content that are, and should be, expressed within curriculum documents. A recent in-depth study of primary education (Alexander, 2010) revealed that the issue of the curriculum attracted more comment than any other of the themes being researched. Aside from teachers and parents, many different groups of people are interested in what is represented in a curriculum, including government ministers, policy makers, industry leaders, subject specialists and academics. It is hardly surprising, therefore, that a vast array of literature has been written about curriculum issues. It is beyond the scope of this chapter to do justice to the range of debate, although some of the key issues will be touched on. The main focus of this chapter is to explore the different layers of influence with regards to the curriculum, from government through to classroom teachers. First, we consider the *national* level and decisions about the purpose, aims and content of a national curriculum. We then consider the *school* level and possible approaches to curriculum development that might support the notion of a 'broad and balanced' curriculum. The final section draws on examples from the *classroom* and decisions teachers make about how they can implement the intentions of a curriculum framework and how these decisions impact on the learning experiences of the children. The starting point, however, is to clarify what the term 'curriculum' might mean.

WHAT IS MEANT BY THE TERM 'CURRICULUM'?

reflection point

At this point, what does the term 'curriculum' mean to you?

What is your experience of 'curriculum'?

There are many definitions of the term 'curriculum'. The Latin derivation of the word refers to a 'course' or 'track' to be followed. A very basic definition of the word in the context of education is, therefore, a course or a 'plan for learning' (Taba, 1962). A more detailed definition is provided by Wyse (2014: 12): 'planned human activity intended to achieve learning in formal educational settings'. Within this definition is the notion of 'intentionality' and the suggestion that intentions may not always match with reality. This distinction is made explicit by the terms used by Kelly (2009) – the *planned* versus the *received* curriculum. The *planned* curriculum represents what is laid down in syllabuses, medium-term plans, and so on; the *received* curriculum is the reality of the children's experience. Inevitably, there is a dissonance between expectations on paper and the way the plan is enacted by the teacher. A related set of distinctions made by McCormick and Murphy (2008) refer to the *specified* curriculum (e.g. the national curriculum), the *enacted* curriculum (what teachers do with the curriculum and changes that might occur to it through this process) and the *experienced* curriculum (how the curriculum is experienced in the classroom). These differentiated terms are useful for this chapter, in terms of thinking about the different levels of influence that affect the curriculum process.

This chapter focuses mainly on the 'national curriculum' for primary and the equivalent framework for early years in England (for a comparison of national curricula in Northern Ireland, Scotland and Wales, see Wyse et al., 2013a). A national curriculum is designed to ensure equity and entitlement to what children learn; it is compulsory in schools, except academies, free schools and private schools. The EYFS framework is compulsory for all early years providers, including reception and nursery classes in maintained and independent schools, day nurseries, childminders and playgroups.

It is important to stress that the national curriculum denotes the content and standards of a range of subjects, but the 'wider school curriculum' refers to the *total* programme of an educational institution, for example aspects like assemblies, intervention programmes, outdoor learning, after-school clubs and community events. This distinction between the school curriculum and the national curriculum can become blurred, perhaps exacerbated by the high levels of prescriptive details in recent forms of the national curriculum in England and some other countries of the world. The introduction to England's national curriculum, however, reminds us to maintain this distinction:

> The national curriculum is just one element in the education of every child.
>
> There is time and space in the school day and in each week, term and year to range beyond the national curriculum specifications. The national curriculum provides an outline of core knowledge around which teachers can develop exciting and stimulating lessons to promote the development of pupils' knowledge, understanding and skills as part of the wider school curriculum. (DfE, 2013, para. 3.2)

THE PURPOSE OF A CURRICULUM

A curriculum is underpinned by a set of values and aims, although they might not be explicitly stated. Aims are intended to convey a curriculum's overall purpose – for example, to provide a skilled workforce for the future, to develop moral citizens or to encourage life-long learning. As will be seen from the following discussion, the overarching purpose of a curriculum influences its structure and content.

In the 1970s, when schools could decide their own curriculum, White (2010) reports that aims invariably linked to children being happy, enjoying school and being able to develop in their own ways. These aims convey a curriculum purpose that foregrounds the personal development of the child. This theoretical tradition dates back to ideas expounded by the 18th-century French philosopher Rousseau. He stressed that children should be enabled to learn what they wish to learn when they are ready to do so and he emphasised the importance of play and first-hand experiences in this process, enriched by the unobtrusive guidance of a teacher or facilitator. This perspective was central to the specialist early childhood curriculum that Froebel developed in the early 19th century, and by the 20th century educationalists like Jean Piaget, John Dewey and Maria

Montessori were also advocating the need for children to be actively involved in the construction of knowledge through hands-on learning. Here, the emphasis is on the processes rather than the products of learning.

Alternatively, a curriculum might focus on more instrumental purposes, for example equipping pupils with pre-determined knowledge and skills, perhaps to improve a nation's educational performance against other countries or to prepare pupils for the job market in the future. A curriculum that reflects an instrumental purpose tends to be more focused on the outcomes of learning, set against clearly defined objectives and systems of targets and testing. Influential to this movement was the American educator Ralph Tyler, who had an analytical, technical approach to curriculum planning and was a key figure in the introduction of testing and assessment in schools. He suggested that curriculum planning consists of four dimensions: objectives, content, methods/procedures and evaluation (Tyler, 1949).

The two curriculum positions that have been outlined are summarised by Kelly (2009) as 'process and development' versus 'content and product'. Evidence of these two positions is very clear in debates about the early years curriculum. One view is that the EYFS should focus on the instrumental purpose of 'school readiness' and core skills that set a foundation for later learning. This view is supported by the evidence that some children start school unready to learn – an initial disadvantage that is considered to bear influence throughout the rest of schooling and indeed life (OECD, 2006). The contrasting view is that children should be free to enjoy their early years without the pressure to learn to read and write at a young age: 'early childhood is valid in itself not simply as preparation for work, or for the next stage of education' (Early Years Curriculum Group, 1989: 3).

Ideas about the curriculum can become entrenched by these polarised positions. Instead of viewing the curriculum as a static end-product, Moore (2015) argues for a more flexible, dynamic concept of curriculum. He suggests that tensions around the curriculum open up the possibility for discussion, innovation and creativity. Flexibility is seen, for example, in the way teachers mediate between the curriculum they are 'given' and the curriculum as they practise it. It is this more dynamic concept of curriculum that underpins the discussion in the chapter. In the next section, we look at the introduction of a national curriculum and its subsequent revisions.

THE DEVELOPMENT OF A NATIONAL CURRICULUM

The national curriculum in England has become a well established element of teaching, but there was a time when this was not the case. Prior to 1988, there was no statutory curriculum for primary schools in England; instead, schools were free to choose what they believed teachers should teach and children should learn. But this situation of schools having control over their own curriculum came under increasing pressure by the late 1970s. A debate began amongst politicians, journalists and academics about what was happening in the nation's primary schools. There was dissatisfaction that a lack of accountability in schools meant they were too free to do as they pleased; there was suspicion (not necessarily grounded) that educational standards were being affected by a supposedly too unstructured, 'child-centered' approach in classrooms.

In 1988 the Education Reform Act introduced a national curriculum for the first time, placing what was being taught in primary schools firmly under the control of the government. It set out the statutory requirements for each subject (the 'core' of mathematics, English and science and the other 'foundation' subjects), as well as non-statutory guidance. Each subject area had a detailed programme of study, delineating the content, skills and processes to be taught; there were also attainment targets defining progress and standards to be met in every subject, as well as arrangements for assessing each pupil at the end of a key stage. Crucially, the national curriculum did not provide prescriptive details about pedagogy. Pedagogy is a term that encompasses the act of teaching and the underpinning educational theories, values and evidence (Alexander, 2004). The new curriculum was introduced with the statement that 'it is the birthright of the teaching profession, and must always remain so, to decide on the best and most appropriate means of imparting education to pupils' (NCC, 1990: 7).

Reviews and revisions

The primary curriculum proved burdensome for teachers. Not only were there the increased demands of planning, content coverage and assessment, but also a sense of loss of teacher autonomy (Wyse et al., 2010). Pressure grew from teachers, teaching organisations, local authorities and researchers for the purposes of the national curriculum to be more clearly spelt out and for a vision to be provided of what the different parts were designed to achieve. A curriculum without an underlying rationale or vision lacks direction and purpose, making it harder for teachers to have a sense of what they are trying to achieve through their teaching. The government ordered a review to ascertain how the curriculum could be improved and following this the *National Curriculum Handbook for Primary Teachers in England* (DfEE/QCA, 1999) came into force. It was a slimmed down version of the original curriculum, with the introduction of two new subjects – Personal, Social and Health Education, and Citizenship. Crucially, it included a two-page introduction that outlined the values and aims of the curriculum, addressing the lack of explicit rationale in the previous document. The outline of a vision in the newly revised curriculum did not result in any major changes to the specifications for each subject; it appears that it was there to justify what had already been decided about content rather than be the driving force for change. The emphasis in dissemination of the handbook to the teaching profession was on the content prescription for each subject, with some teachers not even knowing that the section on aims and values existed (White, 2010). An opportunity, it seems, was lost.

Under the government of New Labour, education became a high priority. In 1998 the *National Literacy Strategy* (NLS) was introduced, followed by the *National Numeracy Strategy* (NNS) in 1999. These documents provided very detailed additional curriculum guidance (alongside the actual national curriculum) and specified pedagogical strategies. Until this point, schools were not subject to any prescription concerning pedagogy, for this was viewed as the product of professional judgement (McCulloch et al., 2000). The levels of prescriptive detail in the NLS and NNS were contentious, so in 2003 the policy was adjusted with the claims that 'teachers have the power to decide how they teach' and 'the Government supports that' (DfES, 2003: 16). Part of the reason for the change, it seems, was a growing sense of failure of the 'standards' agenda and a slowing down in the rate of improvement in literacy and numeracy as measured by statutory tests (Brehony, 2005). In 2006, the NNS and NLS were amalgamated and revised under the *Primary Framework for Literacy and Mathematics*. A detailed history of this period of the NLS in schools is provided by Wyse et al. (2013b).

During the period 2008–2010, three different primary curriculum reviews were conducted. Here was a chance to think about how the curriculum might be radically changed to best prepare children for life in the 21st century; after all, the basic subject structure of the curriculum had changed little since 1988. One review was the 'official' *Independent Review of the Primary Curriculum* (Rose, 2009), which was commissioned by the then New Labour Government to look at how the curriculum could be modernised, including how the aims of life-long learning, emotional well-being and social skills could best be met, whilst reducing content prescription and giving teachers greater flexibility. A key recommendation of this report was the idea that the curriculum should be re-structured around six broad areas of learning to replace individual subjects. Meanwhile, an independent review, the *Cambridge Primary Review* (Alexander, 2010), was also being conducted, led by Robin Alexander. The wide-ranging and in-depth research was welcomed by the teaching profession. The team reported that the curriculum should be opened up to become broader, deeper and more balanced, and with a greater emphasis on oracy. It argued for the establishment of a coherent set of aims, values and principles for 21st-century primary education that would drive, rather than follow, the curriculum, teaching, assessment and policy.

The recommendations of these two reviews were not acted on, for when the Conservative–Liberal Democrat Coalition was in power in 2010, the then education minister, Michael Gove, set up his own review. Here, the rationale behind curriculum reform lay in an interest in what other countries were doing, more especially those that were out-performing English pupils in the numeracy and literacy tests used for international comparison. A panel of experts was established to advise on the process of establishing a new curriculum, although there were deep concerns amongst this group that Michael Gove did not act sufficiently on the research evidence, particularly in terms of broadening curriculum content and reducing curriculum prescription (James, 2012). In 2014 a revised version of the National Curriculum came into effect (https://www.gov.uk/government/collections/national-curriculum) which remained structured around the same subject areas, with a focus on the 'core' of mathematics, English and science and less prescriptive detail for the other foundation subjects (see Table 8.1). Religious education remains a statutory subject but with no nationally agreed syllabus.

Web Link

Further information about the national curriculum in England can be accessed through this web link, available on the companion website: www.gov.uk/government/publications/national-curriculum-in-england-framework-for-key-stages-1-to-4

With its focus on 'core skills' and 'standards', the national curriculum for England represents many elements of a 'content and product' curriculum. The aim that introduces the document is succinct:

> To provide pupils with an introduction to the essential knowledge they need to be educated citizens. It introduces pupils to the best that has been thought and said, and helps engender an appreciation of human creativity and achievement. (DfE, 2013, para. 3.1)

Table 8.1 The statutory elements of the Primary National Curriculum in England, 2014

'Core' subjects (and their programmes of study)	Foundation subjects
English *Speaking and listening* *Reading* - word reading and comprehension *Writing* - transcription (spelling and handwriting); composition (specific features of vocabulary, grammar, punctuation and spelling listed as appendices)	Art & Design Computing Design & Technology Languages (KS2) Geography History Music Physical Education
Mathematics *Number* - number, place value, addition, subtraction, multiplication, division and fractions *Geometry* - properties of shapes, position and direction *Measurement* *Statistics* (Ratio/proportion and algebra in Year 6)	
Science Both KS1 and KS2 include: *Working scientifically, plants, animals (and humans), materials, living things and habitats* KS1 includes seasonal changes. KS2 includes states of matter, rocks, forces and magnets, light, sound and electricity, earth and space, evolution and inheritance	

The early years curriculum

In 1996 the government published a document entitled *Desirable Outcomes for Children's Learning on Entering Compulsory Education* (SCAA, 1996). It provided guidelines for all early years settings in England and it described the 'learning goals' that children should achieve before they enter compulsory education. It emphasised early literacy, numeracy and the development of personal and social skills, although it stopped short of claiming to specify an actual curriculum. What it did mark was the creation of a more cohesive, centralised system of early childhood education and therein a framework for assessment and inspection, as had already been established in the primary sector.

Concerns had grown in many countries about standards of performance in compulsory school education and questions were raised about the difference early years provision could make to academic outcomes, especially for disadvantaged groups of children. A major longitudinal study ('The EPPE project', Sylva et al., 2010) was undertaken to investigate the effects of pre-school education, collecting a wide range of information on children's development between the ages of 3 and 7 years. This influential research demonstrated the positive effects of high quality pre-school provision on children's intellectual and social development to the end of Key Stage 1. Notably, these effects were also seen with disadvantaged children. Early childhood education became an important issue on the national policy agenda and by the turn of the millennium there had been a radical transformation of provision, from something that was poorly financed and rather patchy to full government involvement across the maintained, private, voluntary and independent sectors. The Foundation Stage became a distinct phase of education for children aged 3–5, and there was the publication of a curriculum (*Curriculum Guidance for the Foundation Stage*, QCA, 2000). It was divided into six areas of learning, each of which had a series of developmental goals. Originally, these were not devised as assessment criteria, but the introduction of the *Foundation Stage Profile* (QCA, 2002) used the 'early learning goals' as the basis for a complex assessment system. The Education Act 2002 saw the national curriculum extended to include the Foundation Stage, at which point the six areas of learning became statutory.

In 2011, a review was published of early years education (Tickell, 2011). The result of the review was a revised framework, which took effect from September 2012 (https://www.gov.uk/.../early-years-foundation-stage-framework) The framework has a reduced number of early learning goals (ELGs), greater emphasis on the main areas of learning and a simplified assessment for children aged 5, shared with parents/carers and the receiving Year 1 teacher. The overarching principles from the 2008 document remain: that every child is *unique*, learns through *positive relationships*, in *enabling environments*, with recognition that children *develop and learn in different ways and at different rates*. There are three prime areas of learning: communication and language; physical development; and personal, social and emotional development. Further to this, there are four specific areas – literacy; mathematics; understanding the world; and expressive arts and design. Practitioners have welcomed the slimmed down assessment profile; more controversial has been the introduction of the Progress Check for 2-year-olds, the raised expectations of the ELGs and the undue pressure this may have in using a 'too formal, too soon' approach, for example through using phonics teaching as the main driver for developing early reading and writing skills.

Take time to become familiar with the current curriculum requirements for the EYFS and primary schools and consider the progression from 3 to 11. Looking at either the EYFS curriculum or the primary national curriculum, reflect on the content and consider areas that you think are missing. What could be the potential impact on children's development of the missing areas?

THE DEVELOPMENT OF A SCHOOL CURRICULUM

So far, we have looked at the wider influences on a curriculum, such as social, political and economic concerns, and how they affect the aims and content of the statutory curriculum for primary and early years. When it comes to constructing the school curriculum, there are many areas for decision making – for example, teaching methods and pedagogy, how the curriculum is organised, the distribution of the curriculum across each phase group, the daily timetable, the length of each lesson, resources for learning, and so on. This section explores three key areas of influence: the school vision; the curriculum structure; and the strategic management of each subject.

The influence of a school vision

We have discussed the importance of a national curriculum being founded on clearly articulated aims that relate to an overall purpose – the same can be said of a school curriculum. Most schools will have a vision statement that provides a sense of shared purpose and direction to inform decisions made about all aspects of school life, including the curriculum and its related policies. This vision may also include a clarification of the school curriculum's relationship to the national curriculum. It is more than likely that a vision statement about the curriculum will include the terms 'broad' and 'balanced'. These are concepts that have been used as referents in the curriculum debate since the introduction of the national curriculum (Morrison and Ridley, 1988). It is worth thinking about what these commonly used terms mean.

The idea of a 'broad' curriculum suggests that learning is extended beyond the core subjects, to include a focus on all subjects of the national curriculum. Breadth might also be extended to cover pedagogic styles and classroom organization, for example the use of different grouping strategies, rather than children always working alongside the same peer group. Different pedagogic strategies could also be looked at in terms of 'balance', to make sure that activities like collaborative group work, speaking and listening and use of technology, resources and specialist equipment occur across the *range* of subjects in the curriculum. More typically, 'balance' is related to time, so that each subject receives the appropriate weighting of hours in the weekly timetable. Perhaps more neglected is the idea that balance can also refer to quality of teaching. Since the introduction of a national curriculum, it has invariably been the 'core' subjects that have received the most attention from national initiatives, local authority support and school professional development. So balance also means ensuring that other curriculum areas are not neglected in terms of teachers' subject knowledge.

In addition to a curriculum being broad and balanced, it should also be 'relevant'. This immediately raises the question of 'relevant to *whom*?' and 'relevant to *what*?' Relevance might relate to the interests and motivation of the child; the problem is, however, that what constitutes relevance for one child might represent irrelevance for another. Who decides what is relevant for the individual? Is it the child, the teacher, the school leadership? The concept of relevance might go beyond the child to refer to the social and cultural context of the school, or wider still, the needs of society and national priorities. Relevance might also be in conjunction with the school ethos, aims and organisation.

A frequent complaint is that the national curriculum is overcrowded and this situation challenges aims of breadth, balance and relevance. The pressure from high-stakes testing means that 'core' subjects have been protected but aspects of the wider curriculum have been squeezed out. What has been borne out by HMI and Ofsted evidence, however, is that a broad and balanced curriculum is not a threat to achieving standards in maths and English, rather it is the prerequisite for those standards – 'the evidence could not be clearer. If breadth is attained, so are standards. If breadth is sacrificed, so are standards' (Alexander, 2010: 215).

Decisions about curriculum structure

If schools are to attain breadth and balance within the curriculum, there are key decisions to be made about how the curriculum is organised. The national curriculum outlines the content for each subject, but schools have flexibility over *how* subject knowledge and skills are taught. A key debate in this area is the benefit of subject-based teaching versus a topic-based approach. The former relates to teaching through discrete subjects, whereas topic learning involves a thematic approach that crosses conventional subject boundaries. The argument in favour of a topic-based curriculum is that it better reflects children's view of the world, which is holistic, rather than divided into arbitrary subject areas. If topics relate to children's lives and the world around them, for example 'festivals' or 'travel', children can be encouraged to see meaning and relevance in curriculum knowledge and make connections between areas of learning. One such approach is 'The International Primary Curriculum', which has been taken up by increasing numbers of primary schools in England, as well as by international schools around the world. It takes a thematic, creative approach to teaching the foundation subjects (including science) for children aged 3–11 and includes goals related to personal learning and international mindedness. Against this approach, the benefit of maintaining clear subject boundaries is that children need to be able to grasp particular concepts and skills for each subject and see how to progress from one level of knowledge, understanding and skill to another within that subject. This becomes much more difficult with a topic-based curriculum.

Web Link

The International Primary Curriculum website is a great source of information and can be accessed through this web link, available on the companion website: www.greatlearning.com/ipc

Decisions about implementation and change

The regular alterations to the statutory curriculum by different governments mean that the management of this change is a real challenge to schools and early years settings. It is an impossible task for head teachers to be specialists and influence change in every subject; it is therefore typical in most schools for the head teacher to delegate responsibility for the coordination and development of subjects to different members of the staff team. The following case study provides a snapshot of coordinating mathematics in a primary school.

spotlight on practice

Subject leader for mathematics

In the lead up to the 2014 national curriculum being introduced into primary schools, I (Rachel) was mathematics subject leader in my school. This presented a challenge. I knew that I needed to have a good grasp of the subject content of the new curriculum before I could support change at my school. My main point of reference for support was the online guidance from the National Centre for Excellence in the Teaching of Mathematics (www.ncetm.org.uk), which has useful tools, videos and articles to support subject leadership and also teachers' subject content and pedagogical knowledge. I also attended a local network meeting for mathematics subject leaders. Back at school I established a working group with two other experienced teachers, to look at what was already working well in the school, but also where the challenges lay. Adapting our medium-term plans to take account of the changes to expectations for each year group was our greatest task. Linked to this we looked at the extra resources that would be required to support the new framework. There were some key areas of subject knowledge, for example fractions, where expectations had changed significantly. A plan for professional development and staff meetings over the course of an academic year was made, to address these specific areas of subject knowledge. Once the teachers had started to use the new framework, my role was to provide classroom support to help with the particular concerns of individual teachers in teaching mathematics. Alongside this I worked with other members of the senior leadership team to monitor the impact of the new mathematics curriculum, particularly in terms of children's learning and progress.

Reflect on what you need from peers/colleagues at this stage of your journey as a teacher in order to embrace the current national curriculum. Identify areas of strengths where you can contribute and areas where your knowledge and understanding are more limited.

IMPLEMENTING AND EXPERIENCING THE CURRICULUM IN THE CLASSROOM

In this final section, we reach what is arguably the most important aspect of the curriculum – how policy documents and national requirements are enacted by the teacher and how the subsequent experiences of the children are affected. For all the words that are written on paper, this is where the curriculum really counts. The 'enacted' and 'experienced' curricula are located within the contexts of individual schools and classrooms and therefore each teacher's and child's experience will be different. The focus of this section considers classroom practices that have been shown to have a positive impact on teachers' implementation of the curriculum: developing creativity and metacognition.

Developing creativity through children's curriculum experiences

Creativity is considered by many to be an important feature of the curriculum; for some, it is seen as an essential characteristic of human thinking, whilst others take the more instrumental view that it contributes to a nation's economic prosperity (Wyse, 2014). During the late 1990s, considerable attention and funding were given to developing creativity in schools – for example, 'creative thinking skills' was identified as a key skill in the National Curriculum (DfEE and QCA, 1999), and the National Advisory Committee on Creative and Cultural Education (NACCCE) was established in 1998 to promote creative projects in schools. However, in the most recent national curriculum in England, there is a much reduced profile for creativity, which does little to counter the widespread feeling that opportunities for children to express themselves creatively are being eroded (Alexander, 2010). Creativity does feature more prominently in the early years framework (DfE, 2013), albeit subsumed within the three underpinning characteristics of learning:

- playing and exploring – children investigate and experience things, and 'have a go'
- active learning – children concentrate and keep on trying if they encounter difficulties, and enjoy achievements
- creating and thinking critically – children have and develop their own ideas, make links between ideas, and develop strategies for doing things. (DfE, 2013: 9)

Making space in the curriculum for creativity is possibly less of an issue for early years practitioners, since there is the emphasis on processes and exploration in the EYFS. Primary teachers, however, might be worried that they cannot fit another element into an already pressurised timetable. However, Craft (2005) believes that successful primary teachers can find a way of making pedagogical decisions that support creativity, across all subjects, even when the curriculum menu has an emphasis on knowledge. Part of the issue is having a deeper understanding of what 'creativity' actually means.

Claxton (2006) highlights a version of creativity that tends to circulate in primary education: it is often treated as if it were specially related to the arts, involving a concentrated period of manic activity, and it is something that everyone can engage in equally, provided they are allowed or encouraged. This partial, misleading view is typified by bolt-on approaches to creativity like 'arts week' and does little to appease teachers' concerns about fitting it into a crowded timetable. But if we relate creativity to *how* the curriculum is made available to children, then the teacher can influence creative approaches to learning, even within the limitations of the statutory framework. It need not require finding extra space in the timetable, nor compromise the school curriculum. It can involve any domain of activity.

Definitions of creativity are linked to concepts of 'originality' and 'value' (Wyse, 2014), but these do not necessarily involve the dramatic light bulb moment of a major breakthrough or the discovery of something that is new to the world. Creativity can be a much more subtle, personal and gentle process. For example, Craft (2005) makes a distinction between 'big C creativity', associated with the exceptional talent of the gifted few, and 'little c creativity', which is connected with the resourcefulness and agency of ordinary people. Core to this idea is the notion of 'possibility thinking' – this involves the posing of questions, not necessarily consciously voiced, to help focus the mind on innovative possibilities to counter a perceived problem or obstacle. It contrasts with an attitude of being 'stuck'. When children are engaged in creative thinking, they are questioning and challenging, making connections and seeing relationships, envisaging what might be, exploring ideas, keeping options open and reflecting critically on their ideas, actions and outcomes (QCA, 2005). The following Spotlight on Practice provides a taste of what this might look like.

spotlight on practice

Science in Reception

Four children were asked by their teacher to sort a collection of objects into groups; they were able to choose their own criteria for doing this. They had amassed a group of 'things made of wood', 'things made of metal' and had begun to put together 'things made of plastic'. One boy confidently put the hard plastic items together, but baulked when a girl placed an acetate sheet into the same group: 'That's not plastic because plastic things don't bend', he confidently asserted. The teacher listened to his remark and handed him a piece of plastic tubing - more rigid than the acetate sheet, yet still able to be flexed: 'where does this go?' she asked the boy. He knew it was plastic, but it did not fit with his current concept about rigidity. After a period of reflection, he adjusted his thinking to take account of this conflicting object and he revised his original generalisation. 'This is plastic. Only *some* things that are plastic don't bend that easily', he stated, at which point he conceded that the acetate sheet could go in the same group.

reflection points

Consider the learning taking place in the 'Science in Reception' case study. What key aspects can you identify?

How does this form of learning fit with your ideas about how children learn?

What is the role of the teacher in this example of children learning?

Closely linked to the idea of creativity is that of play. Luff (2014) notes how in both play and creativity there is a focus on process, rather than product; both involve exploration, making meaning and self-expression; both are characterised by choice, motivation, experimentation, experience, imagination and open-ended possibilities. Giving children play-based or open-ended activities does not mean the teacher must remain uninvolved. Often, creative thinking requires careful intervention from the teacher – it is perhaps a timely-asked question that will help develop a child's thinking, or a reminder to the children to draw on what they have already learnt, or the careful selection of objects to challenge misconceptions. This sensitive intervention to guide conceptual understanding requires strong subject knowledge from the teacher. Further to this, Claxton (2006) believes in the importance of allowing children time to mull things over, because creativity is often a slow and hazy process. The teacher might encourage children to share their preliminary thoughts, value their 'working out' as much as their 'neat copy' of work or create 'working walls', where successive drafts of, say, a design, a painting or a mathematics investigation can be seen. Creativity can also be encouraged by adjusting how an activity is presented, for example using collaborative group work so that children can actively engage in the process of negotiating meaning. This is seen in the History in Year 5 case study in the following Spotlight on Practice.

History in Year 5

A group of four children were working collaboratively. They had been given a selection of photographs showing Roman archaeological artefacts and been asked to discuss what the artefacts might reveal about life in Roman Britain, before presenting their ideas to the rest of the class. The following extract is taken from the point when the children were studying a photograph of the damaged remains of a mosaic floor. Interestingly, they became focused on how the floor came to be damaged:

Girl 1: I think this was burnt because half of it is burnt.
Boy 1: No, I think it's broken.
Boy 2: Ah, like what about the heating from under the floor?
Girl 2: Maybe they turned on the heating and the fire burnt it.
Boy 1: No, when it was under ground, when it was under ground it might have rotted.
Girl 1: Like maybe it got water on it.
Boy 1: I think this shows that the Romans were here to stay.
Boy 2: Yeah, they wouldn't make it for no reason. If they're in a war, they shouldn't be thinking about making a mosaic.
Girl 2: Maybe they were walking on it too much and afterwards it just rubbed.
Boy 1: Yeah, like as something gets old. So they must have been living there for about 20 years.

There was a sense of purpose and value to the group's discussion and the ideas were novel. But these ideas were not the result of guessing or wild fantasy; instead, the children crucially drew on their prior knowledge (for example, that Roman villas often had under-floor heating) and built on each other's ideas. Shaping new knowledge cannot occur without some understanding of what already exists. Aside from drawing on their knowledge of Roman Britain, these children were also learning about the nature of history – that it is not a body of inert, objective facts, drawn unproblematically from archival material, but rather it represents socially constructed knowledge, which is open to interpretation and subjective responses.

Are you unsure about planning collaborative group work? Are you concerned about the teacher's role in this? Are you encouraged and excited about working in this way in your classroom?

Developing metacognition through children's curriculum experiences

> If I think about what I need to think about then I get good ideas about how to do it. If I talk to my group about my thinks then they get ideas too. And if I listen to their thinks then that helps me more. (Abdul, aged 5)

This pupil had been a participant in a collaborative group where metacognitive strategies were included on a weekly basis during the academic year. In September, he had very little knowledge and understanding of English and the class teacher had questioned the value of his inclusion in the group, preferring to send him out to work with a teaching assistant to learn English. She was encouraged to allow him to be a participant in the group and by March was more than convinced that his participation was the key aspect of his time in school that was making a difference to his English, his thinking and his confidence in himself as a learner. The quotation from Abdul suggests the value of collaborative group work with an element of metacognition included.

Metacognition can be hard to understand, but Flavell (1976) demonstrates three key aspects of it:

- where children learn to identify situations in which intentional, conscious storage of information is important
- where they learn to keep in mind the relevant information related to the problem
- where they learn to make deliberate systematic searches for information.

Hacker (1998) went further and included in his definition the importance of understanding, monitoring and regulating one's own cognitive and affective processes and states.

Teachers have been hearing and reading about metacognition and talking about how to include this aspect of thinking in their teaching for many years. However, it continues to be an aspect which is given little time and perhaps little value in many classrooms, even where teachers have had professional development sessions aiming to promote metacognition (Robertson, 2014). The reasons for this lack of commitment to metacognitive aspects of learning are unclear. Teachers quote a lack of time as one reason. However, it can be demonstrated that engaging at this level makes a strong positive impact on children's thinking and learning (Robertson, 2014). Time is used more effectively when children are able to take control of their memory and thinking, when they make connections efficiently and when they engage with questions, curiosity and each other.

For those who are committed to developing children's thinking and to encouraging a conscious awareness of being an effective learner, it is essential to include metacognitive elements in lessons on a regular basis. The impact on children has been seen to be at its greatest when aspects of metacognition are used at various points during lessons, when metacognitive strategies are used as normal and standard, therefore embedding themselves in children's repertoire of learning behaviours, and where it becomes routine to consider how to think about a task, monitor the strategies throughout the task and evaluate the thinking being used (Robertson, 2014).

In our experience, the one key aspect that convinced teachers of the value of developing metacognitive strategies in their classrooms was of hearing how their Year 1 children understood what helped them to learn. The teachers were participants in a project to establish and develop a programme aimed at raising children's thinking ability. The professional development associated with the programme had spent a considerable amount of time on developing knowledge and understanding of metacognition, and yet classroom observations showed that this aspect of the lessons was being neglected. It seemed that teachers' priorities were more focused on getting the children to address the challenges of the lessons and to discuss those task-level ideas with each other. Some of the teachers asked questions at the end of lessons that stimulated metacognitive thinking but then didn't capitalise on what the children had found helpful and use this in a future lesson. Teachers did not seem to turn to metacognitive strategies naturally as an important aspect of their own learning.

The challenge was to enable teachers to understand the value of metacognitive strategies. Two main tasks were completed in order to address this issue. First, children's ideas about what they considered helpful or unhelpful in relation to their learning were collected and collated over the course of a year. Lesson observations were transcribed and analysed to identify metacognitive elements of lessons. Children's ideas, or 'constructs', showed a limited number of references to metacognitive functioning. However, when it was mentioned by children, it was clear that they could explain how this level of thinking helped them to learn.

The third task in the project with the teachers was to find a constructive way to involve them in discussing the findings so that they could consider any changes they wanted to make to their pedagogy, in order to improve the learning environment for their children. The teachers agreed to participate in an intervention group to examine transcripts alongside children's constructs. The result was that teachers recognised their own limited use of metacognition, and they acknowledged the children's clear explanations as to how this level of thought and discussion helped them to learn. The teachers themselves chose to target this area of work and determined to include more metacognitive aspects in their teaching the following year. The results showed that explicit use of metacognitive strategies during lessons increased significantly the following year. The children's references to metacognition also increased when providing their constructs about what helped them to learn. The next Spotlight on Practice illustrates some of the responses of the children.

Examples of what metacognition means to 6-year-olds

Aurora said that she liked to **think of other views**. When asked how this helped her to learn, she said:

> If you look at things from different ways you'll probably find a best way of looking at it. Then if you tell the others like what you're thinking then that helps too 'cos they share and you see lots of different ideas then. When we do that we always sort our puzzles out.

Joshua reported:

> When I think about a puzzle, I **look** and see which way will I do it and I **listen** to Aurora and she says something else and I think Oh that's another way but I don't think it will work and I tell them and then we say all the ways what might work that we can see in our brains.

When asked how that helped him to learn, he said:

> Well you can **think** about all the ways the next time you have a puzzle and one of them other ways might be the one to go.

Anna said:

> You need to get like inside your head, you know, and think and say what you are thinking and then you need to like get inside the others' heads too and think what they think and that helps you to understand.

When asked how that helped, she reported:

> Well, if you can sort of think what they might think then you can ask them or like a question 'cos sometimes they don't say what they think so you get their ideas if you like tell them you want to know 'cos it helps. If you just try to solve the puzzle without thinking you're thinking then you probably won't get it.

Philomena also came up with the strategy of asking others, so this may well have been promoted in this particular group. She said:

> I **ask what the others think** sometimes 'cos then that helps me to **know what I think** and if you know what you think then you might know if you're thinking the right way or you might need to change your mind about your first idea.

It seemed as if having confirmation of others' thoughts gave her the confidence to either continue her line of thought or to re-evaluate her thinking and perhaps change to someone else's suggestion. Also, Philomena said that all her constructs were connected and that this helped her to learn. She said:

> If you had some string, I could take these cards [with constructs written on] and I could tie them altogether like lines [she drew with her finger on the table connecting lines between all the construct cards] to show that all them ideas what helps me learn are all joined up, like, you know, in a sort of picture thing.

reflection points

What aspects of metacognition can you identify through these children's responses?

How do you think being able to articulate their thinking in this way helps children in their learning and in being a learner?

---

https://study.sagepub.com/wyseandrogers

Creativity and metacognition

In this section, we have looked at promoting creativity and metacognition in curriculum experiences. Creativity and metacognition reflect different aspects of learning, but they are closely linked and there are elements of practice which help develop both. Here are some ideas about how to get started:

- Recognise that sometimes the process may be as important, or more important, than the product of learning. Look at how your planning reflects this.
- Present activities and experiences to emphasise exploration, active participation and discussion on the part of the children. Provide children with opportunities to make choices and their own decisions.
- Reflect on your intervention during a lesson or activity. Perhaps ask a colleague to record or transcribe your interactions with children during a focused part of learning. What type of questions do you ask? Are there questions that encourage children to reflect on their thinking and the processes of learning? Do you give children time to respond to questions and comments?
- Think about your classroom environment. Include displays that show processes of learning, as well as the finished outcomes. Look to see if children can access resources and materials easily and independently to support their learning.

SUMMARY

This chapter has shown some of the decisions that are part of planning and implementing a curriculum. At a national level, decisions relate to the overall purpose of a curriculum and its aims, structure and content. Debates can become polarised between those who argue for a curriculum focused on 'process and development' and those who believe it should have aims relating to 'content and product'. These different positions reflect the various purposes that become attached to a curriculum, from personal development through to vocational preparation. We have argued that a curriculum should not be viewed as a static end-product, because the school and the individual teacher can influence how it is implemented in the classroom. Everyday curriculum content and experiences can be shaped by effective pedagogical features, the specific examples looked at in this chapter being creativity and metacognition.

companion website

To access additional online resources please visit: **https://study.sagepub.com/wyseandrogers**

Here you will find a classroom activity, author podcasts, free access to SAGE journal articles and links to external sources.

further reading

Kelly, A. V. (2009). *The curriculum: theory and practice*, 6th edition. London: Sage. This has become a classic text. It focuses on the philosophical and political dimensions of the curriculum. Chapters 3 and 4 unpick in more detail the ideologies encapsulated in different forms of curriculum, from 'content and product' to 'process and development'.

Moore, A. (2015). *Understanding the school curriculum: theory, politics and principles*. London: Routledge. For those interested in gaining critical insight into curriculum issues at a deeper level, this book explores a range of educational, philosophical and sociological theories and thinks about how school curricula might be shaped to respond to the demands of the age in which we live.

Soler, J. and Miller, L. (2003). 'The struggle for early childhood curricula: a comparison of the English Foundation Stage curriculum, Te Whāriki and Reggio Emilia', *International Journal of Early Years Education*, 11 (1), 57-67. An interesting journal article to read if you want to learn about international comparisons between curricula. It focuses on the way that visions for early childhood are expressed through the curricula of three different contexts: England, New Zealand and Italy.

REFERENCES

Alexander, R. J. (2004). 'Still no pedagogy? Principle, pragmatism and compliance in primary education', *Cambridge Journal of Education*, 34 (1), 7–34.

Alexander, R. J. (ed.) (2010). *Children, their world, their education: final report and recommendations of the Cambridge Primary Review*. London: Routledge.

Brehony, K. J. (2005). 'Primary schooling under New Labour: the irresolvable contradiction of excellence and enjoyment', *Oxford Review of Education*, 31 (1), 29–46.

Claxton, G. (2006). 'Thinking at the edge: developing soft creativity', *Cambridge Journal of Education*, 36 (3), 351–62.

Craft, A. (2005). *Creativity in schools: tensions and dilemmas*. Abingdon: Routledge.

Department for Education (DfE) (2013). *The national curriculum in England: Key Stages 1 and 2 framework document*. London: DfE.

Department for Education and Employment (DfEE)/Qualifications and Curriculum Authority (QCA) (1999). *The national curriculum handbook for primary teachers in England*. London: HMSO.

Department for Education and Skills (DfES) (2003). *Excellence and enjoyment: a strategy for primary schools*. London: DfES.

Early Years Curriculum Group (EYCG) (1989). *First things first: educating young children*. Oldham: Madeleine Lindley.

Flavell, J. H. (1976). 'Metacognitive aspects of problem solving'. In L. B. Resnick (ed.) *The nature of intelligence* (pp. 231–5). Hillsdale, NJ: Lawrence Erlbaum Associates.

Hacker, D. J. (1998). 'Metacognition: definitions and empirical foundations'. In D. J. Hacker, J. Dunlosky and A. C. Graesser (eds) *Metacognition in educational theory and practice* (pp. 1–23). Mahwah, NJ: Lawrence Erlbaum Associates.

James, M. (2012). Background to Michael Gove's response to the report of the expert panel for the national curriculum review in England. BERA. Available at: www.bera.ac.uk/promoting-educational-research/issues/background-to-michael-goves-response-to-the-report-of-the-expert-panel-for-the-national-curriculum-review-in-england

Kelly, A. V. (2009). *The curriculum: theory and practice*, 6th edition. London: Sage.

Luff, P. (2014). 'Play and creativity'. In T. Waller and G. Davis (eds) *An Introduction to Early Childhood*, 3rd edition. London: Sage.

McCormick, R. and Murphy, P. (2008). 'Curriculum: the case for a focus on learning'. In P. Murphy and K. Hall (eds) *Learning and practice: agency and identities*. London: Sage.

McCulloch, G., Helsby, G. and Knight, P. (2000). *The politics of professionalism*. London: Continuum.

Moore, A. (2015). *Understanding the school curriculum: theory, politics and principles*. London: Routledge.

Morrison, K. and Ridley, K. (1988). *Curriculum planning and the primary school*. London: Paul Chapman.

National Curriculum Council (NCC) (1990). *Curriculum guidance three: the whole curriculum*. York: National Curriculum Council.

Organisation for Economic Co-operation and Development (OECD) (2006). *Starting strong II: early childhood education and care*. Paris: OECD.

Qualifications and Curriculum Authority (QCA) (2000). *Curriculum guidance for the Foundation Stage*. London: QCA.

Qualifications and Curriculum Authority (QCA) (2002). *Foundation Stage profile*. London: QCA.

Qualifications and Curriculum Authority (QCA) (2005). *Creativity: find it, promote it! – promoting pupils' creative thinking and behaviour across the curriculum at Key Stages 1, 2 and 3 – practical materials for schools*. London: QCA.

Robertson, A. (2014). Let the Children Speak: Year 1 Children Inform Cognitive Acceleration Pedagogy. Phd thesis, UCL Institute of Education, London.

Rose, J. (2009). *The independent review of the primary curriculum: final report (Rose Report)*. London: DCSF.

SCAA (1996). *Desirable outcomes for children's learning on entering compulsory education*. London: DfEE/SCAA.

Sylva, K., Melhuish, E., Sammons, P., Siraj-Blatchford, I. and Taggart, B. (2010). *Early childhood matters: evidence from the Effective Pre-school and Primary Education project*. Abingdon: Routledge.

Taba, H. (1962). *Curriculum development: theory and practice*. New York: Harcourt Bruce.

Tickell, C. (2011). *The early years: foundations for life, health and learning*. London: DfE.

Tyler, R. W. (1949). *Basic principles of curriculum and instruction*. Chicago; London: University of Chicago Press.

White, J. (2010). 'Aims as policy in English primary education'. In R. Alexander (ed.) *The Cambridge Primary Review research surveys*. Abingdon: Routledge.

Wyse, D. (2014). Creativity and the curriculum. An inaugural professorial lecture. London: IOE Press.

Wyse, D., Baumfield, V., Egan, D., Gallagher, C., Hayward, L., Hulme, M., et al. (2013a). *Creating the curriculum*. London: Routledge.

Wyse, D., Jones, R., Bradford, H and Wolpert, M. A. (2013b). *Teaching English language and literacy*, 3rd edition. Abingdon: Routledge.

Wyse, D., McCreery, E. and Torrance, H. (2010). 'The trajectory and impact of national reform: curriculum and assessment in English primary schools'. In R. Alexander (ed.) *The Cambridge Primary Review research surveys*. Abingdon: Routledge.

9

ASSESSMENT AND LEARNING

Louise Hayward and Sharon Hayward

LEARNING AIMS

This chapter will enable you to:

- better understand the relationship between assessment and learning
- provide a definition of the three main purposes of assessment and explore possible tensions that can exist between these three purposes
- suggest examples of assessment for formative purposes as a natural part of learning and teaching
- reflect on recent policy on assessment in the early years and primary education.

Assessment is a word that has struck terror into the hearts of each and every one of us at some point in our lives. When the term assessment is associated with high-stakes experiences, ones that matter to us – examination results in school, college or university, driving tests, sports competitions, music grade exams – it can seem very intimidating. Personal experiences of high-stakes assessment mean that assessment associations of passing or failing, winning or losing have often become deeply embedded in our collective consciousness. Assessment and testing have become synonymous with one another and there is a danger that passing/failing and winning/losing become central ideas in our schools and classrooms. All too often, the language of passing or failing tests moves to become part of the description of individuals and, even though the words may never be used, the idea of having children who are successful or unsuccessful learners emerges in our classrooms and early years settings. By the end of secondary school education, successful learners are seen to be those who attain the highest number of qualifications with the best grades; unsuccessful learners have few, if any, qualifications of any significance to them and have developed an identity as people who are unable to learn. The assessment experiences that young people have in the early years and at primary school will play a major role in shaping their identity as learners. If as educators we are to work with young learners to encourage them to remain optimistic learners, then we need to think about assessment in a different way. Instead of thinking of assessment as a means by which we judge individuals, we can focus on the ways that assessment can be used to inform learning. Any assessment that is used to inform learning is formative. When assessment information is used to sum up what has been learned over a period of time, then it is summative. Observation, evidence from children's conversations, tasks, products and tests can all be used to inform learning, and are, therefore, formative; or used to sum up learning and are, therefore, summative. Throughout our lives, we develop our identity and how we see ourselves. Early years settings and schools play a role in helping to shape our views of ourselves as learners. For example, we may describe ourselves as doing 'well' at school or doing 'badly', being 'good' at Music or 'bad' at Art, as 'hard working' or 'lazy'.

Assessment of learners in schools is part of the wider social role of schooling in education. The sociologist Basil Bernstein (1971), whose work examined the nature of education in society, identified what he called the three main *message systems* of education: curriculum, pedagogy and assessment (or evaluation). As the message systems are interconnected (see Wyse et al., 2016), it is necessary to keep all three in mind as we work through this chapter (see also Chapter 8: The Curriculum). In this chapter, we define these message systems in the following way. Curriculum we define as a conversation across generations about what one generation in a given society believes to matter in learning for a young child to progress to become an educated citizen (we will explore ideas of conversation later). Pedagogy involves bringing together learners to engage with ideas in early years settings and primary schools, and using particular approaches to learning and teaching. Assessment is the process by which we discern the extent to which learning is taking place or has taken place. Understood in this way, assessment also provides information about the starting point for what a young person might learn next – their next steps in learning. Next steps should build on what learners already know, say or are able to do, and should help them to grow both as people and as learners.

Individually: Think of an occasion when you had a positive assessment experience and an occasion when you had a more negative assessment experience. What made the difference? Identify three things.

With a partner or in a group: Compare the three things you have identified individually as important in making a difference between assessment as a more positive and more negative experience. What were the similarities and differences? What implications might there be for your practice with learners?

ASSESSMENT PURPOSES: POTENTIAL AND PITFALLS

Assessment, as defined in this chapter, is focused on learning (Hayward, 2015). It may be helpful to think about the relationship among curriculum, assessment and pedagogy as a triangle (see Figure 9.1). Note that assessment is at the bottom of the triangle. Assessment should support curriculum and pedagogy. It should not drive them. Learners and learning are at the centre of the triangle. Everything that we do as educators should be focused on learners and learning.

ASSESSMENT FOR DIFFERENT PURPOSES: FORMATIVE, SUMMATIVE AND ACCOUNTABILITY

Information from assessment can be used to inform learning and teaching as they are taking place, in the *formation of learning*. This is assessment for formative purposes. A second assessment purpose is when information from what children say, write and do is used to look at what has been learned over a period of time and an attempt is made to summarise or *to sum up what has been learned*. This is assessment for summative purposes. The third purpose is where assessment evidence is used to discern the quality of an aspect of an education system. This might relate to the quality of a teacher, a school, an education authority or a country. The use of assessment to hold individuals, schools or education systems to account, i.e. how well the teacher, school, authority or country is performing, has a long history. This is assessment for purposes of accountability. Internationally, over the past two decades there has been an increasing interest in the use of assessment to judge school performance. Commonly, test data are used to judge the quality of a teacher or a school and, from time to time, test results from different schools have been used to construct league tables of schools. Internationally, there are a number of testing systems used to provide evidence to judge how individual countries are performing in relation to one another. The most famous of these, PISA (Programme for International Student Assessment), is organised by the Organisation for Economic Co-operation and Development (OECD). When the results of this survey are reported, commonly there is a great deal of press interest as

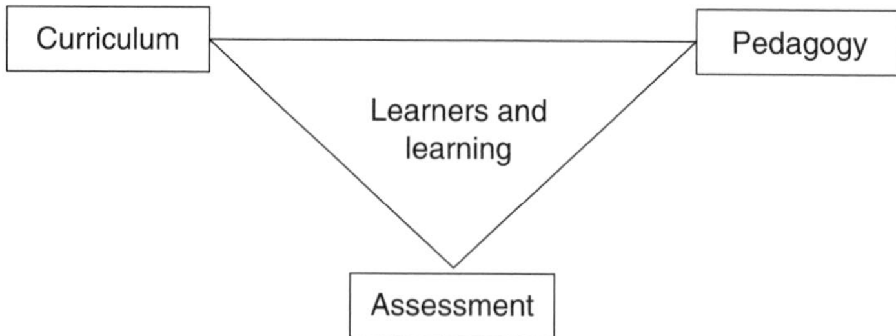

Figure 9.1 The learning triangle

the performance of countries is presented in league tables and governments are eager to see whether or not their country has risen or fallen against other countries internationally. The fact that this survey is carried out by an organisation concerned with economic matters is significant. It demonstrates the way in which education is seen as a major economic driver, and governments internationally believe that there is a connection between improving their education system and improving their economy, even though this is a deeply contested area (Hermannsson, 2015).

This chapter focuses mainly on assessment used to improve learning in early years settings and in primary schools. However, all three assessment purposes (formative, summative and accountability) should contribute to learning, albeit in different ways and for different communities. For example, good assessment information will come from high quality interactions, thoughtful questions, careful listening and reflective responses. The evidence gathered by early years practitioners should always begin with a focus on identifying what children can do and, in discussion with the young person, on what s/he might do next as an individual or as a member of a group. Primary practitioners will also focus on high quality interactions. Thoughtful questions, careful listening and reflective responses are just as important. Although a greater range of sources of evidence may be available from written tasks, it is through interaction with the learner(s) or between learners that the most important learning will take place. Conversation matters. It is through discussion that humans make sense of their world and link existing knowledge, understanding and skills to new knowledge, understanding and skills. Evidence from a variety of sources should be used to discern that learning is taking place, to identify what future learning priorities should be. Assessment is learning. Teachers also have a variety of reasons for wanting to sum up what has been learned over time, such as to show learners the progress they have made, to share information with parents on their children's progress or to offer information to the child's next teacher. When the purpose of assessment is summative, then teachers and young people should collect evidence over time – for instance, examples to show what a child knew or was able to do at the beginning of a term and evidence of what the child can do at the end of a term. Local or national policy makers also want to learn. They want to learn about the education system, about how well it is progressing and to identify areas where the system might need to improve. These areas could then become a focus for future action where teachers, or teachers working with researchers and policy makers, can identify research-informed actions that might be developed in classrooms that would lead to improvement. This is called assessment for purposes of accountability. Care has to be taken with assessment when it is used to hold people to account for the quality of the education system. Gathering and reporting evidence will not by itself lead to improvement. Building from assessment evidence, research-informed action has to be taken if learning and teaching are to improve. All good assessment is focused on improving learning.

There are, however, circumstances where tensions arise between different assessment purposes and this can lead to assessment driving the curriculum or even distorting it. For example, children may be asked to take tests in school, with the evidence of their test results collected at school, local authority or national level. Most commonly, these tests are used to measure performance in language and mathematics. There are statutory tests of English and arithmetic in England that will be discussed later in this chapter. Although a test may be described as a literacy or English test, it cannot deal with the whole language and literacy curriculum, and in many cases can be rather narrow (for example, the phonics screening test in England is a test of phonics but reading is much more than phonics. It includes a need to pay attention to the reader's attitude and motivation, their understanding of the text and, as they progress, an awareness of the author's use of language – see e.g. Hayward and Spencer, 2006). It is most likely that such tests will include some parts of the reading curriculum and aspects of the writing curriculum. Within the reading or writing curriculum, the test will only collect evidence of aspects of each. This raises questions of validity: the extent to which the evidence supports the interpretation of the test scores. Tests are designed to be time limited. This means that most tests will measure only a limited number of aspects, often those that are most easily measured. For example, it is more difficult to test for deep understanding of reading than it is to test a child's ability to answer simple questions to show literal understanding or their ability to read single words of vocabulary lists. Nevertheless, the scores from tests demonstrating evidence of children's performance in limited areas of one aspect of literacy are sometimes used in an uninformed way as a proxy measure for the whole curriculum or for the quality of education across an entire school. This is not a valid use of test data.

In some ways, the use of a test of reading as an indicator of performance may seem innocuous. Evidence from educational history across the UK and from the history of innumerable countries internationally suggests otherwise (see e.g. Klenowski and Carter, 2015 on the impact of NAPLAN on education in Australia). Despite the best intentions of those responsible for designing test systems, tests often become more dominant than anyone would wish. There is international evidence to show that any instrument used to judge teachers' performance, or the performance of a school, a local authority or a country, will automatically be attributed a level of importance whether, as a test, it merits it or not. The stakes for any instrument used to gauge performance in schools and local authorities over time will be high. Schools and local authorities will naturally want to demonstrate improvement. All test results are susceptible to improvement through test practice and it is inevitable that high-stakes tests will be practised by teachers under pressure to hit targets. Publishers will also produce materials for schools to use to improve their test scores.

Scotland does not have a history of using high-stakes national testing in primary schools. However, in the 1990s a new curriculum and assessment system, Education 5–14 (SOED, 1991), was introduced, including national testing that was intended to be low stakes. The policy on Assessment 5–14 (SOED, 1991) was clear. The most important assessment purpose was to support children's learning. Assessment decisions to support children's learning were best taken by teachers using professional judgement. There were five levels of attainment, A–E, over nine years of schooling. Teachers were asked to report children's levels of attainment once per year, accompanied by an indication of their strengths and areas for development across the curriculum. The policy recognised that only teachers could assess children's progress across the whole curriculum and that only teachers knew the individual learners well enough to understand what was appropriately challenging for different children. However, to allow teachers to relate their judgements to national expectations, there was a second part of the policy. National tests, developed by teachers, would be available for teachers to use when they thought that a child was ready to move on to the next level. The tests were designed to be 'light touch' (although they only covered a limited number of areas of the reading, writing and number curricula). The policy explicitly stated that if a difference emerged between a teacher's professional judgement and the national test, the teacher's judgement would be the result reported (although the school was encouraged to review such cases on an individual basis to try to understand the reasons for the difference).

What happened in reality was very different. Test results were collated across the school and collected by local authorities and by national government. Schools were judged by their performance on test results. Soon, the tests were not used to support professional judgement – they replaced it. Teachers stopped making professional judgements and the tests were used to discern whether or not a child had 'achieved' a level. Although the policy recommended that teachers test when ready, i.e. when the evidence they had gathered suggested to them that a particular child was ready to move on to the next level, practice in schools across the country was very different. Schools commonly rehearsed children for tests, had testing weeks when every child took a test and children were reported as 'passing' or 'failing' the test. Some schools sent home award certificates. A few schools took all the children into the school hall and ran tests as if they were national examinations (Hayward and Hutchinson, 2013). Patterns of behaviour such as this, related to tests that are perceived to be high stakes, described as *washback effects*, can now be found in a number of countries internationally. This example illustrates what can happen when there is a tension between two purposes of assessment – to support learning and assess for accountability. If the accountability stakes are high, then that purpose can distort what happens in schools and classrooms, limiting the potential for assessment to support learning.

In 2003, the Scottish Government stopped collecting test information in primary schools and initiated the Assessment is for Learning programme, which transformed assessment in Scotland and brought back the focus on assessment to support learning (Hayward and Spencer, 2010). Where, in Scotland, the focus on testing decreased, in England testing has remained a feature of the education system to a point where Hutchings (2015), in a research report commissioned by the National Union of Teachers, describes schools as exam factories where pupils are under pressure, where there is a disproportionate effect on children who are disadvantaged and where education has been narrowed. However, Scotland is not immune from debates on national testing. In August 2015, the First Minister once again raised the question of whether or not children in primary schools should take standardised tests.

ASSESSMENT TO INFORM LEARNING: ASSESSMENT FOR FORMATIVE PURPOSES

The most important purpose of assessment is to support learning. The phrase 'assessment is an integral part of learning and teaching' is often used but what does it mean? In every conversation, and every observation involving a teacher and a learner, the process of assessment is taking place. Whilst interacting with learners, a teacher is gathering evidence that they will use to make an informed decision about what is happening, what is being achieved and what to do next. The quality of interactions in early years settings and in primary classrooms is crucial to the quality of evidence gathered about children's learning.

Gathering evidence to gauge how much and how well learners are learning is a natural part of teaching and learning. The process does not begin from what can be assessed; it begins from the learners and the curriculum. As part of the planning process, a teacher will have a clear idea of the main learning aims for the class. Previous assessment information will come from her/his knowledge of individual learners. Part of the plan will have come from knowledge of the curriculum translated into learning aims for the class or group of learners agreed between the teacher and, as appropriate, other adults and the head teacher. A second source of information will be the children themselves, what the teacher knows about learners' previous achievements (both individual learners and groups), talking with and listening to learners, asking them what kinds of things they might want to learn, watching their learning and analysing the products they have produced. By bringing together information from these different sources, the teacher, working with learners, will have aims for the class and different aspirations for individual learners. The teacher will create a range of learning opportunities to enable the young people to develop, to deepen understanding and to build skills in the context of the main learning aims. For example, the teacher may begin a topic with an introductory discussion where they will explore what the learners already know about that topic; they may design tasks to allow children the opportunity to engage in activities where they can work together to explore ideas or solve a problem or design a product, a painting or a model or engage in role play. Each of these tasks provides an opportunity to engage learners in learning and becomes a source of assessment evidence for teachers and classroom assistants. These are real opportunities in real primary classrooms or early years contexts. They occur naturally as part of the teaching and learning process. As they work with the children engaged in these tasks, teachers and other adults may be listening to what learners are saying, asking questions to explore their understanding, observing what they are doing, or they may use a combination of different approaches. What teachers hear learners say and what they watch them do is evidence to help them discern progress. This kind of evidence, as part of learning and teaching, informs their professional judgement about the progress that children are making in their learning. This information should also be used to inform what next steps in learning might be appropriate for a child or for children in a group. It may also point to areas where it might be helpful for teachers and other adults to change aspects of the curriculum or approaches to teaching and learning to promote more effective learning.

The two snapshots below offer examples of assessment designed to support learning in practice. The first Spotlight on Practice is set in an early years setting and the second in a primary school.

Assessment for learning in the early years

Diane is a nursery nurse responsible for coordinating a block of planned learning for six groups of children aged 3–5. During early years team discussion time, it was noted that the children had been showing increased interest in new toys that had been set out: outdoor toys, a set of vehicles and a set of animals were all attracting attention. As the nursery nurses began to consider planning a new learning theme, Diane gathered two children from each of the pastoral groups and met with them in 'the boardroom' for a planning meeting. The children had a conversation around the main learning theme in the coming weeks. The ideas of outdoor play, vehicles and animals were proposed by the children and discussed. The children decided that they would like to learn about 'Moving in different ways'. Nursery nurses responsible for each group worked with the children to help them report this idea back to their groups. A consultation week began where all children shared what they already knew and what they would like to learn about. These ideas were displayed in a 3D mind map using toys, pictures, photos, drawings and text to represent 'Big Questions', for example:

How do giraffes bend down?

How long can I bounce on the space hopper for?

Is a lion faster than a car?

The team of practitioners created a set of key learning outcomes, based primarily around understanding the world and mathematics. These linked to curriculum outcomes relevant to the different groups of children and were based on team members' knowledge of children's previous progress. These were adapted for individual children who required greater support or challenge. Specific outcomes were identified and related to success criteria. The team planned clear, moderated assessment tasks that would allow them to check children's ongoing progress. A range of rich learning tasks was created to allow the children to explore the questions they had set.

After the learning experience, the early years team reflected on the evidence they had from learning in real situations and discussed the evidence with the children. Observations, learning conversations using higher-order questions, and discrete observations all contributed to each nursery nurse's knowledge of how well the children were progressing in their learning related to the outcomes and success criteria established as part of the planning process. At the end of the block, the team discussed the progress of all children, sharing evidence and agreeing standards.

When considering the approach of the nursery featured in the above Spotlight on Practice, several aspects are of particular note. First, members of the early years team had regular conversations with and about the children and their learning. They knew how important it is to know their children well – their interests and their skills and attributes – and to discuss this information together. Children were central to the planning process. The teaching team understood how important it is to engage children in learning so they included them in the planning, making sure that their voices were represented and feeding back decisions to the groups. These children were used to having their voices heard and respected (Lancaster and Kirby, 2010). The early years team saw planning as a joint venture, recognised that new learning is built on what is already known about the children's learning, and made room for this within the planning process, giving the children a chance to share and showcase what they already knew. Opportunities were given to capitalise on the creativity and imagination of young learners in setting the 'Big Questions'.

The chance to plan learning which is personalised and motivating to children will ensure that their engagement with learning is maximised. The early years practitioners were mindful of ensuring that moderated assessments, agreed by the team as reliable, valid and appropriate to the standards expected, were identified at the planning stage. It is also worth noting that the team recognised that children themselves are the best evidence of learning. Evidence was generated naturally in the playroom or outdoor space and the nursery nurses saw their role as facilitating and providing the space for children to show how they were progressing. The use of good questioning allowed the staff to build on their own knowledge of individual children's understanding of the new theme and skills and their ability to apply them in other situations. This knowledge would be used to complete the planning cycle in the next planning block. Assessment was incorporated into the planning, teaching and learning process and used to identify next steps in learning for future planning.

Assessment for learning in primary school

Hilary is a teacher with 29 7-year-old children in her class. They vary greatly in the progress they have made across the curriculum to date. One child in the class, Sophie, requires additional challenge in her learning, particularly in English. Her health is sometimes of concern as Sophie

(Continued)

(Continued)

has type 1 diabetes. During transition conversations with the previous teacher that had focused on the children's progress across the curriculum, and their possible next steps, there had been a discussion about the complex home circumstances of a number of children who lived in homes where money was extremely limited and whose only hot food was eaten in school.

During this first learning block of the session, Hilary planned a study in Health and Wellbeing called 'Food: Farm to Fork'. She wanted to build on the early learning experiences her class had had in identifying and tasting a range of foods, and considering healthy food choices, particularly in the school dining hall. Hilary began by showing the class some pictures of food in a variety of contexts: celebration meals, potatoes in a sack, fields of corn, bottles of fizzy drinks, supermarket shopping trolleys. She took the class through a 'thinking routine' called 'I see ... I think ... I wonder ...' to help them engage with the pictures and articulate what they already knew about this theme and what they would like to know. This was collated into a set of 'I can' statements which the children wanted to be able to demonstrate at the end of their study. The children then identified 'experts' who might help them with their research and fact-finding. The school catering manager was quickly identified. Hilary asked who might advise them on topics such as food allergies and diabetes. Sophie, a confident girl who managed her insulin pump under limited supervision, offered to be an expert advisor.

As part of her planning process, Hilary met her stage partner and identified appropriate learning outcomes for the theme. Whilst they were generic to the class, she created two different sets of success criteria to support the learning across the class. She added additional criteria for Sophie, relating to literacy across learning:

> I am learning to present information to my group. I will include things to show them to make my presentation more interesting.
>
> I am learning to share facts with my group – keeping my presentation short.

Assessment tasks were moderated and agreed with her stage partner and linked to health and well-being outcomes and literacy across learning.

Over the course of the learning experiences, Hilary collected a variety of evidence to illustrate that the children were making progress. This evidence came from the children's normal work and could be found in their normal folders and activities. She observed them, listened to them and spoke with them. She provided appropriate feedback on their progress through written comments that focused on key aspects of learning and conversation. She provided daily opportunities to reflect on learning using mid-way and end-of-lesson 'let's stop and think' sessions. The children also reflected on their learning at key checkpoints using the 'I can' statements established at the start of the theme to self-evaluate and track their own progress.

Hilary concluded her learning and teaching block by reflecting on the impact of her teaching, thinking about what she had planned with the children, how her teaching strategies assisted learning (or not) and the progress in learning made by her class, as individual learners. She identified clear next steps for the class and identified some children who required further support in their application of the skills – for instance, two children who had thought of questions for the school catering manager but during the interview had not asked them. She would work with the pair, encouraging them to ask questions in small groups, thus building their confidence.

It is interesting to note the effective practice in this second Spotlight on Practice, where the teacher used previous assessment information as the basis for the next planning block, collecting naturally produced assessment information throughout the teaching block, reflecting on it to inform future learning at the end of the theme.

Hilary planned her teaching and learning, recognising that the children already had relevant experiences to bring with them. She used information from transition discussions with the children's previous teacher well to plan learning that recognised where the children were within the school's curriculum progression pathways, but also taking cognisance of the social context for some of the children and identifying those who required additional support or challenge.

Including children in the planning in this way allowed Hilary to assess the children's prior knowledge, as well as to provide evidence about their abilities to cooperate in groups and share their learning. Supporting the children in articulating their own intended outcomes enabled them to develop their own 'learning assessment vocabulary' and kept the process transparent: the children knew what they were going to learn and, if their learning was successful, what this should 'look like'. Whilst planning with her stage partner, Hilary identified overarching outcomes for the class but recognised that 'success' might look different for different groups or individuals. She kept her separate criteria for Sophie specific and manageable: the products being a presentation to her classmates showing her blood sugar monitor and insulin pump, whilst creating a leaflet for staff about diabetes. Hilary used the children's normal work as evidence of learning and assessment. Judgements were made many times each day as she observed, gave feedback and reflected with the children. This information allowed her to reflect on their progress at the end of the teaching block with confidence and use the information to comment on both their progress and their next steps in learning. Lundy (2007) argues for the importance of children's voice. If we believe that children's voices matter, then she argues we need to pay attention to Space (an opportunity to express their views), Voice (someone to facilitate their views), Audience (their views should be listened to) and Impact (where appropriate, their views should be enacted).

Assessment as part of learning and teaching can also be used to build a positive classroom ethos, helping children to develop their social skills. The next Spotlight on Practice exemplifies this.

Assessment to develop a more supportive ethos

John has a lively class of 10-year-old children. He has observed over a period of time that a group of children within his class are finding it difficult to work well with others. Members of the class are very critical about the work of some of the other children. This

(Continued)

(Continued)

is having an effect on the self-concept of the other learners who are becoming less willing to contribute to class discussion. This observation becomes a focus for learning. John builds a series of lessons on the topic, 'Helping one another to learn', and as part of the topic engages in conversation with the class about what helps children to learn really well. He shares one or two possible ideas with them and then asks them to work in groups to generate a number of ways to complete the phrase: 'In our classroom, to help one another to learn we will...'

John holds a plenary session where each group presents its ideas. Through discussion, pupils develop a list of characteristics of how, in their classroom, they will support one another's learning. These characteristics become the focus for assessment. Evidence for how well the children are progressing in relation to these characteristics comes from a range of real places: observation in the classroom when the children are working with one another; in the sports hall and in the playground; and when the children are playing. John observes what is happening, noting when the children do something well, and reflects on what a child or group of children might work on next. Evidence also comes from the children themselves. At key points in an activity, John asks them to stop and to reflect, using the list of characteristics developed by them. In this conversation, pupils think about what they are doing well and where and how they might want to act differently next time.

There are a number of important points to note in relation to the above Spotlight on Practice. The first is the link that John makes between the needs of the learners and the focus for learning. He uses evidence from observation to identify an area where the children need to develop their understanding and to change their interactions, i.e. the importance of supporting one another's learning, and sets out to build their skills in how to do that effectively. Second, he provides a stimulus to help develop the children's thinking and builds in opportunities for them to think through ideas for themselves, providing space for dialogue where the young people can develop and articulate their ideas. Third, the ideas of both pupils and teacher are valued and respected. They are brought together and become the focus for assessment. These assessment criteria, the characteristics of what supporting one another's learning might mean, are developed together. They are co-constructed. Fourth, the co-constructed criteria are used as the framework within which children can reflect on their own behaviours. They provide a basis for identifying what is being done well and where there might be a need for future action. They provide a basis for self-assessment and/or peer assessment. All of this happens as part of the natural learning environment. Assessment, again, is integral to the processes of learning and teaching.

The Putting it into Practice box below focuses on how assessment can be used to support the learning of an individual child, where a particular issue has arisen within a classroom context in an inclusive way that does not make significant additional demands on the teacher.

Using assessment to help learners support learning manageably

Jessica works with a class of 31 10-year-olds. They are a mixed ability group and Jessica has to plan to recognise different learning aims for different learners across the curriculum. This term she has planned work to develop maths problem-solving strategies. The vehicle for this is collaborative groupwork where children work together to solve problems and puzzles and explain their thinking to one another. Jessica worked with a colleague to plan moderated assessments at the start of the teaching block, ensuring they were at an appropriate standard and would provide real evidence of progress that she could use to plan next steps in learning. She planned to collect a range of evidence to inform her decisions, focusing on observation and listening to children's interactions. Mid-way through the block, she reflected on the range of evidence she had so far and considered how this might prompt her to modify the plans for the groups. She observed children as they worked, considering the learning outcomes and success criteria they had set together to discern progress. Jessica spent time listening to children's conversations with one other as these conversations offered information on how the children were thinking and insights into the strategies they were using. It was during one of these observations that she became concerned about Daniel's progress. Although a boy usually 'on track' with his learning, she had concerns that he was not engaging with the group and not offering any opinions, thoughts or explanations. His was withdrawn and it was difficult to tell whether he truly understood the concepts being explored by the learners.

Jessica decided to set 'pairs tasks' for the children the following day. She created a task where children were set a problem and then encouraged to work with a partner to discuss their thoughts. Child A was *the explainer* and explained their thoughts to Child B who was to listen without interruption. Child B was *the checker* whose role was to check what they thought Child A meant, and add to or extend Child A's thinking. For the next problem, the children had to swap roles. During this task, Jessica observed Daniel and his partner carefully. She noted that in this one-to-one situation, where his partner did not interrupt, Daniel was able to choose a strategy to try, explain why he thought it was the best one, and estimate the outcome. On swapping roles, Daniel listened intently to his partner, nodding approval, and asked a good question of her when she had finished speaking.

Jessica now had evidence that Daniel was making progress in his use of problem-solving strategies and had a good understanding of when to use each one. He had a well-developed mathematics vocabulary and could reason well. She also identified that Daniel required further support when in large group situations with 'big personalities' as he found it difficult to have his voice heard. She used this assessment information to inform her future planning, and decided to assign group roles in the next teaching block, appointing Daniel as group leader.

What is interesting to note in the above Putting it into Practice was the way in which Jessica gave assessment evidence a central role in the planning process. At the start of the block, she identified appropriate assessment tasks, success criteria and possible evidence. She ensured the evidence was generated naturally from the assessment tasks and that no 'special assessment task' was created.

Jessica knew that children themselves are a key source of evidence and planned in this context to observe and listen to them as her primary evidence-gathering strategy. Not all of her observations were noted in her planning folder and she did not go to the lengths of recording children's conversations. She simply interacted with her class as she normally would, being mindful of the success criteria she had set in partnership with the children and seeking evidence of the extent to which they were meeting these.

Jessica had taken time mid-way through her teaching block to reflect and, as a result, was able to adapt her plans to better match the needs of all the children; in this instance, she had to seek further evidence about Daniel. She looked at the range of evidence available through observations and reached the conclusion that Daniel was not showing sufficient evidence of understanding the mathematical concepts. Jessica did not note this down in an assessment record and wait until the next teaching block to address this. Instead, she used the assessment evidence to plan an intervention the next day. By changing the context and looking for different evidence, she had grounds to allow her to be confident that Daniel did indeed understand the mathematical concepts but had some difficulty in managing to have his voice heard within big group situations.

Jessica used assessment evidence to plan next steps in learning, identifying where children required a different context or intervention to enhance their progress.

The four Spotlight on Practice boxes offer examples of how assessment can be used to support learning in ways that also reflect current research on assessment. The characteristics of high quality assessment for learning emerge from socio-cultural theories of learning. James with Lewis (2012) describes key characteristics of what she calls third-generation assessment:

- Third-generation assessment involves building knowledge as part of engaging with others.
- Learning involves both thought and action in context.
- Thinking is conducted through actions that alter the situation and the situation changes the thinking – the two interact.
- Learning is a mediated activity – tools and objects have a crucial role, e.g. books, equipment, language.
- Learning is social and collaborative – people develop their thinking together.
- Learning is distributed within the social group.
- The collective knowledge of the group is internalised by the individual.
- As an individual creates new knowledge, he/she will externalise it in communicating it to others who will put it to use and then internalise it (an expansive learning cycle).

reflection point

Mary James suggests that third-generation assessment is not yet common across schools. Choose one of the Spotlights on Practice or the Putting it into Practice box in this chapter. With another teacher or a small group of teachers, reflect on your chosen case study. To what extent can you see examples of the kinds of characteristics described in the bullet points above? Can you identify ways in which the case study might be developed to be more consistent with the ideas above?

ASSESSMENT IN THE EARLY YEARS AND IN PRIMARY SCHOOL IN POLICY IN ENGLAND

Assessment as part of day-to-day teaching, if developed in practice in the ways described in this chapter, will continue to provide high quality information to support children's learning. However, statutory assessment arrangements, including tests, are changing in England. In September 2015, the Department for Education (DfE) introduced a new baseline assessment in reception year, called the 'reception baseline'. The DfE indicated that the intention in introducing this initiative is to improve how primary schools' progress is measured.

Web Link

More information about this new baseline assessment in reception year can be accessed through this web link, available on the companion website: www.gov.uk/reception-baseline-assessment

The DfE argues that this new approach will be more effective in taking into account the differences in schools with a more challenging intake. The DfE also indicates that the creation of this reception baseline assessment is intended to recognise the important work that goes on in reception and in Key Stage 1 (ages 6–7). Although the DfE will ask schools to collect data from 2015/16, it will not use the data to hold schools to account until 2022 or 2023. After each young person has taken the reception baseline assessment, they are given a score. These scores are not used to track the progress of individual pupils. The purpose of the reception baseline is to provide a score for each pupil at the beginning of their educational journey. The DfE is interested to determine how much value each school has added to young people's learning. When children reach the end of Key Stage 2 (ages 7–11), the reception baseline score will be used to calculate how much progress each young person has made. The information on individuals will be compared to others who had similar scores on the reception baseline test. The DfE will use this evidence to decide on the quality of the school by taking an average of the progress made by all the pupils in the school and comparing that average with the average data from other schools.

In the first phase of the initiative, the DfE will offer schools options. Where a government-funded school has chosen to use the reception baseline assessment from 2015, then in 2022 the DfE will judge the school's performance by the measure which shows the school's performance in the best light – either the progress made between reception baseline and Key Stage 2 or the development between Key Stage 1 and Key Stage 2. From 2016, primary schools will only be able to use reception baseline to Key Stage 2 results to measure progress. If they decide not to use the reception baseline, then from 2023 primary schools will be held to account by pupils' attainment at the end of Key Stage 2. It is an interesting feature of this new system that if independent schools choose to use the reception baseline, then the DfE will not collect the data gathered.

Schools can choose which reception baseline they will use. The DfE makes explicit the criteria used to assess the suitability of reception baseline assessments. These include a need for the test to be informed by research and to have a rigorous framework for analysis. They also offer a list of approved reception baseline centres. It is interesting to note that approved centres offer different tests. Comparing data from tests from different testing bodies will have to be treated with some caution as no two tests are the same, and even if the tests from different bodies are intended to explore the same areas of the curriculum there will be differences in emphasis that may make direct comparison tricky. At a national level, where data are collected from all schools, this may be less of a problem but for individual schools it will be important to monitor the system to ensure that schools are treated fairly. This is particularly important since funding will follow data. From 2016, low prior attainment funding will be allocated using reception baseline data, i.e. additional funding will be made available to schools to support children whose attainment was below the expected level before reception year.

These policies are contentious. Many early years practitioners are concerned about the impact of testing on very young children. For example, the Association for Professional Development in the Early Years (TACTYC) and the British Education Research Association (BERA) offer a powerful critique of the proposals. They recommend that schools should not use a baseline assessment scheme as it will not provide the breadth and depth of information on children's learning that can be obtained if schools follow the principles of the Early Years Foundation Stage assessment. The TACTYC/BERA paper provides an analysis of the tests from each of the providers and demonstrates the areas where each test misses key elements of the profile of a child's learning (e.g. where a test does not provide information on areas of the curriculum – Understanding the World; Expressive Arts and Design).

There are also changes in the arrangements for assessment in primary schools. Recent reforms to the national curriculum have resulted in the system of 'levels', around which progression in the previous curriculum was built, being removed. This decision will have a number of advantages. Learners who find learning hard are often those who receive feedback from schools using letters or numbers that simply confirm the learner's view of him/herself as an unsuccessful learner. Even when the letter or number is accompanied by supportive text, it is the letter or number that is the more powerful communicator. There has been convincing evidence of this for some time (Black and Wiliam, 1998). To encourage children who find learning hard to make progress, the assessment for learning approach that seeks to point to something that the child has done well or has tried hard with, identifies a limited number of areas where the child might take forward their learning and suggests strategies as to how the child might begin to make progress, is most likely to be effective. One challenge that emerges from this change is how best to communicate progress to parents/carers. Some schools have found that sharing the kind of evidence described in the case studies above with parents, letting them see what their child could do at the beginning of a session, and what progress they have made, offers parents insights into progress and identifies ways in which they might support their child more effectively at home.

The DfE believes that by removing levels teachers will have greater flexibility in the way that they plan and assess pupils' learning. There is a framework for progression in the programmes of study where expected progress is made explicit at the end of each key stage within the revised National Curriculum. There are also new Key Stage 1 and 2 tests in English, mathematics and science. Pupils will first take these tests in 2016.

Web Link

A video highlighting the key changes to tests and assessments can be accessed through this web link and is available on the companion website: www.gov.uk/government/news/new-video-published-on-changes-to-2016-tests-and-assessments

At Key Stage 1, new tests will include a grammar test, a punctuation test, a spelling test and an arithmetic paper. At the end of Key Stage 2, the mental maths test will be replaced by an arithmetic test. New performance descriptors will be used to inform statutory teacher assessment at the end of Key Stages 1 and 2 in summer 2016.

Tests where the stakes are high, i.e. where teachers and schools are judged by the performance of their pupils, will create washback effects. The areas that the tests measure will become more prominent in the school curriculum as teachers prepare children for the tests. If teachers, parents and policy makers believe that there needs to be an increased focus on grammar, punctuation, spelling and arithmetic, then these tests will help to accomplish that. However, if the aspirations of the English curriculum are broader than that, then there may be cause for concern, as other important areas are likely to be neglected in the drive to increase test scores. There is one further area to be considered. Testing a particular skill, for example spelling, does not mean that children's spelling will automatically improve. Increasing scores in a spelling test is not the same as improving a child's ability to spell on a regular basis. For that to happen, work has to be undertaken in context as part of day-to-day classroom activities.

reflection point

Look back to the section in this chapter on the three purposes of assessment. How might teachers and schools work to pay appropriate attention to all three purposes? Identify two things that you might do in your classroom to keep a major focus on assessment to support learning. Can you identify ways in which you might try to minimise tensions between the different assessment purposes?

SUMMARY

This chapter began by exploring the relationship between assessment, curriculum and pedagogy, and argued that if we conceptualise assessment as being concerned to support learners, and to discern the nature and quality of the learning that is taking place, then assessment changes character. Its focus is decision making rather than judgement. Assessment is entirely integral to learning (Hayward, 2015). In the second section, we provided a definition of the three main purposes of assessment: formative, summative and accountability, and explored examples of the tensions that can exist between these three purposes as assessment data are used for purposes beyond learning. In the third section, we offered examples of assessment for formative purposes as a natural part of learning and teaching in practice, and reflected on key underlying ideas and how these link to theories of learning. Finally in the fourth section, we presented information on recent policy on assessment in the early years and primary school in England. Education is a public enterprise and politicians are interested in how the education system is performing. The kinds of evidence collected often lead to tensions between the various purposes of assessment, and if we are not careful the most important purpose of assessment, to support learning, can be drowned out in the 'noise' surrounding accountability data (Mansell et al., 2009). Understanding the nature of these different assessment purposes and the tensions that can arise is a first step towards keeping a better assessment balance in your school and in your classroom. By reading this chapter you have taken your first step.

companion website

To access additional online resources please visit: **https://study.sagepub.com/wyseandrogers**

Here you will find a classroom activity, free access to SAGE journal articles and links to external sources.

further reading

Black, P. & Wiliam, D. (1990). *Inside the Black Box*. London: King's College London. This is a series that has stood the test of time. It explores the implications for classroom practice of ideas from assessment for learning.

Hattie, J. & Timperley, H. (2007). The power of feedback. *Review of Educational Research*, 77(1), 81–112. Feedback is one of the most powerful influences on learning. This article reviews the evidence on what makes for good feedback – feedback that really does improve learning.

Klenowski, V. & Carter, M. (2015) Curriculum reform in testing and accountability. In Wyse, D., Hayward, L. & Pandya, J. (eds) *The SAGE Handbook of Curriculum, Pedagogy and Assessment*, Vol. 2. London: Sage, pp. 790–804. In this chapter, Klenowski and Carter examine the impact that accountability measures have had on teaching, learning and assessment across the world. They use Australia as a case study to illustrate the kinds of problem that emerge consistently.

The slides from a presentation by Mary James used in this chapter can be found at: www.mantleoftheexpert.com/wp-content/uploads/2008/05/mary-james-assessment.pdf

The Education Scotland website has a wide range of resources, advice, toolkits, examples from practice and research evidence on assessment, available at: www.educationscotland.gov.uk/learningandteaching/assessment/about/index.asp

For up-to-date reading on the new arrangements for testing and assessment in England, see www.gov/uk/government/news/new-video-published-on-changes-to-2016-tests-and-assessments

For guidance on new baseline assessment arrangements in England, see www.early-education.org.uk/sites/default/files/BaselineAssessmentGuidance.pdf

REFERENCES

Bernstein, B. (1971) On the classification and framing of educational knowledge. In Young, M.F.D. (ed.) *Knowledge and Control: New directions for the sociology of education*. London: Collier MacMillan, pp. 47–69.

Black, P. & Wiliam, D. (1998) Assessment and classroom learning. *Assessment in Education: Principles, Policy and Practice*, 5(1), 7–73.

Hayward, L. (2015) Assessment is learning: the preposition vanishes. *Assessment in Education: Principles, Policy and Practice*, 22(1), 27–43.

Hayward, L. & Hutchinson, C. (2013) Exactly what do you mean by consistency? Exploring concepts of consistency and standards in Curriculum for Excellence in Scotland. *Assessment in Education: Principles, Policy and Practice*, 20(1), 53–68.

Hayward, L. & Spencer, E. (2010) The complexities of change: formative assessment in Scotland. *Curriculum Journal*, 21(2), 161–77.

Hayward L. and Spencer E. (2006) There is no alternative to trusting teachers. In Sainsbury, M., Harrison, C. & Watts, A. (eds) *Assessing Reading — from theories to classrooms*. Slough: National Foundation for Educational Research, pp. 222–40.

Hermannsson, K. (2015) Economic impact of education: evidence and relevance. In Wyse, D., Hayward, L. & Pandya, J. (eds) *International Handbook of Curriculum, Assessment and Pedagogy*. London: Sage, pp. 873–94.

Hutchings, M. (2015) *Exam Factories: The impact of accountability measures on children and young people*. London: NUT.

James, M. with Lewis, J. (2012) Assessment in Harmony with our understanding of learning: problems and possibilities. In J. Gardner, *Assessment and Learning* (2nd edn). London: Sage.

Klenowski, V. & Carter, M. (2015) Curriculum reform in testing and accountability. In Wyse, D., Hayward, L. & Pandya, J. (eds) *The SAGE Handbook of Curriculum, Pedagogy and Assessment*, Vol. 2. London: Sage, pp. 790–804.

Lancaster, Y.P. and Kirby, P. (2010; 2nd edn) *Listening to Young Children*. Buckinghamshire: Open University Press

Lundy, L. (2007) Voice is not enough: conceptualizing Article 12 of the United Nations Convention on the Rights of the Child. *British Educational Research Journal*, 33(6), 927–42.

Mansell, W., James, M. and the Assessment Reform Group (2009) *Assessment in Schools: Fit for purpose? A commentary by the Teaching and Learning Research Programme*. London: ESRC.

Scottish Office Education Department (SOED) (1991) *Assessment 5–14: Improving the quality of learning and teaching*. Edinburgh: SOED.

Wyse, D., Hayward, L. and Pandya, J. (Eds.) (2016) *The SAGE Handbook of Curriculum, Pedagogy and Assessment*. London: SAGE.

10

DIVERSITY AND INCLUSION

Chandrika Devarakonda and Liz Powlay

LEARNING AIMS

This chapter will:

- develop an understanding of the concept of inclusion and relate to children in early years and primary education
- explore current policy and legislation influencing diversity and inclusion from the perspective of early years and primary education
- raise awareness of the changing contexts of children attending early years and primary provision
- develop an understanding of the 'unique child' and its significance in practice.

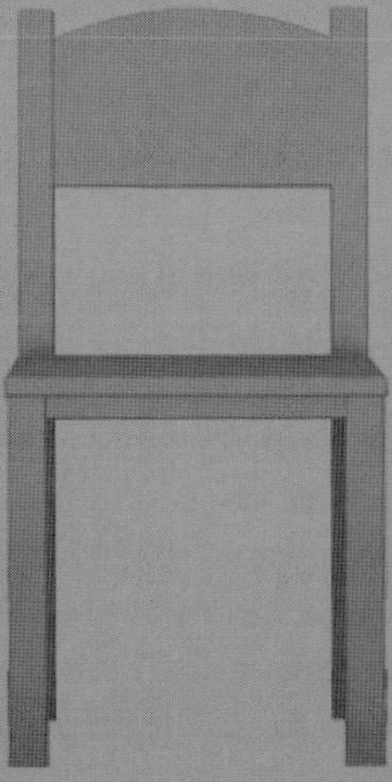

The Organisation for Economic Co-operation and Development (OECD) (2010) defines diversity as 'characteristics that can affect the specific ways in which developmental potential and learning are realised, including cultural, linguistic, ethnic, religious and socio-economic differences' (p. 21).

Another perspective provided by Paine (1990) proposes four orientations to diversity: individual difference, categorical difference, contextual difference and pedagogical difference. The first concept of diversity relates to individual differences between children that are based on their psychological and biological perspectives. In the second, categorical difference, diversity is observed through repeating patterns of variation across individuals. The categories relate to key characteristics of children such as their social class, race and gender. The third category, relating to contextual diversity, is influenced by social construction in different communities and societies, especially in relation to expectations and behaviour that impact on their education. The fourth category relates to causes and implications of difference for children, in terms of how teaching and learning styles differ according to differences in the needs of children.

The increasing diversity of children found in primary school and early years settings will challenge teachers to be aware of the differences and provide appropriate opportunities and experiences to all children. However, a teacher might judge based on their stereotype of the child's attributes such as gender, race, background, ethnicity, EAL, social class, SEN and/or disability. An individual attribute or a combination of these attributes may influence a child's ability to achieve or not. Children from diverse families might possess a wide range of proficiencies in literacy and numeracy due to their family background or to being first, second or third generation of migrants. To illustrate, the following case study will show the ways in which a child's needs are unique. It will encourage you to suggest ways in which a teacher or practitioner might consider the child from a holistic perspective with his/her multiple attributes. However, this can be challenging so an important question for you to consider is: How feasible is it for an early years educator or primary teacher to be aware of the diverse and changing needs of children and provide appropriate opportunities?

There have been several dilemmas arising from the meaning and nature of inclusive education (Norwich, 2007). Some authors have described inclusion to be elusive (Devarakonda, 2013), fuzzy (Göransson and Nilholm, 2014), a conceptual muddle and a complex and problematic concept (Mitchell, 2008). Furthermore, Hardy and Woodcock (2015: 141) understood inclusion to be obscured, camouflaged or insufficiently valued and lacking a commonly accepted definition (McLaughlin and Jordan, 2005). International policies have reinforced inclusion to be accepted as a global movement (Peters, 2004) and this is visible in the policies of several countries (Pijl et al., 1997).

The idea of inclusive education is idealistic and also utopian (Croll and Moses, 2000). Slee (2011) believed inclusive education to be a process towards an inclusive and democratic society. The concept is influenced by local contexts or discourses, and perhaps reinforces how it is conceptualised, understood, practised and implemented at grassroots level. However, Dyson cautions that inclusive education is 'not a set of practices whose effects can be evaluated, but is a principle that is embodied in different ways in different contexts' (2014: 282).

The terms 'inclusion' and 'inclusive education' have been used interchangeably. A wide range of definitions and interpretations of inclusion are discussed below. Slee (2011) suggests that inclusive education is concerned with schools adapting to the diverse needs of all children and not just with accommodating those who are different. Ainscow (1999: 218) elaborated the concept of inclusive education as:

> The agenda of inclusive education has to be concerned with overcoming barriers to participation that may be experienced by any pupils... the tendency is still to think of inclusion policy or inclusive education as being concerned only with pupils with disabilities and others categorized as having 'special education needs'.

Furthermore, inclusion is often seen as simply involving the movement of pupils from special to mainstream contexts, with the implication that they are 'included' once they are there. In contrast, I see inclusion as a never-ending process, rather than a simple change of state, and as dependent on continuous pedagogical and organisational development within the mainstream (Ainscow, 1999: 218). Slee (2011) suggests that inclusive education is concerned with schools adapting to the diverse needs of all children and not just with accommodating those who are different.

Some authors have identified common themes from various definitions and perspectives. Göransson and Nilholm (2014) have categorised the definitions of inclusion under various themes as follows:

- placement definition – children with disabilities or in need of special support in general education classrooms
- specified individualised definition – meeting the social/academic needs of pupils with disabilities/pupils in need of special support
- general individualised definition – meeting the social/academic needs of a pupil
- community definition – the creation of communities with specific characteristics.

A different perspective of inclusion focuses on meeting the outcomes of all children. Farrell (2012) believes that inclusion refers to all children, irrespective of their abilities, disabilities, ethnic origin, social class or gender in mainstream settings, and that full inclusion involves meeting all four pupil outcomes:

- Presence – the degree to which pupils attend lessons in mainstream settings with other children. This is similar to the concept of integration.
- Acceptance – the extent to which staff and pupils accept all pupils, irrespective of their background and abilities, and have opportunities to welcome them into their settings.
- Participation – the way in which all children are given opportunities to participate actively in the classroom.
- Achievement – all children have to succeed in the goals related to their education, behaviour and work.

Every school should provide opportunities to enable all children to meet all four outcomes. If a setting is unable to fulfil even one of the above conditions, then it is believed that the setting is not truly inclusive.

A magic formula for successful inclusion is proposed by Mitchell (2008). Inclusion is a balanced mixture of some key ingredients such as Vision (V) of staff members, Placement (P), Support (S), Resources (R), Leadership (L) and the 5 As (Acceptance, Access, Adapted curriculum, Adapted assessment and Adapted teaching). The formula for inclusive education = V + P + S + R + L + 5As. This formula might be interpreted by individual professionals and organisations according to the contexts, values and beliefs they are influenced by. Furthermore, inclusion is also believed to be a philosophy. The diversity of strengths, abilities and needs of individuals is viewed as natural and desirable in that it enables all communities to respect and value every member, resulting in the growth of the whole community (Alliance for Inclusive Education, 2000). Hodkinson and Devarakonda (2009) referred to inclusive education as a statement of fashion (p. 97) or a politically correct concept (Devarakonda, 2013). Wilson articulated his dilemmas on the shelf life of the concept of inclusion. He warned that:

> If inclusion is based primarily on ideological feeling, it may suffer the fate of most ideologies by running out of steam when social or political conditions and fashions change. We may wish to continue to promote it, we may even - such is the power of fashion - be stuck with it and be obliged to make it work as well as we can; but if we are to do it justice, we have also to clarify and evaluate it. (Wilson, 2000: 304)

Diverse definitions and interpretations of inclusion by practitioners have sometimes resulted in tokenistic inclusion. In order to encourage good practice, Booth and Ainscow (2002, 2011), influenced by social models of inclusion, developed an index for inclusion – a guide on inclusive practice. This is a resource that includes a set of materials to help schools and early childhood settings to develop inclusive practice. This document is relevant to inclusive practice in the staffroom, classroom and playgrounds, and has been translated into several languages to ensure practitioners from different countries can implement good practice. However, Mitchell (2005: 19) cautioned:

> Since there is no one model of inclusive education that suits every country's circumstances, caution must be exercised in exporting and importing a particular model. While countries can learn from others' experiences, it is important that they give due consideration to their own social economic-political-cultural-historical singularities.

- Discuss the definitions and list the key themes suggested by the concept of inclusion.
- Which of these definitions are most relevant in early years and primary settings and why?
- List the ways in which inclusion is relevant in your own setting or placement.

POLICIES AND LEGISLATION

This section focuses on the policies and legislation that influence inclusion. Policy includes plans, decisions, documents and proposals which are legal, formal and written, with a wide range of interpretations at different levels. Further to this, practitioners at grassroots level interpret policy influenced by their past experiences, values, ethos and the contexts of their settings. These contexts influence how the policies are interpreted and implemented in practice as the policy travels from one level to another. As shown in Figure 10.1, the pyramid represents how global policy developed by experts, academics, researchers and policy makers is influential, and how the impact of practitioners on children's services is stronger at the grassroots level at the bottom of the pyramid.

At global or universal level, the United Nations Convention on the Rights of the Child (UNCRC) and the Salamanca Statement (UNESCO, 1994) proposed the right to inclusive education, and expected schools to adapt to and meet the needs of children. At national level, these policies have been embraced, and this has been cascaded to grassroots or setting level through regional and local policies.

UN CONVENTION

The UN Convention on the Rights of the Child (UNCRC) 1989 is an international agreement. It includes a series of articles that list the rights of children and young people up to the age of 18 years. At global level, the UNCRC has granted all children a comprehensive set of rights that has been signed and ratified by the UK government. Some of the articles that relate to inclusion are 2, 3, 12, 13, 23, 28, 29, 30, and 31, which recommends that the government should ensure all children can access their right to challenge discrimination.

Web Link

The Unicef website provides lots of further information on the UNCRC and can be accessed through this web link, available on the companion website: www.unicef.org/crc/

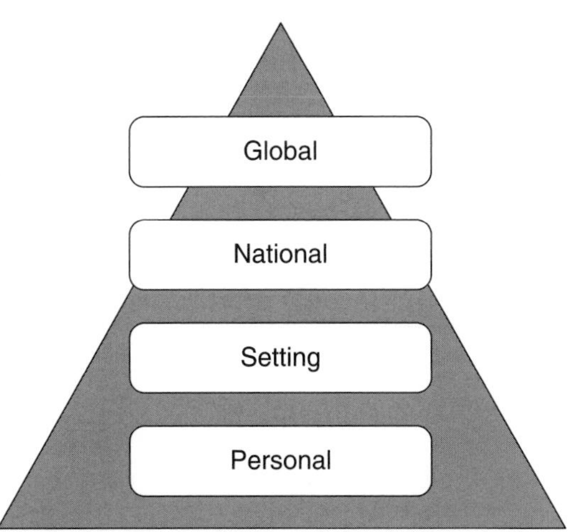

Figure 10.1 Policy pyramid

The UN Convention on the Rights of Persons with Disabilities (2008) affirms the rights of the disabled. The Convention suggests a shift in attitudes and approaches to persons with disabilities from being treated as 'objects' of charity, to 'subjects' who can access their rights and are able to make decisions (p. 20). Global-level polices have been ratified by a majority of governments. These policies seem to be interpreted and implemented at national level, although the focus and priorities of various countries have been different.

SALAMANCA STATEMENT

UNESCO's Education for All (EFA) is committed to providing basic education for all children around the world. In 1994, government representatives from 92 countries and 25 NGOs met in Salamanca, Spain and developed a **statement** about the education of all disabled children in a mainstream school to be the norm. The conference agreed on a new **Framework for Action,** based on the guiding principle that ordinary schools should accommodate all children, regardless of their physical, intellectual, social, emotional, linguistic or other conditions. The Salamanca Statement from UNESCO, adopted in July 1994, emphasised every child's right to education. All children have diverse and unique characteristics and needs that have to be taken into account to overcome discriminatory attitudes and to achieve inclusive education for all.

EQUALITY ACT 2010

The Equality Act 2010 is applicable in England, Wales and Scotland, but with a few variations. For example, in England and Wales the Act applies to all maintained and independent schools, including academies, and to maintained and non-maintained special schools. In Scotland, it applies to all schools managed by education authorities, independent schools and schools receiving grants under section 73(c) or (d) of the Education (Scotland) Act 1980.

According to the Equality Act 2010, schools should not discriminate against children based on a number of protected characteristics. Those relevant to school pupils are disability, race (including colour, nationality, ethnic or national origin), religion or belief (including lack of religion/belief), sex and sexual orientation. This legislation replaced all existing equality legislation around discrimination such as the Race Relations Act, Disability Discrimination Act and Sex Discrimination Act.

Web Link

A DfE document providing information on the Equality Act 2010 to schools can be accessed through this web link, available on the companion website: www.gov.uk/government/uploads/system/uploads/attachment_data/file/315587/Equality_Act_Advice_Final.pdf

CHILDREN AND FAMILIES ACT 2014

The Children and Families Act 2014 came into effect on 1 September 2014. This legislation encourages the participation of parents, children and young people (CYP) in decision making about special educational needs and disabilities (SEND). The Code of Practice provides statutory guidance on duties, policies and procedures relating to Part 3 of the Children and Families Act 2014. This legislation supports children and young people with special educational needs or a disability and their families. One of the significant changes is the replacement of a single statement of SEN with Education, Health and Care plans at local level, to meet the needs of children and young people. Statements were transferred over to Education, Health and Care (EHC) assessments and plans from September 2014, usually during an annual review or at a key transition point, such as a child preparing to go into reception class.

Key points in the Children and Families Act 2014 relevant to early years settings and primary schools include the following:

- involvement of children, young people and parents
- duties apply to all state-funded schools and early years providers
- coordinated assessment
- 0–25 years – Education, Health and Care Plan
- local authorities, health and care services to commission services jointly
- a clear, transparent local offer of services for all CYP with SEND
- offer of a personal budget to parents, giving more choice and control. The SEND Local Offer provides information for parents, in a single place, which helps them to understand what services they and their family can expect from a range of local agencies, including their statutory entitlements.

Table 10.1 Key changes from the SEN Code of Practice, 2001

SEN Code of practice 2001	Code of practice 2014
0-19 years	0-25 years
Guidance for SEN	Guidance for SEN and disabled
Legally binding - education	Legally binding - education, health and social care
Early years or school action and early years or school action plus	Graduated approach - Assess, Plan, Do and Review
Professionals in education	Joint approach - professionals from education, health and social care
Decisions made by professionals, and parents can be involved	Clear focus on the views of children and young people and their role in decision making
Definitions of special educational needs remain the same	Definitions of special educational needs remain the same
Statements and learning difficulty assessments (LDA)	Education, Health and Care plans for children with complex needs
Individual Educational plan	Individual provision map

Policies at settings or schools

The implementation of policies varies and is dependent on the context of the setting. Further, implementing policies around inclusion at grassroots level has been influenced by the ethos of the setting. For example, policies relating to inclusion are called SEN policy, SEN and inclusion policy or inclusion policy. The focus of the policy seems to vary across different schools in the UK, even in a single local authority. For example, some schools relate to children with special educational needs and/or disabilities, whereas the SEN policy of some settings would include vulnerable learners, pupils with English as an additional language, pupils who are very able and/or talented, and pupils who are looked after in local authority care. It is also important for settings to consider what is not SEN but may impact on the progress and attainment of children.

Curriculum and inclusion: Early Years Foundation Stage

The Early Years Foundation Stage (EYFS) is a statutory framework for educating children aged from birth to 5 in England. All settings engaged in promoting learning, development and care of children from birth to 5 are required to follow EYFS. 'Inclusive practice' is one of the commitments to the EYFS principle of 'a unique child'. This relates to all the child's rights to be treated fairly, regardless of race, religion or abilities. All early childhood settings must promote positive attitudes to diversity, irrespective of the context of the local community or even if the setting caters to a specific religious group.

Tickell (2011) reviewed the EYFS and made key recommendations based on feedback from practitioners to retain key elements of the EYFS, especially 'Unique child', endorsing the inclusiveness of the Foundation Stage curriculum. The Early Years Foundation Stage profile is a valuable way of understanding children's attainment and progress, by assessing young children's learning and development outcomes throughout EYFS. Practitioners have to ensure they consider the needs of individual children to make correct assessments – for example, the age of children, special educational needs and disability, children for whom English is an additional language, children from minority groups. Guidance on the EYFS profile (2014) advises practitioners to have 'meaningful' conversations with Year 1 staff to ensure the child makes a smooth and successful transition from the Foundation Stage. From September 2016, the EYFS profile will not be compulsory.

BASELINE ASSESSMENT

Baseline assessments were introduced to track the attainment and progress of children in primary school. In order to improve standards, the government introduced baseline assessments given in the first six weeks of starting reception class. The DfE recommends that the assessments must be age-appropriate and linked to EYFS learning and development requirements – communication and language, literacy and mathematics.

Web Link

Guidance on baseline assessment can be accessed through this web link, available on the companion website: www.gov.uk/guidance/reception-baseline-assessment-guide-to-signing-up-your-school

There are three DfE-approved providers, and schools can choose the scheme that best fits within the ethics and pedagogy of their setting. The baseline tests can be given on computers, tablets or face to face with teachers. The baseline tests include oral and touch-based questions and take 10–30 minutes to complete. Several teachers, practitioners and academics are against baseline assessment tests. Some of the challenges against such tests have included:

- a child's (in)ability to concentrate for up to 30 minutes
- teachers' awareness of unique needs of children with special educational needs and disabilities, EAL, disadvantaged children and shy children
- children without pre-school experience
- settling-in time for children and its impact on performance
- summer-born children
- restricted time of teachers to give the test on a one-to-one basis
- reliability of the test.

A campaign by Early Education, the British Association for Early Childhood, warned that these assessments could harm children's development and that those who perform less well could be 'stigmatised and labelled as failing' within weeks of starting school. The association also believed tests to be 'unnecessary, costly, unreliable, statistically invalid, damaging for children, misleading for parents, stressful for teachers'.

Web Link

A website for an alliance of early years organisations and teaching unions that are opposed to the introduction of baseline assessment can be accessed through this web link, available on the companion website: www.betterwithoutbaseline.org.uk/about.html

NATIONAL CURRICULUM

Inclusion is a high priority in the national curriculum of England:

> Setting suitable challenges
>
> 4.1 Teachers should set high expectations for every pupil. They should plan stretching work for pupils whose attainment is significantly above the expected standard. They have an even greater obligation to plan lessons for pupils who have low levels of prior attainment or come

> from disadvantaged backgrounds. Teachers should use appropriate assessment to set targets which are deliberately ambitious.
>
> Responding to pupils' needs and overcoming potential barriers for individuals and groups of pupils (DfE, 2014: 9)

[These include duties under equal opportunities legislation, and preventing barriers to learning for all pupils.]

One of the key challenges faced by all teachers is to ensure the needs of all children are met and provide appropriate opportunities to achieve. Further, it is essential to raise awareness of and provide training on the diverse needs of children and how to meet them.

The following activity is based on the book *The Very Hungry Caterpillar* and suggests how the individual needs of children can be met in a setting.

putting it into practice

Helping children understand diversity

An activity called 'Fruity Very Hungry Caterpillar scone pizza' is an effective way of helping young children understand the benefits of sharing and taking turns, as well as broadening their understanding of different diets and foods.

You will need a copy of *The Very Hungry Caterpillar* by Eric Carle, fruit mentioned in the story, baking equipment, recipe and ingredients to make a sweet scone base, individual cards of foods the caterpillar eats in the story, one with the happy-looking caterpillar and one of the caterpillars with a tummy ache. Check for allergies and dietary requirements and adapt the fruit and scone base if necessary, asking the children if they would like to suggest any alternative fruits.

The teacher reads the story of the hungry caterpillar to the class, and the children are asked to talk about how the caterpillar eats a mixture of healthy foods that we can eat a lot of, for example fruit, and those that are better eaten occasionally or as a treat.

The children are then invited to take turns to sort out the pictures of the foods. Place those that are healthy next to the 'happy' caterpillar and the others with the 'tummy ache' caterpillar. As the children talk about how people like to eat different things and how some people have reasons for not eating certain foods, for instance allergy, culture and religion, they also begin to share ideas together about what healthy eating is.

Together as a class, taste the fruit from the story, and invite the children to make a 'caterpillar pizza' to share. Follow a recipe and take turns to make a simple scone dough. Ask the children to share out the dough and then shape their dough into segments, using cutters or hands, arranging them on baking paper so they touch and overlap slightly. Decorate the segments with fruit from the story or fruit the children suggest and bake according to the scone recipe.

Talk with the children about how they can share out the pizza so everyone has some to try and can eat it. This activity allows children to be aware of diverse needs and how they can be met in a setting.

Changing contexts and relevance of inclusion

It has been reported that the demographics of the UK have changed significantly (ONS, 2015) due to the migration of populations from several countries, particularly from conflict and war zones for safety as well as for work and a better lifestyle, and from Eastern European countries following the expansion of the European Union. ONS (2011) reported an increase in ethnic minority populations, although the white ethnic population is still a majority group with 86%. According to ONS (2015), the number of school children speaking English as an additional language has increased by a third in the last five years.

Are early childhood settings and schools able to meet the needs of children from EAL and ethnic minority backgrounds? The recent influx of the migratory population has highlighted two issues around skin colour and proficiency in English. Are schools and teaching staff likely to stereotype the lack of proficiency in English of all children from ethnic minority backgrounds? Does colour of the child's skin have any impact on the expectation of the school staff? The abilities and proficiency in English of children from ethnic minority groups could vary and not support the stereotypes.

Schools are expected to provide education to children from a wide range of backgrounds, including children from migratory families. Are all schools able to meet the needs of all children? Does the stereotype around children from ethnic minority groups influence teachers to wrongly identify these children as having SEN? Are teachers equipped with the knowledge and understanding and skills to teach and assess diverse groups of children? An Ofsted (2010) report indicated that children were wrongly identified as having SEN as it compensated for poor teaching and support provided in schools and also added value to the school. The inconsistency in identification of children with SEN has been found not only between local authorities but also within them. In the report, some schools used SEN to broadly refer to those children whose achievement was low or below average, irrespective of whether they had learning difficulties or not. Is it because SEN defined in the legislation was misinterpreted? The Ofsted report indicated the reasons for wrong identification of SEN, including misinterpreting terms such as 'additional and different', 'progress is not adequate', 'differentiated learning opportunities', 'behaviour management techniques usually employed in the setting', 'significantly greater difficulty in learning than the majority of children of the same age' and 'educational provision made generally for children of their age'. Ofsted (2010) also highlighted that early childhood practitioners and teachers might consider the needs of all children as a homogenous group influenced by stereotypes. Classifying children with similar attributes as a homogenous group can be challenging as every child is unique.

The number of children identified with SEN has been disproportionate across gender, race, age groups and school types (Strand and Lindsay, 2009): 19.2% of boys are identified as having SEN without statements compared to 11.4% for girls; prevalence of SEN is 3.5% for black pupils with a statement of SEN; and Indian pupils are least likely to have SEN, at 1.8%. The prevalence of both Speech, Language and Communication Needs (SLCN) and Autistic Spectrum Disorders (ASD) has also increased substantially over the period 2005–2011, from 0.94% to 1.61% for SLCN (an increase of 71%) and from 0.48% to 0.87% for ASD (an increase of 81%). The increases for SLCN and ASD may be due to clarity in the definition of ASD, the expansion of diagnostic criteria, the development of services and improved awareness of the condition. Fernandez and Inserra (2013) warned that communication, speech and language difficulties could be a result of misinterpretation or an inability to speak in English due to EAL.

On the contrary, the DfE (2014a) has reported a decrease in the percentage of pupils identified as having SEN from 18.3% in 2010 to 15.1% in 2014. The decline in the number of children with SEN could be a result of better identification of those children who have SEN and those who do not.

It is important for teachers to realise the differences between what is and is not SEN. In its latest advice on updating the SEN policy of settings, the National Association for Special Educational Needs (NASEN, 2014) has suggested including factors which do not come under SEN but which may impact on progress and attainment: Disability, Attendance and Punctuality, Health and Welfare, EAL, being in receipt of a Pupil Premium Grant, Being a Looked After Child, or Being a Child of a Serviceman/woman.

reflection point

How does your setting or placement define SEN? What factors influence a child being identified as having SEN? Are children who do not achieve or progress likely to be identified as having SEN? Is a child with a disability or a medical condition labelled as having SEN?

spotlight on practice

Supporting children and their families

Lisa, a single mum of three young children - Peter (6 years), Ella (4 years) and Emma (2 years), is worried about her eldest son, Peter. Peter's teacher has often praised him for the enthusiasm and interest he has shown for all the school activities. In the last few weeks, Peter has been throwing tantrums and disrupting other children in their activities, especially when the teacher is giving them attention. Lisa has been invited for an informal meeting with the teacher and the head teacher, but she is reluctant to attend this meeting because she feels embarrassed and not confident to discuss the issues affecting Peter. She has separated from her husband and is aware of the effect of her husband's absence on all the children, especially Peter. She has had a few letters from school informing her about the changes in Peter's attitude. She is worried that Peter's learning and development will be affected. Points for discussion include:

- What are the issues that the school and the teacher have to consider in order to support Peter and his mum, Lisa?
- What strategies can the school use to ensure parents of all children can access school and communicate with school staff without hesitation?
- How can the school support Lisa and Peter during the multiple transitions?

Teacher training

Teachers and practitioners working with children are expected to treat every child with respect and as a unique child. In order to meet the diverse needs of children from different backgrounds, teachers have to be appropriately prepared (Darling-Hammond, 2003).

A recent survey indicates that newly qualified teachers' (NQTs') perceptions of their preparation to work with children from ethnic minority backgrounds and EAL learners have reached a nine-year high, but only 45% of NQTs felt their training was good or very good in this respect (Adewoye et al., 2014). The OECD TALIS survey (2009) highlighted that teachers are unable to cope with the challenges of teaching pupils with SEN. Ferreira and Graça (2006) recommended a list of topics around the wide range of diverse needs of pupils to be covered in the teacher education programme, such as learning difficulties and disabilities, emotional and behavioural problems, communication techniques and technologies; symbolic representation, signification and multi-culturalism, different curricula; teaching methods and techniques and educational relationships.

Jordan et al. (2009) stress the need for opportunities for hands-on experience for teachers to reflect on and analyse their attitudes and perceptions about how to support students with diverse needs. Forlin et al. (2009) warn that if negative attitudes are not addressed in teacher education programmes, this may affect inclusive teaching practices in the future. It can be argued that a stand-alone module focusing on diverse perspectives of inclusion in addition to SEN and disabilities, would enable the trainees to develop their values underpinning inclusion.

The principles of inclusion should be built into teacher training programmes, which should be about attitudes and values not just knowledge and skills (WHO/World Bank, 2011). Merryfield (2000) pointed to teacher educators' lack of knowledge, experience, commitment and understanding that may be impacting on the inclusive practice of future teachers. Lewis and Kaplan (2013) advocate that all teacher training programmes should embed issues around inclusive education such as rights and equality in all modules rather than in standalone modules. A specific module on inclusion may encourage the trainee teachers to limit their understanding of inclusion to SEN and disabilities.

Further, the successful implementation of inclusion in a school or an early years setting will depend on the school's understanding of diversity. It is crucial to be aware of the diverse characteristics of children with SEN/D – their gender, ethnic groups, EAL, Gypsy Roma and traveller families, asylum seekers or refugees. Standard 5 in the Teachers' Standards makes recommendations about inclusion. Every teacher must adapt teaching to respond to the strengths and needs of all pupils. They must *'have a clear understanding of the needs of all pupils, including those with special educational needs; those of high ability; those with English as an additional language; those with disabilities; and be able to use and evaluate distinctive teaching approaches to engage and support them'.*

Web Link

A DfE document providing information on the Teachers' Standards can be accessed through this web link, available on the companion website: www.gov.uk/government/uploads/system/uploads/attachment_data/file/301107/Teachers_-Standards.pdf

---

Building on strengths

Maana, a 5-year-old girl, has recently arrived in the UK with her family. She joined school six weeks ago. She has been found to be showing inappropriate behaviour with other children in the class, as well as with their teacher. All the teaching staff were disappointed, as several behaviour modification techniques did not have a significant impact on Manaa. One of the teaching assistants in the school recognised Manaa's interest in maths and music through her observations. Following this interesting revelation, the teaching assistant and the teacher tried to introduce Manaa to several activities based on maths and music. For example, she was asked to count all the children in her group. She was also given opportunities to sing during circle time, and whilst the class was going outdoors or to lunch. Points of discussion are as follows:

- Manaa's individual needs related to transition may not have been addressed. The teaching staff and the SENCo might have overlooked the changing contexts and diverse background of Manaa. Partnership and appropriate methods of communication used with Manaa and her parents might have resulted in a smoother transition.
- Building on strengths - following discussions with the child, her parents and the teaching staff, the school's SENCo suggested responding to Manaa's behaviour rather than reacting to it by penalising her. Manaa's behaviour was considered to be poor and inappropriate. The SENCo encouraged teaching staff to incorporate maths and music throughout the day.
- The teaching staff could develop a chart that displayed the strengths and weaknesses and likes and dislikes of all children. This would enable the teaching staff to tailor activities appropriately and meet the needs of all children.

Challenges and dilemmas

The concept of inclusion has several definitions and interpretations, resulting in a lack of clarity at national and regional and at setting levels. Teachers are confused by diverse perspectives and are frustrated when they are not able to include all children (Allan, 2008). Teachers are expected to meet the needs of all children and enable them to achieve to the best of their potential. Teachers are faced with the challenge of the ever-changing social, cultural, legislative and political contexts.

Are all teachers able to cope with the diversity of children's backgrounds and provide opportunities to meet their needs? Are teachers influenced by their own stereotypes and prejudices about children from different countries and contexts? Are teachers given appropriate training in their undergraduate courses encouraging them to keep an open mind?

Other challenges relate to negative attitudes of some teachers towards including all children and the influence of stereotypes and prejudices on provision. Sometimes, the pressures around the drive to provide the best quality provision result in teachers struggling to meet the needs of all children. Teachers have pressures of time, affordability and availability of appropriate resources. Teachers have also complained about their lack of knowledge and experience and request for more training (Adewoye et al., 2014). NQT surveys in the past few years have indicated that newly qualified teachers have been consistently reporting their low self-confidence in teaching children from BME families, EAL and children with SEN (Adewoye et al., 2014).

The following activity allows all children from diverse backgrounds to participate in a setting, whether early years or KS1. It could also be adapted to suit children at KS2.

Helping children understand inclusion

An activity called 'People Pebble Dominoes' helps encourage children aged 5-7 to explore their personal, social and emotional development.

The teacher will need washed rounded pebbles or cobbles around 40-60mm in size (available from garden centres, DIY stores or builders merchants), face paint, paint brushes, black permanent marker pens, two or three portrait photographs for each of the feelings happy, sad, worried and angry, or as appropriate for the children, outline drawings for these expressions, and an example of a 'people pebble'.

Split the children into groups and give each one a photograph showing the different feelings, ask them to talk about times when they have felt this way and why.

Encourage the children to look at how the eyes and mouth can change to show the different feelings. Introduce the drawings and ask the children to name the feelings and lay them out. Sort the photographs by asking each child to select a photograph and place it next to the appropriate drawing, talking about why they think the face shows that feeling. Support the children where needed by drawing attention to the eyes and mouth.

Then the teacher introduces the idea of making 'people pebble dominoes', with each end showing a different feeling.

Ask the children to select two paint colours and paint half their pebble one colour and the other half the second colour. When dry, ask one child to draw a different expression on each end of the pebble with the marker pens, using the outline drawings as guidance. Ask another child to copy one of the expressions onto their pebble and then draw a different expression on the other end. Repeat for all the pebbles. Make some extra ones if necessary to ensure that dominoes can be played.

When this has finished, use the completed 'people pebbles' to play dominoes where children take turns to lay their pebble and name a time they felt that way.

The outcome of this activity is that the children will learn about the benefits of talking about feelings and listening to other children's views.

SUMMARY

This chapter has explored inclusion and diversity from the perspective of early years and primary education. The term inclusion is constantly evolving with diverse perspectives and interpretations around who is included (children with SEN and/or disabilities or all children, parents, teachers and/or practitioners), where – the placement, such as mainstream or special school, meeting the holistic needs of all individuals, treating everybody with respect and providing opportunities for all to achieve their full potential. Despite a range of strong policies advocating inclusion at all levels, there is still a lack of clarity and consensus in policies and legislation at global (UNCRC), national (Equality Act 2010, EYFS), regional, local (local authority policies) and settings level. As a result, some teachers may experience tensions and dilemmas, which in turn may impact on their practice and lead them to adopt a tokenistic approach. The rapidly changing political, social and cultural context in the UK and elsewhere means that early years and primary education settings are highly diverse and culturally rich learning communities. This requires that teachers appreciate children's diverse backgrounds. Although research suggests that NQTs may lack the confidence to teach children from ethnic minority backgrounds and those from EAL families in particular (Adewoye et al., 2014), the changing context also presents opportunities for new teachers to acquire new knowledge, skills and cultural awareness. This will also require adequate resourcing for professional learning and leadership in the field of inclusive practice. Such resources will ensure that all teachers are well equipped to meet the challenges and opportunities of teaching in a truly diverse classroom.

companion website

To access additional online resources please visit: **https://study.sagepub.com/wyseandrogers**

Here you will find a classroom activity, author podcasts including Chandrika Devarakonda's top tips for employability, free access to SAGE journal articles and links to external sources.

further reading

Bhopal, K. & Rhamie, J. (2014) Initial teacher training: understanding 'race', diversity and inclusion. *Race, Ethnicity and Education*, 17(3): 304–25. This article explores students' understandings of 'race', diversity and inclusion on ITT courses as complex and multifaceted. The article argues that greater training is needed in relation to the practical assistance that student teachers require in terms of increasing their understanding of diversity and dealing with racism in the classroom.

Casey, T. (2010) Understanding inclusive play. In *Inclusive Play: Practical Strategies for Children from Birth to Eight* (2nd edn), pp. 1–15. London: Sage. This book provides practical strategies supported by sound theory. Some of the student-friendly features such as 'quick actions for change' are thought-provoking.

Devarakonda, C. (2013) *Diversity and Inclusion in Early Childhood: An Introduction*. London: Sage. This text covers issues around inclusion and diversity comprehensively on a wide range of issues such as gender, race, culture, English as an additional language (EAL), traveller families, special educational needs and disability.

European Agency for Development in Special Needs Education (EADSNE) (2010) *Teacher Education for Inclusion: International Literature Review*. Brussels: EADSNE. This report reviews literature to inform further work on the Agency Teacher Education for Inclusion project, with an emphasis on initial teacher education for mainstream teachers. The review highlights: changing conceptions of inclusion, the European context for teacher education for inclusion, policy frameworks to support teacher education for inclusion, effective practice in initial teacher education for inclusion with a focus on models of training, and curriculum, teaching practice and assessment. Further, the review expects teacher education courses to prepare teachers to engage with learner diversity arising from age, gender, sexual orientation, ethnic, cultural, linguistic or religious background, socio-economic status, disability or special educational needs.

Gehrke, R. S. and Cocchiarella, M. (2013) Pre-service special and general educators' knowledge of inclusion. *Teacher Education and Special Education: The Journal of the Teacher Education Division of the Council for Exceptional Children*, 36(3): 204–216. This article reports on a lack of confidence in implementing inclusion due to a lack of consistency between knowledge of inclusion and students' experience of inclusion across teacher preparation programmes in the USA.

Martin-Denham, S. (ed.) (2015) *Teaching Children and Young People with Special Educational Needs and Disabilities*. London: Sage. This is a comprehensive book written by SEND experts with up-to-date information and examples of good practice from special and mainstream settings.

Trussler, S. and Robinson, D. (2015) *Inclusive Practice in the Primary School: A Guide for Teachers*. London: Sage. This is a book that covers teaching of the whole 0–25 age range, with lots of practical strategies. It supports trainee and new teachers by providing insightful and practical ideas on helping children with SEN in mainstream schools. It also conveys a strong message, emphasising giving importance to the child rather than the label.

REFERENCES

Adewoye, M., Porter, S. and Donnelly, L. (2014) *Newly Qualified Teachers: Annual Survey 2014 – Research report NCTL*. London: DfE.

Ainscow, M. (1999) *Understanding the Development of Inclusive Schools*. London: Falmer Press.

Allan, J (2008) *Rethinking inclusion: the philosophers of difference in practice*. Dordrecht: Springer.

Alliance for Inclusive Education (2000) *Notes for Students on Inclusive Education*. Bristol: Centre for Studies in Inclusive Education.

Booth, T. and Ainscow, M. (2002) *Index for Inclusion: Developing Learning and Participation in Schools*. Bristol: CSIE.

Booth, T. and Ainscow, M. (2011) *Index for Inclusion: Developing Learning and Participation in Schools* (3rd edition). Bristol: CSIE.

Croll, P. and Moses, D. (2000) Ideologies and utopias: education professionals' views of inclusion. *European Journal of Special Needs Education*, 15: 1–12.

Darling-Hammond, L. (2003b). Keeping good teachers: Why it matters, what leaders can do. *Educational Leadership*, 60(8): 6–13.

Department for Education (2010) Equality Act 2010. Retrieved from: www.legislation.gov.uk/ukpga/2010/15/pdfs/ukpga_20100015_en.pdf

Department for Education (2011) Teachers' standards, accessed from https://www.gov.uk/government/publications/teachers-standards

Department for Education (DfE) (2012) Ethnic disproportionality in the identification of speech language and communication needs SLCN and autism spectrum disorders 2005–2011. Retrieved from: www.gov.uk/government/publications/ethnic-disproportionality-in-the-identification-of-speech-language-and-communications-needs-slcn-and-autism-spectrum-disorders-asd-2005-to-2011

Department for Education (DfE) (2014a) *Special Educational Needs in England: January 2014*. London: DfE.

Department for Education (DfE) (2014b) Children and Families Act 2014. Retrieved from: www.legislation.gov.uk/ukpga/2014/6/contents/enacted

Department for Education (DfE) (2014c) 'National Curriculum'. Retrieved from: www.gov.uk/government/collections/national-curriculum.

Department for Education (DfE) (2014d) *Special Educational Needs and Disability: 0–25 Years*. London: DfE.

Department For Education and Employment /Qualification and Curriculum Authority (1999) The National curriculum handbook for Primary teachers in England – Key Stages 1 &2, London: The Stationary office.

Devarakonda, C. (2013) *Diversity and Inclusion in Early Childhood: An Introduction*. London: Sage.

Dyson, A. (2014). A response to Göransson and Nilholm. *European Journal of Special Needs Education*, 29(3): 281–282.

European Agency for the Development of Special Needs Education (EADSNE) (2010) *Teacher Education for Inclusion across Europe: Challenges and Opportunities*. Odense, Denmark: EADSNE.

Farrell, P. (2012) Inclusive education for children with special educational needs: current uncertainties and future directions. In G. Squires and D. Armstrong (eds) *Children with Special Educational Needs: Considering the Whole Child*, pp. 79–98. London: Routledge.

Fernandez, N. and Inserra, A. (2013) Disproportionate classification of ESL students in US special education. *Teaching English as a Second or Foreign Language*, 17(2). Retrieved from: www.tesl-ej.org/wordpress/issues/volume17/ej66/ej66a1/

Ferreira, H. and Graça, R. (2006) Special educational needs: an experiment in teacher education in Portugal. In Gash, H. (ed.) *Beginning Teachers and Diversity in School: A European Study*. Instituto Politécnico de Bragança. Report of research undertaken within Comenius Project 94158-CP-1-2001-FR.

Forlin, C., Loreman, T., Sharma, U. and Earle, C. (2009) Demographic differences in changing pre-service teachers' attitudes, sentiments and concerns about inclusive education. *International Journal of Inclusive Education*, 13(2): 195–209.

Göransson, K. and Nilholm, C. (2014) Conceptual diversities and empirical shortcomings: a critical analysis of research on inclusive education. *European Journal of Special Needs Education*, 29(3): 265–80.

Hardy, I. and Woodcock, S. (2015) Inclusive education policies: discourses of difference, diversity and deficit. *International Journal of Inclusive Education*, 19(2): 141–64.

Hodkinson, A. and Devarakonda, C. (2009) Conceptions of inclusion and inclusive education: a critical examination of the perspectives and practices of teachers in India. *Research in Education*, 82(1): 85–99.

Jordan, A., Schwartz, E. and McGhie-Richmond, D. (2009) Preparing teachers for inclusive classrooms. *Teaching and Teacher Education*, 25(4): 535–542.

Lewis, I. and Kaplan, I. (2013) Promoting Inclusive Teacher Education. Retrieved from: http://unesdoc.unesco.org/images/0022/002210/221035e.pdf

McLaughlin, M. J. & Jordan, A. (2005) Push and pull: forces that are shaping inclusion in the United States and Canada. In D. Mitchell (ed.) *Contextualizing Inclusive Education: Evaluating Old and New International Perspectives* (pp. 89–113). London: Routledge.

Merryfield, M. M. (2000) Why aren't teachers being prepared to teach for diversity, equity and global interconnectedness? A study of lived experiences in the making of multicultural and global educators. *Teaching and Teacher Education*, 16(4): 429–443.

Mitchell, D. (ed.) (2005) *Contextualising Inclusive Education: Evaluating Old and New International Perspectives*. London: Routledge.

Mitchell, D. (2008) *What Really Works in Special and Inclusive Education? Using Evidence-based Teaching Strategies*. Abingdon: Routledge.

NASEN (2014) NASEN Help Sheet: Updating SEN Policy for Schools 2014. Retrieved from: www.nasen.org.uk/uploads/publications/329.pdf

Norwich, B. (2007) *Dilemmas of Difference, Inclusion and Disability: International Perspectives and Future Directions*. London: Routledge.

OECD (2009) Creating Effective Teaching and Learning Environments: First Results from TALIS. Retrieved from: www.oecd.org/dataoecd/17/51/43023606.pdf (accessed 22/03/15).

OECD (2010) *Educating Teachers for Diversity: Meeting the Challenge*. Paris: OECD CERI. Retrieved from: www.oecd-ilibrary.org/education/educating-teachers-for-diversity_9789264079731-en (accessed 23/03/15).

Ofsted (2000) *Educational Inclusion: Guidance for Inspectors and Schools*. London: Ofsted.

Ofsted (2010) *The Special Educational Needs and Disability Review*, ref. 090221. London: Ofsted.

ONS (2011) Ethnicity and National Identity in England and Wales 2011. Retrieved from: www.ons.gov.uk/ons/dcp171776_290558.pdf (accessed 24/12/14).

ONS (2015) Migration Statistics Quarterly Report, February. Retrieved from: www.ons.gov.uk/ons/dcp171778_396645.pdf

Paine, L. (1990) *Orientations toward Diversity: What do Prospective Teachers Bring?* East Lansing, MI: National Center for Research on Teacher Education.

Peters, S. (2004) *Inclusive Education: An EFA Strategy for all Children*. Washington, DC: World Bank.

Pijl, S. J., Meijer, C. J. W. & Hegarty, S. (1997) *Inclusive Education: A Global Agenda*. London: Routledge.

Slee, R. (2011) *The Irregular School: Exclusion, Schooling and Inclusive Education*. Abingdon: Routledge.

Strand, S. & Lindsay, G. (2009) Evidence of ethnic disproportionality in special education in an English population. *Journal of Special Education*, 43(3): 174–90.

Tickell, C. (2011) *The Early Years: Foundations for Life, Health and Learning – An independent review of the Early Years Foundation Stage*. London: DfE.

UNESCO (1994) *The Salamanca Statement and Framework for Action on Special Needs Education*. Paris: UNESCO.

United Nations (1989) *Convention on the Rights of the Child*. New York: United Nations.

United Nations (2008) *Convention on the Rights of Persons with Disabilities*. Retrieved from: www.ohchr.org/Documents/Publications/AdvocacyTool_en.pdf

Wilson, J. (2000) Doing justice to inclusion. *European Journal of Special Needs Education*, 15(3): 297–304.

WHO/World Bank (2011) World Report on Disability. Retrieved from: www.who.int/disabilities/world_report/2011/en/index.html, p. 29.

11

PARTNERSHIP WORKING

Amanda Ince and Josh Franks

LEARNING AIMS

This chapter will:

- consider different interpretations of partnership in early years and primary teaching
- enable you to understand the different roles and responsibilities involved in working across different types of organisations from the perspectives of those involved in partnership, including: students, school-based mentors, school communities and initial teacher education providers
- help you to consider the advantages and tensions of partnership working
- present examples of different types of partnership working
- develop knowledge and understanding of effective partnerships informed by research.

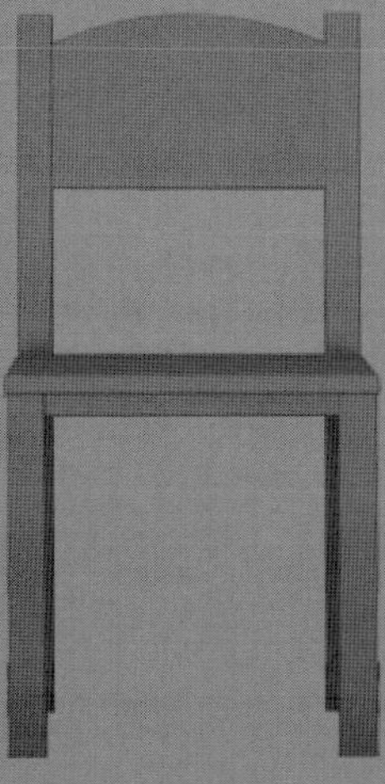

Partnership is a term commonly used in a variety of contexts, from civil partnerships to business partnerships. On first acquaintance, 'partnership' may seem simple and straightforward, and yet in the field of education the term may be subject to a myriad of interpretations, rendering the term problematic to define and research (Clifford and Millar, 2007; Rosenberg et al., 2009). Whilst the idea of educational partnership has been in existence for many decades, more recently partnership has become central to teacher education and development through changes in government policy and the introduction of teaching schools (Greaney et al., 2014). This chapter sets out to clarify the term 'partnership' and to address three key aspects:

- what partnership working means
- building successful partnerships
- future developments in partnership.

Case studies and activities are used to illustrate how partnership might be experienced, developed and established in primary and early years contexts to support teaching and learning. Reflective questions are offered to help you to think about what working in partnership might mean to you as a teacher.

This chapter is written in three sections. Each section takes a key aspect of partnership and relates it to contemporary issues around the what, how and why of partnership working.

Section one considers definitions of partnership and the background to its prominence and current importance. It draws on international literature to discuss different interpretations of partnership and those adopted most widely and prominently in primary and early years.

The second section shifts from a theoretical overview to how partnership in practice operates. Case studies from partnerships and across different viewpoints are used to analyse the features that contribute to successful partnerships and how these might be developed within different contexts.

In section three, the chapter looks ahead to possible future developments in partnership policy and discusses the tensions and issues that can create challenges in implementing partnership working. The summary draws the chapter together and suggests readings and activities for early years and primary colleagues to consider when developing, establishing or embedding partnership working.

DEFINING PARTNERSHIP: WHAT DOES PARTNERSHIP WORKING MEAN?

More recently, research has focused less on the ability to provide a tight definition and more on the features of successful partnership working (Menter et al., 2010; Greaney and Brown, 2015).

In their meta analysis of research into partnership, Clifford and Millar (2007) found a lack of clarity in terminology and suggest that the complexity of partnership and different interpretations according to context have led researchers to shy away from definitions. Perhaps in response to the issues raised by Clifford and Millar, Rosenberg et al. (2009) recognise goal-focused and structure-orientated frameworks for defining partnership (Clifford and Millar, 2007: 3–4). Central to successful partnership seems to be the understanding that partnership itself entails 'joint interests' (Websters, 1996). Unpicking what these might be sheds light on the different types of partnership and how these work.

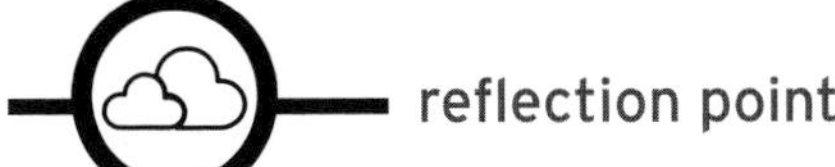

Think about people that you are partners with in everyday life. What are the 'joint interests' that link you with them?

Establishing links between schools is one type of partnership. Schools from very differing cultural and social contexts could make a link (Bourn and Cara, 2013). These links are sometimes based on teachers visiting a school in Africa, for example, making a personal link and then setting up a penpal system, email buddies or similar so that the children can see what life is like in a different country and context. The link supports topic work, raises awareness of social issues affecting children and the school in the less well developed context perhaps gains additional resources through fundraising from the partner school. Sometimes these links are made more formally through charitable institutions or international bodies. The interests of each school are perhaps different, one being social and international awareness and the other resources. Such school links have been encouraged, although not consistently for many years, through external funding, European Union projects, non-governmental organisations (NGOs) and the personal interests and social awareness of teachers.

A development of this is the international placement partnership. Here, higher education institutions (HEI) or colleges make a link with a school (or schools) and send groups of students for short placements. For example, a further education college gained EU funding to send a group of NVQ3 childcare students to Finland for a three-week work placement across the equivalent range of early years and primary provision. A HEI organised a self-funded two-week placement for student teachers to work in a school in Bangalore. The students benefit from working in a different culture and from seeing alternative approaches to pedagogy. Additional adults working in the settings benefit the hosts. These international placements are rarely reciprocal and are different from a student exchange. Both these types of partnerships whilst valuable are not necessarily the type of partnerships anticipated by student teachers and government departments when they emphasise the desire or need for deeper partnership working (Rosenberg et al., 2009).

In the context of primary and early years teaching, partnerships tend to centre on Initial Teacher Education (ITE) and the relationship between schools and providers, in order to offer placements to students wishing to become qualified as teachers or early years practitioners. Within this context, research suggests that a successful partnership is one of positive relationships and good communication (Harlow et al., 2013), where the joint interests are clearly articulated and partners are clear about the benefits or otherwise.

What's in it for me? Alongside daily responsibilities for educating and caring for children are the ever-increasing accountability agenda and external pressures on early years and primary practitioners. So when the invitation to become involved in partnership working is issued, it is reasonable to ask, 'What will this bring to my practice and setting?' The answer seems to depend on who is asking and what partnership might mean in any particular context.

One of the most common partnerships in education is that between ITE providers and schools, although there is a debate currently about the balance between them. This chapter focuses on the partnership aspects of those relationships and not the policy or political debates around the pros and cons of various routes into teaching or the different types of ITE provider. Instead, it focuses on the fundamental issue of placement in school as a key part of any ITE programme, leading to partnership between schools and ITE providers. It is interesting that whilst school experience or placement is a fundamental and core component of any ITE programme, there is no legal or policy directive that requires schools to provide such experiences for would-be teachers. This is made more complex by the nature of ITE whereby host class teachers, school mentors and early years practitioners were once students themselves needing a placement. Once qualified, they often see partnership and hosting students on placements from a different perspective. This raises tensions between the requirements on providers and the reality of school and setting capacity to offer such learning experiences to student teachers.

On one hand, there are ITE providers with a direct requirement to provide school experience for all their students for a minimum of 120 days, in order for the students to be compliant with guidance and achieve qualified teacher status. This is a relatively recent change (DfE, 2010), requiring a renegotiation between schools and universities to account for the shift in balance of time for students. On the other hand, the main duty of schools is the education of children to the highest standards, and they are accountable to both parents and a range of external bodies such as the school governors and Ofsted. The value of partnership in ITE seems obvious for the students and ITE providers but schools understandably have to consider a wide range of responsibilities and priorities. Being able to positively answer 'What's in it for me?' becomes important for schools in their voluntary engagement with ITE providers. Each of the stakeholders, whether schools, ITE providers or students, needs to have a clear view of the benefits or otherwise to them of such partnerships. Figure 11.1 illustrates these experiences and perspectives, alongside ways of working that seem to be successful for all those involved.

These perspectives resonate with Husbands (2012) who identifies the differing perspectives on ITE for schools and ITE providers. On a more pragmatic basis, ITE providers often find that the chance of placing a student in a school or early years setting is strongly related to the success or otherwise of the previous student placed. But with placement at the heart of all routes into teaching there are some key features of partnership working which can support the relationship, regardless of student outcome. Knowing what these are and how to create a successful partnership is discussed in the next section.

What does partnership mean to you? What has informed this view and has it changed over time?

Student: I want a placement in an excellent school local to where I live. It will have worked in partnership with my ITE provider for a number of years so I will be fully supported through a strong relationship.

School 1: We can't take students, we don't have capacity and the payment the ITE provider makes is tokenistic and doesn't cover the time my staff have to invest in the students.

School 2: We'd love to have students but we have NQTs; my school mentor is going on maternity leave and we are due an Ofsted inspection soon.

School 3: What's not to like about having students?

For our teachers:	**For our school:**
Recognition and a reminder of my own expertise.	Staff development. Being a mentor develops staff and can offer a rewarding alternative to out-of-class responsibilities.
Encouragement to think carefully again about what I'm doing – and why.	Opportunities to influence the next generation of teachers.
Prompting to question the rationale behind things I've taken for granted.	Access to latest thinking about teacher education.
Opportunity to observe my own class – learning about their learning.	Coaching and mentoring to impact on pupil learning as well as develop staff expertise and confidence.
Scope to teach in more creative or challenging ways – exploiting the fact that there are two, or more, teachers.	Access to new knowledge, new skills, new ideas.

Figure 11.1 Partnership perspectives

Web Link

A Sage Knowledge video called 'Community and Family' by Jonathan Cohen (Professor in Psychology and Education, Teachers College, Columbia University) can be accessed through this web link, available on the companion website: http://sk.sagepub.com/video/community-and-family

BUILDING SUCCESSFUL PARTNERSHIPS

Relationships and communication

Recognising the tensions between ITE providers looking for placements, students wanting the best experience and schools balancing the needs of their children with the moral imperative to support a future generation of teachers is complex. In many instances, partnership success is based on relationships and communication (Many et al., 2012), a discussion of joint interests, of how the partnership might work and why it is needed. This might include a very basic request for placements. ITE providers do this in different ways, from asking students for contacts to emails and telephone calls. Often, personal relationships and contacts to make the initial relationship are most successful. But there is a risk in partnership being solely within the relationship between two professionals. Teacher retention and changes to organisations can easily alter roles and responsibilities, leading to seemingly solid partnerships disintegrating. A more strategic approach to partnership can avoid some of these issues by making partnership an integral way of working, rather than one based on a loose personal relationship between a school mentor and an ITE tutor, for example. This has been recognised in a range of studies, reports and literature (Harlow et al., 2013). Emerging from this are several practical approaches to developing successful partnerships between schools and HEIs. The next section focuses on two of these approaches in particular: boundary spanners and hub working.

Boundary spanners

The role of the boundary spanner is to work across the school and the ITE provider, brokering, negotiating, understanding and mediating the tensions between the differing perspectives. How can a class teacher host a student when they have so much to do in raising standards, meeting the needs of their class, liaising with parents and developing their own practice? Where will the time come from for meeting the student, for working with them so that they understand planning, assessment and the need for children to make progress? Is it fair that ITE providers expect students to be observed and assessed, and why are supervising tutor visits so infrequent? Personal experience of the boundary spanner of working within the different contexts and experiencing the same legitimate concerns and issues, allows them to build a relationship through a shared understanding. In colloquial parlance, to not only 'talk the talk but walk the walk' creates a foundation of trust that supports joint working for mutual benefits. It mitigates against a potential barrier to partnership working through a perceived inequality in power within the relationship. For example:

> Equality of voice and sharing of power are two components especially important to this process. We must understand that all participants have something to teach and something to learn. This is important, not only to the specific partnership, but also to the field of education as a whole. (Morgan-Fleming et al., 2010: 64)

Class teachers and school mentors have established relationships based on trust and professional respect with colleagues in their organisation. Seconding these staff to work as ITE tutors or creating joint-funded positions across organisations maintains these relationships and transfers the trust into the new organisation. There are clear joint understandings of the pressures on school staff and the issues that hosting students on placement might create. Knowing that the ITE tutor is familiar with these and sympathetic to the school perspective makes communication potentially easier, and frank discussions about issues can be held from professional perspectives. This avoids the potential for a 'them and us' situation to develop, undermining partnership working. Partnership in this instance has the shared goal of supporting students to be successful, working together from an equal and mutually respectful understanding. Underpinned by a similar premise, the School Direct salaried model builds on the now redundant Graduate Teacher programme. Schools recruit and support trainee teachers that will, after a year's training, become colleagues.

Benefitting from partnerships

Seeing how you can benefit from a partnership between an early years setting or primary school and an ITE provider can seem challenging. This might be especially so if no formalised hub or boundary spanner type support exists in your setting. The following suggestions provide potential ways in which to optimise partnership:

- Look through session outlines from a university module. Ask your school mentor to recommend a teacher in the school who has a particular strength in this area. Arrange to observe and interview this teacher.
- Keep a journal to record reflections in practice that enlighten literature and theory from your ITE provider.
- Consider how you would like partnership to operate when you are qualified.

Research by Many et al. (2012) identified three beneficial themes to boundary spanner working: the ability to understand the other perspective, the ability to deconstruct traditional power relationships through dialogue, and the ability to draw on prior knowledge to shape the way teachers engage with colleagues in their new spaces. Whilst boundary spanners have been established for a number of years in the USA, Australia and New Zealand (Many et al., 2012), the term is not recognised in the UK in the same way. Instead, it is interesting to note how schools and ITE providers have developed other ways of working which mirror many aspects of the boundary spanner approach under different terminology. One such iteration is hub working.

Hub working

Hub working is one way that an HEI has developed to support partnership working and to meet the needs of schools, students and tutors. This resonates with the 'boundary spanners' approach from the USA and Australia (Many et al., 2012), in that the ITE tutor works across ITE in an HEI and as a class teacher in school. A group of schools with shared values and approaches creates a hub which welcomes students across local schools. This is also similar to the teaching schools approach for Schools Direct in England, but is more informal as there is no financial link. The schools host students and offer professional development sessions, share the same ITE tutor/s and welcome opportunities to develop innovative approaches to practice. The Spotlights on Practice below illustrate how hub working operates from each perspective.

The student and partnerships

Caroline has previously worked in a school for two terms as a teaching assistant. She has just begun her PGCE and feels confident about working with small groups of children. However, she is very apprehensive about fulfilling the expectations of the university and about taking responsibility for the learning of the whole class. She is the only student in her placement school, she is extremely conscientious and has lots of questions about what the school and the university expect of her. However, she worries about bothering her class teacher, the school mentor or the university tutor.

Caroline has been told that her placement school is one of nine local schools in a hub set up by the university. Her university tutor will supervise all 14 of the students placed in these schools and they will meet fortnightly on a Friday afternoon. The sessions will take place in one of the hub schools and will include input from school staff, the university tutor and time for informal discussions with fellow students.

At the first hub meeting, Caroline is able to compare experiences with her fellow students. Before the session, informal time is given and she discusses positives and worries about her placement. She also has time to discuss ideas about paperwork. Caroline begins to feel more confident that she is progressing well. It becomes clear to Caroline that one of her concerns - regarding expectations of her in-class role - is shared by the majority of the group. The university tutor begins by addressing these concerns.

The focus of the session concerns productive in-class observations. Caroline has been feeling overwhelmed by the amount of information she feels she needs to report and realises that all the students feel similarly. Her tutor encourages the group to have one or two foci for each lesson observation and to prioritise analysis relating to the focus over description. The tutor arranges for students to take part in a school exchange. Caroline is to visit a local school, with a very different intake and philosophy, and observe with Paul, the student placed in the school. In turn, he will join Caroline for an afternoon in her placement school.

Caroline hears from an NQT working in the school and hosting the hub session and is able to spend some time asking candid questions about how to deal with work demands.

Caroline leaves the hub session with many of her concerns addressed. She has a network of fellow students whom she can email, she has experienced a different local school and knows she will be visiting another in the coming week. Caroline also feels confident that she is on the right track with her in-class work. She has another three weeks before returning to university but knows that the hub will meet again in a fortnight, that any concerns that crop up are valid and that she has a tutor who she can contact if necessary.

spotlight on practice

The Initial Education tutor and partnerships

Simon is in his third year as a part-time university tutor. His core role is to supervise PGCE and Schools Direct students. He visits them in schools, observes teaching, assesses paperwork, runs tutorials, gives formative and summative feedback and has a regular online dialogue with the students in response to their reflective journals, as well as responding to emails when questions and concerns arise.

Simon felt a degree of frustration last year for two reasons. First, face-to-face time with his students was limited further as the proportion of university time on the ITE course decreased. Second, Simon had established positive relationships with staff in a number of schools only to discover that some of these schools had decided not to continue taking students due to pressures from external bodies, competition from alternative ITE routes and institutions and, in some cases, reluctance towards hosting students amongst school staff.

In response, before the current school year began, a senior member of university staff approached Simon about setting up a hub of schools. Simon also works part-time in an inner-city primary school and has built a relationship with staff in a number of schools within the same borough, as well as with schools in which he has supervised students. He approached nine schools/children's centres within a 3-mile locality about joining the hub.

Simon informed school staff that he would be supervising all students placed in hub schools. Students would meet fortnightly on a Friday afternoon. He asked that sessions could take place in one of the hub schools and include input from school staff, as well as from him. All nine schools were very positive about joining the hub and showed excitement at the prospect of hosting sessions and sharing the expertise of the staff in their schools.

By the end of the autumn term, Simon felt that he had established very strong working relationships with the students in the hub. As compared with the previous year, the face-to-face time with students was greatly increased. Simon felt that he had a more thorough understanding of individual approaches, temperaments, strengths and areas for development. He was able to respond to questions and concerns as they arose and, in many cases, pre-empt difficulties related to university expectations for teaching practice and paperwork. The dedicated time for students on visit days had become significantly more productive as general queries had been addressed and, therefore, more time could be dedicated to analysing pedagogy, developing planning and assessment and setting achievable targets.

(Continued)

(Continued)

Simon also felt that the relationship with school staff had become very strong. He was now familiar to all staff in the hub schools, rather than 'just' the student mentor, many of the staff had contributed to hub sessions or were keen to participate in future and he felt like more of a collaborative colleague than a visitor taking what he needed for the university.

Simon now has a very strong understanding of the ethos, approaches and particular strengths of the hub schools. When he wants to give students relevant input to support their stage of school experience, he is confident about which school(s) and which staff members to approach.

Simon has also been able to promote the further development of the partnership between the university and the hub schools by facilitating student visits, tutor visits and action research within the hub schools. The number of school staff participating in interviewing prospective students and working on support sessions within the university has also increased.

Schools within the hub are keen to continue and develop the relationship with the university. Simon knows that for the coming years he will supervise students in the same schools, working collaboratively with the same school staff.

spotlight on practice

The school mentor and partnerships

Jenny has been a class teacher for seven years. She has mentored students in her class before and has also had overall responsibility for working with ITE students at the school for two years. Jenny was enthusiastic about working with students as she has an interest in mentoring as well as in keeping up to date with developments in research and pedagogy.

Jenny had hoped that the work in school with students would build a relationship with the university but until this year she had been left frustrated. Previously, Jenny had set up weekly meetings with the students placed at her school and observed them teach once a fortnight. She had followed the guidelines set out by the student handbook and had supported students very well.

However, until this year, Jenny had no relationship with the students' university tutors. Three different tutors had visited the school during her time in the role and whilst the visits had been positive and productive for the students, Jenny felt that her role and the role of the school were far less of a priority.

At the start of the academic year, Jenny's school was invited to join a hub of schools. It was explained to Jenny that the university valued the support that the school had given to students in the past and that the school had strengths that would fit very well with those of the other local schools in the hub.

Jenny accepted the invitation to join the hub of schools. Immediately, the tutor assigned to the hub made contact with the school and spoke to Jenny about how the school could/would like to benefit from working in the hub. Jenny expressed her wish to vary her work with students and the university and asked for clarification about a number of issues related to student placements.

This year Jenny hosted a hub session on Assessment for Learning (AfL). Students from across the hub observed Jenny teach her class, employing a number of strategies for AfL. Jenny then ran a practical workshop with the students to follow up. Jenny has since been invited to run a similar session at the university. Jenny and a colleague have also been involved in interviewing prospective ITE students alongside university staff this year.

Jenny has now built a strong working relationship with the tutor responsible for the hub. She is in contact immediately if there are questions and concerns about students in her school and increasing numbers of her colleagues have expressed an interest in being involved with hub work.

The Spotlight on Practice case studies above suggest that boundary spanning or its iteration as hub working is one approach that enables partnerships between schools and ITE providers to develop to mutual benefit. These rely on partners overcoming potential barriers to such working. They include the challenge of setting up such relationships in sufficient time to host students in the required numbers and being able to maintain the same staffing. Smaller schools can be enthusiastic participants but may find they are unable to host students due to reduced capacity through staff maternity leave or illness. Dropping out for a year can make the longer-term relationship harder to maintain and affects the number of placements and potential funding available to maintain the allocation of ITE provider staff to the school or the secondment of school staff to the HEI or ITE provider. Grappling with organisational issues can be challenging and for students can seem incomprehensible when, from their perspective, they see a good local school and not the complexity of factors that can prevent them from being offered a placement.

The themes that emerge from the experiences of students, schools and ITE providers are around communication, relationships, respect and mutual benefits. The same themes are present in other types of partnerships discussed below.

Partnership in early years

An outstanding nursery school works in partnership with a range of organisations. It has links with a local college and university to offer student placements on a range of courses from school experience for sixth form pupils via NVQs to early years teacher training. The same nursery works with a different HEI as a strategic partner to support its research and development projects. These include joint bids for external funding to pursue research into leadership in early years – action research projects across an alliance of primary and nursery schools. The nursery offers opportunities for international students on MA programmes to visit and observe its practice and outdoor learning environment. Partnership for this nursery also includes working with the local community and parents. There is a newsletter to support communications, and there are community events such as fairs and fetes to fund raise and sponsored events for charity. Parents and carers are invited to attend various nursery events throughout the year to share their child's experiences and development. The nursery website plays an important part in supporting communication between the partners, sharing information and promoting opportunities, including offering consultancy and support for other nurseries or early years settings. This nursery sees partnership as important beyond the local and national and is also involved in international work, hosting visitors and visiting early years provision abroad. The consultancy work brings in a little income, which is used to develop opportunities for the children. This proactive approach to partnership across a range of different aspects and all involving practitioner development in some form has been carefully considered, with this nursery identifying the pros and cons of partnership working as follows:

> The only drawbacks in partnership working we can think of are the additional time that this can involve (although this is improved with greater email use) and the current financial restraints that mean participants tend to rely on twilight sessions for face to face meetings (the advantage to this is that people are really committed to the work).
>
> The benefits are the exchange of ideas and good practice that is always part of practitioners' meetings and beyond that is the development of more reflective professionals, constantly planning, testing ideas and reviewing practice. They (practitioners) are also enticed back into the world of theory, reading current research and ideas but with the practical opportunities to explore theory.
>
> The gains for children are that their practitioners are exploring and finding out what really works in school and are involved in a virtuous circle of improvement.
>
> Benefits for the wider society include practitioners using their skills more fully, improving their practice and developing professionally often at little financial cost. (*Source*: Sue Munday, Northfleet Nursery School.)

This nursery sees partnership as much wider than the traditional ITE relationship and its approach has enabled it to position itself as a dynamic organisation, more than equal to taking its place alongside universities, ITE providers and schools at discussions around leadership and learning.

Partnerships can be formalised through contracts, memos of understanding and tighter relationships such as federations and alliances. These are often between schools or between universities and schools and are linked to ITE although not exclusively. This variance in partnerships might be seen as unhelpful in a policy context where external pressures appear to be combining to reduce the range and diversity of organisations involved (Greaney and Brown, 2015). Conversely, the individuality of some partnerships allows them to be dynamic and flexible, which may enable them to respond better to the challenges of future developments.

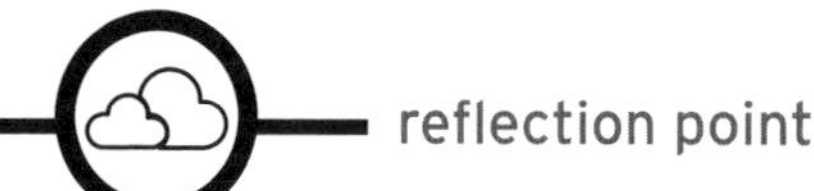

How are you working in partnership currently? What would or could improve the partnership to make it more successful from your perspective (as a student/mentor/school/parent or provider)?

FUTURE DEVELOPMENTS IN PARTNERSHIP

Education is always changing, as celebrity chef Jamie Oliver noted when he ruefully commented that he had met with three education secretaries within an 18-month period during his crusade to improve school dinners (2005). In particular, since the Prime Minister at the time, Tony Blair, famously stated in 1997 that the three priorities for his government were 'Education, education, education' there has been almost constant change and it seems unlikely that, regardless of government, the desire for change will cease. So where does that leave partnership? This section considers the possible future developments for partnership under three Ps – practice, policy and potential: first, the perspective from practice in schools and those involved in partnership to reflect on current partnership and what the next steps might be; second, the policy perspective, and in particular the Carter Review (2015) which makes suggestions for ITE with implications for partnership; and, finally, we consider the potential that partnership may provide for future problem solving.

Web Link

Tony Blair's speech in full can be accessed through this web link: http://www.britishpoliticalspeech.org/speech-archive.htm?speech=202

Practice

There have been an abundance of innovations in partnership working between schools and ITE providers recently and many have been locally set up and initiated in response to local situations such as Teaching School designations, School-Centred Initial Teacher Training (SCITTs) and School Direct. Those involved evaluate their local arrangements and make changes in the light of these. However, such is their newness and localness that there remains a gap in the overall knowledge of the most effective approaches. The National College does collect and collate examples of partnership working and case studies on its website and commissions research and reports. However, many schools engage in partnership without contributing their experiences to the national agenda, citing time and conflicting priorities as barriers to writing up their ways of working or the very local nature of their work which potentially precludes others from replicating it. For example, one large HEI in an urban area is involved as a strategic partner with a very large number of schools, but in ITE recognises a much smaller number of partnerships through its hub working approach. Each hub has a unique culture created by the schools involved and recognising the local issues and nature of the hub. Each hub started from its strengths and own agenda – for some, this might mean a maths focus and a desire to recruit locally, whilst for others it is the challenges of the catchment area and retention or staff development.

Web Link

Find out more about how to use research and development to support school improvement in your teaching by accessing this web link, available on the companion website: www.gov.uk/the-national-research-and-development-network

The programmes they offer students are varied but all based on what the schools consider to be the important aspects of ITE and additional to the ITE provider programme. Anecdotal feedback from schools and students suggests that these are highly successful and the notion of mutual benefits is being fulfilled. Schools are recruiting these students to be NQTs, knowing that they have some insight into the local issues for that school and some preparation for working in that culture and environment. The students are pleased to have a job in a school that they know a little about, with staff that are supportive. But with each hub operating differently and the evidence anecdotal, there are challenges for all the partners in taking what has been a developmental process so far and continuing to build the partnerships strategically so that a staff change does not undermine the whole arrangement. Student feedback is challenging, and the annual NQT survey carried out in early spring by the National College for Teaching and Leadership (NCTL) reports on the whole ITE sector. The level of response is low (20% in 2014) and there are various reasons proposed for this. Successful students are busy being successful NQTs and are unlikely to respond, whilst less successful students have more time and a possible agenda to vent so are potentially over-represented in the survey. Students might be reluctant to give feedback on their placement as they might want a job in the future and wrongly think that their feedback will affect their career. The difficulties for a national survey, supported by national organisations, in obtaining accurate data is indicative of the challenges facing smaller partnerships in accurately evaluating and reviewing their work. Linked to this are the possible challenges for staff working in partnership – where do their priorities and loyalties lie? As a class teacher, the whole focus is on the children in the class and ensuring their progress. For an ITE tutor, the focus is on the student. Where staff work across both roles, as boundary spanners or hub tutors, there is the possibility of a conflict of interests. For example, one teaching school focuses on students' development to fill places in its alliance of schools. This works very well for them as a recruitment tool but is not so helpful for students who do not want to work in the alliance post-qualification. So the mutual interest that initiated the partnership can be compromised and in practice there are challenges for ensuring that these are reviewed and evaluated so that joint interest can be maintained and updated in the light of changes.

Policy

Many of the changes that affect partnership are policy driven. The introduction of teaching schools (TS) (DfE, 2010) required schools applying for TS status to have strategic partners. The application process led to some hasty partnerships forming to fulfil the criteria. The evaluation of partnerships for both teaching schools and others has led to some breaking up and to realignment between partners (Kennedy, 2015; L'Anson and Eady, 2015). Although these relationships are challenging, they illustrate Greaney and Brown's advice for partners to avoid inertia and to renegotiate the terms of partnership if necessary (2015: 35). As we write, the future for teaching schools seems slightly uncertain and will rely on further funding. And the longer-term sustainability for some is clearly a challenge. Such developments have implications for ITE partnerships, with schools asking for additional funding to host students on placement and to offer professional studies sessions. Joint problem solving with bartering of services is one solution adopted by some. Some HEIs have become more involved in partnership with ITE through university training schools or similar. Another solution is consideration of School-Centred Initial Teacher Training (SCITT) working which removes the HEI participation. The uncertainty over numbers for some HEIs is too much and with the latest policy of removing the allocation for ITE, some HEIs have decided not to offer ITE provision. So, from a policy perspective, there seem to be two possible future developments, either to withdraw as a HEI or school totally from ITE partnerships or to go it alone As a school, this might mean setting up a SCITT and possibly a teaching school alliance (TSA) in the future. As a HEI, this might mean investing further in partnership through joint bids that marry practice with theory more closely and provide opportunities through a closer partnership model.

The Carter Review (2015) adds another dimension to partnership working in the future. The report was published prior to the general election and its findings were put on hold. They include:

> Recommendation 10: Wherever possible, all ITT partnerships should build in structured and assessed placements for trainees in special schools and mainstream schools with specialist resourced provision.
>
> Recommendation 11: ITT partnerships should ensure all trainees experience effective mentoring by:
>
> i. selecting and recruiting mentors who are excellent teachers, who are able to explain outstanding practice (as well as demonstrate it)
> ii. providing rigorous training for mentors that goes beyond briefing about the structure and nature of the course, and focuses on how teachers learn and the skills of effective mentoring
> iii. considering whether they are resourcing mentoring appropriately - the resource allocated to mentoring should reflect the importance of the role.
>
> Recommendation 12: DfE should commission a sector body, for example the Teaching Schools Council, to develop some national standards for mentors.
>
> Recommendation 13: All schools should, wherever practically possible, seek out and participate in robust local partnership arrangements. In a school-led system, this recommendation is naturally the responsibility of schools. (Carter Review, 2015: 68-9)

These recommendations appear to place a strong emphasis on partnership working but do not address some of the challenges, such as the tensions between the voluntary nature of hosting placements and the mentoring responsibilities. If these recommendations are adopted, then the future developments for partnership will include working together to manage these developments.

How this is done leads to the third possible future development, that of potential.

Potential

The potential for problem solving in partnership is one of its key strengths. It is identified by the Carter Review (2015) but also in recent research into partnerships. One of the ways forward and one which offers this potential is the notion of a 'third space' which Routledge (1996) explains as:

> This third space involves a simultaneous coming and going in a borderland zone between different modes of action. A prerequisite for this is that we must believe that we can inhabit these different sites, making each a space of relative comfort. To do so will require inventing creative ways to cross perceived and real 'borders'. (p. 406)

Greaney and Brown (2015: 4–5) identify it as one of four factors emerging from recent research into partnership:

- Be clear on what you need and what you can offer.
- Empower leaders to create a 'third space'.
- Accept that effective partnership will take time to develop, but avoid inertia.
- Focus on impact, but be prepared for unexpected outcomes.

The first point resonates clearly with the original notion in this chapter of mutual benefits and joint interests. Understanding the concept of a 'third space' is more complex. One way is to consider the 'boundary spanners' described earlier in this chapter. They appear to inhabit the spaces that Routledge identifies and, when successful, seem comfortable in both. This success suggests that the freeing up of preserved positions, whether as a student, an ITE provider or a school, is important in being able to move beyond potentially entrenched positions and into a space that allows for engagement with ideas and possible solutions. It seems that if there is sufficient will, usually generated through a strong mutual interest in maintaining and developing partnership, then the concept of a 'third space' potentially offers the most promise in terms of opportunities for the future of partnerships. However, experience from Australia (Kruger et al., 2009) suggests that active contributions by schools and governments are required to ensure success – a challenge for us all.

As a student teacher, try to identify what you might need from and what you can offer a partnership.

Can you view partnership from another perspective and create a 'third space' to creatively problem-solve the issues affecting your partnership working?

SUMMARY

Partnership is central to successful working in education but interpreted and experienced in a variety of ways. It is important for all those working in education to recognise and work within agreed structures and to understand the advantages and tensions of partnerships from different perspectives. It seems that principles underpinning successful partnerships can be identified as:

- agreed mutual benefits
- professional trust between partners
- ongoing discussion and renegotiation of the relationship over time
- a willingness to problem-solve.

When partnership is based on joint interests, then there is more imperative to work in creative ways, potentially using a 'third space' to negotiate solutions. The potential problem solving and creativity offered by the 'third space' and the combination of determined partners to move forward together is a powerful tool for change. Despite demands on time and practical barriers, the majority of schools, settings and students express a willingness to engage in and express enthusiasm for educational partnership beyond the sum of its parts. Looking to the future, successful partnership can be a positive and highly productive way to work in primary and early years.

To access additional online resources please visit: **https://study.sagepub.com/wyseandrogers**

Here you will find a classroom activity, author podcasts including Amanda Ince's and Josh Franks' top tips for employability, free access to SAGE journal articles and links to external sources.

Greaney, T. and Brown, C. (2015) *Partnerships between Teaching Schools and Universities: Research Report*. London: London Centre for Leadership in Learning, UCL Institute of Education, pp. 1-40. This report focuses on partnerships between teaching schools and universities. It provides four recommendations for successful partnerships in a self-improving system.

Robinson, C., Dingle, B. and Howard, C. (2013) *Primary School Placements: A Critical Guide to Outstanding Teaching*. Northwich: Critical Publishing. This text will be particularly helpful for ITE students, guiding them through school placements with a range of scenarios from different perspectives alongside clear advice and guidance.

Sorenson, P. (2012) Mentoring and Coaching for School Teachers' Initial Teacher Education and Induction. In S. J. Fletcher and C. A. Mullen (eds) *The Sage Handbook of Mentoring and Coaching in Education*. London: Sage, pp. 201-14. Whilst the chapter is about mentoring and coaching within ITE, it provides a useful political, policy and practical context for discussing mentoring partnerships.

The following website shows how one university has developed partnership across research and development, professional learning and ITE through a more formalised partner award scheme. It includes research bids, case studies and opportunities: www.ioe.ac.uk/about/71489.html

REFERENCES

Bourn, D. and Cara, O. (2013) *School Linking: Where Next? Partnership Models between Schools in Europe and Africa*. London: Development Education Research Centre.

Carter, A. (2015) *Carter Review of Initial Teacher Training*. London: DfE.

Clifford, M. and Millar, S. B. (2007) K-20 Partnerships: Literature Review and Recommendations for Research. Report of the NSF-funded SCALE Partnership. Madison, WI: University of Wisconsin-Madison.

Department for Education (DfE) (2010) *The Importance of Teaching: The Schools' White Paper 2010*. London: DfE.

Greaney, T. and Brown, C. (2015) *Partnerships between Universities and Teaching Schools: Research Report*. London: UCL IOE, p. 34.

Greaney, T., Gu, Q., Handscomb, G. and Varley, M. (2014) *School–University Partnerships: Fulfilling the Potential – Summary Report*. Swindon and Bristol: Research Councils UK and National Co-ordinating Centre for Public Engagement.

Harlow, A., Cooper, B. and Cowie, B. (2013) *Collaborative University and School Partnership Project*, February. Hamilton, New Zealand: Centre for Teacher Education, Faculty of Education, University of Waikato.

Husbands, C. (2012) School–University Partnerships in Teacher Education: Effective Practices and Relationships. 1st June 2012. An Ontario Institute for Studies in Education presentation.

Kennedy, A. (2015) University Teacher Education as a Site of Contestation: School–University Partnerships and Competing Policy Realms. University of Strathclyde EERA/ECER conference paper, Budapest, 9 September.

Kruger, T., Davies, A., Eckersley, B., Newell, F. and Cherednichenko, B. (2009) *Effective and Sustainable University–School Partnerships: Beyond Determined Efforts by Inspired Individuals*. Victoria: Australian Institute for Teaching and School Leadership.

L'Anson, J. and Eady, S. (2015) Partnership: a Wolf in Sheep's Clothing? University of Stirling EERA/ECER conference paper, Budapest, 9 September.

Many, J., Fisher, T. R., Ogletree, S. and Taylor, D. (2012) Crisscrossing the University and Public School Contexts as Professional Development School Boundary Spanners. *Issues in Teacher Education*, 21, 2: 83–102.

Menter, M., Hulme, M., Elliot, D. and Lewin, J. (2010) *Literature Review on Teacher Education in the 21st Century*. Edinburgh: Scottish Government.

Morgan-Fleming, B., Simpson, D., Curtis, K. and Hull, W. (2010) Learning through Partnership: Four Narratives. *Teacher Education Quarterly*, Summer: 63–79.

Rosenberg, M.S., Brownell, M., McCray, E.D., deBettencourt, L.U., Leko, M. and Long, S. (2009). Development and Sustainability of School–University Partnerships in Special Education Teacher Preparation: a Critical Review of the Literature (NCIPP Doc. No. RS-3). Gainesville, FL: National Center to Inform Policy and Practice in Special Education Professional Development.

Routledge, P. (1996) The Third Space as Critical Engagement. *Antipode*, 28, 4: 399–419.

Tony Blair speech (1997) "Education, education, education". Available at: http://www.britishpoliticalspeech.org/speech-archive.htm?speech=202

Websters (1996) *The New International Websters Comprehensive Dictionary of English Language*. Cape Town: Trident Press.

12

REFLECTIVE PRACTICE

Vivienne Marie Baumfield and Raymond Kutscher Viola

LEARNING AIMS

This chapter will enable you to:

- evaluate different perspectives on the role of reflective practice in professional learning and the opportunities and challenges it presents
- be aware of examples of teachers reflecting on their practice in early years and primary school settings
- have access to practical strategies to support engagement *in* and *with* educational research through inquiry into practice.

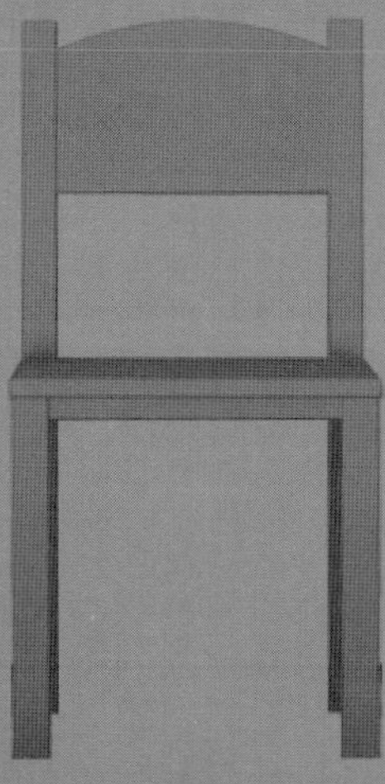

WHAT IS REFLECTIVE PRACTICE?

Teachers need to develop a depth and breadth of knowledge which is embedded in practice as they become expert professionals. The tacit nature of this knowledge means that teachers often know more than they can say, and so sharing it with others can be difficult and can lead to practice-based knowledge and classroom routines not being questioned. Reflective practice aims to develop ways of developing and sharing professional knowledge by looking carefully at what teachers do and how they learn from what they do. It describes a process of bringing what is normally in the background of teachers' thinking to the foreground so that it is accessible both to them and to others. Teachers who make their reflective thinking about their practice visible in this way are able to convert what is otherwise assumed into intelligent action in the classroom because they are aware of what they do and why they are doing it. It is an approach enabling cumulative insight into practice, 'which makes the difference between twenty years of experience and one year of experience twenty times' (Bolton, 2005: 3).

An example of effective reflective practice

A teacher working in a school-university partnership in the North East of England focusing on the infusion of thinking skills into the curriculum, describes the impact of reflection on his practice:

> *I learned more from watching the video of one lesson than I did from 25 years in the classroom.*

With the permission of parents and carers, he had set up a camera in a corner of the classroom and simply let it run. The pupils soon forgot it was there and he used the recordings to look for any changes in patterns of interaction in the classroom. At first, he found the experience of watching himself teaching so embarrassing that he could only watch the video on his own at home, but gradually his interest in understanding what was happening led him to share the videos with colleagues and eventually to showing clips in presentations to staff on teacher development days to get their views on what was happening.

The insight into how the children were responding provided powerful feedback as the teacher and his colleagues noticed changes in who was participating most actively. What was really surprising was that it wasn't the children who normally joined in but the quieter ones or the ones who were usually difficult to engage in learning at all. Another noticeable change was the shift from the teacher dominating the classroom talk to the children taking the lead. Interest in learning about what was happening in the classroom was kindled and everyone wanted to know more.

(You can read about this and similar activities in Baumfield et al., 2013.)

The term 'reflective practice' is associated with Donald Schön who published two influential books on how professionals think in action in the 1980s. He criticized the dominant 'technical-rationalist' view, according to which professional practice was an instrumental process requiring the application of theory in predictable, clearly defined circumstances. He argued that approaches to professional learning based on this view were inadequate to the task of understanding how practitioners make use of intuitive, tacit knowledge to develop their practice (Schön, 1987). Although Schön had studied the work of architects, psychotherapists, engineers, planners and managers rather than teachers, the concept of reflective practice seemed to co-incide with common-sense ideas about how teachers think about classroom situations and so became popular in teacher education. Popularity brought its own problems as people began to use the term loosely, making it hard to pin down exactly what reflective practice meant and, more importantly, how its contribution to our understanding of teachers' learning could be evaluated. Schön admitted that he caused some of this confusion himself by being inconsistent in his use of the term in his early writings, but the importance he gave to an embodied way of understanding professional practice is beyond doubt.

Emphasizing the role of reflection in practice acknowledges the importance of the knowledge teachers have and their ability to make decisions about their work to meet the needs of learners, rather than simply follow the prescriptions of others (Pedro, 2005). It problematizes the idea of best practice as something that can be simply passed on by copying, which 'has become part of international educational common sense' (Lefstein and Snell, 2014: 4) by recognizing that what a teacher does in the classroom is complex and 'prey to ambiguity' (Forde et al., 2006). Practice presents dilemmas requiring sensitive interpretation, and thinking reflectively involves considering multiple perspectives in a process of continuous change and flux. Deciding what to do is not a matter of being told that if 'x' happens do 'y', but requires the exercise of professional judgement. Focusing on how teachers reflect on their practice offers the opportunity to develop a sense of purpose and a stronger professional identity, as closely observed small events, instances in practice, can generate an understanding of wider educational issues. Reflecting on practice extends the range and depth of professional knowledge by enabling connections to be made between the experience of the individual teacher, colleagues in schools and the wider community including educational researchers (Sparrow et al., 2005).

The literature on reflective practice ranges from what can be described as minimalist to maximalist representations according to the extent of the change to the teacher and her teaching that is envisaged. Minimalist representations of reflective practice focus on changes within an individual teacher's sphere of influence, whilst maximalist representations call for a reconfiguration of the whole education system by teachers who, as members of an activist profession (Sachs, 2003), question and challenge every aspect of their experience. Arguments in support of reflective practice highlight the importance of the ability to exercise judgement as integral to any claims that teaching is a profession:

> The consequences for the well-being of the clients of how well things are done are very much more serious in a profession than in most other occupations. Also, in the professions there is a great deal of choice about how to achieve the clearly stated ends. (Tripp, 1993: 130)

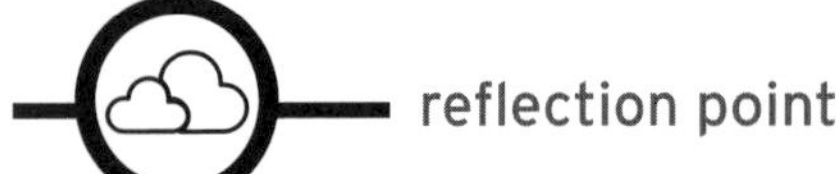

Identify some of the key features of reflection on practice and discuss some examples of these in the context of classroom teaching.

Whilst reflection may be a necessary part of the professional development of teachers, it may not be sufficient (Day, 1993, 2000). The focus and quality of reflection is important as 'flawed reflections, of whatever kind, can inhibit good practice' (McLaughlin, 1999: 18). When teachers are required to demonstrate reflective practice, as is the case on some Initial Teacher Education courses, the accounts are often lacking in the depth of analysis required to demonstrate an impact on learning (Admiraal and Wubbels, 2005). It is difficult in any case to make a direct connection between reflection and any changes in the classroom; too much confidence can be placed in 'the power of language' (Atkinson, 2004), in teachers' descriptions of changes in their thinking. However, given the right opportunities and support, teachers' accounts of reflective thinking can become more analytical, and crucial to this is paying more attention to the context of their practice. It is important to have an understanding of teaching that considers what teachers do and feel as well as what they think. Belonging to a community that encourages inquiry is also important as we know from research into learning in the workplace that the social practices of occupations shape how knowledge is created and shared (Lave and Wenger, 1991).

Teaching is a complex activity requiring an intensity of attention to what is happening as it happens, what Van Maanen (1995) calls 'engaged immediacy', which is exhausting for even the most accomplished teacher; this leads some people to question the feasibility of exercising reflective practice in the classroom. Schön's work has been criticized as although it may describe how practitioners react to situations after the event (reflection *on* action), it has less to say about how practitioners can be proactive in shaping events at the time (reflection *in* action). Whatever the differences, everyone agrees that teaching can never be a completely thoughtless activity and we can, at least for now, put the question of definitions of reflective practice to one side. In the next section, we look at what *kind* of thinking happens in the 'thick of the action' in practice, how it is beneficial and how it can be supported.

REFLECTIVE PRACTICE IN EARLY YEARS AND PRIMARY SCHOOL SETTINGS

> Reflective Practice is only effectively undertaken and understood by becoming immersed in *doing* it rather than reading about it or following instructions. (Bolton, 2005: xv, our emphasis)

What does 'doing' reflective practice look like in early years and primary school settings? The first thing to note is that, as is often the case in education, there may not be anything particularly 'new' about some of the salient features of what practitioners need to do to be reflective about their practice. Building a cumulative and shared body of professional knowledge in teaching is challenging and too often the effects of a kind of 'academic amnesia' mean that we forget what has already been done. The absence of a sense of the history of education obscures how the profession of teaching has developed, how ideas have changed and different theories waxed and waned. We need more detailed narratives of practice to provide this perspective (Alheit, 2009); for example, 'child study' played an important role in the professional formation of early years and primary teachers. One of the earliest champions of child study was the American educationalist G. Stanley Hall who in the 1890s promoted the close observation of interactions with children by teachers in order to understand how their minds were developing and tailor their education accordingly. According to Hall, it was the task of the teacher to have knowledge in two domains: the subject matter to be taught and the nature and capacity of the child. He hoped that child study would prevent 'the mutilation which so powerful an engine as the modern school may inflict upon the tender souls and bodies of our children, and thus upon our entire national future' (Hall, 1891: 121).

Reference here to the task of the teacher as a mediator charged with tailoring experience to meet the needs of the child, resonates with the idea of the teacher building a bridge between the child and the curriculum proposed by the educational philosopher John Dewey at the beginning of the 20th century (Dewey, 1990/1902) and more recent studies of the nature of teacher knowledge (Bereiter, 2002). Child study serves as a reminder that from the beginning of the formal education of teachers there have been approaches to their professional learning that consider how to make sense of experiences in the classroom and construct knowledge that supports the holistic learning of the child – the essential task of the teacher. This argument for improving practice by teachers observing closely what is happening in the classroom and articulating their reflective thinking is expressed in the guidance for the Early Years Foundation Stage (EYFS) in England (DfES, 2003) and in the Early Years Professional Status Standards (Teaching Agency, 2012).

putting it into practice

Tools and examples of your own reflective practice

You will be watching what children do in your classroom all the time and also gathering and recording information about what they do as an integral part of your work. It need only be a small step to finding manageable ways of using this activity to focus an inquiry and then share this with a colleague. The Carnegie Foundation in the USA has an archive of tools and examples on its website (http://specctoolkit.carnegiefoundation.org/category/faculty-inquiry-groups-fig/). In the UK, the Centre for the Use of Research and Evidence in Education (www.curee.co.uk) and the National Foundation for Educational Research (www.nfer.ac.uk) both have ideas, resources and examples you can try out.

Given the opportunity, teachers talk to each other about their experiences in the classroom and most of us can, and do, regale colleagues, family and friends with anecdotes about particularly colourful classroom encounters. The importance of narrative in professional learning has been demonstrated in the work of Clandinin and Connelly (1996) in the USA and Goodson (1995) in the UK. Teachers' stories are a rich source for understanding how they make sense of their experiences and sharing stories is an opportunity for professional learning bound up in the daily work of the classroom.

Embedding opportunities for professional learning: Stories from Australia

The Deputy Head (Learning and Teaching) of a primary school in Sydney, Australia, was looking for a way of effectively embedding opportunities for professional learning within the day-to-day work of the staff in the school. Attempts to provide staff workshops failed because they were scheduled on top of an already busy day and often the teachers did not see the topics as having any immediate relevance. The lack of enthusiasm evident in the responses of the staff to the formal continuing professional development programme was in sharp contrast to the enthusiasm with which teachers would talk about their teaching in the staffroom over coffee or during the lunch break. It was not that they weren't interested in learning how to improve their practice but they were doing this informally by 'talking shop' in conversation with each other. It was decided to harness this interest and direct it towards more structured opportunities to reflect on their practice by building on work on using narrative for professional learning. Using a combination of one-to-one and small group interviews, questions of how and what the teachers were learning in their day-to-day work were explored in conversations that emulated, as far as possible, the informal narrative style of 'shop talk'. The conversations were recorded and transcribed and formed the basis for further discussions as themes and metaphors of learning were agreed amongst the participants. The features of 'how' and 'what' teachers in the school were learning were shared more widely and became the trigger for more conversations and the development of a programme for extending and developing the ideas. Stories proved so powerful because they captured the details of a job located in situations that are 'suffused with specificity'. At the same time, access to the stories and to the themes running through the individual accounts created a culture of collaborative, dialogic inquiry and an appetite to seek an understanding of sources beyond their own classroom and the school. The school also recognized the importance of creating and supporting opportunities and spaces for the spontaneous story telling and 'shop-talk' to continue as a vital part of the professional lives of the staff. (A fuller account has been published in Ambler, 2015.)

Team work is integral to working in early years and primary settings and this is why the opportunity to reflect on practice in collaborative teams is such an important part of teachers' professionalism. The strength of teachers articulating their thinking is the potential for the insights into learning in the classroom to be shared not only with colleagues but also with parents and carers. In this way, a democratic professionalism could develop with 'a similar and broad knowledge base, participatory relationships between all staff and parents, quality interactions with children and effective leadership' (Colwell et al., 2015: 66).

Documenting and sharing what we know

Sixteen teachers in a professional network of six kindergartens in Wellington, New Zealand used an approach known as 'pedagogical documentation' to spend more time considering the purpose and values underpinning their work in early childhood education centres. Pedagogical documentation is a technique developed in Sweden that has close links with the practice of teachers at Reggio Emilia in Italy. The documentation is material recording what the children are saying and doing, their work and how the teacher is relating to the children and to their work. It can take different forms, including video, audio recordings, written notes and children's work. In essence, it is anything that makes the pedagogical work concrete and accessible so that it can be used to reflect on the learning and teaching interactions and transactions. The process is for the teacher to first study the documentation alone and then with others, including the children themselves, their parents and the wider community. In this way, interest is widened to take in perspectives and contributions from outside of the immediate context. The teachers in the network were volunteers and were attracted to join by the opportunity to both improve their own practice and make a contribution to broader policy discussion about provision for the education of young children. The senior management of the kindergartens made a commitment to support the project for 12 months and each kindergarten team chose the focus and types of pedagogical documentation. Belonging to the network also gave the participants the chance to collaborate with a researcher from a local university who was attached to the project. The teachers found the discussion of the pedagogical documentation helped them to 'step out of their shoes' and see things from another point of view. Sometimes the new way of looking at something was a bit of a shock and one teacher speaks of experiencing a 'shake-up' in ideas, but the balancing of autonomy with assistance provided by the collaboration supported change and opened up the kindergarten as a democratic learning community. Three factors were identified as crucial to the success of the network as an 'intellectual space' in which to foster professional growth: combining 'bottom-up' enthusiasm from participants with 'top-down' support for meetings held within the normal working day; the use of pedagogical documentation as a tool for inquiry; and access to external support from the university (Mitchell, 2003).

Practitioners who are confident in their own professional knowledge are more able to respond to educational change and external requirements, such as the Early Years Foundation Stage Profile (DfE, 2014), by deploying four types of mediation:

> *Protective mediation* calls for strategies to defend existing practices which are greatly valued. (This would involve identifying priorities and allocating limited resources appropriately – to protect time for staff to meet together and share experiences, for example.)

(Continued)

(Continued)

> *Innovative mediation* is concerned with practitioners finding strategies to work within the spaces and boundaries provided by new requirements. (By identifying the potential for new requirements to have a dual purpose - record keeping could be adapted to provide opportunities for reflection on practice, for example.)
>
> *Collaborative innovation* refers to practitioners working closely together to provide mutual support in satisfying and adapting new requirements. (Changes to ways of working can be used creatively to encourage working together as it is harder to bring about change when individuals are 'set in their ways'.)
>
> *Conspiratorial innovation* is about adopting more subversive strategies where practitioners resist implementing those aspects of external requirements they believe to be particularly inappropriate.
>
> (Osborne et al., 2000, cited in Colwell et al., 2015: 76)

reflection point

Do you think it is appropriate for practitioners to use their professional knowledge to subvert externally imposed requirements? Can you think of an example of when this might happen?

INQUIRY INTO PRACTICE: ENGAGING *IN* AND *WITH* EDUCATIONAL RESEARCH

What might 'doing' reflective practice actually mean? For Dewey, reflective thinking 'impels to inquiry' through the search for knowledge beyond immediate, individual experience (Dewey, 1997/1910: 7). One of the ten principles for effective teaching and learning identified recently in the summary of the Teaching and Learning Research Programme (TLRP, the largest ever education research project in the UK) also promotes this idea of a journey from reflection to inquiry:

> *TLRP Principle 9: Effective teaching and learning depends on teacher learning* - the need for teachers to learn continuously in order to develop their knowledge and skills, and adapt and develop their roles, especially through classroom inquiry should be recognized and supported. (see www.tlrp.org)

Teachers are problem solvers and faced with puzzling situations in the classroom they look for solutions. A willingness to test ideas by collaborating with other people in a community of inquiry and develop an understanding of what can be done is indicative of a professional attitude and the precursor of intelligent action to promote learning in the classroom. Focusing on inquiry links teachers' professional learning directly to their work with learners in the classroom, creating the expectation that reflection triggers interest and stimulates questions to be answered together through dialogue and research.

putting it into practice

Using lesson study to improve teaching practice

'Lesson study' is an increasingly popular way of linking careful observation and reflection with systematic investigation. Lesson study is similar to quality improvement circles in industry in Japan and takes up the idea that it is the people actually doing the job who can come up with the best ideas about how to do it better. You can focus on a small aspect or issue in your teaching and work with colleagues to trial ways of improving what you do. Resources to support lesson study can be found at http://lessonstudy.co.uk and also at http://tdtrust.org/nten/lesson-study/what-is-ls.

It is this emphasis on dialogue, with other people and with what is already known, that signals the move from reflection to inquiry.

spotlight on practice

A Scottish teacher's journey of discovery

I find most reading schemes unhelpful and, over time, I have developed a personalized reading curriculum framework responsive to learner interests and needs. The framework used metacognitive (thinking about your thinking) strategies to encourage children to work in groups and talk about what they thought and felt about reading. I had found that the chance to talk about the strategies they were using when reading helped them to learn from each other and gave me important clues as to how I could support their learning. I tried to make learning more active and visual by using games, films and role play linked to the books we were reading. I also gave as much choice as possible to the children in the selection of books to read by working with the local library. This was the curriculum that I wanted to investigate by looking at the impact of the strategies on my students and, at the same time, sharing my practice and learning from colleagues.

Scotland's new national curriculum, Curriculum for Excellence (CfE), is explicit in denouncing centralized prescription in favour of promoting teachers' professional capacity to apply guiding principles to design learning experiences that respond to local needs. CfE guidance informs practitioners that literacy development should lead to creative, critical and metacognitive thinking in the classroom and this corresponds to the General Teaching Council Scotland's (GTCS) standards for teachers, which state that systematically responding to learner needs should

(Continued)

(Continued)

instigate professional inquiry. In Scotland, the professional autonomy of teachers and curriculum development to promote learner autonomy go hand in hand. However, that does not mean that teachers won't attempt to adopt central guidance uncritically or ignore the principles when attending to the immediate concerns of classroom teaching. This challenged me to consider how best to share what I was learning with colleagues.

Children's perceptions are important and methods to collect learner feedback should allow them to choose how much and in what way they want to express themselves. Feedback on the experiences of my class was collected using posters of DeBono's Six Thinking Hats (6THs) and Pupil View Templates (PVTs), a cartoon visual of a learning situation with spaces for the children to write what the characters in the cartoon are saying and thinking. The 6THs were used in groups of four as prompts with cumulative responses recorded on the six separate posters and individual feedback was collected using PVTs of distinct stages in a typical learning experience. Both activities gave participants the chance to express themselves in writing or drawing and gather thoughts individually or collaboratively. The feedback was also used to identify any differences between individuals and groups, changes over time and evidence of learning.

I gave an introductory presentation on the approach I was trying to develop to my colleagues and asked for volunteers to provide formal and informal feedback. I also asked a critical friend (a member of senior management at a different school) to review the themes I identified as emerging from the feedback of my pupils, their parents and my colleagues. One core feature of active professional learning in the standards for teachers in Scotland is the opportunity for teachers to observe expert teachers, or be observed teaching in their own classroom and obtain feedback. I provided colleagues with a guide for observations with questions on two dimensions of instructional quality: cognitive activation and personal learning support posed as prompts. The specific times for the observations were opportunistic, reflecting the need not to interrupt the flow of teaching and learning, and the learning experiences observed were: summarizing, inference and visualizing.

The power of feedback: listening to the students

For the learners, the two most salient means for supporting their understanding of the texts were acting out scenes and craft-based activities in collaboration with peers:

> *I am going to make a board game just like [M]onopoly*
>
> 'This is going to look good!!!'

Talking to others helped the learners plan, create, decide and remember. Another finding from the PVTs was that many learners recalled experiences where ideas were challenged, causing a sort of positive conflict:

> 'Well they went up the tree they could have fell'
>
> 'Nah it would ruin it'

The learners' feedback demonstrated that interaction helped understanding directly and indirectly:

> 'I like this book because it has good jokes and it says "flipping" a lot!'

It appeared that the more personalized the choices were, the greater the learners enjoyed their experiences of reading, although one learner revealed their feelings of conflict between accepting the majority decision and wanting something more suitable to their (the learner's) tastes:

[Groupmate:] 'I have liked reading Don't Look Now! I liked it because there are not many words'

[Groupmate:] *I love this book because it has loads of pictures.*

[Learner:] 'Uh, yeah ... I ... like this book too. (Under my breath) NOT.'

[Learner:] *I want to get a better and more challenging book but I don't want to spoil my group's fun.*

On the other hand, peers' opinions of the texts appeared to be important to the learners. This learner's new appreciation for Tom Gates was based on a friend's insistence that she try it:

[Responding to friend's suggestion:] *I will hate Tom Gates*

[After reading:] 'It's great'

The learners demonstrated that they were using strategies to engage with the text. It appeared that by providing an enjoyable context for learning, through the use of authentic texts and relevant tasks to support strategy use, the learners were stimulated to learn:

'I have learned to pick books that are right for me.'

One learner indicated plans to buy new books over the summer to read based on developing preferences.

The PVTs also showed that once in pairs they independently planned to keep in line with their partner:

'We are talking about our reading plan and what page we are going to read up to.'

Another learner, who had convinced their partner to read a particular text, still had to maintain their own conviction that it was the right choice; the learner's friend learned to enjoy the book in the end.

There were also indications that attempts to promote engagement and provide structure did not always improve learning outcomes:

'I think strategies are useless.'

Also, not all learners agreed that reading was worthwhile and were conflicted between being motivated to read and just wanting to go out and play all the time:

'[Reading for enjoyment] takes up personal time.'

(Continued)

(Continued)

On the other hand, some of the more confident and experienced readers grew impatient whilst the use of a strategy was modelled and instructions given:

> 'You just need to let us get on with it!'

The power of feedback: listening to my colleagues

Although being introduced to the idea of using any strategy seemed to be beneficial to learners, some were perceived to have more value than others. The teachers thought that they were more able to evaluate comprehension and that the strategies could be transferred to other contexts, beyond reading. Providing resources (both books and supporting materials) for everyone to take part in a shared experience posed a problem. Solutions were found by sourcing material online and editing it to suit local needs. With the right resources, it was believed that learners could access the learning better and in turn demonstrate their understanding more effectively. Evidence of learning was vital in further responding to learners' needs, and quality interaction, both with the teacher and amongst the learners, was seen as an important form of support:

> 'it's always a great thing for us to look at different things.'

All teachers appeared to greatly value sharing practice, primarily through observation and the joint development of resources. They recognized that this may not just improve practice but also ease a teacher's workload, allowing them to build on colleagues' previous work. New approaches and materials that had been discovered were integrated into existing practice, rather than replacing them.

What have I learned from the journey so far?

- Affiliation: making meaningful choices together

Inclusive practices are central to professional expectations, and ensuring that everyone benefits from reading instruction was at the heart of much of the dialogue. All the teachers (myself included) were proactive in developing their daily practice in concrete ways. The approach seemed reasonably successful in facilitating effective, enjoyable reading habits. However, packaging up an instructional programme would surely be doomed to the same fate as many other, better researched approaches. This struck a chord as I was reminded of the scepticism shown near the beginning of this journey, when several colleagues stated their fear that this approach was just another short-term initiative. To be successful, literacy programmes must provide opportunities for quality professional development and making meaningful choices together.

- Agency: doing meaningful things

It is important that the learners themselves value the reading comprehension strategies, enjoying learning them now and being optimistic for their use independently in future. The strategies had a range of utilities, providing deeper access to reading, varied opportunities to talk and write about understanding, transfer to other mediums than the written word and support with summative assessment. Another outcome was the affordance of an objective view of the teachers' practice. Supporting the learners to ask each other questions that they had created prompted one of the teachers to reflect on the detail she thought most important to the learners. It would appear that both learners and teachers want to do meaningful things their own way.

- Autonomy: awareness of self to make informed choices

It is hoped that I helped the learners on their road to becoming a reader. At best, the learners were aware of some metacognitive strategies to employ to understand their reading; at worst they knew what they enjoyed doing in relation to their reading. The flexible boundary of choosing how much to read seemed meaningful to the learners, with many seen each week encouraging (or castigating) their peers so that they were all at the same point in the book before discussion. Ultimately, I wanted the children to fall in love with books and to be able to find appropriate books for themselves, and the strategies provided a language for the learners to demonstrate their enthusiasm for texts. Formal and informal feedback prompted reflection amongst the teachers, making them more aware of their practice; as teachers and learners became more aware of themselves and their choices, they became more autonomous.

Teachers are under pressure to accept the use of pre-packaged reading programmes, in light of accountability measures and high-stakes testing; however, this comes at the expense of teacher autonomy and individualized learning. With the freedom that CfE offers comes the responsibility to design bespoke curricula. Furthermore, for all learners from primary to professional, relationships matter, as do having a say in objectives and getting support with them. Teachers need a sense of affiliation with fellow professionals to build psychological strength, agency in facilitating innovation to develop professional wisdom, and autonomy in deciding what aspects of content knowledge and pedagogy to develop. This is key to professional empowerment.

This account of my journey may be viewed as a type of reconnaissance for future inquiry or as an insightful anecdote into contemporary primary teaching in Scotland. CfE has offered me the chance to design a reading comprehension curriculum that has promoted affiliation, agency and autonomy in my classroom. I have also experienced affiliation, agency and autonomy - through relationships with my students and with my colleagues. Hopefully, a teacher with similar values and an inherent interest in reading comprehension will gain something from reading about it.

SUMMARY

Teaching is an immediate and practical activity and if it is to be educative, the teacher requires the wisdom to make decisions in the best interest of the child in complex and uncertain situations: 'The essence of professionalism in early years practice is being able to make high quality judgements' (Colwell et al., 2015: 58).

Current global trends towards the professionalization of early childhood educators is a welcome development given the tendency, at least in the UK and the USA, to devalue the status of teachers in general and those who work with young children in particular. Research demonstrating a high degree of consensus that higher staff qualifications are correlated with higher quality in early childhood provision (Peeters and Vandenbroeck, 2011) has led to the recognition that we need specialist practitioners with specific knowledge, skills and understanding. Less welcome is the increase in regulation and professional development that, by not taking into account the particular features of the context, could stifle rather than promote good practice (Swim and Isik-Ercan, 2013). Teachers' professional learning has never been more important and never more open to debate and this presents both opportunities and challenges. Reflective practice is a concept that continues to be widely used but not always understood and has become 'more a metaphor for representing a process of learning from experience than a term that might be subject to more detailed analysis (Leitch and Day, 2000: 180). We do, however, know more about the process of learning from experience and reflective thinking remains the key to accessing the embodied knowledge of practitioners. We also know what matters in the process of learning from experience: we need to engage in dialogic inquiry as members of a strong professional community with access to pedagogical tools to facilitate refection on complex classroom interactions. The term 'tool' can excite concerns that we are proposing a technicist approach to 'what works', but as the Spotlights on Practice in this chapter illustrate, these are tools in the sense of being practical strategies that help to make learning visible and open to discussion. Tools should not be part of 'how to' guides for reflective practice but form part of narratives of practice, which both illuminate and problematize their use.

Reflecting on practice requires teachers to look closely at the specifics of their own context, looking inside, but also to follow a trajectory of inquiry that leads outside, to the experiences of others and to what is already known. It also requires us to consider general trends and events 'outside' our classroom and our school, and their impact on our professionalism – how the outside shapes our inner world and identity. Reflective practice is, above all, a dynamic, active process far removed from caricatures of teachers 'navel-gazing' and losing themselves in a spiral of endless introspection.

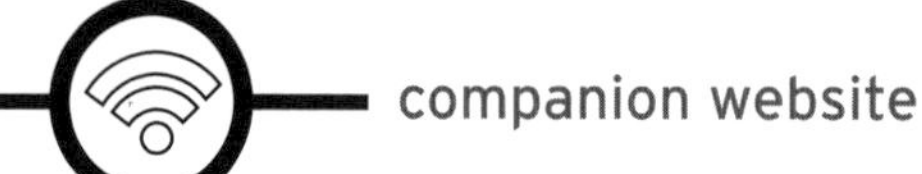

companion website

To access additional online resources please visit: **https://study.sagepub.com/wyseandrogers**

Here you will find a classroom activity, author podcasts including Raymond Kutscher Viola's top tips for employability, free access to SAGE journal articles and links to external sources.

further reading

Baumfield, V.M., Hall, E. and Wall, K. (2013) 'Exploring your own and your colleagues' professional knowledge' (Chapter 6), in *Action Research in Education*, 2nd edition. London: Sage. This book draws on over 15 years of working collaboratively with teachers investigating their practice in the classroom. Each chapter takes a different stage in the process of inquiry and aims to provide a practical guide on how to conduct an inquiry but also tries to explore the processes and relationships to promote a better understanding of what is involved. Chapter 6 offers examples from the experiences of teachers engaging in inquiry as to how the practical knowledge of teachers can be articulated and shared, and suggests some tools for exploring what is happening in your classrooms.

Education Scotland (2014) *Career-long Professional Learning*. Livingston: Education Scotland. (Also available to download from the educationscotland.gov.uk website.) This is guidance supporting teachers' professional learning so that there is maximum benefit to them, children and young people, their colleagues, their individual school and across other schools in the wider learning community. The document also has links to a range of resources available as pdfs.

McLeod, M. (2015) Reflecting on reflection: improving teachers' readiness to facilitate participatory learning with young children. *Professional Development in Education*, 41(2): 254–72. This journal article, in a Special Issue of the journal of *Professional Development of Education*, focuses on early years education and develops an argument about the importance of creative and emotional aspects of professional learning. The author connects the ideas of readiness to learn and openness to experience as important for learners of any age.

http://assessment.tki.org.nz/Assessment-in-the-classroom/Teaching-as-inquiry/Teaching-as-inquiry-practical-tools-for-teachers – this is a very rich, practical guide with freely available templates and tools to support inquiry. Don't be put off by the reference to assessment – it goes much deeper into learning and has excellent links to other innovative work in New Zealand that is relevant to teachers everywhere.

REFERENCES

Admiraal, W. and Wubbels, T. (2005) Multiple voices, multiple realities, what truth? Student teachers learning to reflect in different paradigms. *Teachers and Teaching: Theory and Practice*, 11(3): 315–29.

Alheit, P. (2009) Biographical learning: within the new life-long learning discourse. In K. Illeris (ed.) *Contemporary Theories of Learning: Learning Theorists … in their own Words*. Abingdon: Routledge.

Ambler, T.B. (2015) The day-to-day work of primary school teachers: a source of professional learning. *Professional Development in Education*, 1–14.

Atkinson, D. (2004) Theorising how student teachers form their identities in initial teacher education. *British Educational Research Journal*, 30(3): 379–94.

Baumfield, V.M., Hall, E. and Wall, K. (2013) *Action Research in Education*, 2nd edition. London: Sage.

Bereiter, C. (2002) *Education and Mind in the Knowledge Age*. Mahwah, NJ: Lawrence Erlbaum Associates.

Bolton, G. (2005) *Reflective Practice: Writing and Professional Development*, 2nd edition. London: Sage.

Clandinin, D.J. and Connelly, F.M. (1996) Teachers' professional knowledge landscapes: teacher stories–stories of teachers–school stories–stories of school. *Educational Researcher*, 19(5): 2–14.

Colwell, J. with H. Beaumont, H. Bradford, J. Canavan, E. Cook, D. Kingston, et al. (2015) *Reflective Teaching in Early Education*. London: Bloomsbury

Day, C. (1993) Reflection: a necessary but not sufficient condition for professional development. *British Educational Research Journal*, 19(1): 83–93.

Day, C. (2000) Effective leadership and reflective practice. *Reflective Practice*, 1(1): 113–27.
Dewey, J. (1990) *The Child and the Curriculum*. Chicago: University of Chicago Press. [Originally published in 1902.]
Dewey, J. (1997) *How We Think*. New York: Dover. [Originally published in 1910.]
Department for Education (DfE) (2014) *Early Years Foundation Stage Profile*. London: DfE.
Department of Education and Skills (DfES) (2003) *The Early Years Foundation Stage*. London: DfES.
Forde, C., McMahon, M., McPhee, A.D. and Patrick, F. (2006) *Professional Development, Reflection and Enquiry*. London: Paul Chapman.
Goodson, I. (1995) *Storying the Self: Politics and the Study of the Teacher's Life and Work*. San Francisco, CA: American Educational Research Association.
Hall, G.S. (1891) Editorial. *Pedagogical Seminary*, 1 (June): 121.
Lave, J. and Wenger, E. (1991) *Situated Learning: Legitimate Peripheral Participation*. Cambridge: Cambridge University Press.
Lefstein, A. and Snell, J. (2014) *Better than Best Practice: Developing Teaching and Learning through Dialogue*. London: Routledge.
Leitch, R. and Day, C. (2000). Action research and reflective practice: Towards a holistic view. *Educational Action Research*, 8(1): 179–193.
McLaughlin, T.H. (1999) Beyond the reflective teacher. *Educational Philosophy and Theory*, 31(1): 9–24.
Mitchell, L. (2003) Shifts in thinking through a teachers' network. *Early Years*, 23(1): 21–34.
Pedro, J.Y. (2005) Reflection in teacher education: exploring pre-service teachers' meanings of reflective practice. *Reflective Practice*, 6(1): 49–66.
Peeters, J. and Vandenbroeck, M. (2011). Childcare practitioners and the process of professionalization. In L. Miller and C. Cable (eds), *Professionalization, Leadership and Management in the Early Years* (Vol. 3, pp. 62–76). London: Sage.
Sachs, J. (2003) *The Activist Teaching Profession*. Buckingham: Open University Press.
Schön, D. (1987) *Educating the Reflective Practitioner: Towards a New Design for Teaching and Learning in the Professions*. San Francisco: Jossey-Bass.
Sparrow, J., Ashford, R. and Heel, D. (2005) A methodology to identify work-place features that can facilitate or impede reflective practice. *Reflective Practice*, 6(2): 189–97.
Swim, T.J. and Isik-Ercan, Z. (2013) Dispositional development as a form of continuous professional development: centre-based reflective practices with teachers of (very) young children. *Early Years: an International Research Journal*, 33(2): 172–85.
Teaching Agency (2012) *Early Years Professional Status Standards*. Nottingham: Teaching Agency.
Tripp, D. (1993) *Critical Incidents in Teaching: Developing professional judgement*. London: Routledge.
Van Maanen, M. (1995) On the epistemology of reflective practice. *Teachers and Teaching: Theory and Practice*, 1(1): 33–50.

13
BEHAVIOUR

Sue Roffey, Lucy Jamison and Corinne Davis

LEARNING AIMS

This chapter will:

- help you explore alternative ways of thinking about behaviour in the classroom
- identify ways to promote a positive emotional environment for learning
- outline strategies for teaching classroom behaviour
- show how emotional literacy facilitates effective responses to challenges
- identify unusual behaviours so you know when to ask for further advice
- explore ways of working collaboratively with families
- emphasise the importance of teacher well-being.

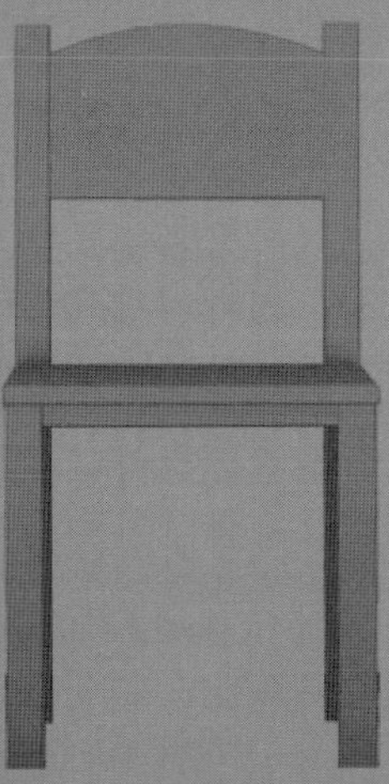

New teachers starting out may have concerns about behavioural issues in the classroom, as these seem to regularly hit the headlines. The reality, however, is reassuring. The latest figures indicate that 92.3% of all schools in England were judged good or outstanding for standards of behaviour and only 0.3% were considered to be inadequate. Much of the literature suggests that low-level disruption is of most concern to teachers and more extreme behaviour comparatively rare. Incidents of verbal and physical abuse do occur but are more usually directed at other pupils rather than teachers (DfE, 2013).

Any unwanted behaviour, however, can undermine both teacher effectiveness and well-being. It is worth knowing how to promote a positive classroom environment, as well as dealing effectively with challenges when they occur. How you position your pupils, the relationships you build, how well you look after yourself and maintain your professional integrity all make a difference, as do school culture and expectations. Although there is no single solution or quick fix, small daily changes make big differences over time. Choosing what works sometimes means reflecting on long-held beliefs.

reflection points

'The purpose of education is to enable every child to become the best they can be.'

'Your role as a teacher is to create a positive and flexible learning environment in which every child, regardless of ability or background, can make optimal progress.'

Make a few notes on these statements and then discuss them with a colleague.

This chapter is built on both evidence-based practice and practice-based evidence. In order to best meet the needs of all pupils, we need to identify factors that promote resilience and strategies that make a positive difference for children who challenge.

TEACHERS MATTER

A significant protective factor is having someone believe in you – someone who lets you know you are worthwhile (Werner, 2004). Families usually provide this security, but for some individuals it can be a teacher. Biographies are full of anecdotes about teachers who were inspirational and/or encouraging, enabling someone to have a future that may otherwise have been out of reach. Teachers these days are judged on academic outcomes but rarely on the difference they make to someone's life:

> Mrs Harvey, my 6th grade teacher, made every student feel like the most important person in the room ... (she) nurtured the human spirit, and she made me want to achieve more than my circumstances would predict at the time.
>
> It takes a very special person to be a teacher. (NSW Federation, 2014)

Web Link

You can watch the NSW Federation's new campaign 'The Graduate' on YouTube, accessible through this web link and available on the companion website: www.youtube.com/watch?v=OdreCYJMyUU

reflection point

Talk to a partner about a teacher you remember, someone you admired and who made you feel good about being in school. What did they do and say?

POSITIONING CHILDREN WHO CHALLENGE

There are various ways to think about pupils who are hard to manage. Some educators believe unwanted behaviour is deliberate and children should know better. Feelings of anger and frustration follow. Even though they may have differing genetic predispositions such as sensitivity, cheerfulness or energy levels, no child is just 'born bad'. They have either learnt to behave that way, are responding to experiences or have difficulties beyond their control. Caring teachers may position a child as 'sad' and their behaviour an outcome of negative life events. Although more compassionate, this can lead to helplessness, blame and resentment towards families. Labelling children with psychiatric 'disorders' may secure funding but positions a child as 'abnormal', suggesting there is something innately wrong with them that requires 'treatment'. The critical focus on the environment then diminishes (Johnstone, 2013).

A more useful way of thinking focuses on what the teacher can do. If a child has a hearing impairment, you would take this into account. A child struggling with social and emotional issues also needs an adapted and supportive environment to access learning.

spotlight on practice

Case study of a child struggling with social and emotional issues

Jack is 10. He regularly comes to school late and often looks tired and crumpled. He is easily distracted and rarely finishes his work. When he does manage to get homework done, this is also scrappy. His teacher gets irritated because she sees Jack has ability that is just not being

(Continued)

(Continued)

reflected in his attainments. She tells Jack that he really needs to pull his socks up and take more responsibility. Last time this happened, Jack told her to 'f... off' and was given detention. He didn't turn up and got into more trouble.

Jack's parents never come to parents' evenings and letters home are unanswered.

Jack is an only child in a single-parent family. His mother has multiple sclerosis and is also depressed. Before he comes to school, Jack has dressed his mum, taken her some breakfast and sorted out her medication for the day. On his way home, he does the shopping. Usually he makes dinner for them both and often needs to do a wash - his mum is not very reliable going to the toilet. Jack has been doing this for a couple of years and is constantly worried his mum might take another overdose.

reflection point

Nearly a quarter of a million children in the UK are carers for a relative with a physical and/or mental disability; 23,000 are under 9 years old (Children's Society, 2013).

Discuss with a colleague actions you might take to support Jack at school.

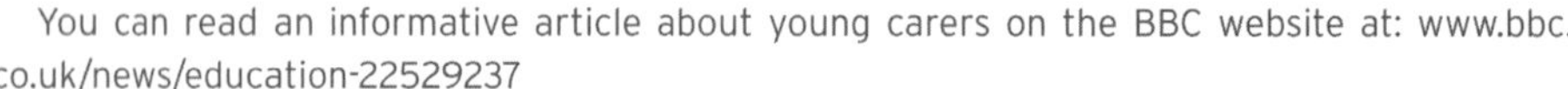

You can read an informative article about young carers on the BBC website at: www.bbc.co.uk/news/education-22529237

N.B. From April 2015, young carers are entitled to an assessment of their needs by the local authority. This includes consideration of the impact of their caring role on their educational opportunities and emotional well-being.

WHAT CHILDREN BRING WITH THEM TO SCHOOL

Most pupils are keen to learn. It is the unsettled, the distressed and the non-compliant that we are concerned with here. Many children whose behaviour is hard to manage have experienced stressors in their young lives, sometimes including challenging relationships within the family. When children struggle with adversity, they often have difficulty with concentration, cooperation and friendships; they don't feel good about themselves or others. This potentially sets up a negative spiral. Early teacher intervention can make all the difference, not only to their behaviour and overall well-being but also to their learning. There is little you can do about what has happened in the past or a child's family circumstances, so use your precious energy on things you can change or influence. The following gives some ideas to build on. Most are not about doing extra but doing differently. Children may have come to see themselves as a nuisance, a failure – or a superstar, depending on the conversations around them. You can do much to promote a positive and healthy self-concept in all your pupils. Help students identify what they can do and who they are becoming.

putting it into practice

Using strength cards to improve behaviour

Strengths cards and other games help pupils identify their own strengths and those of others. Use the phrase 'I have noticed that ...' to refer to a pupil's positive behaviour and the characteristic that goes with this - for instance, 'I noticed you helped Josh pick up the rubbish yesterday - you are becoming a helpful person - and a good friend. What do you think?'

Strength cards and other excellent resources can be found on the Innovative Resources website (www.innovativeresources.org) and also on the At My Best website (www.atmybest.com).

Feeling controlled, unloved, insecure or not heard are not conducive to learning or cooperative behaviour. Positive feelings such as feeling valued, included, comfortable and safe promote creativity and problem solving as well as resilience (Fredrickson, 2009). When you acknowledge and validate strong emotion, children no longer need to express it more strongly: 'I can see you are feeling a bit down/cross today'. Giving children a say helps those who need to wrest control back into their lives. Create a classroom where positive feelings are actively promoted.

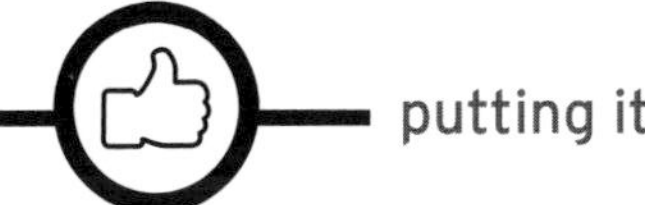

putting it into practice

Helping children to express emotions

Help children develop a language for feelings without asking for personal information. In a circle session, mix and pair children up and hand out cards with pictures of faces illustrating different emotions. Ask children to identify what this person might be feeling and what might have happened to them.

Ask groups to think about what it feels like to belong somewhere and what it might feel like to be left out. What might they say or do to help someone feel they belong? Put ideas on the wall under the headline: We All Belong Here.

One teacher asks her pupils to indicate how they are feeling when they arrive in the morning. All they do is indicate with their thumb. She then knows which children will need longer to settle and maybe a moment of extra attention.

Some early years centres provide a foam 'cocoon' comfort corner with cushions and soft music that distressed children can retreat to if they choose. This helps them begin to learn coping strategies and is never used as a sanction.

Where children have had positive attachment experiences, they are more likely to be confident and friendly. Young children who have poor attachment may be clingy, rejecting or attention seeking. They need reassurance, comfort, understanding and positive role models that are both predictable and responsive. Where relationships have been inconsistent, they may see others as a threat or want to cling to them. Aggressive behaviour is difficult for teachers.

An activity to help boost friendship skills and inclusive practices

The best way to address social issues is to boost friendship skills and inclusive practices. Activities that enable children to discover what they share limits prejudice and fosters connection.

Try this: Children make two concentric circles, facing each other. They are given a topic of conversation such as 'my journey to school' and have one minute to talk about it and find something in common. After the minute, one circle moves three paces to the right and pupils repeat the conversation with a new partner.

Many children are not fluent in English when they first come to school. For some, English is not their first language, whilst others have had limited interaction with adults who may have poor language skills themselves or a developmental impairment. Children with communication difficulties often get confused and frustrated and find it hard to make friends. They are also more frequently bullied. Use all means of communication at your disposal to get a message across. Where possible, show children what to do rather than just tell them. When a child does not comply with instructions, check first that they have understood.

Web Link

The I Can booklet *Speech, Language and Communication Needs and Primary School Aged Children* can be accessed through this web link, available on the companion website: http://bit.ly/1zhEHNI

There are often so many things for children to pay attention to that they cannot focus. Others cannot settle into directed tasks because of anxiety. Some children need to learn the concept of a beginning and an end. They may not know what 'finished' means. Some children have learned to get powerful attention when they are badly behaved. Teachers, especially those working in the early years, often have to reverse this by teaching children how to gain attention by positive behaviours. This takes time to be effective and may get worse before it gets better.

Children with attention difficulties need structure, clear and brief instruction, manageable tasks, if necessary broken into smaller components, and an environment with minimum distractions. Small steps with breaks may keep pupils going and lead to better task completion. Acknowledgement by teachers alongside self-evaluation of progress will help. Checklists and charts for older children can be motivating. Develop the strength of self-control, acknowledging whenever this is demonstrated.

Young children have an innate drive to make sense of the world. This may be messy and not always welcome. Some may have learned not to try new things as this brings disapproval. We need to value and build on the developmental drive for finding out. Confidence builds resilience so children need to know it is OK to have a go and not be perfect. When children are given the opportunity to explore and share their unique insights, they contribute to collective learning.

Using the flipped classroom approach to improve engagement

With older primary school children, you may like to try some flipped lessons. Rather than teachers imparting information in class followed by pupils doing assignments, children are given video clips of the topic to view at home or in the library and then work on their understanding and application in class. This stimulates curiosity without the immediate pressure to perform, enabling children to go at their own pace. Teachers are then able to address questions and issues for groups and individuals.

The research indicates higher levels of engagement though it is still early days. There is an interesting article about this online, entitled 'Research Says Evidence on Flipped Classrooms Still Coming In', which can be accessed through this web link, available on the companion website: http://bit.ly/1z7BQ4x

Children's natural urge to do things for themselves may have been inhibited by over-protective or over-busy parents who do everything for them. This can lead to children becoming passive and helpless. Some children will respond well to being asked to start independently and then given help to finish. Others may need help to start and then be asked to complete an activity themselves. The pupil needs to feel proud of what they have achieved on their own and encouraged to do even more next time.

Case study: encouraging children to take responsibility

Luca was 5 but everything was done for him and he had become reluctant to take any initiative. His teacher suggested to Luca's mother that he could perhaps take responsibility for putting his packed lunch into his school bag. For a couple of weeks, this went well and Luca was beginning to be more independent in other ways. One day, he forgot his lunch but was happy with the piece of fruit his teacher offered. Then his mother knocked frantically on the door with the lunchbox in her hand. All the progress disappeared and it took several weeks to get back on track.

Free play is essential for both mental health and the development of empathy. Play is the vehicle for early years cognitive and social development, so where pupils in school have not had the chance to play, their behaviour may reflect this.

Giving children a wide range of opportunities to play may fulfil a need that will enable them to move on to the next stage of directed activity.

Play encourages risk-taking within a safe environment. The more you can find a play/fun element in directed activities, the more engaged pupils are likely to be.

Web Link

Peter Gray talks about the vital importance of play for healthy development on a video on YouTube, which can be accessed through this web link, available on the companion website: www.youtube.com/watch?v=Bg-GEzM7iTk

reflection point

What are the benefits of a playful classroom?

Some children will have learnt that having a tantrum gets them what they want and others may have had poor models of social and emotional skills. Being shocked or angry in school is not helpful. Children copy what they see and hear around them so may need consistent modelling of respectful behaviour, as well as direct teaching of emotional and social skills (Roffey, 2014). Work on what is wanted (e.g. kindness) rather than on what isn't (e.g. bullying).

Web Link

This Sesame Street clip shows how breathing can help reduce anger, and can be accessed through this web link, available on the companion website: www.youtube.com/watch?v=_mZbzDOpylA

Conversations children hear at home influence how they respond in the classroom. This highlights the importance of developing positive home–school relationships. Learning will have been encouraged where pupils have had adults around them talking and asking questions about their experiences, such as going to the park. Children need to see themselves as successful learners. If necessary, you need to construct 'success experiences' in which pupils address sequential parts of a task to make incremental progress. Tasks that are too big can seem overwhelming. Provide opportunities for practice – mastery is a motivator. Introduce the concept of 'personal bests' – a familiar term in sport (Arief et al., 2012).

Fixed mindset vs. growth mindset

When children hear themselves or others praised for their ability ('you are a clever girl'), they see themselves as either having this ability or not. This is known as a fixed mindset. When children are praised for their efforts, they have a growth mindset which encourages them to try harder (Dweck, 2006).

Children who are tired, hungry, cold or unwell are unlikely to learn or behave well. Undiagnosed sensory impairment may also lead to inappropriate expectations.

Your first questions about a child who is not doing well at school will be about their health and well-being and include revisiting sight and hearing checks. Initial and ongoing information to parents about children's sleep needs and healthy eating – especially having breakfast – can be invaluable.

PROMOTING THE POSITIVE: MAKING WELL-BEING CORE BUSINESS

If the management of unwanted behaviour is your main focus, you will find yourself doing this day after day. Creating a positive environment for learning so your classroom is a safe, respectful and engaging place will minimise difficulties, even if it doesn't eliminate them altogether.

Promoting resilience

It is children experiencing adversity who have greatest difficulty with pro-social behaviour and engaging with learning. This is most evident when the adversities are multiple and chronic, such as living in poverty with parents who are not coping. Resilience research (Werner, 2004) provides guidance on factors that promote the ability to function well despite challenges. Personal qualities include a positive outlook, a sense of humour, confidence, not being overly gender defined (e.g. 'boys don't cry'), persistence and friendliness. Intelligence is protective if used constructively for problem solving. Environmental factors are:

- having someone who thinks you are worthwhile
- high (but appropriate) expectations – and help to meet these
- feeling you belong.

Teacher-student relationships

The quality of teacher–student relationships is a central feature of Hattie's (2009) meta-analysis of effective education. This includes the importance of respecting pupils with ideas of their own and not giving up on anyone. Teachers who work at relationships have a better time in the classroom, are more effective and less stressed. Spending time in the first few days of the school year getting to know students and establishing class guidelines with them will save hours of crisis intervention. This is a better idea than imposing class rules.

A recipe for a safe and friendly classroom – Years 2-6

Intro: the recipe is an action plan mixing different ingredients together to make something good.

Equipment: give groups of 3-4 pupils a large piece of paper and felt tip pens.

Ingredients: what will need to go into the mix and how much – a cup, a spoon, a sprinkle? How will these be mixed and cooked? Will the mix need checking to see how it's doing? How will you know when it is done? What will this look like, feel like and sound like? How will you share a safe and friendly classroom with everyone?

When this activity is finished, display everyone's work for a week, then take the issues that have been mentioned by everyone and write them up for permanent display.

As it can be hard to have relationships that respond to differing needs, here are some basics that are applicable universally. Think about how you communicate both verbally and non-verbally with your class:

- Be approachable – smile a lot.
- Friendliness does not mean being a friend – you are first and foremost a teacher.
- Model the behaviour you want to see in your pupils. Children copy significant people in their lives.
- Learn and use pupil names – it really does help.
- Talk up the positive to your whole-class group – how proud you are of them, how well people are doing, the efforts you have noticed.
- For both the positive and occasionally the negative, make use of an imaginary child drawn on the window or a class mascot/teddy. Talk to this person about the class: *Hey, Teddy, what do you think of that clearing up then, so much better than last week! … You know, Paula Pane* (outline of child on window), *I can hardly hear myself today there is so much noise. I wonder what I can do to get everyone working quietly*.
- Show pupils that mistakes are part of learning by making a few yourself and acknowledging what you have learned from them.
- Apologise when you haven't got something quite right or have been grumpy.
- Get pupil attention by non-verbal means rather than by raising your voice – try hands on head, fingers on noses, clapping a rhythm.
- Discover what most of the class are viewing on TV and watch it yourself so you can share in a group interest. This will also provide a hook for lessons, building on what children know about or are interested in.

- Use whole-class learning for social development and inclusion. Social skills' training for individuals does not change the perceptions of others, and gains can be short-lived.

Web Link

A photo film on Circle Solutions offers a great example of whole-class intervention and can be accessed through this web link, available on the companion website: www.youtube.com/watch?v=2mruLmlySIU

Relationships with individuals

Children who are hard to reach are often the more challenging.

Find something you like about these pupils and let them know – if you can do this through a third party all the better. Tell someone else who will tell them that you thought well of them about something.

Without being intrusive, find out something about their lives and ask the occasional question about this. If you can discover something you have in common, even better. Do you like the same music, support the same team? This gives you opportunities for short positive conversations that are not just about how they are doing at school. Investing these few moments of your time repays great dividends over the longer term. Circle activities in which teachers take part will give you insight into children's lives and interests without appearing nosey. For instance, you could start the day with a brief mix-up and pair share – for example, something you have grown out of, the highest you have ever climbed. Once you have established a positive relationship with a pupil, just being disappointed with poor behaviour may be enough. Rather than tell them what they have done wrong, ask why this wasn't acceptable and check how they are feeling. Give them time to think about what they can do to 'do sorry'. All is not lost, tomorrow is another day and you believe they can do better.

Web Link

Restorative approaches take more time but lead to sustainable outcomes. A brief summary can be found online, entitled 'Restorative Approaches in Schools in the UK', and can be accessed through this web link, available on the companion website: www.educ.cam.ac.uk/research/projects/restorativeapproaches/RA-in-the-UK.pdf

The power of positive feelings

No one attends well to a task when they are awash with negative emotions. Positive feelings, on the other hand, open cognitive pathways for both problem solving and creativity (Fredrickson, 2009). Positive emotions include feeling you belong and you matter, being valued, having a voice and choice, feeling safe, being liked and feeling you can achieve.

Oxytocin is the 'feel good' neurotransmitter that supports connectedness and increases resilience. It can be generated by humour in the classroom, especially shared laughter. Try cartoons, YouTube clips, funny stories and identifying deliberate mistakes. Not only does this reach out to engage disaffected young people, it also strengthens class cohesion and boosts learning for everyone.

Physical activity also boosts brainpower so get your class to stand up and stretch for a minute every so often – or perhaps do a silly dance! It might look crazy to an outsider but will pay dividends with children who find it hard to sit still, and enable all students to renew their focus (Sibley and Etnier, 2003).

TEACHING BEHAVIOUR

Like everything else, behaviour can be taught. Sometimes young children need to unlearn behaviours that are not helpful to them in school or early years settings. The task that teachers routinely perform at the beginning of the school year to transform a motley group of children into a cohesive, functioning class is rarely acknowledged. Skills and routines need to be introduced in a clear and concise way, with opportunities for practice and reinforcement. The following may help in remembering best practice in teaching behaviour.

Behaviour begins with a 'C'

Give pupils good models to **COPY**: you are the most powerful teaching tool in the classroom.

CATCH the child being 'good': be deliberate in acknowledging the positive to limit children trying to get attention in negative ways. Tactical ignoring is where you give minimal attention to disruptive behaviour in order to focus attention on the positive. When a lot is going on you have to choose your battles! What matters most?

Be **CLEAR** about expectations: children need to know what is wanted. As soon as someone hears 'don't think of an elephant', an image of an elephant is imprinted on their brain. Avoid telling children what NOT to do – phrase what is expected in terms of what they should be doing.

CONSTRUCT a positive self **CONCEPT**: if you tell a child she is naughty, then that is how she will think of herself; if you tell him he is helpful, then that is how he will think of himself.

Be **CARING**: show the child that what they do matters to you, and how pleased you are with their efforts and progress. Ask how they are going from time to time.

Be **CONCISE**: use language that pupils understand and keep it short. So often, adults use words that are not in a child's vocabulary, give too many instructions at once and then get cross because the child has not complied.

Be **CONSISTENT**: children need to know where they stand. Changing your expectations with your mood is confusing.

Give pupils **CHANCES** to practise new behaviours to embed their learning.

When kids muck up!

CLASS COMMUNICATION: whenever possible, address the whole class rather than individuals, e.g. *I need everyone to listen to the next instruction, some of you are doing this already, I need everyone, thank you.*

Keep **CLOSE**: move around the class so that you are standing near those who are not complying. Physical presence helps.

CHECK: bear in mind the mantra 'reminders before reprimands'. Ask a pupil who is not complying what they are supposed to be doing and if they are able to do it.

Give **CLUES**: this promotes support alongside independence and doesn't take as much of your time. You can then genuinely give credit when clues are followed up.

Be **COLLABORATIVE**: do things together or with others where appropriate and possible.

Give **CHOICES**: a limited choice gives pupils more control but not freedom to do as they like.

THE PLACE OF EMOTIONAL LITERACY IN CHALLENGING SITUATIONS

Emotional literacy means taking account of emotions in any given situation and responding in ways that promote resolution. As strong emotions are often present in behavioural issues, this makes sense. Try the following strategies:

- Acknowledge and validate feelings, e.g. 'I can see something has made you very angry.' When a child has been 'heard', it reduces the need to express emotion more loudly.
- Be aware that when someone is having a meltdown, their amygdala (the seat of emotional memory) will have temporarily overwhelmed their neo-cortex (the thinking part of the brain). This means they will not be able to think straight. It is a waste of your time to ask 'why?' until things have calmed down.
- Give permission. If you tell a child that a good cry or yell might be just what they need and you will find a safe place for them to do this, they might decide they don't need to after all!

spotlight on practice

Case study: an example of effective emotional literacy

Four-year-old Jasmine had great difficulty in letting her mother go in the mornings. Her tears and screams were distressing for everyone. For several weeks, her teacher and her mother had done everything they could to try and stop these outbursts. Finally, they tried the permission tactic. Jasmine was told that it was fine for her to cry for as long as she wanted after her mother left and to tell the teacher when she was ready to join the group. Within three days, the outbursts had stopped.

(Continued)

(Continued)

- Present yourself as calm, confident and self-controlled. Rather than reflect the emotion of the pupil who is challenging - easy to do as we have mirroring neurons in our brains (Iacoboni, 2009) - offer a presence for them to imitate. This means speaking slowly and firmly in a low voice and breathing regularly.
- Keep your distance. Invading someone's space with body, face or fingers will be interpreted as threatening.
- Calm does not mean bland. Children need to know that what they are doing matters to you, so you might begin your response with a similar level of energy and then bring this down.
- Being emotionally literate means not taking things personally. What is happening for this child will have little to do with you, though your response can make things worse or better.
- Unless someone is being hurt, moving away from a situation temporarily can take the heat out of a situation and provide a space to calm down and perhaps recover some self-control. It makes you look in charge of proceedings and allows time to attend to others. Looming over someone who is in a high emotional state or demanding they do something 'now' will exacerbate a potential confrontation. You might suggest that they find a safe space in the classroom or perhaps outside, or ask someone to fetch them a glass of water or go with them to do this.
- 'You' statements can be interpreted as accusations - think of a finger pointing! 'I' statements are easier to hear. Some useful statements might be: I would like you to ... I will just give you a moment ...

Remember that your self-respect does not reside in the immediate compliance of others.

GO WITH THE FLOW

Rather than go on the defensive and deny accusations from pupils, partly agree with them. A 'go with the flow' strategy avoids confrontation, establishes you as someone with calm self-respect, can bring humour into a tricky situation and may surprise children out of antagonistic positions.

Table 13.1 Go with the flow

Pupil comment	Teacher response
You can't make me.	No, I can't. What you do is up to you. I can only tell you what the consequences of your decision will be.
It's too difficult, I can't do it.	You're right. Everything is difficult the first time you try. It gets easier. Can you think of anything you have got better at with practice?
You're a rubbish teacher.	So you will have to help me improve. What's one thing I could do better?
You don't like me.	I don't like what you are doing at the moment but you are OK.
You never listen to me.	I am sorry you feel that. I am listening now - what do you want to say?

Experienced teachers know that some children are at their most volatile on a Monday morning when they have had negative experiences at the weekend. Some need time to settle – too many demands too soon may increase anxiety. Others value just getting into the routine of school again and will welcome this.

reflection point

What can you do in a classroom to help pupils feel connected and that they matter?

SPECIFIC ISSUES

Loss and change

Many children find themselves dealing with loss or major change and the impact of this on self-concept, learning and behaviour is often under-estimated. Loss may include the death of family members including pets, family breakdown, parents in prison or long hospital stays, or moving away from a familiar home and friendship network. Bereavement is more straightforward and adults are often sympathetic, but teachers are less likely to be aware of other issues and may be less tolerant of the consequences. Establishing blended families can also be difficult for children to manage and parents do not always handle this with sensitivity. Children may suddenly have to share their bedroom, have less time with a parent who has a new partner and perhaps deal with a range of different expectations.

Young children below the age of 7 almost always believe that the disappearance of a parent is somehow their fault (Dowling and Elliott, 2012). They might then live out their self-concept of being a bad person. They are often confused and angry and it is safer to express this at school rather than at home. They might also push people as far as they can to see if they too will reject them. Others may want to stay at home to be close to the remaining parent and be distracted in school.

How family breakdown is mediated with children is critical. They need to be told it wasn't their fault and given reassurance that the other parent will not be disappearing too.

The range of emotions children experience during parental separation can include high levels of anxiety, deep sadness, self-blame, rejection, conflicting loyalties and confusion. Anger may be expressed as aggression or sometimes self-harm. Children may struggle to make sense of what has happened. Significant adults need to talk to children in a language they can understand.

Schools often provide a refuge for children in such crises. When families are encouraged to inform school of any changes at home, teachers are more able to respond effectively. This includes not taking sides, and showing you understand why someone might be angry but letting them know that aggression towards others is not acceptable.

Can you identify three children who have experienced loss? What have been their reactions and what has helped? What does this tell you about what children need at such a time?

For further information on this topic, *Understanding Children's Needs When Parents Separate* (Dowling and Elliott, 2012) addresses a range of related issues at different developmental stages and how best to respond: useful for both teachers and parents.

Web Link

The Seasons for Growth peer support programme presents loss and change as a valuable part of life. The sessions with trained 'companions' enable children to talk through shared issues in a safe environment. Further information can be accessed through this web link, available on the companion website: http://seasonsforgrowth.co.uk/

Learning difficulties

There are two areas of learning difficulties that may first be identified as behavioural issues. The first is where pupils appear to be less mature than others of the same age, do not grasp new concepts quickly and need a lot of practice to embed them. This is likely to become evident in the early years. In discussion with families, you may find that developmental milestones happened later than expected. Some individuals are born to live life much slower. Other children may have missed out on early emotional nurturing and this will have had consequences for their cognitive development. Whatever the cause, you will need to change your expectations and provide for learning in smaller incremental steps with opportunities for reinforcement. You also need to monitor and record progress as such children may eventually need an Education, Health and Care (EHC) plan.

Another type of learning difficulty becomes evident later on in primary school. You will find that some individuals become the class clown, resist any literacy activities, especially writing, and do not attempt to work independently. These pupils are not otherwise slow to grasp ideas but their attainments do not match their evident cognitive ability. It is likely that these children struggle to decode words so avoid doing so and do everything they can to maintain face with their peers. Silly behaviour may be covering up anxiety. Ensure pupils know the primary purpose of a task – content, accuracy or presentation. If it is ideas that are wanted, they can tidy up the spelling later. Maintain a positive sense of self and motivation by valuing their innate ability and finding ways for them to demonstrate this.

Difficulties which may require a referral

Most children will respond to the interventions suggested above but others may not. Some individuals behave in ways that are bewildering or extreme and this can be especially distressing for caring teachers who don't understand what more they can do. Two specific issues are discussed here: autism and trauma.

Autism

It is possible a child is on the autistic spectrum. You need to tread carefully. When a child is diagnosed with any serious difficulty, parents suffer a loss and may experience denial, anger, despair and deep sorrow. It takes time to accept that a child is in some way different and empathic support to move forward (Roffey and Parry, 2014, Chapters 1 and 4).

The autistic spectrum is wide and some individuals may exhibit only a few behavioural anomalies and occasionally also have some exceptional abilities, whilst others have difficulties in many areas. To confuse matters further, some children not on the spectrum occasionally exhibit autistic-like behaviours for other reasons.

One indicator of autism in young children is the lack of symbolic play (NICE, n.d.): toy cars will be pushed backwards and forwards or lined up but few imaginary scenes will be played out. Language is often delayed and when it does develop it is factual and concrete – jokes and metaphors are simply not understood. There may also be a flat voice intonation. Autistic children do not recognise non-verbal communication so the use of raised eyebrows, for instance, will not have any impact.

Children may treat peers as objects and simply take what they want. This can seem callous but the lack of 'theory of mind' in autism means not being able to understand that someone else may think differently. Many children on the spectrum are comfortable and make progress playing or working alone. Any encouragement to interact needs to be gentle. Learning basic social skills however can be helpful. Carol Gray's *The New Social Stories Book* (2010) is a good start. A further indicator of autism is the need for routine. The more structured the day the better. The fear of change, however, can result in a meltdown when something different or unexpected happens. Warnings are essential.

Other behaviours indicative of autism are: a single-minded interest bordering on obsession, sensory sensitivity (loud noises or touching certain textures, for example, can cause great distress), unusual behaviours such as eating mud or smelling everything and poor motor coordination.

If you monitor a child who is exhibiting some of the above, you will know whether you need to seek the advice of a specialist. Although you need permission from parents to refer a child directly, most professionals will talk through issues of concern and offer general advice on ways forward. You might also pay a visit to a specialist school to see what you could incorporate into your classroom.

Trauma

Trauma may arise from multiple and varied sources, such as sexual abuse, witnessing violence, being involved in a major accident or disaster, or having been caught up in a war zone. Whatever the trigger, it has been an overwhelming experience resulting in terror and helplessness. The thoughts, feelings and images engendered by the event may intrude into everyday life and affect the ability to function. Sometimes a child appears to be coping and then something triggers a re-traumatisation. This can be as simple as a smell, a sound or even someone wearing a particular piece of clothing. It could also be an anniversary. You will not know why a child is suddenly out of control and they will barely know themselves, so there is no point in asking 'why?'

Factors surrounding the trauma will make a difference to recovery, such as who was involved, how well the family is coping and whether the trauma was a one-off incident or more pervasive. The following will therefore apply to some but not all children:

Hyper-vigilance: being fearful, anxious and alert all the time

Sleep difficulties: leading to very tired and irritable children

Separation anxiety: panic at a parent being out of sight

Intrusive thoughts: resulting in an inability to focus on directed activities and reduced pleasure in play; play scenarios may include re-enactment of the event

Regression: behaving as a younger child, including toileting accidents and lack of self-control in managing feelings

Physical complaints: typical of younger children less able to express emotional and psychological pain

Reduced optimism and ability to enjoy anything

Self-blame: children may believe an event was their fault; this is especially true of children below the age of 7 who have an ego-centric interpretation

Recklessness: a lack of caution and taking greater risks with safety.

It is likely you will come across traumatised children in your classroom but will not necessarily be aware of the events that have led to the trauma, especially if they include abuse or family violence. So what can you do?

By following the guidance in the section above on promoting the positive, you will already be helping with the healing process:

- Children need a sense of calm and as much normality as possible. A positive and purposeful classroom environment with a clear routine and structure provides a predictable and safe place.
- Children look to trusted adults for help, so the relationship you establish with them is critical. Some may be rejecting but do not take this personally.
- Consistency and the gentle establishment of appropriate boundaries show that the adult is in charge of a situation but is not controlling the pupil. This difference is critical (Roffey, 2013). Unchecked negative behaviour is not helpful to anyone, including the child.
- Validate feelings and give reassurance that bad feelings will shrink in time. Remind children that they are in a safe place now.
- Bring children back into the moment when intrusive thoughts seem to be occurring. Point out what they can see and hear in the vicinity – offering food or drink may help.
- Provide physical outlets when negative feelings build up a high level of energy. This relieves tension and inhibits angry outbursts.
- Accept regressive behaviour and reassure children that they will feel more like themselves in time and be able to be more grown up.
- Physical comfort may relieve bodily tension. When a child asks for a hug, don't reject

them but ensure you are in a public place and keep it brief.

- Appropriate expectations – ask children to do as much as they can manage. Be pleased with their efforts and encourage a little more next time.
- Parents are the most significant factor in a child's recovery. Work with them as much as possible. Some children may value a 'transition' object to cling onto when a parent is unavailable.
- Children may need to play out roles in which they re-enact what happened, sometimes putting themselves in control of events. This can be scary for their classmates. Without shaming them, gently intervene in any aggressive or sexualised play and tell them this is frightening for their friends and needs to stop. Ask them to draw some pictures instead and then take the opportunity to talk to them about what they have drawn.

A referral to a psychologist, play therapist or counsellor would provide the child with an opportunity to talk about their feelings in more depth and to use play as a therapeutic intervention under guidance.

Having traumatised children in the class can be exceptionally challenging. Teachers need to look after their own well-being and look out for each other to maximise the positive outcomes for everyone.

WORKING WITH FAMILIES

The first step is to make all parents feel welcome so that when issues need addressing a positive relationship has already been established.

Web Link

You can read examples of good practice in Scotland on welcoming families of new arrivals, in a report on the Education Scotland site, which can be accessed through this web link, available on the companion website: www.educationscotland.gov.uk/images/cuimnnus_tcm4-618947.pdf

It is easy to blame parents when children are exhibiting uncooperative or distressed behaviour and although understandable this approach leads nowhere. Parents themselves are often confused and at a loss to know what to do. They may appear angry or demanding but this probably emanates from anxiety – the same feeling that keeps other parents away from school.

reflection point

Most parents want the best for their children and do the best they can with the knowledge, skills and resources at their disposal, including emotional resources. What are the advantages of taking this position? What difference would it make to your approach?

Talking to parents about behavioural difficulties

Parents appreciate an informal approach in the first instance - perhaps just a quiet word in the playground checking on how things are going. If you want to ask them in for a chat, invite families as experts on their child. You need their help to understand the child better. If the child's mother is likely to come on her own, encourage her to bring someone for support. This is especially important if meetings become more formal and other professionals become involved. It is emotional talking about your children - and how this reflects on you as a parent. Begin the conversation with something positive that shows that you do not see their child as all bad and you have their best interests at heart. Then ask an open question about how things are at home. Active listening involves giving your full attention (put phones on silent and a do not disturb notice on the door), clarifying meaning, not interrupting with concerns about other children and giving verbal and non-verbal encouragement to continue. Ask what they have tried and if anything has worked, even a little bit. By this time you will have a clearer idea of ways you might move forward. Decisions about actions need to be made jointly - parents may want to please and agree things they can't manage. Take into account that some parents have poor English, others cannot read well and some will be experiencing family violence or have mental health concerns. Before you end the conversation, agree on a review to see how things are going. Ask how best to stay in touch.

All conversations with and about children with behavioural difficulties need to be solution-focused: What do you need the child to do, how much can they do already and what would be the next small step?

TEACHER RESILIENCE AND WELL-BEING

Behavioural issues in the classroom can be wearing. It is critical that teachers maintain their own well-being in order to support the children they work with. However caring or well prepared you are, you will not be able to sustain a positive relationship or respond effectively in challenging situations if you are exhausted and over-stressed. Stress becomes problematic when it demands excess resources. Maintaining well-being means either increasing resources or limiting demands. This brief section outlines what teachers can do to help themselves and what they can do for each other.

What helps you bounce back after a really tough day? What can you do for yourself and what do you need others to do for you? What does this say about what you need?

Looking after yourself

Physical well-being: not only do you need to eat and sleep well, you also need to take regular exercise – even walking every day will make a difference to serotonin levels; the occasional massage also boosts oxytocin.

Cognitive strategies: how you think about your role and your pupils makes a difference to how you feel. Keeping things in perspective is valuable. There is increasing evidence that mindfulness and meditation also boost well-being (BPS Research Digest, 2015).

Emotional support: who can you de-brief with, who will give you a hug, who are your reliable emotional supports? Look after the relationships that are most important to you. Accept any mistakes as part of learning, as you would expect your pupils to.

Social support: friends who will take you out of yourself are to be treasured. Getting away from the job means that you return refreshed.

Time management: take account of how the term runs so you can manage expectations. Think about what you need to do to the best of your ability and what is less of a priority.

Looking after each other

Schools where well-being is core school business ensure that teacher well-being is high on the agenda and social capital actively promoted. This means that everyone feels valued for the work they do and their efforts are acknowledged; colleagues look out for each other, share resources and find time to socialise.

SUMMARY

Most children are happy in school and their behaviour reflects this. It is the vulnerable and the distressed who present difficulties. This chapter has explored what teachers can do to help those individuals become engaged with learning and choose more pro-social behaviour. There are also ideas of how best to respond when challenges arise. In order to do this well, teacher well-being and collegial support matter.

companion website

To access additional online resources please visit: **https://study.sagepub.com/wyseandrogers**

Here you will find a classroom activity, author podcasts including Sue Roffey's top tips for employability, free access to SAGE journal articles and links to external sources.

further reading

Burningham, J. (2007). *Edwardo: the Horriblest Boy in the Whole Wide World*. New York: Random House. This book provides a light-hearted understanding of how deficit labels embed a negative self-concept and ways to help a child think differently about themselves.

Gerhardt, S. (2003). *Why Love Matters*. London: Routledge. This book summarises the neurological impact of attachment. It is fascinating, informative and easy to read.

Spratt, J., Shucksmith, J., Philip, K. and Watson, C. (2006). 'Part of who we are as a school should include responsibility for wellbeing': links between the school environment, mental health and behaviour. *Pastoral Care*, 14–21 September. This piece is an excellent overview and summary of the issues.

REFERENCES

Arief, G. Liem, D., Ginns, P., Martin, A.J., Stone, B. and Herrett, M. (2012). Personal best goals and academic and social functioning: a longitudinal perspective. *Learning and Instruction*, 22(3): 222–30.

British Psychological Society (BPS) Research Digest (2015). *The Psychology of Mindfulness Digested*. http://bit.ly/1KeaR2o (accessed 25 June 2015).

Children's Society (2013). *Hidden from View: The experiences of young carers in England*. http://bit.ly/1HjrzLb (accessed 25 April 2015).

Department for Education (DfE) (2013). *Pupil Behaviour in Schools in England*. Education Standards Analysis and Research Division. London: DfE.

Dowling, E. and Elliott, D. (2012). *Understanding Children's Needs when Parents Separate*. Milton Keynes: Speechmark Publishing.

Dweck, C.S. (2006). *Mindset: The new psychology of success*. New York: Random House.

Fredrickson, B. (2009). *Positivity: Ground-breaking research to release your inner optimist and thrive*. Oxford: OneWorld Publications.

Gray, C. (2010). *The New Social Stories Book*. Arlington, TX: Future Horizons.

Hattie, J. (2009). *Visible Learning: A synthesis of over 800 meta-analyses relating to achievement*. London: Routledge.

Iacoboni, M. (2009). Imitation, empathy and mirror neurons. *Annual Review of Psychology*, 60: 653–70.

Johnstone, L. (2013). Alternatives to Psychiatric Diagnosis: Psychological Formulation. Global Summit on Diagnostic Alternatives. http://dxsummit.org/archives/1208 (accessed 24 June 2015).

National Institute for Care and Health Excellence (NICE) (n.d.). Recognising Possible Autism in Children and Young People. http://bit.ly/1LtcPwb (accessed 23 June 2015).

NSW Federation (2014). TV ad campaign 'Teachers Make A Difference'. http://teachersmakeadifference.org.au (accessed 27 March 2016).

Roffey, S. (2013). In Control or in Charge. *21st Century Learning*. https://learning21c.wordpress.com/2013/02/26/in-control-or-in-charge/

Roffey, S. (2014). *Circle Solutions for Student Wellbeing*. London: Sage.

Roffey, S. and Parry, J. (2014). *Special Needs in the Early Years: Supporting collaboration, communication and co-ordination*, 3rd edition. London: Routledge.

Sibley, B.A and Etnier, J.L. (2003). The relationship between physical activity and cognition in children: a meta-analysis. *Pediatric Exercise Science* 15(3): 243–56.

Werner, E.E. (2004). 'What can we learn about resilience from large scale longitudinal studies?' in *Handbook of Resilience in Children*. New York: Kluwer Academic/Plenum.

14

NEW TECHNOLOGY

Steve Higgins and James Siddle

LEARNING AIMS

This chapter will:

- provide you with information about educational technology use in UK schools
- enable you to understand research evidence in relation to digital technologies and learning
- help you to relate examples of children's learning with technology to theories of learning
- present examples of how digital technology can support teaching and learning
- develop knowledge and understanding of e-safety issues in schools.

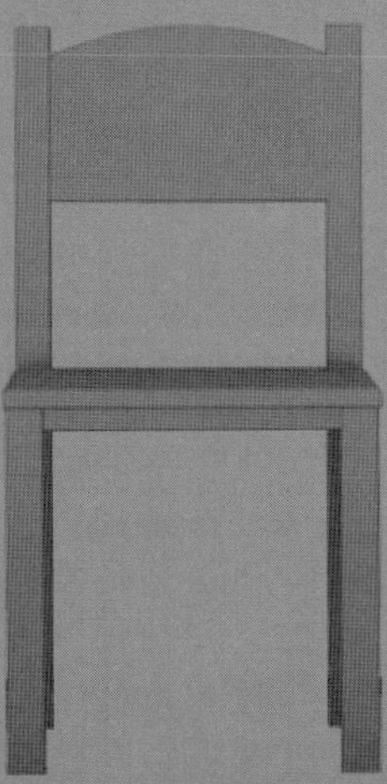

The first section of this chapter presents an overview of the history of digital technology use in schools in the UK from the BBC Micro to interactive whiteboards and iPads, with some case study examples of technology use explicitly linked to theories of learning. Digital technologies are here to stay – the important questions are not *whether* to use them, but *which* technologies to use and for *what* purposes?

A SHORT HISTORY OF DIGITAL TECHNOLOGY IN SCHOOLS IN THE UK

The UK has always been at the forefront of computer technology use in schools. In the 1980s the Microelectronics Education Programme (MEP) aimed to promote the study of microelectronics and its effects within the school curriculum and to encourage the use of the technology to support teaching and learning. It ran from 1980 to 1986 and supported the use of British technologies such as Acorn (producing the 'BBC' computers), Research Machines and Sinclair (such as the 380Z and the ZX Spectrum) computers in both primary and secondary schools. A continuation project, the Microelectronic Education Support Unit (MESU) from 1985, then funded 600 advisory teachers with Education Support Grants to help local authorities across England to purchase hardware and software and develop training for teachers. By the end of the 1980s, a new national curriculum had been introduced, setting out the information technology capabilities expected of pupils aged 5–16 and another body, the National Council for Educational Technology (NCET), provided guidance, advice and support for schools and colleges in England, Wales and Northern Ireland on the use of educational technology, in particular the use of computers for teaching and learning. Shortly before the Labour Party came to power in 1997, it commissioned the Stevenson Report on ICT in UK schools (Stevenson, 1997), which concluded that 'the state of ICT in our schools is primitive and not improving'. After the election, the government replaced NCET with the British Educational Communications and Technology Agency (BECTA) to bring it closer to government with two main roles: (1) to influence the strategic direction and development of the national education policy so as to best take advantage of technology; and (2) to develop a national digital infrastructure and resources strategy leading to greater national coherence. This was developed from 1998 through the National Grid for Learning (NGfL) and the provision of linked educational resources on the internet. The NGfL was specifically set up to support English schools, with separate 'grids' for schools in Northern Ireland, Scotland and Wales. You can still find a number of these 'grids for learning' as websites with ideas and resources for teaching.

Subsequent national initiatives have included providing training to nearly half a million serving teachers and school librarians in the use of ICT between 1999 and 2003 at a cost of £231 million from the Big Lottery 'New Opportunities Fund', and the promotion of interactive whiteboards (IWBs) by 'embedding ICT' in the literacy and numeracy strategies and subject teaching, such that by 2007, Becta's Harnessing Technology Schools Survey indicated that 98% of secondary and 100% of primary schools had IWBs.

These initiatives were driven by a number of goals – a combination of the educational and the economic. An important driving force has been a political commitment to economic competitiveness and supporting UK manufacturers and industries, as well as providing a skilled workforce for these industries, as evidenced by the involvement of the Department for Trade and Industry in the initial micro-electronics initiative. Of course, the political and economic aims have been allied with educational ones, such as a curriculum which is more responsive to changes in society, or an emphasis on skills such as collaboration and problem solving, and more recently computational thinking. These elements are now more explicit again in the curriculum with the three distinct aspects of computing: computer science, information technology and digital literacy. This has brought the curriculum full circle, back to the 1980s, with an emphasis on computing and programming now firmly back on the agenda.

reflection point

What was your experience of technology and computers at school? Which aspects do you feel you are confident to teach? Are there areas where you think you need to learn more?

Today, we see the explosion of more individual devices such as smartphones with computing capability and tablets, such as the iPad. The recent uptake of these has not been driven by central initiatives, unlike with older technologies, indeed it is unlikely that we will see a central commitment to the provision of equipment for schools such as micro-computers in the 1980s, to teacher training with local authority advisory teachers or to lottery-funded courses in the current economic and educational climate. Even allowing for a cost estimate of £100 per device, with a lifetime of three years, a typical class would need an investment of £1000 pounds a year, every year, to keep a set of small tablet computers renewed and this does not take into account Wi-Fi network maintenance, broadband internet costs (about £2000 per year for a small to medium-sized primary school in an urban area) and technical support.

THEORIES OF LEARNING AND THE USE OF TECHNOLOGY

It is important to understand how digital technologies can help in schools and one way to do this is to look at different learning theories and how they might be understood in relation to digital devices. Early attempts to develop computer technology for learning were heavily influenced by behaviourist theories of learning, aiming to provide corrective feedback to learners to help them remember or master specific content. Drawing on the work of researchers like Skinner and Bloom and the development of early mechanical teaching machines, this led to the creation of learning labs, perhaps most used in language learning through the 1980s and 1990s. Another example of the influence of this theoretical approach was the development of 'integrated learning systems' in the 1990s where pupils answered questions on screen, typically in mathematics or English lessons, and were provided with automatic feedback about their responses. A content management system directed the learner through the materials and also provided information on students' progress to the teacher. These approaches are characterised by the breaking down of learning content into specific discrete objectives, with the computer or digital environment providing both content and feedback to the learner on these small steps. Current software designed on these principles includes RM Maths.

In the 1960s, Seymour Papert, who had studied with Jean Piaget at the University of Geneva, created a programming language with colleagues in the USA called Logo as a tool to improve the way children think and solve problems. A small mobile robot called a 'Turtle' was developed and children were shown how to use it to solve simple problems in an environment of play and exploration. The programming language was designed to have a 'low floor' and be easily accessible, but also a 'high ceiling', capable of extending experts. Papert drew on Piaget's learning theory of constructivism, but developed a version which focused on programming and creativity called constructionism where the emphasis was on learning through making things or digital creation (Papert, 1980). This linking of the precision of programming with creativity is part of the current computing curriculum.

Other approaches, such as Dawes, Mercer and Wegerif's (2000) 'Thinking Together' or Naylor and Keogh's (2005) 'Concept Cartoons', use digital technology to present activities or scenarios for active discussion and agreement or resolution by learners, based on the social constructivist ideas of Vygotsky. Here, the digital content is used to provoke discussion with a picture or puzzle which learners discuss through 'exploratory talk', sharing and building on each others' ideas to resolve the puzzle or problem or move to the next step in the software. The central idea is that collaborative support for learning in a group develops skills and knowledge which the learner will be able to use in the future by themselves, independently without peer support.

The growth of video clips for independent learning, such as with the informal posting of 'how to' guides on YouTube, as well as the more organised collections such as Khan Academy for learning mathematics, reflects yet another learning theory developed by Albert Bandura and called social learning theory. This approach is based on the idea that learning is a cognitive process but one which takes place in a social context and can happen purely through observation or direct instruction, even in the absence of immediate practice or direct reinforcement and feedback. Bandura's ideas drew on behaviourism, but aimed to explain the influence of social context and the role of the individual in actively interpreting what they see as part of their learning. Today, many young people will search for a video online to show them how to do something they want or need to learn.

Computers and digital technologies have always been closely linked with various learning theories, but no particular theory has turned out to be the most influential or persistent. The emphasis has been on theories of learning and, only by implication, ideas for teaching and instruction. Most theories consider learning, however, at an individual level or learning as an individual participant in a small group. None of the main theories of learning have been developed as part of a theory of teaching, particularly teaching classes of 20–30 children. As a result, it is difficult to provide clear recommendations for how teachers might get the best from technological innovations when thinking about their role as a class teacher.

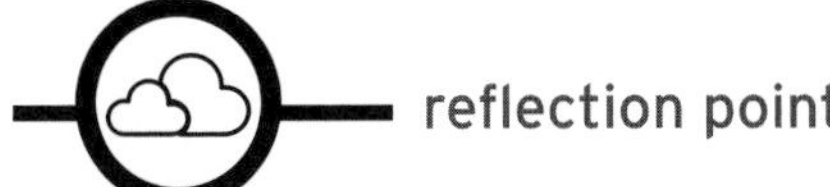

reflection point

Which theories of learning are you familiar with: Behaviourism? Constructivism? Constructionism? Social Constructivism? Social Learning Theory? Which learning theory best explains how you have learned with computer technologies? Read through the four case studies below and consider how different learning theories might help us understand what is happening in terms of children's learning.

spotlight on practice

Learning to count or learning to play the game?

Danny is 5 and is in a reception class. He enjoys playing 'NumberMaze', a counting and calculation program for young children. He likes to choose the racing car so he can drive it through the maze on screen with the mouse and get a printed certificate when he crosses the finish line with the chequered flag. Every time he comes to a dead end in the maze, he is given a counting challenge, a picture of a number of objects he has to count, and then he is supposed to type the number in the box on the screen. Danny has worked out, however, that if he runs his finger along the numbers at the top of the keyboard, it puts in the numbers one by one into the box, each numeral replacing the last: 1, 2, 3, 4, 5, 6, 7, 8, 9. One of these will be correct and he will be able to progress through the maze more quickly than if he stops to count. For Danny, the object of the game is to race through the maze. All of the clues on screen support this - the car, the sound effects, the 'Well done!' or 'Good job!' verbal feedback when he overcomes a challenge, the chequered flag at the end of his turn and the certificate he proudly takes home. These all reinforce his view that the game is about getting his car out of the maze. The teacher had planned this activity to help Danny to practise touch counting as he knows the number names to ten, but cannot coordinate his touch and count reliably. Danny does not share this objective, however.

spotlight on practice

Audio feedback with iPads

Ellie, who is in Year 5, has completed a piece of written work and handed it in to be marked. That evening, her teacher audio records comments on the work on an iPad and identifies its strengths and weaknesses in terms of the agreed learning objectives and some next steps to improve what Ellie has

(Continued)

(Continued)

written. The sound file is uploaded to a free cloud storage site, 'SoundCloud', and the teacher prints out a QR code (Quick Response Code) with a link to the audio file which she sticks on Ellie's book. The next day, Ellie scans the QR code with a class iPad and listens to the audio file with headphones as she reviews her work. She likes the spoken feedback as she finds the teacher's voice reassuring, and she listens to the feedback several times as she edits and improves her writing. She says she finds it easier to link the recorded comments with the sections of her work that it refers to than with written comments where she has to look at what the teacher has written and what she wrote in turn.

spotlight on practice

Creating and counting

Sophie and Emily are both 4 years old and attend a nursery class in an early years unit. They are using a children's painting program, KidPix, to design 'counting pictures' in an early years setting. The aim is to create a picture or a scene where you can count different things you can see, such as houses, flowers, cars, animals or people. The children can choose different stamps from a toolbar and place the little pictures on screen to make a scene with plants and flowers or animals or other objects. They can also choose a numeral stamp which says the name of the number they select in a funny voice so they can place this next to their collections of objects to show how many there are. As they decide how many flowers to place, they count and recount the objects on screen until they have the number they have agreed. They like choosing the numeral stamp and repeat the number name in unison, copying the funny voice in the software. As they finish the picture, the teaching assistant (TA) helps them to save their picture and to print out three copies. Each of the girls are to take one home. The TA staples a short pre-prepared letter about the counting pictures and what their parent or carer might look for when they share the activity with their child in terms of accurate touch counting, coordinating the touch and counting words and knowing that the last number name gives the total. The letter also suggests some other counting activities they could do at home. The third copy is laminated and added to a collection of these counting pictures stored next to a carpeted area where the children can choose to share their own pictures with their friends or choose other children's pictures along with books and stories. The children enjoy recognising and reading each other's names, as well as counting the different things in the pictures and identifying the matching number stamp.

spotlight on practice

Recording learning

Jack and Harry are in Year 6. They have been practising for their SAT tests and creating short video clips using some iPad software called 'Explain Everything'. This lets you create video guides or tutorials with added sketches and voiceovers. They have a photograph of a geometry question with a diagram on the screen which they annotate in the software and they describe out loud what they are doing as they complete the question to record a model answer. The software saves what they write over the picture with the voice-over as a video clip. They review the finished clip for clarity and accuracy and decide to make another recording before posting what they think is the best version to the school's learning platform for others to use if they are stuck on this particular revision question.

TECHNOLOGY AND PEDAGOGY

This section reviews the research evidence on the impact of digital technologies on learning and considers the different choices about digital technology that teachers can make when using technology. These include approaches which support demonstration, explanation and interaction, as well as technology for use as tools by pupils in their own learning and the planned use of tutorial or practice software.

What does the research evidence say?

Overall, the research evidence over the last 40 years or so on the impact of a wide range of digital technologies on learning has consistently identified positive effects (Tamim et al., 2011). The increasing variety of digital technologies and the diversity of contexts and settings in which the research has been conducted, combined with the challenges in combining evidence from different methodologies, make it difficult to make clear and specific recommendations for educational practice in schools.

Studies which have looked for an association that links the provision or availability of technology with its use in schools or by children and young people in their lives more generally, find small but consistent positive associations with educational outcomes, as measured by test results (Higgins et al., 2012). However, a causal link cannot be inferred from this kind of research. It seems more likely that more effective schools and teachers use digital technologies more effectively than other schools. What we need to know more about is where and how it can be used to improve specific learning outcomes and then investigate to see if this information can be used to help improve learning in other contexts. We do not know from these studies if it is the use of technology that is making the difference. When looking at home use, there is a 'Goldilocks' effect, where those who do best at school have moderate access to and use of technology at home, and those who have no access do less well, but so do those who use technology the most.

Research findings from other kinds of research designs, such as controlled trials and experimental studies and which have been combined in meta-analyses, show that technology-based approaches generally produce just slightly lower levels of improvement compared with the average of all other researched interventions and approaches (such as peer tutoring or those which provide effective feedback to learners). The extent of impact identified in these studies suggests that it is not whether technology is used (or not) that makes the difference, but how *well* the technology is used to support teaching and learning (see Higgins et al., 2012 for a fuller discussion of this). There is no doubt that technology engages and motivates young people. However, this benefit is only helpful for learning if the activity is effectively aligned with what is being taught. If the increased motivation encourages children to work harder, or for longer, or more persistently or with greater understanding, then it may help improve particular learning outcomes. Most of the time, using technology is simply different, and children enjoy the activity, especially if they are using technology with their friends. Here, we need to distinguish between motivation or engagement in learning, and motivation or engagement in activity. The value of the motivation supported by technology is only helpful educationally if it motivates better learning in some way.

Taken together, the correlational and experimental evidence does not offer a convincing case for the general impact of digital technology on learning outcomes. This does not mean that it is not worth investing in new technology to improve learning, but it should encourage us to be cautious in the face of technological solutions to educational challenges. Careful thought is needed to use technology to best effect. What is most important is the teacher's thinking and the decisions about the use of technology in the classroom: the *how* rather than the *what*. This is the key lesson that emerges from the research. The way that you use it is more important than what you use.

SO WHAT IS EFFECTIVE?

The Sutton Trust–Education Endowment Foundation (EEF) Teaching and Learning Toolkit shows that two of the approaches which make the most difference to teaching and learning are effective feedback and meta-cognition combined with self-regulation. Meta-cognition is where learners develop a vocabulary about, and an understanding of, planning, monitoring and reviewing their own learning, along with self-regulation which is where learners take responsibility for managing aspects of these strategies themselves, such as developing approaches to help them persist with and overcome difficulties or challenges in their learning by themselves.

It is therefore helpful to think about how digital technology might help achieve this. How can technology help provide more effective feedback to learners? Can it help close the gap between feedback given by the teacher and that received and understood by the learner? Or how can technology help learners understand how to plan, monitor and evaluate their own learning and take greater responsibility for this? In the early numeracy examples above, the feedback that Danny was getting actually drove his learning in the wrong direction. He thought the aim was to get his car to the end of the maze as quickly as possible and the environment, the computer feedback of 'Well done' and the certificate just reinforced this. For Sophie and Emily, the collaborative activity of making a counting picture encouraged them to talk and check, thus providing feedback and developing their self-regulation of their own counting as well as providing further opportunities for practice and feedback with the printed versions with their peers, and again at home. Ellie was not only receiving feedback from the teacher, but was also taking responsibility to improve her writing using this information. Her awareness of how to improve her writing will help develop both her meta-cognition and her self-regulation. Similarly, Jack and Harry were supporting each other in developing their self-regulation of their learning by collaborating in creating the video tutorials for other children to use. They needed to be aware of the purpose of the clip in demonstrating clearly how to answer the specific mathematics question, and in planning how to answer the question, but also in evaluating how useful the clip would be for helping others. Each of these stages promoted meta-cognitive skills, which the teacher reinforced in discussion.

BEING A DIGITALLY LITERATE TEACHER

It is impossible to avoid digital technology in today's world. Most classrooms have interactive whiteboards and a range of digital devices, computers, laptops, tablets, cameras and voice recorders, with these features also available in school. Even a mobile phone can usually be used to record a short video clip, take a photograph and send this to another phone or computer. Technology can support your teaching right across the various aspects of a teacher's professional life, including preparation and planning, teaching and learning interaction in classrooms or with individual pupils and groups; it can play a part in assessment and record keeping, as well as in the teacher's wider role, such as working with other professionals and parents/carers or on your personal professional development.

Web Link

A really useful website for anyone interested in using technology in teaching can be accessed through this web link, available on the companion website: www.naace.co.uk/

Technology can help with your planning, from the trivial task of copying and pasting objectives and information on planning proforma to the more interesting tasks of researching and designing activities to support children's learning. Technology, and particularly access to the internet, can provide an endless source of inspiration, ideas and activities. The challenge is how to organise the materials and resources that you find or create, so you don't spend ages repeating searches or hunting for things you know you have seen or made. You will need a systematic approach, whether this is using a well-organised digital filing system on your laptop or school learning platform, or using software such as Evernote which lets you tag and connect files and websites.

Web Link

Relevant online classroom resources can be accessed through this web link, available on the companion website: http://ukedchat.com/ictmagic/

The arrival of the interactive whiteboard in classrooms early in the 21st century brought all manner of digital resources into the classroom. Interactive whiteboards have a number of technically interactive features which can support a teacher's presentational skills of demonstration, explanation and questioning, such as drag and drop, hide and reveal, highlighting and annotating. However, it is not the technical capabilities which make the technology *educationally* interactive, it is how teachers use these features to extend their repertoire of presentational strategies and the choices that they make about when to orchestrate different techniques or technical features. It is also now possible to use a wide variety of multimedia in the classroom with presentation technologies, from text to pictures and audio clips, to video film excerpts or software like Google Earth to take a walk in a city on the other side of the globe, or even programs to simulate an interstellar flight – the options are literally limitless. These devices have increased the choices that teachers can make about how to present information, challenge thinking, develop understanding, as well as inspire, enthral and engage young minds. The challenge is how to continue to develop and extend your repertoire and not get stuck in a rut with software like PowerPoint or Notebook, powerful though these can be.

putting it into practice

Extending your repertoire of IWB strategies

Agree to work with two or three of your friends or colleagues who are teaching a similar age group to you over the course of a term or even a school year. Take it in turns once a week to email or post on shared social media like Facebook an idea or a link to an example of an IWB technique you could use in the next week in your teaching. Each person should then post what they tried and what they learned from using the technique, and add a reflection about how and where it might be useful in the near future.

The idea is not just to find out what the interactive whiteboard is good at, but what it helps you do well as a teacher. How can you use hide and reveal to develop deeper questioning? What multimedia resources really develop understanding in science? How can you explain mathematical concepts so that children not only remember them, but can connect them with other mathematical ideas, such as fractions, ratio and proportion, for example? Are there any 'killer apps' for specific teaching techniques or curriculum content?

Technology is also useful for practice and assessment. Some children will just need more time to develop 'mastery' or fluency with aspects of knowledge in core subjects, such as with spelling or number facts and times tables. They are usually willing to practise using technology and you can set challenges which encourage them to persist and succeed with computer software. Other areas of learning may just need learners to spend time productively practising their developing skills. Some practice programs, such as *Skoolbo*, are available for free on the internet and schools can sign up to them so that children can use them both at home and at school. Other programs can encourage learners to stay engaged and practise for longer or more productively. An approach like *Accelerated Reader* gets children to choose books to take home and read; they then take a comprehension quiz on a computer at school where they can obtain points and prizes. As a teacher, you can see what progress they are making and if they are having difficulty with specific aspects of comprehension. Computers and software are not necessary to encourage children to practise, but they are worth considering, particularly for learners who do not see themselves as successful.

You may also find your school has adopted an online assessment system which helps to keep track of progress. What it is important to remember with all of these automated assessment systems is that they are very good at presenting questions and marking them, but you will need to make a judgement about how good or how valid this assessment is. Typically, children will get better at playing the game, like Danny in the case study above. You need to decide how this assessment relates to their overall learning progress. If children are getting their spellings right in a computer game or as a result of learning words out of context, is there evidence of this improvement in their writing? Are they able to apply the knowledge they are gaining through digital practice? What can you do to encourage them to apply what they know in one situation to another?

Accurate assessment is, of course, invaluable in helping you decide on what progress children are making and where they might need more help or more practice. Don't just rely on one source of information, but also think about the broader learning progression of your pupils. All kinds of information can be useful here. One valuable source of information is the children themselves. You could develop a digital portfolio of information with your pupils where they decide, with you and perhaps with their peers, which activities or pieces of work best demonstrate their progress in different areas of the curriculum. They will enjoy looking back at things they did earlier in the year and will be able to see the progress they have made. A digital environment saves keeping copies of everything and also enables you to make copies to share with parents or the school they move on to. In the early years, parents will also often be very willing to take short video clips of their own child demonstrating particular skills at home which will help you understand the children's development and engagement outside of school. For older pupils, you may be able to send a photograph of a good piece of work or a successful achievement to parents, either by email or text, if your school uses this kind of technology. Used in this way, digital technology can also facilitate the flow of assessment information from pupil to teacher, making their own recordings such as the maths clips already mentioned or by using immediate feedback technology such as 'Plickers' (www.plickers.com/).

This brings us to the use of technology in your wider professional role. Technology is invaluable for keeping in contact with other professionals involved in the broader development of children, whether this is special needs expertise or health or social care, subject, of course, to any data protection regulations. Online sources are also a valuable source of professional news, information and development, whether through informal means such as Facebook and Twitter or more specific websites for particular interest groups, subject associations through to formal continuing professional development courses from a range of providers including higher degree courses at universities. You are likely to need to take responsibility for your own professional development. Some opportunities will be provided by the school that you work at, but you should also think about which areas of teaching you would like to develop expertise in and pursue some of these yourself. In addition, digital technology such as Iris Connect can also facilitate greater collaboration and enable teachers to explore effective practice without always having to leave their own school. Skype and webinars (such as those used by the National College) can enable professional learning communities to be developed.

The curriculum: computing, information technology and digital literacy

The curriculum separates aspects of technology use by pupils into three strands (see Figure 14.1), bringing back programming which first appeared in the 1980s, but also reflecting how pervasive

	KS1	KS2
Computing	Understand what algorithms are; how they are implemented as programs on digital devices; and that programs execute by following precise and unambiguous instructions. Create and debug simple programs. Use logical reasoning to predict the behaviour of simple programs.	Design, write and debug programs that accomplish specific goals, including controlling or simulating physical systems; solve problems by decomposing them into smaller parts. Use sequence, selection and repetition in programs; work with variables and various forms of input and output. Use logical reasoning to explain how some simple algorithms work and to detect and correct errors in algorithms and programs. Understand computer networks including the internet; how they can provide multiple services, such as the World Wide Web. Appreciate how search results are selected and ranked.
Information Technology	Use technology purposefully to create, organise, store, manipulate and retrieve digital content.	Use search technologies effectively. Select, use and combine a variety of software (including internet services) on a range of digital devices to design and create a range of programs, systems and content that accomplish given goals, including collecting, analysing, evaluating and presenting data and information.
Digital Literacy	Recognise common uses of information technology beyond school. Use technology safely and respectfully, keeping personal information private. Identify where to go for help and support when concerned about content or contact on the internet or other online technologies.	Understand the opportunities that networks offer for communication and collaboration. Be discerning in evaluating digital content. Use technology safely, respectfully and responsibly; recognise acceptable/unacceptable behaviour; identify a range of ways to report concerns about content and contact.

Figure 14.1 Breakdown of the technology curriculum

digital technologies are in our world. The most challenging of these is the computing strand, though the purposeful use of technology is important.

The final section in this chapter looks at the issue of e-safety, part of digital literacy, in more detail.

Getting started with programming

The most important thing to remember when starting with computer programming is that the basic ideas are very simple but that we need to understand the key terms used in the curriculum. An 'algorithm' is nothing more than a sequence of precise instructions, such as 'move forward one step, make a quarter turn right, move forward two steps' and the like. The best way to get this idea across is not with a tablet or a computer but through robot role play in the classroom in pairs (director and actor) or teams of three (director, actor and producer, the latter being an observer who gives feedback).

Have one pupil (the director) instruct a partner (the actor) to build a particular object from Lego or tie their shoelaces or some other straightforward task. Through the laughter that follows, children will learn about precision and clarity, and you should draw out some of the most important ideas in programming:

- Computers are not intelligent; they do exactly what they are told.
- You have to be really precise and exact with your instructions to achieve your goals.
- You can improve or 'debug' when things go wrong, by finding the precise step which caused the problem and correcting it.
- When a simple routine or program works, it can be repeated as many times as you need and built into other programs to create more complex ones.

Web Link

For guidance and advice about getting started with programming in primary schools, have a look at the 'Barefoot Computing' initiative, which can be accessed through this web link, available on the companion website: http://barefootcas.org.uk

E-SAFETY

E-safety is a very real and important concern for teachers and schools. E-safety risks to children and young people have proved real in relation to cyber-bullying, invasion of privacy, communicating with strangers and accessing inappropriate materials such as pornography or websites advocating hate. This section sets out the key legal and safety issues and the importance of following school policies, which draw on Department for Education (DfE) and Ofsted guidance. The use of a wide range of digital technologies, including communication tools and social networking or other online activities, can support and enhance learning. Pupils need to be taught how to use them in a safe and responsible way. It is also important that they learn how to behave appropriately online and to know what they can do if they are at all worried about something someone says to them in a digital environment or something that they see or something that is sent to them electronically which makes them feel uncomfortable.

Two independent reports were commissioned by the government to look at children and new technology and the risks they face online (Byron, 2008, 2010). The reports argue for a shift away from the viewpoint that new technology causes harm to children and young people towards an understanding around how they can be empowered to manage the risks. The initial report set out a national strategy for the government, industry and families to work together to help keep children safe online. Two years later (Byron, 2010), the report reviewed the recent progress that had been made regarding e-safety and emphasised the need to embed these approaches across the curriculum and not just cover them in ICT or PHSE. The report also noted significant developments in initial teacher training, with a TDA survey (2009) showing that over three quarters (77%) of newly qualified teachers thought they understood the e-safety risks pupils faced and almost the same number (74%) felt that they could use this knowledge in their teaching practice.

School policy and ethos

The first and most important issue is that schools should create an environment where pupils feel confident to tell any member of staff about online experiences which made them feel uncomfortable. Every school should have an e-safety policy that has been read and understood by all staff and which is regularly reviewed. The DfE recommends, following the first Byron report (2008), that schools should also have an 'acceptable use policy'. This should provide guidance on how different digital technologies are to be used, how any incidents of misuse will be recorded and what sanctions or consequences will apply should use be considered unacceptable. This should cover the use of mobile or 'smart' phones and other mobile devices and should be updated to keep pace with new and emerging devices and software, particularly communication technologies.

It is important that all teaching and non-teaching staff are appropriately trained for e-safety and that they are confident to recognise e-safety issues and take action where this is needed. It is a good idea for schools to promote helplines and other sources of information so that pupils know where they can get help if they do not feel able to talk to someone at school.

What are your school's responsibilities?

The Ofsted guidance 'Inspecting E-Safety: Briefing for Section 5 Inspection' (2013) outlines a school's responsibilities and also what inspectors will be looking for in terms of e-safety. Schools need to demonstrate that they educate and protect both pupils and staff in their use of technology and have appropriate procedures to intervene and to support any e-safety incident. Ofsted focus on three areas identified as posing the greatest risk. The first of these is *content* in terms of exposure to illegal, inappropriate or harmful online materials. This includes online pornography and sexual images, sites which promote violence and hatred, as well as sites which advocate or condone substance abuse, anorexia, self-harm or suicide. The second is *contact*, which means being subjected to harmful or potentially harmful interaction with others online. This includes grooming, cyberbullying and things like identity theft and the dangers of sharing passwords or using those which are easily guessable. The final area is *conduct*, which is about personal behaviour which causes or might cause harm, such as the disclosure of personal information, health and well-being, sexting, copyright and data protection issues.

Good practice for schools

Ofsted has also identified some examples of good and outstanding practice to help identify different roles and responsibilities for effective e-safety in schools. First and foremost is the importance of a consistent whole-school approach, which is the responsibility of the leadership and management of the school, but which also requires the involvement and active engagement of the whole school community, such as by providing workshops for parents and planning sessions where pupils can teach parents. Policies, including an 'acceptable use policy', should be regularly reviewed and updated, with the involvement of pupils in the development of policy. The school infrastructure should be secure, with actively monitored filtering and use of a recognised internet service for schools. It is also important for schools to have robust and integrated reporting procedures, which might include online approaches to report concerns or incidents, but also the use of peer mentoring and support from fellow pupils. Monitoring and evaluation should be routine, with appropriate risk assessments and use of data to assess the impact of e-safety procedures. Each school should have an e-safety curriculum that is relevant and appropriate for pupils of all ages and that engages them and teaches them how to stay safe and protect themselves and others. Finally, training for all staff is essential, in all of these aspects plus instruction in the management of personal data in accordance with the Data Protection Act 1988, as is maintaining a professional code of conduct in their own use of technology and online behaviour.

reflection point

Have you seen examples of acceptable use policies in the schools you have spent time in? Would you know what to do if a child reported seeing inappropriate content online or has been a target for cyber-bullying?

FUTURE DEVELOPMENTS

It is hard to predict which areas of our lives are going to be affected by new technologies as they emerge and embed in our contemporary world. Digital technologies are like a deciduous tree which annually sheds it leaves, as new technologies emerge and are replaced by another generation of digital devices. The tree continues to grow and develop with new branches and opportunities, as other technologies fade and are forgotten. Who remembers the quinkey, the Palm Pilot or Apple's e-mate computer? (Google these if you are curious!)

What we can predict is that the invention of new digital devices and technologies will continue, with greater integration and transferability of digital information and resources. Do you wish you could flick an activity from your interactive whiteboard to each of the tables where your pupils are sitting? Or that you could easily pick up what some children are doing on their table and display it to the class, and get them to explain their ideas as they continue to improve it, modelling the process for other children, then copy and send this example back to everyone to work on in their separate groups? This can already be done: a project called SynergyNet at Durham University, funded by the Teaching and Learning Research Programme's Technology Enhanced Learning fund, has created a digital classroom where teaching and learning materials can be moved easily from whole-class display to large interactive tables to tablet computers, to develop greater digital flow of information, even assessing aspects of children's learning automatically in the background and summarising this information on the teacher's iPad.

Web Link

The fascinating 'Re-imagining School' Ted Talk can be accessed through this web link, available on the companion website: www.ted.com/playlists/24/re_imagining_school

Flipped learning is also being explored. This is where learners do much of the preparation and learning of materials outside of the classroom, at home or working with their peers from video or other online resources. The teacher then addresses any issues which arise and can focus on developing understanding or application of the material, rather than more basic acquisition of knowledge and information.

'Bring your own device' or 'BYOD' is also influencing technology use. Most children own or have access to a smartphone with a range of digital capabilities. The advantage of BYOD is that the learner is responsible for learning the specific skills of using the device, and this frees up the teacher to focus on the curriculum and the specific learning objectives for the lesson, without getting bogged down in specific instructions about operating a particular device. There are significant issues about equity and the exclusion of children from disadvantaged backgrounds who may not have access to the latest technology or even any technology of their own (Longley and Singleton, 2009). However, the cost savings made by not owning and renewing a stock on individual devices, even with the costs of helping some families to buy technology, can reduce overall expenditure and technical support costs so a number of schools, particularly at secondary level, have started to explore this option.

Technology will always be full of fads, fashions and new-fangled ideas. You are likely to get the best from these if you keep your sights firmly focused on the learning that the latest gadget can help you do better than before. What people forget is that when you start doing something new with technology, you have to stop doing something else, so you need to be sure that the 'something else' that you stop is actually worse than what you can achieve with the latest gadget.

SUMMARY

Technology is here to stay, and although the evidence on the benefits of technology use is generally positive, it is important to focus on the learning outcomes and to understand what role new technologies can play as they develop and are used in schools. It is easy to be fooled by superficial engagement in the activity and the use of technology without reflecting on how the technology is contributing to children's engagement in learning. Analysing what is happening in terms of different theories of learning can help to focus attention on what is important in terms of how it is contributing to children's learning.

Digital technologies are flexible and powerful tools which can support all aspects of a teacher's professional life. Different tools can help with planning and preparing engaging and effective activities, supporting and enhancing interaction skills such as with an interactive whiteboard, and in the areas of assessment and recording of progress or reporting to and engaging with parents. Professional development can also be made more accessible and applicable with the use of online materials and courses.

The curriculum separates aspects of technology use by pupils into three strands: Computing, Information Technology and Digital Literacy, with an emphasis on programming, on using technology to manage information and on learning to live in and with a digital world productively and safely, reflecting how pervasive digital technologies are in our world. The most challenging of these for many teachers is the computing strand, though the purposeful use of technology as pupils learn to learn at school is also important. However, the issue of e-safety, part of digital literacy, is clearly crucial in ensuring the well-being and security of children in your care. Digital technologies can connect children and classrooms to the outside world in a way which can enhance and enliven countless educational activities. However, there are also risks associated with this connectivity, both educational and personal.

Overall, technology is integral to our world. New technologies are going to continue to emerge at a rapid pace, with both predictable and unforeseen consequences. It is the educational professional's role to take responsibility for ensuring that the inclusion and embedding of digital technologies in school enhances the educational opportunities for the children and young people that they teach.

To access additional online resources please visit: **https://study.sagepub.com/wyseandrogers**

Here you will find a classroom activity, author podcasts including Steve Higgins' and James Siddle's top tips for employability, free access to SAGE journal articles and links to external sources.

further reading

Savage, M. and Barnett, A. (2015) *Digital Literacy for Primary Teachers*. Northwich: Critical Publishing. This book provides a good introduction to digital literacy from both a professional perspective and in terms of covering the curriculum for primary-age pupils.

The Barefoot Computing initiative aims to help primary school teachers get started with programming: http://barefootcas.org.uk

The BBC has resources to teach children and young people about the dangers that are present online: www.bbc.co.uk/cbbc/topics/stay-safe

The British Computer Society (BCS) has a website to support Computing at School: www.computingatschool.org.uk

The Sutton Trust-EEF Teaching and Learning Toolkit is a good source of information from research and has a specific section on digital technology: https://educationendowmentfoundation.org.uk/index.php/toolkit/

REFERENCES

Byron, T. (2008). *Safer Children in a Digital World: the Report of the Byron Review – be safe, be aware, have fun*. London: DCSF.

Byron, T. (2010). *Do we have Safer Children in a Digital World? A Review of Progress since the 2008 Byron Review* (DCSF-00290-2010). London: DCSF.

Dawes, L., Mercer, N., and Wegerif, R. (2000). *Thinking Together: A Programme of Activities for Developing Thinking Skills at KS2*. Birmingham: Questions Publishing Company.

Higgins, S., Xiao, Z., and Katsipataki, M. (2012). *The Impact of Digital Technology on Learning: A Summary for the Education Endowment Foundation*. London: EEF. Available at: http://bit.ly/10xRmZ4

Longley, P. A., and Singleton, A. D. (2009). Linking social deprivation and digital exclusion in England. *Urban Studies*, 46(7), 1275–98.

Naylor, S., and Keogh, B. (2005). *Concept Cartoons in Science Education*. Sandbach: Millgate House.

Ofsted (2013) *Inspecting E-Safety: Briefing for Section 5 Inspection*. London: Ofsted.

Papert, S. (1980). *Mindstorms: Children, Computers, and Powerful Ideas*. New York: Basic Books.

Stevenson, D. (1997) *Information and Communications Technology in UK Schools: An Independent Inquiry*. London: Independent ICT in Schools Commission.

Tamim, R. M., Bernard, R. M., Borokhovski, E., Abrami, P. C., and Schmid, R. F. (2011). What forty years of research says about the impact of technology on learning a second-order meta-analysis and validation study. *Review of Educational Research*, 81(1), 4–28.

TDA (Training and Development Agency for Schools) (2009) *Results of the newly qualified teachers survey 2009*. Manchester: TDA.

15

YOUR FIRST JOB

Joanne Waterhouse and Rachel Miller

LEARNING AIMS

This chapter will enable you to:

- know the key elements to effective preparation for starting your first teaching job
- understand the common expectations of parents, children and colleagues of an effective classroom teacher
- understand the processes of classroom observation for professional learning and accountability
- consider the attributes of teacher leadership and collegial practice that constitute teacher professionalism.

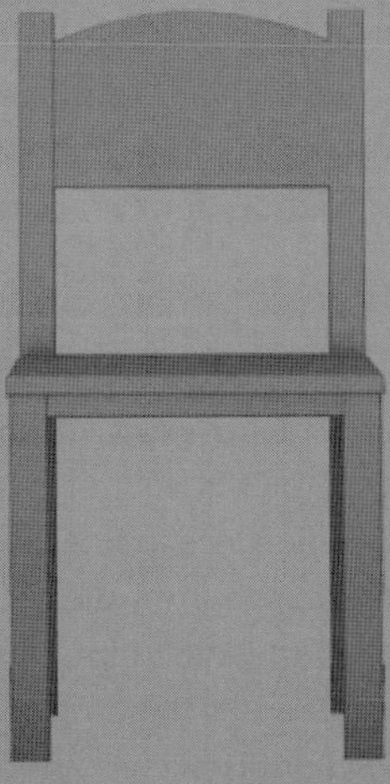

It is a privilege to be a teacher and your first job is likely to represent the most formative stage of your career. Lessons learned in your first job will remain with you long after the anxieties have faded. This chapter is not intended to be a manual for the first year nor a definitive guide to all that you are likely to encounter. Rather, it is designed to offer a reflective discussion on key elements for success in the acquisition and settlement of your first teaching post. Our premise is that making a success of your first job is essentially the act of becoming a professional. Teaching is a dynamic, interpersonal and dialogic profession. It requires the application of theory with an awareness of the nature of classrooms and schools as complex environments. We understand professionalism to be the conscious, reflective rendering of theory into practice as a career-long endeavour, which will begin in the specific cultural context of your first job. This positions the professional teacher as a learner, first and foremost.

This chapter is a reflective guide to managing the reality of the teaching task, and a consideration of how to make the theory work. It is structured in two parts. *Part 1: Getting started* is designed to encompass the period from initial contact and preliminary visit to becoming settled in your first job. The specific art of 'contextual literacy' is emphasised as key to making sense of your experiences in navigating the organisation in the initial weeks and months. *Part 2: Becoming a professional* includes discussions on the practicalities and realities of becoming a reflexive practitioner in the broader cultural contexts of continuous professional development, inspection and collaboration.

PART 1: GETTING STARTED

There are diverse ways to train to become a teacher. Increasingly, the route is one that places the trainee within the school from the outset. Traditional university courses remain and are the preferred choice for many, allowing as they do for sustained periods of reflection and study. Alternative school-based schemes are encouraged as part of the extended remit of schools to lead learning for the profession. The routes to your first job will therefore differ, with some trainees based in university and seeking employment at the end of a course and others immediately placed in their school either as a trainee or, in some cases, as an employee. This makes for a complex picture of how to get started. However, the essential components of making contact, effective preparation, navigating the cultural context and establishing positive relationships will all remain significant.

Prior to making contact, it is important to know the possible types of school that you could occupy in your first job. Table 15.1 contains a summary of the types and governing arrangements for state school provision in England.

In addition, there are numerous independent public schools in which you could work for your first job. Unlike state schools, these do not require you to acquire qualified teacher status in order to apply. Traditionally, age phase arrangements exist within a two-phase primary and secondary model, although there are increasing initiatives to create 'all through' models that incorporate provision from nursery to sixth form. Some areas in England have first, middle and upper school arrangements and some favour separate sixth form colleges. Schools vary enormously in size and there is a diverse range of faith schools. The issue of inclusive education and selection is debated and variously provided for. There is also an understanding of rural, urban and inner-city schooling. You will need to decide which type of school is likely to suit you best.

Table 15.1 Governing arrangements for state schools in England

Type of school	Arrangements
Community (or maintained) schools	The local authority employs the school's staff and owns the school's land and buildings, although the governing body has responsibility for most employment matters and has day-to-day control of land and buildings. The local authority has responsibility for deciding the arrangements for admitting pupils.
Foundation and Trust schools	Employ their own staff and set their own admissions criteria within a national framework. Buildings are usually owned by either the governing body or by a charitable foundation. Trust schools are foundation schools with a charitable trust drawn from an outside organisation.
Voluntary aided (VA) schools and voluntary controlled (VC) schools	In VA schools, the governing body employs the school's staff and has primary responsibility for admission arrangements. The school's buildings are normally owned by a charitable foundation. The governing body contributes towards the capital costs of running the school. In VC schools, the local authority employs the school's staff and has primary responsibility for admission arrangements. The school's land and buildings are normally owned by a charitable foundation.
Academies (convertor and sponsored)	Free from local authority control and National Curriculum requirements. Independently funded and governed. Often part of a larger 'chain'.
Free schools	Free from local authority control and National Curriculum requirements. Independently funded and governed. Usually independent and single entity.

Source: Higham et al. (2007)

Web Link

An article that considers how new teachers might go about choosing the right school can be accessed through this web link, available on the companion website: http://newteachers.tes.co.uk/content/new-teachers-choose-right-school

Beyond governance understood technically, there is the matter of school leadership arrangements. These are also varied and increasingly complex. Academy chains often appoint a chief executive who works with the governing body to oversee the work of school principals in a number of schools. Executive arrangements are becoming more common, in secondary schools but also in networks of smaller, primary schools, and heads of school are often in place with two or more deputy head teachers. School leadership structures can be bespoke to an organisation and school leadership personnel will be an integral part of the leadership dynamic in place. All this will form part of the landscape to be navigated and understood. The key message to anyone seeking a first teaching job is to research the area and type of school that you are considering applying for, and include a visit to the immediate locality if possible. Much of the 'making contact' discussion below will reflect the inherent imperative of matching the individual to the organisation.

MAKING CONTACT

Appearances matter and first impressions count. What is also important is the narrative that you tell about your motivations for becoming a teacher, your understanding of the challenges and privileges involved and your experiences of working with children or young adults. Your knowledge about the school, the locality, the community and the particular route or course will all resonate to impress the people with whom you are making initial contact. The key element to this process is mutuality. It is as much a decision for you as it is a selection of you by others. There needs to be a good fit between you and the school in terms of values, behaviours and character. Another important element is the balance that you can make between the inherent enthusiasm and commitment that you bring, and the sense of humility that comes from an awareness that the school is essentially unknown to you. Each school is a unique environment, comprising a particular history, community, identity and set of values. The job of a newly appointed teacher is to ask questions about this unique place and seek to understand the complexities of tradition and personalities – all this, whilst bringing an invaluable new perspective and fresh insight to bear.

Making contact with staff and children

Visiting a school, with its inevitable noise, pace and energy, can be an overwhelming experience for anyone, let alone a candidate prior to an interview. When I visited my school, I had so many questions buzzing around my mind all leading to 'What do I need to do to make them want me?' and, as importantly but often overlooked, 'Do I want to work at this school?' After the visit, which was fortunately incredibly enjoyable, there remained some unanswered questions but also an over-arching feeling of positivity. My own preparation was hugely assisted by a teacher at my own childhood primary school with whom I had contact and I will always share their advice.

There was a point in my own visit when I was asked whether I wanted to eat lunch with the staff (whom I had already spent time with at break) or eat with the children? Taking the latter option, it proved invaluable. In speaking to the pupils, you are able to elicit how behaviour is managed and what inspires them at the school, whilst gauging if they seem curious, polite and engaged.

Considerations when choosing a school

First, do your research. Look at the school website – alongside reading any curriculum guidance, learning explanations or policies, make sure you browse the photographs, read the newsletters and look at the PTA events, as all of this will indicate the values that underline the school. Locate the most recent Ofsted report - reflect on how it matches the current situation. What can you learn from that perspective? On the day, as you navigate the school look at the displays, peer into classrooms - what does the presentation say about the style of the school? Is it all triple-backed and neat or organic and formative? Introduce yourself to staff members and ask them how they are. Do they seem happy and positive? Are there signs of collegial collaboration? Proudly talk about your experience to date and why you are looking to join their school. Always remember that you are interviewing the school as much as they are interviewing you. When you are finished, take a breath and consider if this is the school for you to follow the career you imagine - whatever that may be.

EFFECTIVE PREPARATION

Elsewhere in this book you will read about curriculum theory and practice, about effective learning environments and how to manage behaviour. Your first job is the first time when these things need to be synthesised and to be realised in the context of helping your first class of children to learn. There will be various forms of induction and institutional preparation organised by your colleagues, both prior to you starting a teaching job and subsequently. It is important that you also think about your own needs for preparation. This is likely to include one or more informal visits when you are able to design your classroom environment and begin to get to know the people with whom you will be working. Effective preparation includes learning who is responsible for allocating resources for your class, your team or your department. What are the expectations on you with regard to resourcing and preparing your teaching space? What will be required to be in place prior to any children or students entering the space? How will you make it 'emotionally inviting' (Wyatt and White, 2002)? Visit other people's spaces, asking them what is generally expected. You may wish to be innovative, but it is always useful to be aware of the school's norms when planning innovations so that you can anticipate what will be required to support the young people in navigating your space safely. Similarly, it will be useful to plan how you will manage the curriculum. You cannot know everything so will need to plan the process of preparing content and the necessary resources incrementally throughout the academic year. Identify who is responsible for the various subjects or for the elements within your department, and establish what sources of information are currently mined for ideas and activities. Such effective preparation can be a blueprint for your ongoing professional behaviour throughout your first few terms and going forward.

reflection point

Your classroom should be an emotionally inviting space ...

You must give respect and expect respect.

(Wyatt and White, 2002: 7, 107)

(Continued)

(Continued)

- What do these two statements mean for you?
- What are the implications for the way you organise and illustrate your classroom?
- How much can you establish by structures and how much is established by attitudes and behaviours?

UNDERSTANDING THE CONTEXT OF SCHOOLS

Although schools each have their own unique contexts, different schools also have some similar features such as the customs and practices of registration, assemblies, duty at break times, and so on. Common practices also arise more systematically as a result of formal links with other schools. There are also common practices that arise through the subjects of the curriculum, supported by local and national organisations. Increasingly, schools are networked variously and extensively. Academy chains (academy schools linked through the organisations that manage them) will often have shared policies for a range of procedures. Whatever the scale of the organisation you join, you will need to learn about the cultural context. Espoused values are seen in a school's vision or mission statement. The underlying values and beliefs can be guessed at by studying rituals and traditions, as well as other pointers such as role systems and hierarchies, pedagogical trends and social relationships. These can refer to:

> those aspects of the school setting that are viewed by school personnel as 'givens' or essential features, which they would strongly defend against elimination or marked change, and which to them reflect psychological concepts and value judgements. (Sarason, 1995: 71)

Then there are the norms of behaviour – the 'unspoken rules for what is regarded as customary or acceptable behaviour and action within the school' (Stoll, 1999: 36). School culture is identified by the way its members behave and yet is also, for the members, a way of understanding and conforming. Hence, some elements are explicit in policies and other school documentation, whilst other elements are implicit so require you to work these things out by being perceptive when you talk to people in school. The school culture is seen in norms of behaviour (for teachers and for pupils) and in teaching strategies. It can vary between teams and departments and it can consist of elements that can inhibit or support innovation. What is important for you in your first job is that you seek to understand the context for your work. Part of your effectiveness as a teacher will lie in how you navigate your way through the school culture to work with colleagues and students harmoniously. This is not to say that there is a requirement to accept all norms and never seek to challenge or innovate; it is rather an acknowledgement that you can be more effective and influential with an understanding of the context. This knowledge will necessarily be incremental, increasing over time through the multiple interactions that will be part of your experience.

Learning about expectations

Each school is required to publish a prospectus that includes the mutual expectations between the organisation and the community it serves. There will be published requirements for communication, formal and informal, and for student dress and behaviour. In addition to published materials about the school and its teachers, the parents will develop a sense of you as a new teacher. It is vital that in your first job you know from the outset what the published expectations are regarding assessment, reporting progress and informing parents and carers of both routine and unusual matters. Similarly, there will be various policies for aspects of school life, such as safeguarding, behaviour, assessment and curriculum.

The school is required to formulate a 'school offer' comprising curricular and well-being elements. These cannot all be known and absorbed prior to taking up a teaching post, but it is important that in your first job you have a strategy for accessing published documents and learning how they work in your school. It is likely that your role has a job description and person specification attached. Both will provide you with knowledge of how the position is perceived theoretically within the organisation. Take advantage of partnerships, mentors and team colleagues to discuss published policies with them, in order to learn how they are realised in practice.

Schools often publish their stated aims and values. This may include a vision statement. Part of the navigation of the cultural context is learning how these are manifest in the daily lives of the school community. This in turn will indicate the expectations on teachers to represent those stated values and aims. Part of your professional practice will be to understand these aims and values, and to engage in dialogue with colleagues to develop your understanding of them.

Accountability measures, including formal inspection procedures, make explicit the expectations on teachers with regard to outcomes for students and the ways in which teachers and schools are judged. Schools will vary in the extent to which they adapt and interpret national accountability regimes. What is crucial is that you learn how your school manages the processes of professional development, appraisal and inspection. In your first job, the key requirement is to establish yourself within your team or department as someone who knows and understands the internal expectations and strives to meet them. If you adopt the stance of a learning professional, you will have an enquiring mind, be interested in trying new ideas, will engage in discussions and have the confidence to both reflect on things you do well and seek to understand things that do not go well. We will discuss this further in a later section.

The ways in which you conduct yourself and how you sustain positive working relationships are also part of your professional practice. Teaching strategies and less formal expectations of teacher behaviour are likely to be implicit rather than the explicit subject of policy or prospectus. This is where navigating the cultural context is crucial. Expectations of appearance and behaviour can vary between organisations but are usually immediately understood by initial observations and preliminary interactions. This will have been part of the mutual choosing that occurred at the first meeting. You may wish to join a union and make connections with various networks of support for your phase, subject or organisation.

Web Link

An interesting article about getting to know your new school can be accessed through this web link, available on the companion website: http://newteachers.tes.co.uk/news/getting-know-your-new-school/23184

ESTABLISHING POSITIVE RELATIONSHIPS

Teaching is relational. It is about communicating successfully and making connections with others in order to achieve a changed state in the learner. Those others include children and students, colleagues both within the classroom and beyond, and those with knowledge of the child beyond the school, such as parents and carers. To this end, the establishment of positive relationships is crucial. There are two elements to the establishment of positive relationships that are highlighted here. One is the dynamic between home and school, in which the child can increasingly play an active part. The other is the issue of managing adults in the classroom in your first job.

The home/school dynamic

Your school will have developed a culture and practice for home–school contact and communication. There are likely to be policies, and the school year will have its own rhythm for meetings and reporting to parents, formal and informal. A constructive home–school dynamic will impact on the trust and confidence that you gain in relationship with parents and carers, as well as with the children themselves. Rather than viewing the relationship with home as a partnership that is essentially one-way, such as instructions going from school to parents/guardians, it can be conceived more creatively with the child as an important person whose voice is significant. In this way, the relationship may be imagined as a triad, involving the teacher, parent and child. The child moves daily between the different social worlds of home and school. As an integral and equal member of the triad, the child can be seen as a key player, routinely sought out and included in the communication. From this perspective, the child 'mediates' the message, acting both as a conduit and a participant as they 'select and act upon' the information being shared (Scanlon, 2011: 264). Activities for this include shared display boards, the making of DVDs and photo collections using disposable cameras, and the collection of significant artefacts in a shoebox which is compiled at home and shared discursively at school.

> You will be used to thinking about children having individual needs and preferences. It is therefore important to keep this uppermost in your mind when thinking about parents and carers too. (Albon, 2011: 57)

- What do you think are the particular challenges of interacting successfully with parents and carers?
- How will you access the invaluable insights that they can bring?
- How can you organise the learning environment to include shared spaces for communicating with home?

Managing other adults

Entering the teaching profession new to a school and its community is challenging. One of the challenges is establishing your authority as a professional when you are inexperienced and probably a relatively young person yourself. This issue has been characterised as a significant dilemma: 'To be able to lead practice in situations where practitioners may have different values, beliefs and approaches at a point in one's career when one is still developing one's own!' (Cable, 2011: 280). The new teacher may bring changes to practice that others find confusing or threatening because the new practice can be seen as implicitly challenging their usual ways of working. Your confidence in the classroom can be undermined by thoughts that everyone else seems to know more than you about school procedures. Increasingly, there are other adults in the room working alongside you, some of whom you are expected to manage. This requires teamwork and a commitment to shared knowledge.

Teaching assistants (TAs) are often experienced, trusted and effective members of the community. Their roles are various and nuanced, frequently placing them with the most vulnerable or apprehensive members of the class. It is a wise teacher who recognises the skills of TAs who 'may well have highly developed skills in communicating with pupils, observing pupils at work, and acting as advocates for marginalised or disaffected pupils' (Cajkler and Suschitzky, 2011: 186). A new teacher will establish authority by having the learning environment well-resourced and organised, the lessons well prepared, and by being open to learning from those around, whilst confidently dealing with their responsibilities, including safety and welfare. A good strategy is to actively engage with the people you work with and demonstrate a willingness to make adjustments if required. Collaboration is a strength, not a weakness.

There are a range of other adults you may need to liaise with in the course of preparing appropriate support for individual children and students. These may include other professionals such as interpreters, advisors, therapists, specialist teachers, educational psychologists and social workers. In your first job, you will need in a short time to be confident to contribute to joint planning and decision making because you are necessarily at the heart of the process (Walker, 2011). Developing this confidence will be a matter of time, experience and learning from others.

reflection point

It is a teacher's professional responsibility to find out what TAs bring to the classroom: linguistic, pedagogic, musical, technical, and personal/social. (Cajkler and Suschitzky, 2011: 187)

- How will you work with the TAs in your classroom to ensure you learn about their interests and skills?
- What routines and habits of communication will you establish?

PART 2: BECOMING A PROFESSIONAL

Your first job is a key time when you take forward your professional identity. Becoming a professional can be characterised in the twin terms of teacher as learner and teacher as leader. In both regards, it is a time of taking on responsibility and of '*emotional labour*' (Corbin, 2010). A research study into the perspectives of new teachers focused on the emotional aspects of the process of becoming a teacher and of 'feeling professional' (Corbin, 2010). The emotional labour was centred around the process of becoming 'strictly nice' and the new teachers reported how they scrutinised experienced teachers for clues as to how they 'personify what appear to be impossibly simultaneous practices of both control and affection' (2010: 52). Early professional learning was comprised of the act of becoming more relaxed and resilient whilst developing confidence and reputation. Another perspective from the same study illuminates responsibility as 'an unrehearseable aspect of professional performance' (Stronach, 2011: 203). The rapid professional learning of new teachers is characterised by key dynamics of rapid and uncertain change, amid development that was incremental, recursive and disruptive (2011). The first months of teaching plunge the neophyte into 'an unavoidable gap between the reach of induction and the grasp of initiation' (2011: 215). There is arguably an inevitable, and enduring, gap throughout the first months of teaching between what you can be inducted into and what you can confidently know and understand. It is in this context that new teachers learn to assume responsibility for their class, or classes, and can become participants in collaborative practices to lead change in their organisations.

Feeling apprehensive

It is two weeks until the start of my first teaching post and I am noticing the tinge of envy in the voices of friends as they discuss my long summer break. I sit there smiling and agreeing that indeed I am lucky, however in all honesty I am feeling far from lucky. I am feeling a little apprehensive. My thoughts include:

- How will I get a child to do their work if they don't want to?
- Marking over 90 books per night and lesson preparation – will I have a life beyond that?
- How do I ensure all 30 children are appropriately catered for?
- What if a parent disagrees with my approach to teaching their child?

I didn't conquer any of these concerns before the start of term but I did take some action that helped. I prepared my classroom and teaching sufficiently so it felt like my own, whilst understanding it would be developed throughout the year. I read the behaviour policy of the school because, personality and style aside, if you follow a consistent plan then behaviour management becomes a lot easier than envisaged. I discussed planning with colleagues but soon realised that my first week, whilst planned, would need to be dealt with in a flexible manner. I familiarised myself with the topics and subjects that I would be covering. I enjoyed updating my knowledge of some areas, such as the exact dates for the Stone Age and current strategies for teaching times tables! I considered how I wanted to be considered as a teacher and took small steps to achieve this. Most importantly, I took guidance from my new colleagues. And, by the way, I did other things in my life for enjoyment and relaxation! It is OK to be apprehensive: it shows you care, and with care you will start to become the teacher you want to be.

reflection point

The emotions of becoming a professional

Taking on responsibility as a new teacher in your first job has been described as 'an unrehearseable aspect of professional performance' (Stronach, 2010: 203).

- Think about some steps you will take to enhance the way you feel emotionally about teaching and the taking on of new responsibilities.
- What support might you need from colleagues to help you deal with the new experiences that you will encounter?

TEACHER AS LEARNER

There are two discrete practices in your first job that emphasise the role of teacher as learner. These are the act of being mentored and the participation in observing lessons – as both observer and the observed. We would argue that both practices are mutual acts of engagement which involve reciprocity and shared understanding. The new teacher must take responsibility for their own learning and be encouraged to act as a peer from the outset of the process. The act of mentoring may comprise a series of relational features: trust and rapport; benevolence; honesty; openness; reliability and competence. Concerns of beginning teachers have been classified in terms of: Management – the expectations and behaviour of senior members of staff; Personal – the development of their role and reputation; Instructional – the challenges of managing pupil progress and behaviour; and Socialisation – the development of relationships in and out of the classroom (Daresh, 2003; Tschannen-Moran and Tschannen-Moran, 2010). Effective mentoring develops over time in response to context and the progress of the individual. Mentoring is relational and best enacted collaboratively. It brings to mind an axiom of teacher learning, that 'Teachers don't care how much we know until they know how much we care' (Tschannen-Moran and Tschannen-Moran, 2010: 28).

Mentoring

> Effective, regular, planned and sympathetic communication between you and your mentor is quintessential to your success as a beginning teacher and will go a long way to making you feel needed, valued and supported, oh, and happy. (Dillon and Maguire, 2007: 8-9)

- How will you ensure 'planned communication' with your mentor?
- What do you think are your strengths as a communicator?
- How do you think your needs for support from your mentor might change over the course of the initial two terms in your first job?

Learning from observation

A new teacher needs to take advantage of any opportunities to observe the practice of others. This is a vital tool for broadening understanding about practice and invaluable for developing strategies and resources. In your first job, you are likely to have additional opportunities to visit others' classrooms and other schools and it is imperative that you take advantage of this. When you agree targets for development, these can often be realised by visiting other people's spaces and asking questions of more experienced colleagues. Additionally, in your first job you will be involved in a series of observations made of your practice from the outset. These should not be onerous or unexpected, so it would be understood that you always agree the time and purpose and that no more than one or two observations each term would be arranged. Observations may be enacted by team or department peers, your mentor, the lead colleague in your team or department, or a member of senior management. Occasionally, it may be that an outside advisor or consultant is deployed to visit your classroom and there is the possibility that an Ofsted inspection will take place. In your first job, it is the responsibility of senior members of staff to induct you into their processes for accountability, as discussed above. What you need to focus on is what you can gain from the process of being observed. This can be knowledge about curriculum, increased understanding of teaching strategies and a better appreciation of your own practice in the context of a particular group on a particular day. What is crucial is how you engage with the process – how you plan, how you listen and how you question. Observers will watch students, scrutinise work and listen to how you interact with others. A good strategy is to agree a focus for an observation in your own classroom, and then take that focus into others' classrooms to 'triangulate' your learning.

spotlight on practice

Learning from observation

In any job, if you were asked to complete a task to the best of your ability, with your manager watching each move and making copious notes, it would be normal to feel under pressure. If the task was not under your full control (e.g. because 30 children have their own ways of acting), the challenges of lesson observation become clear.

One observation I had with my head teacher early into my first post gave me some key learning points that I have always remembered. Yes, resources matter, yes, a colourful flipchart can help, yes, music can add to the lesson, but be sure of your objective and what you want each child to learn. If the children were asked, could they tell the observer what they were learning? If not, the likelihood is you have over-complicated the lesson through trying to show too much about your teaching. I found myself not being able to tell my head teacher the precise learning outcome - not through lack of preparation but due to insufficiently focused preparation. I can vividly remember at one point in my feedback feeling wronged that the observer was not taking my class into account.

putting it into practice

Learning from observation

Talk yourself through the modelling: what are the clear sections of the lesson and what will learning look like for all of your class? Consider extensions and support but don't over-complicate things; the most impressive lessons I have seen are streamlined, clear and unfussy. Contextualise the entire learning setting for the person observing you. Write a detailed plan not only of the lesson but also a page stating where you are in a unit; the number of children in the class; the achievement levels of the children; your classroom organisation; and the target children, including of course any behavioural concern. The extended plan for your observer allows them a needed insight that will enhance the likelihood of genuinely useful feedback. Lastly, ensure you leave the feedback meeting with no more than two immediate and measurable targets and ask for these if not given. Targeted feedback is vital for our pupils and vital for you, so ensure you have it. Most of all, through it all, accept that you will feel personally affected by the formal grading but take a breath and know that observations are formative, and that it will all become more routine as your career develops.

Judgements on lessons that are observed will have their focus on pupil progress as well as effective teacher behaviour. For a lesson to be judged 'outstanding' (in Ofsted terms), it will need to be clear how your resources have been planned and deployed to maximum effect so that the students have evidently made progress. Increasingly, such judgements are made about a series of lessons, a unit of work or a collection of work under scrutiny. Certainly, Ofsted judgements are broader than a single lesson. The inspectors are interested in more sustained efforts and effects. Observations need to be contextualised in a process of dialogue and engagement, characterised by the new teacher's reflective practice and improved confidence.

TEACHER AS LEADER

There is an increasing emphasis on teachers as leaders. You can see this in the approach taken to early career paths by the organisation Teach First, but also by proponents of the recognition of teachers as being at the frontline of student progress and efforts to change practice. Teacher leadership is conceived as 'parallel leadership' – a process whereby 'teacher leaders and their principals engage in collective action to build school capacity' (Crowther, 2009: 53) – and as 'extended professionality', whereby teachers are leaders through their relationships with each other and through 'school based research and enquiry strategies' (Law, 2011: 408). In a recent study, teacher leadership was defined as: 'Leadership activity occurring within teachers' individual classrooms and through the informal interactions and relationships among teachers where teachers were leading with others' (Fairman and Mackenzie, 2015: 63).

In your first job, it is likely that there will be many opportunities for collaboration with immediate colleagues in your team or department. For those in small schools or otherwise isolated, there may be opportunities to collaborate in networks and online forums. From collaboration through shared planning, observations, evaluation and pupil assessment can come the motivation to engage in further dialogue and enquiry. Common activities and dispositions comprising teacher leadership include: mutual respect and the recognition of colleagues' individual strengths; establishing positive, professional relationships; modelling a commitment to professional learning; courage to challenge the status quo; and sharing ideas and practices (Fairman and Mackenzie, 2015). Aspiring new teachers recognise these attributes as a commitment to the daily life of schooling, in which change is constant and improvement efforts are an expectation on all members of the community.

spotlight on practice

Being a reflective leading teacher

I often think that each topic has 100 different ways to be approached and each approach has 100 different objectives and these objectives can be achieved in 100 different ways and every time you make a decision there could have been another route to take. To make sense of this, you must be reflective. You must take positives from all that went well but be honest about what could be better and focus on honing this in your classroom practice. You will constantly find different ways to do something and to ignore these because they may not fit into your prescribed style is to halt your own learning journey. Recently, I was able to give some advice to a senior member of SMT about how to approach a particular History lesson. I was astounded: why would she need to know my thoughts? However, on reflection, how fantastic that someone who appears so 'sorted' in her teaching still dedicates time to improve. If we want our children to hold a growth mindset and continue to push themselves, then we must model this ourselves. Liaise with a colleague, read a new educational book, research online, attend an education-related event or even speak to your children. How could things continue to get better? If you are trying to get 'there', stop and smile at the fact that you never will but will instead always be part of the most privileged journey.

reflection point

Teacher as leader

> The most salient learning for most of us comes when we don't know how to do it, when we want to know how to do it, and when our responsibility for doing it will affect the lives of many others with whom we live and work. This is where teacher leadership and professional development intersect. (Barth, 2001: 81)

- Discuss with some of your peers what this quote means for you.
- Reflect on how you learned something new.
- How could you influence and lead your colleagues?

Collaboration, trust and well-being

'Teachers as leaders' is a concept and practice that needs a context in which to thrive. The extent to which the school or organisation in which you settle in your first job has a culture of collaboration and collegiality among all members of the community, adults and students, will be an indicator of the degree of leadership influence that you can immediately aspire to. One important aspect that keeps featuring in the discourse for new teacher learning is trust. The significance of trust as an element of relationships is crucial. It is founded on ideas of *social capital* as a quality of interpersonal ties across a community. Social capital theory builds on the work of Putnam (1998) and Szreter (2002) and their ideas of social capital as 'generalised reciprocity' infused with 'widespread and transitive trust and trustworthiness' (Ibid: 574). Bridging social capital is focused in particular on pro-action for equality and 'depends crucially on context' (Ibid: 576). Trustworthiness has been identified as 'a property of the relational ties among individuals within a social system through sustained social interactions' (Bryk and Schneider, 2002: 12). This has been defined as 'relational trust' and is to be found in the 'nature of the interpersonal exchanges among members who comprise that community' (Ibid: 14). These authors assert that relational trust can be viewed as a key factor for motivating and influencing change, a 'moral resource for action' (Ibid: 26). In this way, such trust can be understood as the source of school improvement efforts. Relational trust has been further understood as 'the willingness of individuals to rely upon others and to make oneself vulnerable to others in that reliance' (Mayrowetz et al., 2007: 89). Trust is comprised of respect, personal regard, competence and personal integrity. So in your first job, building trust and collegial relationships will be key to your ongoing efforts to lead learning in your class and beyond.

Building collegial relationships

Collaboration can be seen as a lynch-pin for success in teaching, however it is an approach that can often be lost behind the closed doors of a classroom. I once heard teaching described as a 'frequently lonely pursuit', which puzzled me when thinking of the plethora of people you deal with on a daily basis. However, one term into my first job I appreciated that when the pupils leave the classroom and you are faced with your mountain of work, it can result in a feeling of isolation.

Building collegial relationships

In my first term, I was approaching an impending PE topic that was causing me anxiety due to my own inexperience. As opposed to approaching this alone, I took two deliberate courses of action. First, I set out my ideas and concerns and clarified what was worrying me and what I required to feel confident. Second, I arranged an informal 'coffee and biscuit' after-school meeting with an experienced phase leader and our school sports coach. Simply in sharing my thoughts, accepting their suggestions for both resources and approach, and listening to their own anecdotes, after a 20-minute discussion I left with an enthusiasm and excitement that I could not have achieved alone. Nothing made me feel more settled in my first job than the feeling of being part of a unified team.

The, yet unmentioned, spectre at the table is how you can maintain your efforts and retain your good spirits and health. Teaching is a demanding job conducted in a public sphere with constant scrutiny as a norm. The implication throughout this chapter has been that the various elements – effective preparation, positive relationships, teacher as learner, teacher as leader – are collectively designed to comprise a framework for support and success that can work for the good of children and teachers alike. However, the high expectations of teachers, from others but also, and more importantly, from themselves, can incur unique pressures that make teachers particularly vulnerable. It is important to plan for social interaction and out-of-work activities that allow for relaxation and which act as a counterpoint to the intensity and inherent seriousness of your first job. The reflexive practice of effective pedagogy must extend to knowing yourself beyond the classroom and appreciating what you need for personal and professional nourishment. Teaching is a generous, giving profession. You need nourishment to replenish your energy for the emotional work involved.

Professional and personal nourishment

Late one windy, cold Friday evening in the middle of my second term, my mother came to stay and her first words when she saw me were 'You do look very tired'. Being a retired teacher herself, she said this with a knowing tone. At this point, I did feel that 7.00 am to 7.00 pm at school, then working until 11.00 pm at home was the only option. To make matters worse, I ate poorly, did not exercise and took it upon myself to exclude myself from weekend social activities due to the necessity to work. After reaching rather a crisis point, I made two small yet invaluable changes. I joined a gym and forced myself to go once during the week and once at weekends. I also had one evening a week where I would stay at school until 6pm and take no work home. The actual days were of course variable based on the timetable of my week but I stuck to it. Weeks into my plan, I was enjoying the routine and found myself with a fresher approach to my working week.

Professional well-being

> When we feel a sense of well-being, we are not under stimulated and bored, nor are we suffering under the burden of excessive stress and pressure. We have a sense of control over our work and even over our destiny in life. (Holmes, 2005: 6)

- What action can you take to ensure your well-being in your first job?
- How will you conserve energy over a weekend and throughout the week?
- How will you preserve some social time?
- How will you negotiate the expectations of work beyond the classroom?

SUMMARY

Teaching is a privilege and a huge responsibility. It is emotional and suffused with the requirement to create, maintain and sustain positive relationships. Your first job is an incremental process of becoming a professional. This involves identity formation and the rapid acquiring of new knowledge. It is unrehearseable. If you position yourself as a learner and seek opportunities to be a leader, you will have the maximum opportunity to flourish in a contemporary context of complexity and change. Above all, take care of yourself. The children who reside at the heart of this process need teachers who can sustain their attention and maintain their good health.

companion website

To access additional online resources please visit: **https://study.sagepub.com/wyseandrogers**

Here you will find a classroom activity, author podcasts including Joanne Waterhouse's top tips for employability, free access to SAGE journal articles and links to external sources.

future reading

McNally, J. and Blake, A. (eds) (2010) *Improving Learning in a Professional Context*. Abingdon: Routledge. An edited book that is part of a book series that builds on projects funded by the ESRC as part of the large-scale Teaching and Learning Research Programme (TLRP).

Pollard, A. (2014) *Reflective Teaching in Schools*, 4th edition. London: Bloomsbury.

Pollard, A. (ed.) (2014) *Readings for Reflective Teaching in Schools*. London: Bloomsbury.

Classic texts from the popular Reflective Teaching series that have recently been expanded to include the teaching of younger children.

REFERENCES

Albon, D. (2011) The importance of partnership with parents and carers. In J. Moyles (ed.) *Beginning Teaching, Beginning Learning in Primary Education*. Maidenhead: Open University Press.

Barth, R. S. (2001) *Learning by Heart*. San Francisco: Jossey Bass.

Bryk, A. S. and Schneider, B. (2002) *Trust in Schools: A Core Resource for Improvement*. New York: Russell Sage Foundation.

Cable, C. (2011) Exploring Leadership in the Classroom. In J. Moyles (ed.) *Beginning Teaching, Beginning Learning in Primary Education*. Maidenhead: Open University Press.

Cajkler, W. and Suschitzky, W. (2011) Teamwork in the Primary Classroom. In J. Moyles (ed.) *Beginning Teaching, Beginning Learning in Primary Education*. Maidenhead: Open University Press.

Corbin, B. (2010) Feeling Professional. In J. McNally and A. Blake (eds) *Improving Learning in a Professional Context*. Abingdon: Routledge.

Crowther, F. (2009) *Developing Teacher Leaders*. London: Sage.

Daresh, J. C. (2003) *Teachers Mentoring Teachers*. London: Sage

Dillon, J and Maguire, M. (2007) Developing as a beginning teacher. In. J. Dillon and M. Maguire (eds) *Becoming a Teacher*. Berkshire: Open University Press

Fairman, J. C. and Mackenzie, S. V. (2015) How Teacher Leaders Influence Others and Understand their Teacher Leadership. *International Journal of Leadership in Education*, 18(1), 61–87.

Holmes, E. (2005) *Teacher Wellbeing*. Abingdon: RoutledgeFalmer.

Higham, R., Hopkins, D. and Ahtaridou, E. (2007) *Improving School Leadership: Country Background Report for England*. Paris: OECD.

Law, E. H. F. (2011) Exploring the Role of Leadership in Facilitating Teacher Learning in Hong Kong. *School Leadership and Management*, 31(4), 393–410.

Mayrowetz, D., Murphy, J., Seashore-Louis, K. and Smylie, M.A. (2007) Distributed Leadership as Work Redesign: Retrofitting the Job Characteristics Model. *Leadership and Policy in Schools*, 6(1), 69–102.

Putnam, R. D. (1998) *Bowling Alone: The Collapse and Revival of American Community*. New York: Simon Schuster.

Sarason, S. B. (1995) *School Change: The Personal Development of a Point of View*. New York: Teachers College Press.

Scanlon, M. (2011) Reading Out: Fostering Partnership with Parents. In J. Moyles (ed.) *Beginning Teaching, Beginning Learning in Primary Education*. Maidenhead: Open University Press.

Stoll, L. (1999) School Culture: Black Hole or Fertile Garden for School Improvement? In J. Prosser (ed.) *School Culture*. London: Paul Chapman.

Stronach, I. (2010) The invention of teachers: how beginning teachers learn. In J. McNally and A. Blake (eds) *Improving Learning in a Professional Context: A research perspective on the new teacher in school*. Abingdon: Routledge

Szreter, S. (2002) The State of Social Capital: Bringing Back in Power, Politics and History. *Theory and Society*, 31(5), 573–621.

Tschannen-Moran, B. and Tschannen-Moran M. (2010) *Evocative Coaching*. San Francisco: Jossey Bass.

Walker, G. (2011) Beginning to work with other agencies. In J. Moyles (ed.) *Beginning Teaching, Beginning Learning in Primary Education*. Maidenhead: Open University Press.

Wyatt, R. L. and White, J. E. (2002) *Making Your First Year a Success*. London: Sage.

16

LEGAL ISSUES

Dominic Wyse, Steven Ford QC,
Charles Hale QC and Christine Parker

LEARNING AIMS

This chapter will:

- provide information about key areas of law that affect teachers
- explain key legal ideas such as 'duty of care' and relate these to teachers' classroom practice
- present ways in which teachers must safeguard children in the context of a children's rights perspective.

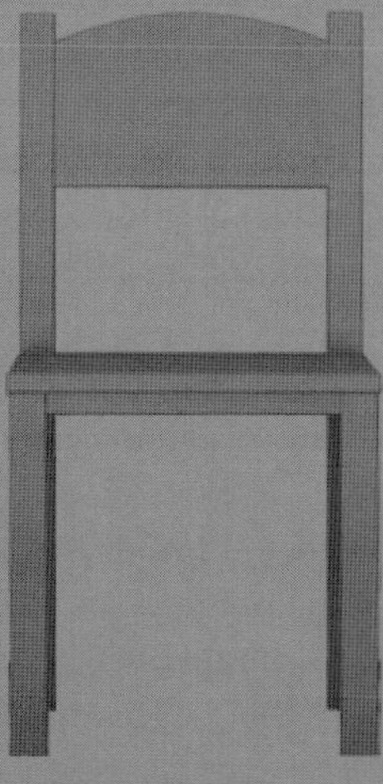

There are many laws that affect teachers. Some of these laws are specifically relevant to teachers in the course of their work, whilst other laws apply to teachers as they do to all people in society. For example, there are laws covering pay and conditions that are specific to teachers, and there are laws that apply to all people's workplaces such as health and safety legislation. There are two main areas of law that affect all people: civil law and criminal law.

One important distinction between the two is the *standard of proof* required before a court can make a finding. In a civil law case, the standard of proof is the *balance of probabilities*. The balance of probabilities has been defined by case law in what was the highest court for deciding cases in England and Wales, the House of Lords (now the Supreme Court). In the case, B (Children) [2008] UKHL 35 (this is the conventional way that court cases are cited), the court was asked to consider the test that one or other of a child's caregivers had deliberately injured a child, with respect to serious allegations made in care proceedings. The consequences of the judge getting that decision wrong for a parent or the child are clearly very serious indeed. Baroness Hale considered that 'the balance of probabilities' meant 'more likely than not', no more and no less than this. Even the seriousness of the allegation (such as sexual abuse or deliberately injuring a child) did not alter the test to be applied. She explained it in this way:

70. My Lords, for that reason I would go further and announce loud and clear that the standard of proof in finding the facts necessary to establish the threshold under section 31(2) or the welfare considerations in section 1 of the 1989 Act is the simple balance of probabilities, neither more nor less. Neither the seriousness of the allegation nor the seriousness of the consequences should make any difference to the standard of proof to be applied in determining the facts. The inherent probabilities are simply something to be taken into account, where relevant, in deciding where the truth lies.
71. As to the seriousness of the consequences, they are serious either way. A child may find her relationship with her family seriously disrupted; or she may find herself still at risk of suffering serious harm. A parent may find his relationship with his child seriously disrupted; or he may find himself still at liberty to maltreat this or other children in the future.

The standard of proof in criminal cases is different from in civil cases. For a criminal case, the standard is the more familiar concept of 'beyond reasonable doubt'. In other words, a judge or jury has to be satisfied so that they are sure the person being accused of the crime did in fact commit it.

The laws that affect people in the UK are derived from two main areas: statutes (legislation) and what is called common law. Statutes are those laws that are debated and then enacted by the House of Parliament. Common law is law that has been developed by judges on a case-by-case basis (through a process of legal precedent) from custom and practice. The common law originated in England during the period after the Norman Conquest in 1066. An important point of consolidation, of what began as regional systems of law, was carried out by King Henry II (Glendon, 2015). Contract law has developed from both statutes and the common law and is applicable to the legal contract that you have as an employee.

This chapter addresses legal issues with the qualified teacher in mind. The legal need to act responsibly and with care also applies to trainee teachers but the most important caveat is that the trainee teacher must seek advice from their class teacher mentor, whose class they are working with. In fact, for more risky activities such as PE the class teacher would normally be present during the trainee teacher's lesson. The presence of the class teacher is considered a reasonable precaution in view of their ultimate responsibility for the children when a trainee teacher is teaching. However, the trainee teacher still has legal responsibility for the children they are teaching, just as teaching assistants and other adults would when accompanying children on a school trip, for example.

DUTY OF CARE

One of the most important overall legal principles guiding the work of teachers is the 'duty of care'. In simple terms, this means that teachers must take reasonable care of the pupils for whom they are responsible. The standard of care expected by teachers is that of a reasonable person, taking into account the school context. One aspect of the school context is that the duty of care to individual pupils depends on the age of the children, the activity being undertaken and the size of the group or class being cared for (National Union of Teachers (NUT), 2013: 3).

Taking a class of children out of school for an educational visit is a valuable educational activity. These school trips can be as straightforward as a walk out of school to some point of interest in the community, or they can involve overnight stays as part of a longer experience, something that is often done in the final years of primary school. The first trip away from home, as a primary school experience, is one that many people remember with fondness. One example of research showing the value of school trips can be seen in a recent rigorous study that found that the combination of a school trip with an approach to teaching writing, that had also been found in previous robust research to be effective, produced a high positive impact on improving the writing of 10–12-year-old children with special educational needs (Torgerson et al., 2014).

Unfortunately, over the last 10 years various myths about the law in relation to school trips have emerged. For example, there is the idea that if there is any injury at all to a child whilst on a school trip, the teacher will always be sued and will lose the case. This has led to some schools being unduly 'risk averse', and in the worst cases simply not taking children out on school trips for fear of legal consequences. The Health and Safety Executive (HSE), who is concerned with criminal prosecutions in relation to health and safety in England, is admirably clear on these matters:

> Key message: 'Well-managed school trips and outdoor activities are great for children. Children won't learn about risk if they're wrapped in cotton wool.'
>
> Key message: 'Teachers should expect their schools to have procedures that encourage participation, are proportionate to the level of risk and avoid bureaucracy.'
>
> Key message: 'Those running school trips need to focus on the risks and the benefits to people - not the paperwork.'
>
> Key message: 'Accidents and mistakes may happen on school trips - but fear of prosecution has been blown out of all proportion.' (Health and Safety Executive (HSE), 2011, pp. 1-3)

As a result of the Compensation Act 2006, courts dealing with civil claims for damages (commonly known as suing for damages) are now required to consider the balance between risk and the benefit inherent in the activity, in order to decide whether a teacher has acted negligently.

Section 1: Deterrent effect of potential liability

A court considering a claim in negligence or breach of statutory duty may, in determining whether the defendant should have taken particular steps to meet a standard of care (whether by taking precautions against a risk or otherwise), have regard to whether a requirement to take those steps might:

(a) prevent a desirable activity from being undertaken at all, to a particular extent or in a particular way, or

(b) discourage persons from undertaking functions in connection with a desirable activity. (Compensation Act 2006)

spotlight on practice

Educational visit to Woburn Safari Park

Year 1 went on an educational visit to Woburn Safari Park in Milton Keynes. The drive from Peterborough took approximately 1½ hours.

Upon our arrival, we separated the year group into our three classes and explored the road safari by foot. We were able to see many different animals, such as penguins, tortoises and sea lions.

There are some exhibits that allow visitors to walk through the animal's caged area, such as the squirrels, monkeys and wallabies. This gave the children the opportunity to experience the animals up close in a relatively natural habitat, and we were able to catch a glimpse of some animals in action, for example a baby wallaby hopped right alongside our path into his mother's pouch.

The school visit programme at Woburn allows for the group to book a talk and demonstration with a staff member. Our year group learned all about lemurs and we were able to see the lemurs being fed.

We then got back on the coach and drove along the car safari road; we saw many foreign animals that the children had only ever seen in pictures, such as bears, lions and tigers. The visit was an excellent experience for our children, who will soon be starting their science learning on different types of animals. They now have had first-hand experience with many different animals and are keen to talk and write about them.

putting it into practice

Educational visit to Woburn Safari Park

Having read the account above, discuss potential risks and plans for the trip then compare with the bullet points on the following page. Discuss the excent to which this advice is applicable to other visits.

- Book the visit to Woburn well in advance, as the park hosts many schools.
- Utilise the free pre-visit option to familiarise yourself with the park's layout. In order to maximise the number of animals the children can see, plan a schedule that follows the park's map so that time is not wasted travelling between exhibits. A pre-visit also helps to assess possible risks, such as car parks and bodies of water.
- Assign each adult a small group of children to ensure that all children are accounted for throughout the day. Every adult should have lists of the children in their group as well as of the other groups in case of an emergency. Adults should be aware of any medical requirements among their children and should have the necessary medical equipment, such as inhalers and epi-pens, on hand. Ideally, adults with medical knowledge, such as first aid, should be grouped with these children. It is helpful if children with more intensive needs have their parent join as an additional adult. Adults should also have the contact information for trip leaders, in case of an emergency.
- If motion sickness is a concern, plan in advance to minimise driving time. For example, it is helpful to start the walking portion of the day upon arrival so that the children can have a rest from sitting on the coach. Each coach should have sick buckets, complete with sick bags, bin bags, towels and water, should there be any problems. Some children benefit from taking tablets before the trip, wearing sickness bands or sitting on newspaper.
- There is no place to leave lunches other than on the coach. Approximately 10 minutes before your planned lunch time, ask some adults to retrieve the lunches from the coach. This saves the children from having to carry their lunches throughout the day. Pack extra lunches in case a child forgets theirs.
- Provide each adult with a safari park map so they can talk about the animals to the children. It gives the adults added knowledge so that the children can learn facts to take back to the classroom after the visit.
- Keep the driving tour interactive and engaging by using the coach's microphone, if available. Spread the adults throughout the coach so they can interact with the children.
- Remember that the driving portion of the safari takes approximately 1 hour and windows must be kept shut. Ensuring a comfortable temperature inside the coach is important and should be a point of consideration when choosing the means of transportation and its features, such as air conditioning.

HEALTH AND SAFETY

The legal responsibility for health and safety lies first with the employer, as the Health and Safety Act 1974 makes clear:

> 2 General duties of employers to their employees.
>
> (1) It shall be the duty of every employer to ensure, so far as is reasonably practicable, the health, safety and welfare at work of all his employees.
>
> (2) Without prejudice to the generality of an employer's duty under the preceding subsection, the matters to which that duty extends include in particular –
>
> (a) the provision and maintenance of plant and systems of work that are, so far as is reasonably practicable, safe and without risks to health;

> (b) arrangements for ensuring, so far as is reasonably practicable, safety and absence of risks to health in connection with the use, handling, storage and transport of articles and substances;
>
> (c) the provision of such information, instruction, training and supervision as is necessary to ensure, so far as is reasonably practicable, the health and safety at work of his employees;
>
> (d) so far as is reasonably practicable as regards any place of work under the employer's control, the maintenance of it in a condition that is safe and without risks to health and the provision and maintenance of means of access to and egress from it that are safe and without such risks;
>
> (e) the provision and maintenance of a working environment for his employees that is, so far as is reasonably practicable, safe, without risks to health, and adequate as regards facilities and arrangements for their welfare at work. (Health and Safety Act 1974)

This means that the head teacher and the governors of a school have a responsibility to ensure the health, safety and welfare of all who work in the school including teachers and pupils. Although these responsibilities lie with the employer, employees also have responsibilities under the Act:

> 7 General duties of employees at work.
>
> It shall be the duty of every employee while at work:
>
> (a) to take reasonable care for the health and safety of himself and of other persons who may be affected by his acts or omissions at work; and
>
> (b) as regards any duty or requirement imposed on his employer or any other person by or under any of the relevant statutory provisions, to co-operate with him so far as is necessary to enable that duty or requirement to be performed or complied with. (Health and Safety Act 1974)

Taking reasonable care of pupils, and of other people who may be working with the teacher, covers a wide range of issues. We have already addressed the particular circumstances surrounding trips outside the school in the section above on duty of care. When starting placement experience or work in a new setting/school, it is important first and foremost to locate any local health and safety guidance (of the local authority and/or the school/setting itself). The contexts of the work of early years and primary teachers tend to have less obvious dangers than say science lessons in secondary schools that involve heating chemicals in laboratory type situations, or power tools for working with wood, metal, etc. However, there are some risks from everyday equipment that require vigilance. Older children may use sharp craft knives so would need clear instructions on how to cut safely. All children, including younger children, will access sharp implements, such as pencils, which can cause unpleasant injuries (if, for example, a child were to fall onto a pencil) and so need vigilance. In addition to being vigilant about safety, there is a duty to report incidents:

> 39. All employers have a duty to report any hazards and potentially dangerous incidents at work and teachers should make themselves familiar with any recording system in the school, academy, free school or college, such as the accident report book. (NUT, 2013: 6)

All early years settings and schools have ways to record accidents that happen to children whilst in the setting. Minor injuries are quite common, for example when children are out in the playground during breaks. The school's or early years setting's designated people for first aid will deal with many minor injuries, and will if necessary call for medical help. The EYFS framework is clear on the requirements for recording incidents and sharing this information with parents:

Accident or injury

> 3.50. Providers must ensure there is a first aid box accessible at all times with appropriate content for use with children. Providers must keep a written record of accidents or injuries and first aid treatment. Providers must inform parents and/or carers of any accident or injury sustained by the child on the same day, or as soon as reasonably practicable, of any first aid treatment given.
>
> 3.51. Registered providers must notify Ofsted or the childminder agency with which they are registered of any serious accident, illness or injury to, or death of, any child while in their care, and of the action taken. Notification must be made as soon as is reasonably practicable, but in any event within 14 days of the incident occurring. A registered provider, who, without reasonable excuse, fails to comply with this requirement, commits an offence. Providers must notify local child protection agencies of any serious accident or injury to, or the death of, any child while in their care, and must act on any advice from those agencies. (Department for Education, 2014a: 26)

It is unlawful for a teacher to interfere with or misuse anything which has been provided to enhance health and safety. For example, propping open fire doors or blocking fire exits, including by leaving too much rubbish in a corridor which would make an escape route less easy to use. It would be quite understandable for someone who is not vigilant not to see a wet patch on a hard floor as a serious hazard, yet severe injury could be caused if someone were to slip on the wet patch and land badly on their spine, for example.

SCHOOL DISCIPLINE

The legal requirement and authority for teachers to appropriately discipline pupils in their care comes from the Education and Inspections Act 2006, and is made clear in the School Teachers' Pay and Conditions requirements at section 52.9 (see below):

> 52.1 A teacher may be required to undertake the following duties:
>
> Teaching
>
> 52.2 Plan and teach lessons to the classes they are assigned to teach within the context of the school's plans, curriculum and schemes of work.
>
> 52.3 Assess, monitor, record and report on the learning needs, progress and achievements of assigned pupils.
>
> 52.4 Participate in arrangements for preparing pupils for external examinations.

Whole-school organisation, strategy and development

52.5 Contribute to the development, implementation and evaluation of the school's policies, practices and procedures in such a way as to support the school's values and vision.

52.6 Work with others on curriculum and/or pupil development to secure coordinated outcomes.

52.7 Subject to paragraph 53.7 supervise and so far as practicable teach any pupils where the person timetabled to take the class is not available to do so.

Health, safety and discipline

52.8 Promote the safety and well-being of pupils.

52.9 Maintain good order and discipline among pupils.

Management of staff and resources

52.10 Direct and supervise support staff assigned to them and, where appropriate, other teachers.

52.11 Contribute to the recruitment, selection, appointment and professional development of other teachers and support staff.

52.12 Deploy resources delegated to them.

Professional development

52.13 Participate in arrangements for the appraisal and review of their own performance and, where appropriate, that of other teachers and support staff.

52.14 Participate in arrangements for their own further training and professional development and, where appropriate, that of other teachers and support staff including induction.

Communication

52.15 Communicate with pupils, parents and carers.

Working with colleagues and other relevant professionals

52.16 Collaborate and work with colleagues and other relevant professionals within and beyond the school.

(Department for Education, 2014b: 42)

Teachers (and any paid staff in schools such as teaching assistants) are legally allowed to discipline pupils, proportionately and reasonably, if a pupil's conduct falls below the standard reasonably expected of children of their age, taking into account any special circumstances such as a disability. Schools should have clear behaviour policies in place which should be consistently and fairly applied. These policies should include rewards to reinforce good behaviour. It is important to remember that specific, meaningful and genuine oral praise for good behaviour is one of the teacher's most important behaviour management strategies. At the same time, behaviour which breaks school behaviour policies should lead to sanctions that are implemented consistently and fairly.

1. Discuss in general some of the implications of imposing the sanctions below on a class you are going to teach.
2. Consider the extent to which the following sanctions are relevant to children in: (a) a nursery class (ages 3-4); (b) a Year 6 class (ages 10-11):

- a verbal reprimand
- extra work or repeating unsatisfactory work until it meets the required standard
- the setting of written tasks as punishments, such as writing lines or an essay
- loss of privileges - for instance, the loss of a prized responsibility or not being able to participate in a non-uniform day (sometimes referred to as 'mufti' days)
- missing breaktime
- detention including during lunchtime, after school and at weekends
- school-based community service or imposition of a task - such as picking up litter or weeding school grounds; tidying a classroom; helping clear up the dining hall after meal times; or removing graffiti
- regular reporting including early morning reporting; scheduled uniform and other behaviour checks; or being placed 'on report' for behaviour monitoring
- in more extreme cases, schools may use temporary or permanent exclusion.

(Department for Education, 2014c)

Corporal punishment is illegal. This means that it is against the law to smack, cane or in any other way use physical means to discipline a child. However, reasonable physical restraint is allowed, for example if a teacher were to physically separate two pupils who were fighting. Male teachers, in particular, should not feel that because of a misplaced understanding of child protection they are not allowed ever to have any physical contact with children. For the youngest children, some physical contact is appropriate, for example young children may want to hold the hand of a teacher or teaching assistant, or a teacher may want to comfort or congratulate a child. These examples and some others are entirely appropriate ways in which teachers sometimes come into physical contact with pupils (for more detailed guidance, see 'Use of reasonable force: advice for head teachers, staff and governing bodies', Department for Education, 2013).

CHILDREN'S RIGHTS AND CHILD PROTECTION

The idea that children have rights can be a difficult one for some people to accept. One of a teacher's duties, as you have seen, is to maintain good order and discipline among pupils. This inevitably puts the teacher in an authoritative role that includes requiring children at times to 'do as they are told', however sensitively this role is undertaken. Children also have powerful rights in international law, which, for example, require society to consult children on all matters that affect them in a way that is appropriate to their development. They also have the right to be treated reasonably, so any discipline carried out by schools should be proportionate and reasonable. The balance between rights and responsibilities can be complex.

The UK is a signatory to the United Nations Convention on the Rights of the Child (UNCRC). The convention consists of 54 'articles' that in theory give all children in the world powerful rights. One of the most basic rights is that children know about the UNCRC in the first place:

> Article 42
>
> States Parties undertake to make the principles and provisions of the Convention widely known, by appropriate and active means, to adults and children alike.

In our view, one of the most important articles implies that schools and teachers should seek children's opinions, and seriously take account of those opinions, as seen in article 12:

> Article 12
>
> 1. States Parties shall assure to the child who is capable of forming his or her own views the right to express those views freely in all matters affecting the child, the views of the child being given due weight in accordance with the age and maturity of the child.

One straightforward way to do this is to genuinely ask children's views on the day-to-day work and practices going on in the classroom.

In 2001 I carried out the first study to research the ways in which children's participation rights in the CRC were being addressed in schools in England (Wyse, 2001). The research took place in two primary schools and two secondary schools in the north west of England. One of the challenges of the research was when it became evident, through talking to the child and teacher participants, that none of them had even heard of the CRC. It is of course almost impossible to uphold rights if you don't know what those rights are. The research found that children's participation rights were not being upheld, and that even where school councils existed (a potentially powerful way to act on children's opinions) these were not operated in ways that best upheld children's rights. More recent work has recommended the northern Italian Reggio Emilia early childhood approach to conceptions of children and childhood, the creation of spaces to allow children's voices to be heard and particular ways to listen to children (Tisdall, 2013).

SAFEGUARDING CHILDREN

For people who have not suffered abuse in their childhood, it can be an idea that is difficult for them to comprehend. However, unfortunately significant numbers of children suffer from abuse. Estimates on the numbers of children who suffer abuse vary widely. At one end of the spectrum are suggestions that as many as one in three children may suffer some form of abuse during their childhood. That means that in a class of 30 children aged 18 as many as 10 children may have suffered from abuse. This figure is difficult to estimate because one of the problems with abuse is that many children don't report that they have been abused. Official statistics based on child protection data confirm that 'one in five children today have experienced serious physical abuse, sexual abuse or severe physical or emotional neglect at some point in their lifetime' (Harker et al., 2013: 4). The following official statistics of data from 2011 to 2012 show some of the extent of the problem:

- 520,000 estimated victims of maltreatment by a parent or guardian in 2011
- 2.5% of under-11s and 6% of 11–17-year-olds had experienced maltreatment by a parent or guardian in the past year
- 1.2% of under-11s and 3.1% of 11–17-year-olds had experienced maltreatment by an adult outside the home in the past year
- 200,000 estimated children in need due to abuse and neglect in 2011/12
- 58,000 estimated children placed on a child protection plan or register in 2011/12
- 50,000 estimated children 'Looked After' due to abuse and neglect in 2011/12
- 23,305 recorded sexual and cruelty/neglect offences against children in 2011/12. (Harker et al., 2013: 5)

So, first and foremost, anybody with responsibility for children, which of course means teachers, must have at the back of their mind the fact that significant numbers of children are abused and therefore vigilance is necessary. Correspondingly, having the idea that abuse is not a real problem is unacceptable. The statistics do of course beg the question: how is abuse defined?

Child abuse is defined in government guidance as follows:

> Abuse
>
> A form of maltreatment of a child. Somebody may abuse or neglect a child by inflicting harm, or by failing to act to prevent harm. Children may be abused in a family or in an institutional or community setting by those known to them or, more rarely, by others (e.g. via the internet). They may be abused by an adult or adults, or another child or children.
>
> Physical abuse
>
> A form of abuse which may involve hitting, shaking, throwing, poisoning, burning or scalding, drowning, suffocating or otherwise causing physical harm to a child. Physical harm may also be caused when a parent or carer fabricates the symptoms of, or deliberately induces, illness in a child.
>
> Emotional abuse
>
> The persistent emotional maltreatment of a child such as to cause severe and persistent adverse effects on the child's emotional development. It may involve conveying to a child that they are worthless or unloved, inadequate, or valued only insofar as they meet the needs of another person. It may include not giving the child opportunities to express their views, deliberately silencing them or 'making fun' of what they say or how they communicate. It may feature age or developmentally inappropriate expectations being imposed on children. These may include interactions that are beyond a child's developmental capability, as well as overprotection and limitation of exploration and learning, or preventing the child participating in normal social interaction. It may involve seeing or hearing the ill-treatment of another. It may involve serious bullying (including cyber-bullying), causing children frequently to feel frightened or in danger,

or the exploitation or corruption of children. Some level of emotional abuse is involved in all types of maltreatment of a child, though it may occur alone.

Sexual abuse

Involves forcing or enticing a child or young person to take part in sexual activities, not necessarily involving a high level of violence, whether or not the child is aware of what is happening. The activities may involve physical contact, including assault by penetration (for example, rape or oral sex) or non-penetrative acts such as masturbation, kissing, rubbing and touching outside of clothing. They may also include non-contact activities, such as involving children in looking at, or in the production of, sexual images, watching sexual activities, encouraging children to behave in sexually inappropriate ways, or grooming a child in preparation for abuse (including via the internet). Sexual abuse is not solely perpetrated by adult males. Women can also commit acts of sexual abuse, as can other children.

Neglect

The persistent failure to meet a child's basic physical and/or psychological needs, likely to result in the serious impairment of the child's health or development. Neglect may occur during pregnancy as a result of maternal substance abuse. Once a child is born, neglect may involve a parent or carer failing to:

- provide adequate food, clothing and shelter (including exclusion from home or abandonment);
- protect a child from physical and emotional harm or danger;
- ensure adequate supervision (including the use of inadequate care-givers); or
- ensure access to appropriate medical care or treatment.

It may also include neglect of, or unresponsiveness to, a child's basic emotional needs. (HM Government, 2015: 92)

reflection point

Read the Spotlight on Practice 'Safeguarding children: Part 1' below and then discuss what you think the teacher should do next. Having finished the discussion, read Part 2 to see what happened.

spotlight on practice

Safeguarding children: Part 1

Clare, a recently qualified teacher, is starting her career as a Year 3 teacher. At the beginning of the school year, basic child protection training was provided, facilitated by the school's designated safeguarding lead, who in this case was the head teacher.

Rose holds the position of high level teaching assistant. Her responsibility is to support children and families in managing complex situations in their lives. She is a member of the school's safeguarding team. Rose briefed Clare about the school documentation for recording 'low level' concerns, and the internal referral form for 'high level' concerns, such as a pupil's disclosure of abuse.

Rose met with Clare, prior to the start of the school year, to inform her of the concerns she had about Ben. Ben is 7 years old and the eldest of four children. He lives with his mother and father. The family occupies a rented two-bedroom flat that is in poor condition. Ben suffers with eczema, so frequently needs to apply his eczema cream at school, and he is overweight. Ben typically arrives at school late and hungry.

Clare noted that Ben found coming into the classroom late everyday difficult, was not always attentive at the beginning of the school day and was becoming increasingly unhappy. He was self-conscious about his eczema and worried about being teased by other children. Every day Ben asked if he could apply his cream.

One day Ben came to school and asked to talk to his teacher during breaktime. He informed Clare that he was 'seriously fed up': 'Mum and dad never get up in the morning. I hate being late. Everyone stares at me. My house smells and I smell. I can't bear it.'

Stop reading at this point in order to discuss what you think should happen next. Then once the discussion has finished, read on.

Safeguarding children: Part 2

Clare made a written record of Ben's worries using as many of the words that Ben used as possible. She also made it clear to Ben that she was required to inform another member of staff. Clare spoke to Rose, whilst a teaching assistant supervised the class. The designated safeguarding lead was informed, who made a referral to Children's Social Care (the relevant council department). Ben's parents were informed that the referral had been made. Although Ben's case did not meet the social services threshold for immediate action, the council safeguarding team knew that the concerns had been reported.

At school, it was arranged to meet with Ben's parents and a 'Pastoral Care Plan' was put into place. The school committed to: providing a place for Ben at the breakfast club; liaising with the school nurse; making a referral for Ben to attend a weight control programme; and supporting the family to access more suitable housing. The Pastoral Care Plan paid careful attention to Ben's wishes by listening carefully to his opinions, including his unhappiness at being late for school.

Tragically, in the most extreme cases of child abuse children die. For every child that dies as a result of abuse, investigations are carried out. Time and time again, it has been the lack of coordination between agencies and people involved with children that has been seen as one of the causes of children not being protected. For that reason, the two key principles in relation to safeguarding children are:

- safeguarding is everyone's responsibility: for services to be effective each professional and organisation should play their full part; and
- a child-centred approach: for services to be effective they should be based on a clear understanding of the needs and views of children. (HM Government, 2015: 9)

Another important fundamental understanding about the legal aspects of child abuse and safeguarding children is that there are two legal systems that apply. One legal system is to do with child protection. Under this system, teachers and other professionals and people involved with children have a duty to report any concerns they have about suspected abuse. These concerns must be reported to the designated *safeguarding lead*. This might be the head of the early years setting or the head teacher of a primary school. (If a head is suspected of abuse, concerns should be reported to the setting's chair of governors. Contact can be made directly with local authority Children's Social Care in cases where serious risk to a child is a concern.) The second legal system is the criminal justice system that is applied in circumstances where a crime has been committed against a child. The important aspect of these two legal systems is that people can and must act to protect children, irrespective of any criminal prosecution that may occur.

Local authorities have overarching responsibility for safeguarding and promoting all children's welfare, but all people who work with children have a duty to work together in children's best interests, including in safeguarding children. Early years and primary teachers are in a unique position to spot the signs and symptoms of abuse because they spend so much time with the children they teach. However, this does not mean that detecting the signs of abuse is easy, not least because children may be scared that the abuser will harm them more if they tell anyone, or the child may not realise that what is happening to them is abuse. The other advantage that teachers have is that they have knowledge of the typical ways that children develop, including the ways their behaviour develops. For that reason, the signs, symptoms and effects of child abuse and neglect are related to children's age, particularly if you remember that under the law a child is someone who is under the age of 18.

Possible signs and symptoms of child abuse

Teachers are in a very good position to notice whether children's development is typical or not. These are some of the signs to be aware of:

How to tell whether behaviour is normal for their age

Children develop and mature at different rates, so what is worrying for a younger child might be normal behaviour for an older child. If a child looks or acts a lot older or younger than their age, this could be a cause for concern.

However, if a child develops more slowly than others of a similar age and there isn't a cause, such as physical or learning disabilities, it could be a sign they're being abused.

All ages

- Talks of being left home alone or with strangers.
- Poor bond or relationship with a parent (appropriate bonds for babies are known as *attachment*).
- Acts out excessive violence with other children.
- Lacks social skills and has few, if any, friends.

Under 5s

- Doesn't cry or respond to parent's presence or absence from an early age.
- Reaches developmental milestones late, such as learning to speak, with no medical reason.
- Significantly underweight but eats well when given food.

5-11-year-olds

- Becomes secretive and reluctant to share information.
- Reluctant to go home after school.
- Unable to bring friends home or reluctant for professionals to visit the family home.
- Poor school attendance and punctuality, or late being picked up.
- Parents show little interest in child's performance and behaviour at school.
- Parents are dismissive of and non-responsive to professional concerns.
- Is reluctant to get changed for sports etc.
- Wets or soils the bed.

Source: NSPCC (2015).

The government's advice for practitioners about identifying and responding appropriately to possible abuse and neglect is summarised in Figure 16.1.

We have already made the point earlier in this chapter that teachers have to be aware of and alert to the possibility that children in their care may be suffering from abuse. However, as the signs of abuse are often not obvious it is important that teachers consider speaking to a child alone in order to question behaviour that appears to be unusual for that particular child (HM Government, 2015). Talking to the child needs to be done sensitively, with particular care for the child's needs and rights, and should reassure the child that any necessary action will be taken to support them. As you will have realised having read the above Spotlight on Practice, there are important things you have to be aware of if a child discloses something to you in relation to potential abuse under any of the categories of abuse: physical, emotional, sexual or neglect. Although teachers will maintain confidentiality, they are not allowed to keep something secret even if the child asks them to, because under the law the teacher has a duty to refer. Teachers must listen carefully to what a child discloses and should make a written record using the exact words that

24. There are four key steps to follow to help you to identify and respond appropriately to possible abuse and/or neglect.

25. It may not always be appropriate to go through all four stages sequentially. If a child is in immediate danger or is at risk of harm, you should refer to children's social care and/or the police. Before doing so, you should try to establish the basic facts. However, it will be the role of social workers and the police to investigate cases and make a judgement on whether there should be a statutory intervention and/or a criminal investigation.

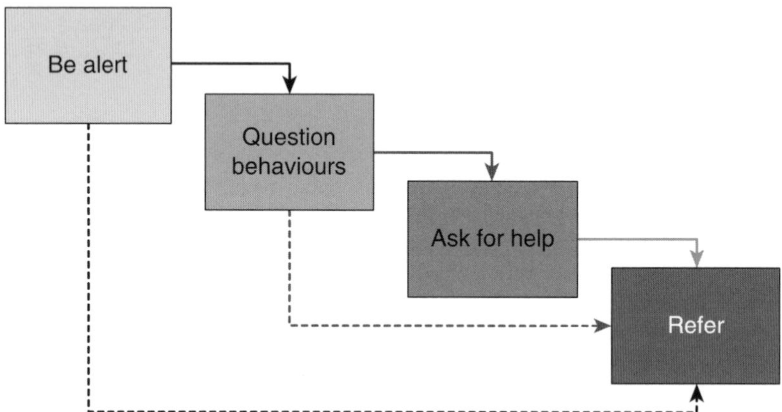

Figure 16.1 Identifying and responding to possible abuse and neglect

Source: HM Government (2015: 12)

the child uses as far as possible. The teacher then has to discuss the disclosure with the school's designated child protection lead.

Although child abuse is a long-standing problem for society, some forms of abuse are more recent. Bullying using social media and/or mobile phones is an example of a more recent form of abuse. Although the texts and images on social media and mobile phones are less likely to be seen by teachers, the origins of bullying begin with social contact between children at the same school (this is different from the risks of grooming behaviour carried out be predatory paedophiles using the internet). Teachers do see the ways that children interact with each other so are well placed to spot bullying, and should assume that this bullying may have the additional dimension of digital forms. As with all bullying, teachers have a duty to act according to school policies on bullying that should be in place.

One system that is designed to minimise the risk of abuse is the Disclosure and Barring Service (DBS). All people who work regularly with children are required to be vetted by the DBS system (so at the beginning of a course of teacher training all trainees have to register). Anyone who has been convicted for offences against children will be registered in the system, and so would be barred from working with children were they to attempt to register for an Enhanced Certificate which certifies that the applicant has no convictions, cautions, reprimands or warnings, and that they are not on the children's or adults' barred list for anything that would preclude them from working with children.

reflection point

Discuss the merits of using an approach like the NSPCC's Underwear Rule for talking to children about staying safe:

> Talk PANTS and you've got it covered. PANTS is a really easy way for you to explain the Underwear Rule to your child to keep them safe:

Privates are private

Always remember your body belongs to you

No means no

Talk about secrets that upset you

Speak up, someone can help

Source: NSPCC (2015).

EQUALITY AND DISCRIMINATION INCLUDING SPECIAL EDUCATIONAL NEEDS (SEN)

Children come to their early years setting or school with experiences that are likely to be rather different from your own experiences. This can make it challenging for you to genuinely empathise with all the children you come into contact with. However, one part of the responsibility of teachers as professional people is to deal fairly with all the people they come into contact with as part of their work. This section of the chapter deals with legal obligations in relation to equality and discrimination, but another important reason for ensuring equality is that children are likely to learn more effectively if they are treated fairly.

The laws on equality and discrimination went through a major change in 2010. The Equality Act 2010 'replaced nine major Acts of Parliament and almost a hundred sets of regulations which had been introduced over several decades. It provides a single, consolidated source of discrimination law, covering all the types of discrimination that are unlawful' (DfE, 2014d: 6). In one sense, the Equality Act 2010 is straightforward:

> Protected characteristics
>
> 1.9 It is unlawful for a school to discriminate against a pupil or prospective pupil by treating them less favourably because of their:
>
> - sex
> - race
> - disability
> - religion or belief
> - sexual orientation
> - gender reassignment
> - pregnancy or maternity. (DfE, 2014d: 8)

There are four kinds of unlawful behaviour defined by the act: direct discrimination, indirect discrimination, harassment and victimisation. Direct discrimination is the most straightforward. Teachers must not treat any person (pupil or any other person they come into contact with as part of their work) less favourably than any other person because of a protected characteristic. Indirect discrimination means carrying out some kind of practice that would, by default, result in less favourable treatment. Harassment includes not just things like bullying behaviour but also the causing of offence. Hence, it would be unlawful to make fun of someone (for example, through jokes) based on the protected criteria if this violates their dignity. It is also unlawful to victimise someone, in other words treat them less favourably, because of something they have done. For example, if a parent made an allegation that a teacher had been racist it would be unlawful to treat that parent less favourably in future, even if the allegation was found not to be true.

In relation to disability, there are some special provisions:

> 1.25 The law on disability discrimination is different from the rest of the Act in a number of ways. In particular, it works in only one direction - that is to say, it protects disabled people but not people who are not disabled. This means that schools are allowed to treat disabled pupils more favourably than non-disabled pupils, and in some cases are required to do so, by making reasonable adjustments to put them on a more level footing with pupils without disabilities. The definition of what constitutes discrimination is more complex. Provision for disabled pupils is closely connected with the regime for children with special educational needs. (DfE, 2014d: 11)

One of the protected characteristics that is new in relation to pupils is gender reassignment. It is unlawful to discriminate against someone if they have undergone, or are in the process of undergoing, reassignment of their sex by changing some of their attributes. Gender reassignment does not just mean a medical procedure; it includes taking steps (or proposing to take steps) to change attributes in order to live in the opposite gender.

SUMMARY

This chapter has explored the main laws that affect teachers' work. The duty of care that is required of teachers includes their vital role in safeguarding children from harm. Examples of practice in relation to taking children on school trips and in relation to child protection have related legislation to the practical steps teachers must take as part of their conditions of service.

Visit the companion website to find an example of an educational visit risk assessment.

To access additional online resources please visit: **https://study.sagepub.com/wyseandrogers**

Here you will find a classroom activity, author podcasts including Dominic Wyse's top tips for employability, free access to SAGE journal articles and links to external sources.

Diaz, N. (2011). Statutory Professional Responsibilities. In H. Cooper (ed.) *Professional Studies in Primary Education*. London: Sage. Provides an account of how statutory and non-statutory regulations affect the work of professionals and how personal values influence the ways in which professionals act.

Lindon, J. (2012) *Safeguarding and Child Protection: 0-8 Years - Linking Theory and Practice*, 4th edition. London: Hodder Education. A popular book written by a chartered psychologist that includes very good advice for work with children under 5 years of age.

Tisdall, K. (2013). Effective Contributors: Evaluating the Potential for Children and Young People's Participation in their Own Schooling and Learning. In M. Priestly & G. Biesta (eds), *Reinventing the Curriculum: Policy and Practice*. London: Bloomsbury. An important contribution to children's rights in relation to education. The chapter, and the book as a whole, also include reflections on Scotland's Curriculum for Excellence.

Wyse, D., Davis, R., Jones, P., & Rogers, S. (eds) (2015). *Exploring Education and Childhood: From current certainties to new visions*. London: Routledge. As part of this book's bold new vision for early years and primary education, including its 'manifesto for change', one chapter address children's rights and another chapter addresses the voice of the child.

REFERENCES

Department for Education (DfE) (2013). *Use of Reasonable Force: Advice for head teachers, staff and governing bodies*. London: DfE.

Department for Education (DfE) (2014a). *Statutory Framework for the Early Years Foundation Stage: Setting the standards for learning, development and care for children from birth to five*. London: DfE.

Department for Education (DfE) (2014b). *School Teachers' Pay and Conditions Document 2014 and Guidance on School Teachers' Pay and Conditions*. London: DfE.

Department for Education (DfE) (2014c). *Behaviour and Discipline in Schools: Advice for head teachers and school staff*. London: DfE.

Department for Education (DfE) (2014d). *The Equality Act 2010 and Schools: Departmental advice for school leaders, school staff, governing bodies and local authorities*. London: DfE.

Glendon, M. (2015). Common Law. Available from: www.britannica.com/EBchecked/topic/128386/common-law

Harker, L., Jütte, S., Murphy, T., Bentley, H., Miller, P., & Fitch, K. (2013). *How Safe Are Our Children?* London: NSPCC.

HM Government (2015). *What to Do if you're Worried a Child is being Abused: Advice for practitioners*. London: HM Government.

Health and Safety Executive (HSE). (2011). *School Trips and Outdoor Learning Activities: Tackling the health and safety myths*. London: Health and Safety Executive.

National Society for the Prevention of Cruelty to Children (NSPCC) (2015). Signs, symptoms and effects of child abuse and neglect: What to look out for, the effects of abuse and support for adults abused as children. Retrieved from: www.nspcc.org.uk/preventing-abuse/signs-symptoms-effects/

National Union of Teachers (NUT) (2013). *NUT Notes 2013–14: Education, The Law and You*. London: College Hill Press.

Tisdall, K. (2013). Effective Contributors: Evaluating the Potential for Children and Young People's Participation in their Own Schooling and Learning. In M. Priestly & G. Biesta (eds), *Reinventing the Curriculum: Policy and Practice*. London: Bloomsbury.

Torgerson, C., Torgerson, D., Ainsworth, H., Buckley, H., Heaps, C., Hewitt, C., & Mitchell, N. (2014). *Improving Writing Quality: Evaluation Report and Executive Summary*. London: Education Endowment Foundation.

Wyse, D. (2001). Felt Tip Pens and School Councils: Children's Participation Rights in Four English Schools. *Children and Society*, *15*, 209–18.

17

RESEARCH AND TEACHING

Pete Dudley, Bernadette Duffy and Gillian Lister

LEARNING AIMS

This chapter will:

- explain why educational research is vitally important for teaching and children's learning
- explain the differences between and the common purposes of quantitative and qualitative educational research and what they are helping us to discover and do
- help you understand how these connect with reflective practice, practitioner-led classroom enquiry, professional learning and the creation and mobilisation of practice knowledge in settings and schools
- enable you to discuss, plan and try out approaches to reflective practice, classroom enquiry, case study development and lesson study in your classroom, setting or school
- provide you with a clear rationale for why you should build reflective practice and practitioner enquiry into the way you practise.

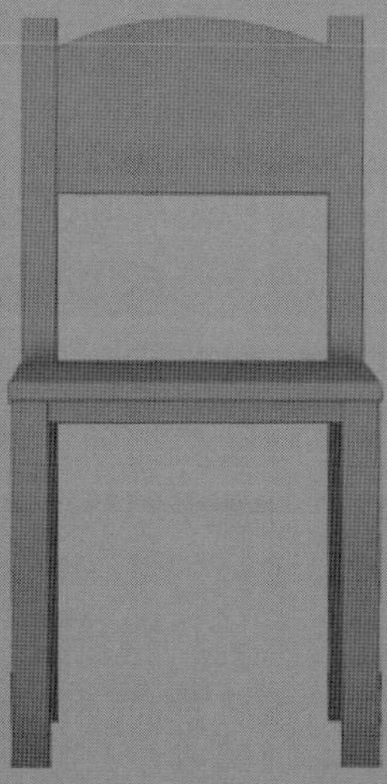

WHY DOES RESEARCH MATTER TO TEACHERS AND PRACTITIONERS?

In the UK, research into medicine has a long and successful history dating back hundreds of years. Admittedly, in the early days of surgery, for example, 'research' was little more than trial and error – but even back in the days of the early surgeons it was, as far as possible, *informed* trial and error. Early British surgeons would perform their operations before an audience with a few fellow surgeons gathered around as well as members of the public. The fellow surgeons were there to contribute helpful professional advice informing the procedure – even if at times it was advice like 'Don't cut that bit off! I cut off one of those last week and the patient was dead two minutes later ... Try cutting off the next one down!' It is no accident that the place where surgeons perform their operations is, to this day, still called an operating 'theatre': a place to practise one's profession before an audience of peers.

Children have attended educational settings for the purpose of helping them to learn for thousands of years. One would imagine then that educational research would have amassed enough volumes of research to dwarf its much younger counterpart – medical research. But this is not the case.

However, one ancient study of successful teaching can be found in the beautiful 2,500-year-old recordings made by Plato of the pedagogical work of his mentor, the Greek philosopher Socrates. Socrates thought a lot about the nature of life and humanity and helped his fellow Athenians to do so as well. He did this by observing them closely over time and then involving them in dialogue through which he explored their perceptions of life, and their espoused and actual motivations or reasons for doing and believing things. Through this guided reflection, he gently helped them to come to realise and even accept some of the false beliefs that they used to govern their lives. Plato's recordings of these conversations formed the core text for the school of philosophy established in Socrates's honour – Plato's Academy. We thoroughly recommend Plato's (2005) *Early Socratic Dialogues* as an early, rare, relevant and readable core text on education, pedagogy and as an example of formative observation of teaching.

However, whilst these early studies focused mainly on the teachers, there are also examples of child studies in which adults, including parents and teachers, observed and recorded children's learning and development, inspired by Rousseau ([1762] 1979) and Froebel. In the 1920s, Susan Isaacs (1929) drew on this tradition to inform her work at Malting House School. She documented the daily occupations of the children, their play and their questioning. By reflecting on her detailed anecdotal insights, Isaacs learned about how children learn, and as a result influenced generations of early years practitioners (Nutbrown and Carter, 2013). We will see later how observation of children's learning and development has played a key role in research into learning and teaching.

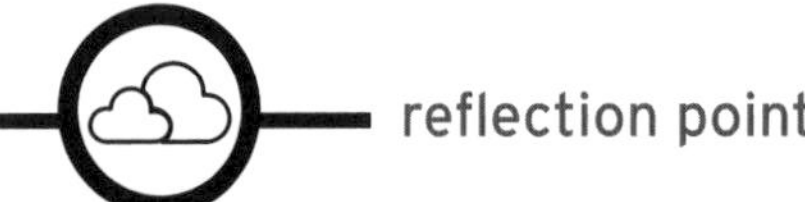

Think of your own childhood or those of children you know. How did the adults in your life record your learning and development at home and at school (for example, photos of key events, videos, pictures you drew, letters/cards you wrote)?

What stories have they passed on about your childhood and their impression of you as a child?

What is research?

At its root, scientific enquiry – research – involves observing nature (which really means observing in normality things as different, for example, as the way in which employees work together in an insurance office or the microscopic formation of synapses in the brain). The observation leads to a recording of what has been seen – for example, in the form of notes, drawings, audio or video recordings: research 'data'! These data are analysed in order to identify patterns, themes, relationships, and explored to find out whether these patterns occur under similar circumstances elsewhere and to form hypotheses about why the patterns occur. The hypotheses are then tested to exclude any possibility that there could be another 'cause' of the patterns than that predicted. The hypotheses that survive the tests are developed into a *theory* that explains the occurrence of the patterns. Researchers will then try to prove, modify or disprove the theory, and if the subsequent body of research evidence supporting the theory grows, the theory becomes accepted as new knowledge – until a new theory is developed that usurps it.

Why is such research important? Because research allows us deliberately to manage discovery and the creation of new knowledge. A text that develops the idea of research as 'work' that creates new knowledge from evidence is Glaser and Strauss's (1967) seminal work on the discovery of grounded theory.

Educational research

Educational 'research', as we indicated earlier, is surprisingly new. The purpose, values and ethics of education have been the subjects of philosophical thought for millennia. Even as late as the 1870s, Matthew Arnold, an architect of the English state system, pursued the philosophical goals of 'sweetness and light' for education. *Scientific* educational research however did not begin in earnest until the early 20th century and even then it was more closely associated with medical science than education. That is in marked contrast to the focus we see from education policy makers today who usually wish to add 'what works' to the philosophical and ideological bases for education (see DfE, 2010 for a recent example of evidence-driven policy; and Sahlberg, 2012 for a critique of 'the great education reform movement').

The growth of confidence in the ability of scientific research to create new knowledge leading to new technologies, meant that in the 20th century advances in funding for science made it possible to carry out very large-scale research projects with sometimes millions of subjects. Using large numbers of subjects means using research methods that are very dependent on the analysis of those numbers and the calculation of levels of confidence in the results. The 'effect size' of the trial is a measurement of the difference it has made – its impact. In education, such quantitative science has mainly prevailed in the area of measurement of educational achievement through tests and examinations.

In the early 21st century, policy makers have tended to discount research that does not have a *quantitative* methodology and to dismiss *qualitative* methods that rely on painstaking observations of particular cases of the phenomenon being researched (Haynes et al., 2012). But painstaking, detailed observation should not be discounted so quickly. It was such processes that led Darwin to develop his theory of evolution, whilst Einstein developed his theory of relativity through his 'thought experiments'.

Research about learning and development is concerned less with how well something has been learned and more with the process of how it comes to be learned. It seeks to answer questions like 'How does learning happen?' or 'How can we best organise educational processes so that children learn most effectively?'

Influential studies that have generated theories of learning that we use as key tools today, have been of very small numbers of children indeed. Vygotsky and Piaget, both 'big hitters' in the field of research into learning, studied the development of no more than a handful of children between them, and like Susan Isaacs they developed profound theories from their observations which, with modification, have held up well over time as countless subsequent studies have put them to the test.

But the vast majority of this later research has taken place in the past half century. The Effective Provision of Preschool Education Project (EPPE), which ran from 1997 to 2003, has demonstrated the true impact that research can have on practice as well as on policy (Sylva et al., 2010). EPPE was funded by the Department for Education and involved 3,000 children aiming to identify the most effective forms of pre-school provision. As well as showing the long-term impact of high quality early education on children's later achievement and life chances, the project introduced many practitioners to the Early Childhood Environment Rating scale (ECERs) and the Infant and Toddler Environment Rating scale (ITERs). These and the identification of strategies such as 'sustained shared thinking' helped practitioners to reflect on and thus better promote children's learning.

We argue in this chapter that a continued emphasis on the observation of learners and learning as a basis for the development of educational knowledge remains important to educational research in the 21st century in schools and classrooms, not just universities.

Why educational research was so late in 'coming of age'

Perhaps this is because no one really thought of education as a serious field of human endeavour worthy of enquiry. For centuries, intelligence was assumed by most people to be fixed, not something that could be developed and increased through education. Whilst medicine and law have been taught in British universities for over 600 years, education was only recognised as a discipline in most UK universities in the past hundred years.

Education is a relatively new science and educational research is a relatively new scientific discipline. This is exciting. It means that there is a lot to play for. Psychology became the first discipline to engage in the scientific development of learning theory, and as a result of early 20th-century educational studies (described above) we have seen rapid developments in the scientific understanding of learning. Recent convergence of many theories into an emerging understanding of how learning happens has subsequently been supported by tangible neuroscientific observations of permanent changes in the brain that occur as we learn (Howard-Jones, 2011).

Thus, we now know that we learn through social processes of 'joining in' and negotiating meaning through talk and that we do this best in the specific places where the new knowledge is needed. We have also observed the physical structures that our brains develop to manage that knowledge.

So for practitioners coming into the profession, it has never been more important to understand the potential for educational research to contribute to the way we as teachers can best help others learn. And there has never been more reason to become actively involved in research *as a practising teacher*. Visionary educator Laurence Stenhouse foresaw the time when education practitioners, like medical professionals, would participate in research throughout their careers for the benefit of learners and would use the classroom and school as a laboratory for improving learning and achievement in the way that research hospitals have done for 200 years (Stenhouse, 1975, 1981).

WHAT IS GOOD RESEARCH?

If research is 'informed trial and error', then good research should be informed by the best possible knowledge and thought. The 'trial' element – the research *methodology* – is designed to provide the best possible answer to the research question. It has to be 'fit for purpose', which might mean that it involves a large sample of subjects and produces the same result enough times to make it 'reliable'. On the other hand, it might mean that a phenomenon under study (say a child's verbal expression of increasingly sustained thinking in dialogue with another) has been observed:

- in sufficient proximity and detail
- with sufficient frequency
- between sufficient numbers of adults and children
- in enough different contexts

to make it capable of detailed description by a researcher. This detailed description may be a basis for analysing the sustained shared thinking. This in turn may yield patterns and relationships that bear interrogation and scrutiny and thus allow plausible theories for the existence of these patterns to be advanced.

The findings from the first example may be expressed in terms of differences in numbers or percentages represented in words and mathematical charts. The findings from the second may be expressed through explanations involving examples of observed dialogic patterns linked with an increase in sustained verbal expression by the child.

The first kind of research is called quantitative, the second qualitative research. Let us explore each of these in more detail in relation to education and learning.

Quantitative research

In marked contrast to the past, the British government has recently favoured funding what some call the 'gold standard' in research – randomised control trials (RCTs) championed in particular by *Guardian* columnist Ben Goldacre (see Haynes et al., 2012). This is a common example of quantitative research.

Take an RTC designed to test whether a new drug is better than the one used currently. A sample will be created of a thousand sufferers of the disease treated by the drug. All are given identical instructions on how and when to take their pill each day. The experimental drug is given to half of the sample selected randomly. The other half – the control group – is given either an identical pill that contains the drug that is currently in use or an identical pill that has no medicinal properties called a 'placebo'. Participants do not know which they are getting. Neither do the researchers. In this way, it is presumed, no researcher bias or human emotions can be present to affect the outcome.

Results are expressed numerically. For example, 'Those taking the experimental drug reported reduced symptoms three days sooner than patients using the existing version whilst the 'placebo' group reported increased symptoms'. RCT data can be interrogated in many ways, so it may be possible to examine the effect of the treatment on different population groups within the study – men, women, younger or more elderly populations, for example.

The Education Endowment Foundation (EEF) was set up in 2010 to oversee the funding of a considerable portion of publically funded educational research in England. It is a condition of the EEF that every project has to be evaluated using a quantitative 'medical' model, such as that described above, conducted by a team from a list of research organisations approved by the EEF.

What kinds of educational research would you see this approach being especially useful for? Can you see any drawbacks in using medical trials like this in an educational context?

However, there are limitations to what RCTs can tell us. They seldom tell us why a treatment worked or not, or how to improve it.

Because educational science is relatively new, our scientific understanding of learning itself is still underdeveloped. Therefore, as well as finding out how *well* a teaching and learning approach, resource or other intervention works, we still need to be concerned with understanding why it works – how it operates in (and what it reveals about) the learning process.

This may be one reason why RCTs have until recently been less common in educational research than in other fields. Another reason for this is that even if an RCT is proposed, practitioners can be more reluctant than doctors to place children in a control group.

Qualitative research

We discussed earlier how observation and reflective, analytical thinking cannot be underestimated in educational research. The influence of Piaget, Vygotsky and Isaacs on practitioners has been powerful and not only because of the insightful theory that they developed from their observational research. Their vivid but compellingly argued accounts of children's development and learning have spoken powerfully to generations of practitioners for whom this research has had face validity, the 'click of recognition' (Lather, 1986) and therefore credibility. Their research has not only convinced practitioners of its veracity, it has motivated them to trust in and use the knowledge.

By observing children and parents, both Vygotsky and Piaget evolved important theory about how learning happens and can be supported. They did not carry out mass observations with huge sample sizes. They studied the behaviours of a few children. Their data were not numbers, they were detailed accounts over time from observations. From these qualitative data sources, they began to discern patterns and themes from which in turn they raised hypotheses. They returned to different areas of their database (their observation notes) repeatedly to seek more examples of patterns that triangulated or corroborated their hypotheses (or alternatively challenged, undermined or disproved them), until they reached a point where some ideas held good, providing plausible explanations for why a child was learning in the manner observed.

A crucial role thus exists for smaller qualitative studies – especially in investigating primary questions such as how or why things happen in relation to learning, teaching, curriculum or settings. However, for such research to be high quality, it needs to make up for the lack of scale in the strength and depth of its observational work and in its theoretical underpinning.

And, of course, 'numbers' exist in patterns in the most naturalistic, observational studies. All patterns repeat somewhere and one can count these repetitions and factor them into a descriptive analysis. This has created 'mixed method' studies which seek to combine qualitative and quantitative approaches, offering findings about how and why as well as how much.

It is also possible to take a number of small-scale studies that examine similar subjects with measurable outcomes and treat each study as a unit of analysis. Studying studies is called 'meta-study' and has recently been dominated by New Zealand researcher John Hattie, whose meta-analyses of thousands of studies from around the world have become the bible of educational policy makers and politicians (Hattie, 2009). Hattie takes educational themes that can affect outcomes such as class size, gender mix or same-sex teaching, setting and mixed ability, as well as 'interventions' such as formative assessment, and curricular models such as teaching phonics in early reading. He studies the best research evidence available on each, giving the reader an 'effect size' of their respective impacts. This is why his work is so popular with politicians keen to make a difference to educational standards.

Web Link

Good, practitioner-friendly information about the findings from a range of such meta-studies as well as RCTs can be accessed through this web link, available on the companion website: https://educationendowmentfoundation.org.uk

REFLECTIVE PRACTICE

So what relevance does research have to a trainee or novice teacher embarking on a career in teaching? It all seems a million miles away.

Far from it. Growing evidence suggests that teachers and practitioners who deliberately and habitually reflect on their practice from the very outset of their training, progress in their teaching expertise more quickly than those who do not (Cajkler and Wood, 2015). And a well established body of evidence explains why classroom practitioners, in particular, need to engage throughout their careers in reflective practice. Something that it is important for novice practitioners to know about is the difference between the professional 'practice knowledge' (James, 2007) of teacher practitioners and that of doctors or lawyers.

The difference is this: most of the practice knowledge that you will develop and use in your career will be invisible to you and you will not know that you know or use it. But when you need it, it will come to you automatically as does all tacit knowledge. Teachers who succeed learn to utilise tacit knowledge systems for storing their practice knowledge (Cooper and McIntyre, 1996; Wragg et al., 1996; Eraut, 2000; Dudley, 2013). This tacit practice knowledge is forged in the classroom: one of the most complex, fast-moving work environments there is. Each day, teachers make thousands more decisions than other professionals.

We use tacit knowledge to deal with rapid decision making. When you are riding a bicycle, you use your conscious knowledge to think about where to go and negotiate the traffic, and you use your tacit knowledge to stay upright – making hundreds of corrections a minute. The same happens in classrooms. You use your conscious knowledge to think about the content you will teach next, to follow your plan, to note points about a child's responses that tell you about their learning and, once sufficiently experienced, you use your unconscious tacit knowledge to constantly 'read' the classroom, to judge when to change your body language or tone of voice and often when to intervene to assist a child's learning.

In the first three years of teaching, we build 'filters' that enable us to navigate our lessons without getting distracted by the fast-moving, unpredictable information we are constantly processing. We filter out everything that can be dealt with unconsciously (Dudley, 2013). Dudley argues that this creates a growing problem for us as we gain in experience because we stop seeing (or being conscious of) much that happens in our classrooms.

putting it into practice

Applying reflective practice to research

Reflective practice is a good habit and it needs to be 'habitual', deliberate, recorded, processed or analysed and to lead to conscious (if small) decisions about a change in future practice (because tiny but correct improvements continually repeated end in transformation).

Some quick and easy reflective actions that you can take alone are as follows:

- Plan, Do, Review: Choose one activity a week to carry out a quick evaluation using questions used by the US army to review operations. The questions are: (i) What was supposed to happen? (List) (ii) What actually happened? (List) (iii) How do you account for the difference? (List) and (iv) What are the implications for the future?

- Each day, identify one aspect of a child's learning behaviour or achievement that exceeded your expectations and another which fell short and try to identify what it was that caused your expectations to be different and also what this means for your work with these two children tomorrow.
- Seek children's views of how well an activity has worked - perhaps by asking them what they liked most about it and how it could be improved if other children in the group do it tomorrow.
- Each day, choose two children who you will observe every hour for a minute each. Sit down at the end of the day with the outcomes of their learning and your five brief notes of each child. List what new things about them you have discovered and what you need to do differently as a result.
- Track one child each day for a week to log who they are interacting with when playing and learning at 15- or 20-minute intervals. Use a timeline to record this and at the end of the week compare all five - for example, the numbers of different interactees and the number of interactions each has with the focus child. You might want to plot socio-grams or charts to make the differences clearer visually. Note any surprises and list any implications or questions the data raise. Use internationally recognised scales such as ECERS and ITERS (Harms et al., 2014) to evaluate your work and to measure provision and teacher-child interactions.

This is why all teachers need to adopt reflective practice and use it regularly throughout their career. Reflective practice sounds passive and contemplative. Reflection that is going to help you improve and learn professionally is always 'effortful' because it involves learning (which is always effortful; Resnick, 1987). However, it can also be tough and challenging, but you will always be a better practitioner for it.

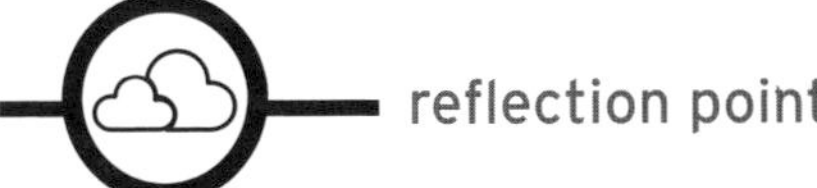

What aspects of your classroom setting would you think might yield interesting insights and perhaps even challenge some of the assumptions that you find you have been making about your children and the effect of your practices or the policies of your setting?

REFLECTIVE APPROACHES

We will now take a look at some practical and relatively straightforward approaches that you can begin to take to become a reflective practitioner. This will be all the better if you get into the habits of reflective practice at the outset of your career, and the evidence shows that you will progress more quickly in your development of expert practice.

Keeping a reflective log

A reflective log is a really simple way of amassing all the observations, thoughts and questions you have as you carry out your reflective practices. You can use your own code to sort your thoughts – for example, thought bubbles for hypotheses about why something may be happening, light bulbs for insights, and panels and diagrams for fuller reflections, decisions or emerging theories. Each month or half term, you can track systematically through your insights, hypotheses, observations, decisions, musings and theories, creating a reflections page where you list the ways your knowledge of practice has improved and what you want to focus on in your and your children's learning over the next half term.

Involving others in reflection and collaborative enquiry

Reflection can be solitary but also collaborative. There are huge bonuses if you carry out some of the ideas above alongside a colleague and compare notes each month. You can also use your reflections to raise talking points with more experienced colleagues or a mentor.

If you are able to identify colleagues who are interested in developing their reflective practice, then you can form a professional learning community and engage in joint enquiries into aspects of children's learning and how to improve them. For more information about reflective practice, please see Chapter 12 in this book.

Two forms of classroom enquiry that are very popular with teacher practitioners are action research and case study research.

Action research

Action research is a strategically planned and deliberate form of reflective practice that may be written up and shared in a formal 'report'. It may be carried out by practitioners exploring aspects of their specific context. For example, a small group of teachers carrying out an enquiry into how they set up and use collaborative group work would almost certainly involve researching their own practices. This is called 'participant research' because they are both subjects of the research and the researchers. In the 1970s, Laurence Stenhouse began what has become a strong tradition of action research in English schools. His vision for teaching was of a profession developing and publishing its continuously evolving professional knowledge, built up through a process of teacher practitioners engaging in *systematic enquiry made public*. This movement was continued by John Elliott, becoming known as *teachers as researchers*.

Proponents of educational action research, such as Carr and Kemiss (1986) and Elliott (1988), have helped to embed this in the hands of collaborating practitioners in schools and classrooms.

Action research involves identifying an authentic enquiry question that, if better understood as a result of enquiry, will improve learning or teaching or leadership, and ultimately benefit children. It involves carrying out small 'reconnaissance' studies to understand the subject of study and then careful design of how the data are to be gathered and analysed. Ways of checking the authenticity of findings are designed-in by seeking evidence of their existence through other means – to ensure findings are 'triangulated' and thus more robust. Triangulation involves using more than one enquiry method to explore the same research question. If a finding is replicated using two or three different methods, it strengthens its veracity.

Research into active exploratory thinking

Rose and Jane were studying their 5- and 6-year-old children discussing aspects of mathematics with 'talk partners', in order to encourage greater engagement in active exploratory thinking. They decided to explore this by gathering evidence of the nature of the talk exchanges between these talk partners. As well as looking at the kinds of ideas and words the children were using to develop their mathematical thinking, Rose and Jane decided to collect numerical data on the numbers of pupils 'putting their hands up' to volunteer answers to the class after the talk partner sessions, and to compare these with the numbers doing so before the talk partners were introduced. This seemed to be another simple and countable indicator of whether the children felt more engaged and confident in their mathematical thinking following the discussion. They also decided to explore the children's perspectives of whether and how they had benefited from the talk partner discussions by interviewing small groups of them and examining their responses. Finally, they collected evidence of the pupils' progress in the areas of mathematics for which the talk partners' approach was used and compared this with progress in these areas when no talk partners had been used. Comparing all these different forms of data gave them deeper insights into what was happening in relation to their children's learning but also helped to 'triangulate' their findings because they detected positive changes across all their different data sources and analytical methods - what the pupils reported, what they were revealing of their mathematical thinking through the paired exchanges, the numbers feeling confident enough to share with the class (by putting their hands up) and the comparative rates of progress of the pupils when talk partners were used. It is harder to dismiss findings revealed in so many sources of data.

Case study research

Case study research originated in medical work where practitioners would (and still do) draw up detailed descriptive studies of how diseases affect specific people. 'Case' here refers to the particular instance of the disease – not to the person suffering from the disease. As we state above, much of our current knowledge about child development and about learning theory comes from detailed studies of learning and development in a very few children – or cases.

Case study is a method frequently used by teacher researchers. This is partly because the origins of much classroom and learner-focused research lie in medical and psychological research. Discussion that takes place between school leaders and teachers about specific pupils or groups can mirror the 'supervision' discussion between a psychologist or a senior researcher and members of their team.

Case studies are often made by teacher researchers observing the effects of pedagogical, curricular or wider school interventions on the learning of children in their classrooms. Classroom observations, semi-structured or structured interviews, discourse analysis of talk, questionnaires, concept maps, climate mapping, sociogrammetry, analyses of children's work samples: all of these can help form part of an action research-based classroom or school-based enquiry (see Table 17.1).

And all can contribute to building an analytical picture of the 'case' being studied. Such a case may be a group of 5-year-olds responding to a new approach being used in the school to working

Table 17.1 Different forms of data gathering

Classroom or pupil observations	Systematic observations of what is happening in a setting or classroom. Factors to 'watch out for' can be predetermined or can emerge from an analysis of what observers note. Observers can be asked to make an observation of specific children at defined time intervals or the process can be left more open. Observers can be asked to focus on the object under study such as how children use a role play area within a half-hour period and what for, or they might focus on sustained adult-child interactions - their focus and how or why they seemed to be sustained.
Structured interview	An interview with children or adults where the same questions are asked of each respondent in order to make them highly comparable and open to quantitative analysis.
Semi-structured interview	An interview where the same main prompts are used but where respondents can develop their ideas and where follow-up questions might be different with each respondent.
Discourse analysis of talk	Where child to child, group or child/adult talk is recorded and then transcribed. There are many different ways of analysing transcribed talk - from focusing on content - what the people were talking about - to examining ways the two 'interlocutors' speak and how adult and child manage to keep a dialogue going so that they respond to each other's thoughts and ideas. They might look for signs/words of encouragement, exploration ('How?') and suggestion (Let's...). See Mercer (2000) or Wells (1999) in conjunction with Watkins (2003).
Concept maps	A process where teachers or children are asked to draw or to arrange objects onto a map to represent how they think about something. For example, children might have pictures of sheep in a field, sheep being sheared, someone spinning yarn from fleece, someone knitting and a child wearing a wooly hat. The children sequence the pictures - if older, perhaps using arrows to show relationships - and then describe what the map is saying. This can reveal conceptions and misconceptions.
Climate maps	Children may be given a picture of different rooms in and around their setting and asked to mark with a smiley sticker the places that make them feel happy and the places that don't with a droopy face. These can then be explored and experimental changes might be made. A further use of the same climate map at a later point can help reveal whether children are feeling differently towards their surroundings.
Socio-grams	As part of a classroom observation, practitioner observers might be asked to draw diagrams of the groupings of children at different points in a day. This may include differentiating between girls and boys or older and younger children in the same space. If you are studying a particular child, the socio-gram diagrams might represent the groupings the child is in at different intervals and how long they were sustained before children moved off or joined.

with non-narrative text. Observational, discourse and work-sample data might be collected monthly during the introduction of a new approach and contribute to an analysis that helps teachers to understand what effect the approach is having on the learning of specific kinds of pupils and how to adjust and modify it further before conducting another cycle of action research.

reflection point

An exploratory case study might be made of how early years practitioners give formative oral feedback to children to help promote sustained shared thinking about relationships with other children. What sort of data would you gather to help you and a colleague to explore the answer to this question?

One skill in analysing data in order to shed new light on a familiar classroom phenomenon is to try to look at the data in ways that disguise the familiar pictures and patterns we see in classroom life. For example, a transcript of an interview of teachers talking about their classrooms may have the effect of burying important issues as a result of the familiarity we have with our classrooms. We therefore need to throw that familiar landscape into a different relief for these issues to become visible. So a study of the specific verbs and adjectives or metaphors that the teachers use may help you, as an analyst, to 'see' some of their talk (and therefore thought) in a new light. Researchers call this 'fracturing' the data in the way a geologist might fracture a stone along different axes in order to reveal vital information about its formation that is not visible externally. Exploring patterns or themes within data sets and then using the same data sets to try to confound or confirm the hypotheses that these patterns suggest, is called developing 'grounded theory' (Glaser and Strauss, 1967), and it is often necessary and always good practice to gather more data from the field and test your ideas out on a second or third data set to see if you can view evidence for them again in the same way.

Often in participant teacher action research, you may need to go back to some of your subjects (teachers or pupils) and explore with them the patterns that you have discerned in their use of language when talking about a particular pupil or subject – using verbs and adjectives and metaphors that differ markedly from those used for others. Engaging colleagues in the process of analysis, speculating and hypothesising about the reasons why this has happened can not only strengthen your evidence but also help people to see the issues themselves. People are more likely to accept, own and, importantly, *act on* the outcomes of school-based teacher research when they have been involved themselves.

Web Link

Online examples of different kinds of school-based action research that have been conducted and reported by teachers and school leaders can be accessed through these web links, available on the companion website: http://lessonstudy.co.uk; http://beta.sharingbestpractice.camden.gov.uk

One powerful aspect of case study research is that if you conduct two or three or more case studies similarly, then they can become units of analysis in a 'cross case' study. If three case studies, like the one described above, conducted in three different schools, yield a common finding, then that finding has to be taken extremely seriously.

OBSERVING AND UNDERSTANDING CLASSROOM INTERACTIONS

Unfortunately, most 'classroom observation' undertaken in schools today still focuses on the teacher and not on the learning. Coe's (2014) finding that 'teaching quality grades', given following lesson observations by inspectors and performance managers, bear no relation to the progress pupils made in those lessons, led Ofsted to abruptly cease using such grades in school inspections in 2014 after 20 years of doing so.

But it is difficult to observe learning because much learning is invisible. So when we are trying to study learning in our classrooms and settings, we have to look for secondary evidence of learning taking place. If the learning we are looking for relates to how a child develops fine motor control, then we can observe the child each week engaging with a task demanding this and compare our observations with those made earlier, looking for signs of progress. If our aim is to discern how a child thinks about being kind to others, we need a different approach. We might, for example, try the strategy of 'catching the child being nice to others' in our day-to-day work. Or we may also need to engage the child in talk about what being kind to people or toys or animals is like. We may discuss examples of being kind and being unkind to others – or encourage the child to do this with their peers following stories featuring acts of kindness through role plays or with puppets and toys. Our job, then, is to 'eavesdrop' on their discussions to see what they reveal about their thinking about and conceptualisation of 'kindness'.

Taking the time to make such systematic observations of children in classrooms – particularly of their interactions – can dramatically increase our ability to 'scaffold' their learning by designing activities (perhaps characters from a story blown up as stick puppets) which allow the children to act out empathetic conversations in which they pretend to be the characters in the story.

Studies into the learning and development of children in the early years (and the rest of their school lives) have significantly helped us to understand learning. The EPPE and EPPSE studies, for example, have done more than almost any other research project to demonstrate just how revealing the deliberate observation of children's and adults' talk and learning behaviours can be of social learning processes (Sylva et al., 2010). It was these studies that first used the phrase 'sustained shared thinking' to describe talk interactions between practitioner and learner or between peer learners to describe a key process that needs to be engineered in learning settings, alongside opportunities for children to struggle with support and for this struggle to be seen as necessary for learning. Studies by Mercer (2000) and Alexander (2005) have shown how capturing and analysing children's talk for learning opens a window on the processes of dialogue and collaborative group work.

THE ROLE OF LESSON STUDY IN CLASSROOM ENQUIRY

There is one classroom enquiry method which has been developed and honed for almost 150 years that provides an ideal approach to collaborative classroom observation and the study of pupil learning. It originated in Japan and its name, *Jugukenkyu*, translates approximately in English as 'lesson study' (LS). In LS teachers collaboratively examine how children learn in 'research lessons' that they have planned together. Then they discuss and analyse what they have seen and begin to plan a subsequent 'research lesson' that builds on their discussions and findings. When they have carried out three or so research lessons, they have usually discovered things about their pupils and about their teaching, pedagogy and curriculum that lead them to make changes in their teaching generally.

The tradition of LS in Japan requires a LS group to make its learning public by sharing it with fellow professionals, either by inviting them to attend an 'open house' lesson or by creating presentations, posters or lesson study case reports. A Japanese teacher will be a member of at least one LS group throughout their career and will carry out one or more lesson studies each year. In the UK, thousands of teachers use social media such as Twitter to publish or follow the outcomes of their classroom enquiries and lesson studies and this approach is growing apace.

LS is a good example of collaborative classroom enquiry and has also proved to be a powerful tool for the profession in leading and implementing curricular and pedagogical changes in the classroom from the roots up (Kuno, 2015). In LS a group of teachers who have something that they want to improve on in their classrooms that is part of their regular curriculum, will agree a 'lesson study focus'. They research the kinds of approaches that the latest literature suggests may work and they set about planning their research lesson. In a model developed recently in the UK (Dudley, 2013, 2015), participating teachers sign up to a protocol, which guarantees that all contributions will be valued, and which makes sure everyone feels safe in contributing to the LS group (see Figure 17.1).

Figure 17.2 then sets out the LS process. LS teachers also identify a sample of around three 'case' children to whom they pay specific attention when planning, observing and discussing the research lessons – but they plan, teach, observe and discuss for the whole class as well. They interview some of the children after each research lesson to gain their perspectives on what worked and what could be improved further. And when they discuss the research lessons afterwards, they make sure to begin the discussion with a comparison of what they had predicted in the planning session that each case child would do and learn, with their observations of what actually happened.

Stigler has described how LS 'slows down' the fast-moving action of the classroom, enabling interactions and evidence of learning to be seen that we are usually too busy to see or which we store in our 'tacit knowledge' reserves and are blind to. Teachers find LS challenging but rewarding and fulfilling, and studies in Japan (Lewis, 1998) have suggested that it is LS that gives teachers great depth and detail of the learning of their children and allows them great and frequent insights into their classrooms. Research is now showing how use of LS by trainee and recently qualified teachers accelerates their practice development (Cajkler and Wood, 2015).

This protocol exists to help create common expectations amongst the LS group members. In doing this it will help the group to form a good working relationship that helps members to share ideas, concerns, challenges and 'wonderings' without fear of criticism. All this will aid the sharing and discovery of new practice knowledge.
At all stages in this Lesson Study we will act according to the following:

- All members of the LS group are equal as learners whatever their age, experience, expertise or seniority in school (or beyond)
- All contributions are treated with unconditional positive regard. This does not mean they will not be subject to analysis, doubt or challenge, it means no one will be made to feel foolish for venturing a suggestion. It is often suggestions that make you feel foolish or vulnerable that are of the greatest value and generate the most learning
- We will support whoever teaches the research lesson(s) and make faithful observations, recording as much as possible what pupils say as well as do
- We will use common tools for Lesson Study – planners, pupil interview prompts and approaches to sharing outcomes with each other
- We will use pupils' work and interview comments to inform the post-lesson discussion alongside our observations
- We will use the post-lesson discussion flow, starting by discussing what each case pupil did compared with what we predicted and let the discussion flow from there
- We will listen to each other and to ourselves when we speak and build on the discussion, making suggestions, raising hypotheses, elaborating, qualifying and at all times being accountable to our lesson aims, our case pupils and our observation and other research lesson data
- We will share what we learn – our new practice knowledge – with our colleagues as accurately and vividly as we can and in such a way that they can benefit from and try it out themselves
- We will share the aims and outcomes of our Lesson Study with our pupils appropriately, depending on their ages and stages of development. Their views, ideas and perspectives will be treated with equal positive regard

Signed and dated by LS group members.

Figure 17.1 Lesson study (LS) group protocol

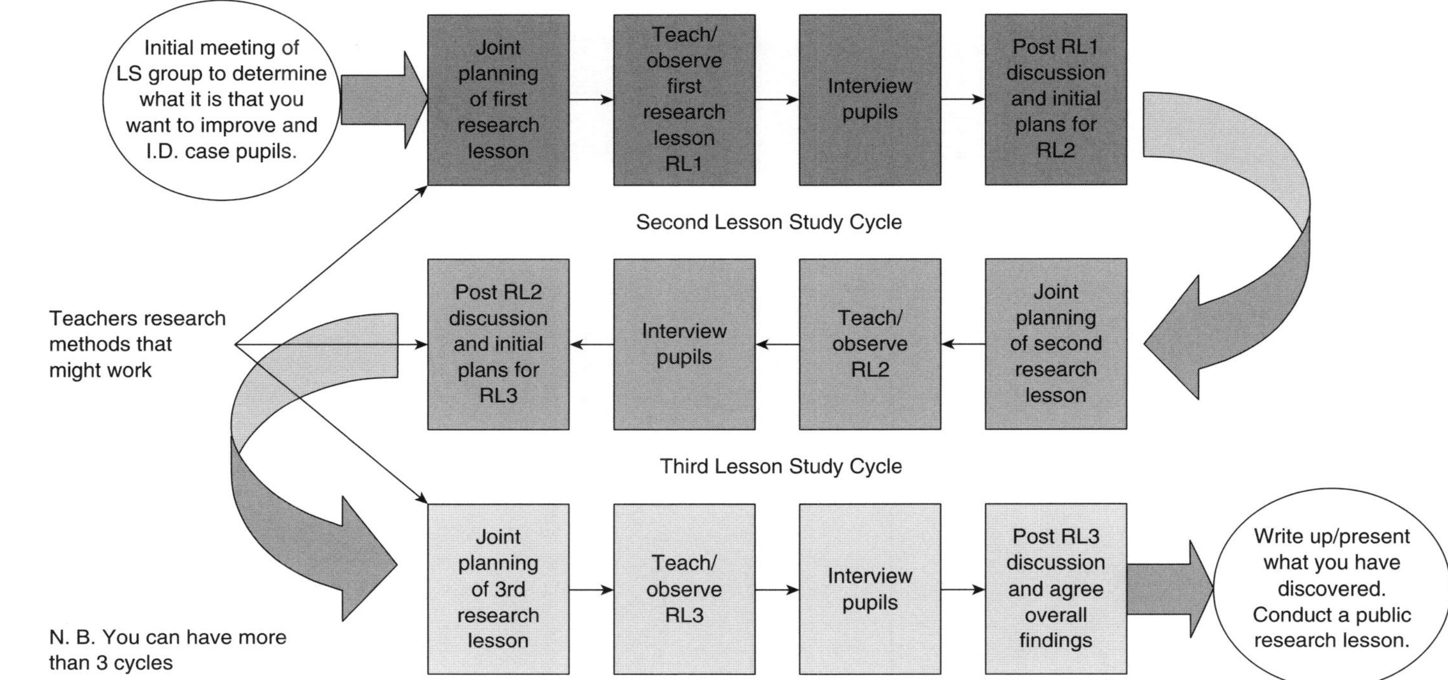

Figure 17.2 The lesson study cycle

Source: Dudley (2011)

Boys and writing: a lesson study

As part of Camden's Early Learning Cluster, a number of reception class practitioners expressed concern about boys in their classes who showed little or no interest in writing, and in many cases actively avoided mark making and writing. They identified boys in each setting they wanted to focus on and over the term used their colleagues from other settings in their lesson study group to observe their target children. This generated detailed moment-by-moment accounts of the children during the observation period. During discussion after a lesson, the observer fed back and the lesson study group shared its thoughts on each child's experience and learning. In many cases, pre-observation views of a child were challenged by the observation findings and led to significant changes in how practitioners encouraged writing in the target children. At whole cluster meetings, each lesson study group shared its observations and thoughts on boys and writing, increasing the range of effective strategies which practitioners drew on to support writing development for all children.

Early years lesson study, Camden, London

Context: Practitioners from early years settings in children's centres and schools in Camden, London came together in mixed children's centre and school staff groups of two from each setting to plan lesson studies that they conducted and analysed together - alternating between a children's centre and a school setting.

Aim: To explore the potential for colleagues from settings with different traditions to learn from each other's practice and to identify areas of common need in promoting the characteristics of learning by conducting lesson studies together.

Outcomes: The project dispelled any myths about over-formal practices in schools or low challenge in children's centre settings. There were many outcomes but a common finding amongst practitioners was that almost every lesson study, whether in a school or children's centre setting, revealed the degree to which practitioners intervened before the learner had 'struggled' enough to learn, and supplied the answer or did it for them.

Future actions: Not only planning activities that address the characteristics of learning but also letting the children struggle enough independently to be able to learn.

Gillian Lister from Thomas Coram Children's Centre and Nursery participated with two other practitioners from early years settings and one from a reception class. She found that the lesson study practice enabled her and her colleagues to see their children's learning in a new light and to learn from and to be inspired by the practice of peers that directly affected her subsequent approach to allowing children more opportunity to learn. She commented thus:

> I really learned how to let the children take a lead rather than expecting an 'end result' in where the children were taking me and to be a bit more courageous in letting go and following what they were actually doing in the lesson. We planned and discussed how the research lesson would be taught and identified case children, usually three but sometimes we had a couple more just in case.

Explaining how she learned to stand back in this way, she says:

> I think it was from observing other practitioners in their practice and also from the feedback from the group that we had when we met as a large group for the project. We learnt ideas that people would feed in to the discussion and, 'Oh I like that idea ... I'll try it myself'. That kind of thing. It's about, with a lesson you might have a plan but it's about being able to go away from the rigidity of the plan. Being able to follow the children and it might take you somewhere different but it didn't matter because people would have observed how the children were learning in that lesson and you'd say, 'Oh! I didn't realise that he was actually listening when he was ...' See what I mean? That kind of thing. And somebody else could actually feed that back to you when you'd been thinking, 'Oh, this isn't going terrible well', when their feed in made it seem different.
>
> Now I think as a result I am relating more to the children and where they are rather than where I think they should be ... People need to not have textbook expectations of how the children are learning and to understand their communications, their language or where they're going, what they're doing. If they suddenly got up from the table to go and do a painting, if you'd mentioned 'paint' you'd realise that that was where they were interested rather than that they should be sitting down – that sort of thing.

Commenting on a view expressed by John Elliott (2009) about the medium-term impact of participation in a lesson study on a practitioner as being like having an 'injection' that sensitises them to their learners and their practice for a period of time, Gillian commented: 'I think that's right, because it motivates you as well and you're thinking more about what you are doing and you put more into what you're doing as well and that's like an injection, yes.'

Web Link

Information (including handbooks for early years and school practitioners about using LS) can be accessed through this web link, available on the companion website: www.lessonstudy.co.uk

There is a growing national and international following on Twitter and other social media linking up lesson studies across the world, which can also be accessed through this web link, available on the companion website: www.walsnet.org

SUMMARY

Reflective practice and praxis

As we said at the start of this chapter, research into learning and teaching is comparatively new when one considers the millennia that children have been taught formally by adults. In his international study of pedagogy, Alexander (2000) laments the fact that 'recitation' is still the 'default' mode of classroom teaching across the globe because research reveals that it has severe limitations in promoting learning. The continued reversion to recitation (telling children) rather then helping them to learn is in part due to the fact that our language, culture and expectations of teaching have, for all these millennia, been based on the notion of the 'transmission' of knowledge from teacher to pupil by 'telling' – storytelling, song, rhyming epic poetry, whereas we know that children need to explore and manipulate the ideas in their minds by talking about them themselves, by encountering them in different forms and explaining them to themselves, by building mental models of them in their minds. Bruner coined the term 'folk pedagogy' to describe these ancient pervasive beliefs and yet it is not uncommon to hear modern educational professionals using terms like 'knowing your stuff', which is an echo of those old beliefs, and it is not hard either to see the way we continue to design classrooms, educational technology or even examination-based assessment systems that facilitate teacher talk or memorisation and (written) recitation by the learner as proof that learning has taken place.

In his seminal work on reflective practice, Donald Schön (1983) promoted the pursuit of *praxis* as an ideal for any group of practitioners that want to be thought of as a true 'profession'. Aristotle used 'praxis' to describe the moral imperative on a practitioner in any field to ensure that she or he is acting on the basis of the best possible information available or gatherable and with the best possible knowledge of how to gain the best outcome for those on whose behalf the practitioner is working – children, parents, other teachers.

There is a consensus that the kind of professional learning that most impacts on practice happens when practitioners work collaboratively together to identify ways to improve children's learning (Cordingley et al., 2004; Dudley, 2013). Hargreaves (2012) called this 'joint professional development' (JPD) and Kazemi and Hubbard (2008) describe this ongoing development and renewal of practice knowledge as the 'co-evolution' of practice (2008). A study of 800 research studies or 'meta-study' carried out by Robinson et al. (2009) revealed that the single action a school leader can take that will have most impact on children's achievements in school is to lead on a collaborative classroom and school-based enquiry into how to improve pupils' learning. Doing this had more effect than the next three actions combined.

In Japan, key educational policies such as the national curriculum are based on what thousands of lesson studies conducted by teachers across the country and collected by university education departments are saying about how children are learning. This national cycle of renewal is repeated every five years.

AN EXCITING FUTURE FOR REFLECTIVE PRACTICE AND JOINT PROFESSIONAL DEVELOPMENT (JPD)

We have described in this chapter examples of such enquiry which, if used regularly, help teachers to build their professional knowledge of their pupils, of learning and of how their teaching affects this. We have looked in particular at the 'case' of 'lesson study' as a form of teacher professional learning that is time-honoured and which harnesses important features of many of these other enquiry models into one highly effective, replicable approach, which is the way practitioners in Japan develop teaching throughout their careers. Japan is surely a 'case' in point, as a country whose educational outcomes have consistently been amongst the strongest in the world – a fact that many in Japan and globally attribute to the widespread pursuit of lesson study and reflective practice.

Thus, we strongly hope that you will commit to and engage in reflective practice as you develop as a practitioner or teacher and pass on what you learn as you go to your fellow professionals and to the profession as a whole, ensuring that your day-to-day trial and error in the classroom is as well informed as it can be, and that the outcomes of your regular, deliberate, reflective 'trial and error' enquiries and lesson studies are conveyed to your colleagues and fellow professionals through your case studies, lesson studies, coaching of colleagues and leadership, engaging others in lesson study and deliberate enquiry throughout your career.

companion website

To access additional online resources please visit: **https://study.sagepub.com/wyseandrogers**

Here you will find Bernadette Duffy's group activity for trainee teachers, free access to SAGE journal articles and links to external sources.

further reading

Dudley, P. (2014) *Lesson Study: A handbook for teachers and practitioners*. Early Years Edition, ed. J. Lang, accessed 22 August 2015 at: http://lessonstudy.co.uk/wp-content/uploads/2014/01/new-handbook-early-years-edition2014-version.pdf

Mercer, N. (2000). *Words and Minds: How we use language to think together*. London: Routledge.

Nutbrown, C. and Carter, C. (2013) The Tools of Assessment: Watching and Learning. In G. Pugh and B. Duffy (eds) *Contemporary Issues in the Early Years*. London: Sage.

Rousseau, J. (1979) *Emile, or 'On Education'* (trans. A. Bloom). New York: Basic Books.

Schön, D. (1983) *The Reflective Practitioner: How professionals think in action*. New York: Basic Books.

Sylva, K., Melhuish, E., Sammons, P., Siraj-Blatchford, I. and Taggart, B. (2010) *Early Childhood Matters: Evidence from the Effective Pre-school and Primary Education Project*. Oxford: Routledge.

Sylva, K., Roy, C. and Painter, M. (1980) Childwatching at playgroup and nursery school. *Oxford Preschool Research Project*, Vol. 2. Ypsilanti, MI: High/Scope Press.

Watkins, C. (2003) *Learning: A sense maker's guide*. London: Association of Teachers and Lecturers.

REFERENCES

Alexander, R. (2005) *Towards dialogic learning*. Cambridge: Dialogos.

Alexander, R. (2000) Improving Oracy and Classroom Talk in English Schools: Achievements and Challenges, accessed 26 March 2016 at: http://www.robinalexander.org.uk/wp-content/uploads/2012/06/DfE-oracy-120220-Alexander-FINAL.pdf

Cajkler, W. and Wood, P. (2015) Lesson Study and Initial Teacher Training. In P. Dudley (ed.) *Lesson Study: Professional learning for our time*. London: Routledge, pp. 87–114.

Carr, W. and Kemmis, S. (1986) *Becoming Critical: Education, Knowledge and Action Research*. London: Taylor and Francis.

Coe, R. (2014) Classroom observation: it's harder than you think. CEM, University of Durham, accessed 22 August 2015 at: www.cem.org/blog/414/

Cooper, P. and McIntyre, D. (1996) *Effective Teaching and Learning: Teachers and students' perspectives*. Maidenhead: Open University Press.

Cordingley, P., Bell, M., Rundell, B., Evans, D., and Curtis, A. (2004) *How do collaborative and sustained CPD and sustained but not collaborative CPD affect teaching and learning?* London: EPPI-Centre, Institute of Education.

DfE (2010) The *Importance of Teaching: the schools white paper*. Department for Education.

Dudley, P. (2011) *Lesson study: a handbook* accessed 25 March 2016 at: http://lessonstudy.co.uk/wp-content/uploads/2012/03/Lesson_Study_Handbook_-_011011-1.pdf

Dudley, P. (2013) Teacher learning in Lesson Study: What interaction-level discourse analysis revealed about how teachers utilised imagination, tacit knowledge of teaching and fresh evidence of pupils learning, to develop practice knowledge and so enhance their pupils' learning. *Teaching and Teacher Education*, 34: 107–21.

Dudley, P. (ed.) (2015) *Lesson Study: Professional learning for our time*. London: Routledge.

Dudley, P. (2014) *Lesson Study: A handbook for teachers and practitioners*. Early Years Edition, ed. J. Lang, accessed 22 August 2015 at: http://lessonstudy.co.uk/wp-content/uploads/2014/01/new-handbook-early-years-edition2014-version.pdf

Elliott, J. (1988) Educational research and outsider–insider relations. *International Journal of Qualitative Studies in Education*, 1(2): 155–166.

Elliott, J. (2009) Lesson and Learning Study: a globalizing form of teacher research. Paper presented at the British Educational Research Association Annual Conference, University of Manchester, 2–5 September 2009.

Eraut, M. (2000) Non-formal learning and tacit knowledge in professional work. *British Journal of Educational Psychology*, 70(1): 113–36.

Glaser, B. and Strauss, A. (1967) *Discovery of Grounded Theory: Strategies for qualitative research*. New York: Sociology Press.

Hattie, J. (2009) *Visible Learning: A synthesis of over 800 meta-analyses relating to achievement*. London: Routledge.

Hargreaves, D. (2012) *Towards a self improving school system*. National College for School Leadership.

Haynes, L., Service, O., Goldacre, B. and Torgerson, D. (2012) *Test, Learn, Adapt: Developing public policy with randomised control trials*. London: Cabinet Office.

Harms, T., Clifford, R.M. and Cryer, D. (2014) *Early Childhood Environment Rating Scales*, 3rd edition (ECERS-3). New York: Teachers College Press.

Howard-Jones, P. (2011) Neuroscience and Education: Issues and opportunities – a commentary by the Teaching and Learning Research Programme, accessed 20 August 2015 at: www.tlrp.org/pub/documents/Neuroscience%20Commentary%20FINAL.pdf

Isaacs, S. (1929) *The Nursery Years*. London: Routledge & Kegan Paul.

Kazemi, E., and Hubbard, A. (2008) New directions for the design of professional development: attending to the coevolution of teachers' participation across contexts. *Journal of Teacher Education*, 59(5): 428–441.

Kuno, H. (2015) Evolving the curriculum through lesson study in Japan. In P. Dudley (ed.) *Lesson Study: Professional learning for our time*. London: Routledge, pp. 128–44.

Lather, P. (1986) Issues of validity in openly ideological research: between a rock and a soft place. *Interchange*, 17 (4): 63–84. Reprinted in Yvonna Lincoln and Norman Denzin, eds. *Turning Points in Qualitative Research*. Rowman and Littlefield, 2003, 185–215.

Lewis, C. (1998). A lesson is like a swiftly flowing river: how research lessons improve Japanese education. *American Educator*, (Winter), 12–17 & 50–51.

Mercer, N. (2000) *Words and Minds: How we use language to think together*. London: Routledge.

Nutbrown, C. and Carter, C. (2013) The tools of assessment: watching and learning. In G. Pugh and B. Duffy (eds) *Contemporary Issues in the Early Years*. London: Sage.

Plato (2005) *Early Socratic Dialogues*. London: Penguin Classics.

Resnick, L. (1987) *Education and Learning Think*. Committee on Mathematics, Science and Technology Education, Commission on Behavioral and Social Sciences and Education: National Research Council.

Rousseau, J. ([1762] 1979) *Emile, or 'On Education'* (trans. A. Bloom). New York: Basic Books.

Robinson, V., Hohepa, M., and Lloyd, C. (2009) *School leadership and student outcomes: identifying what works and why best evidence synthesis*. Auckland: New Zealand Ministry of Education.

Sahlberg, P. (2012) *Finnish Lessons: What can the world learn from educational change in Finland?* New York and London: Teachers College Press.

Schön, D. (1983) *The Reflective Practitioner: How professionals think in action*. New York: Basic Books.

Stenhouse, L. (1975) *An Introduction to Curriculum Research and Development*. London: Heinemann.

Stenhouse, L. (1981) What counts as research? *British Journal of Educational Studies*, 29(2): 103–13.

Sylva, K., Melhuish, E., Sammons, P., Siraj-Blatchford, I. and Taggart, B. (2010) *Early Childhood Matters: Evidence from the Effective Pre-school and Primary Education Project*. Oxford: Routledge.

Watkins, C. (2003) *Learning: A sense maker's guide*. London: Association of Teachers and Lecturers.

Wells, G. (1999) *Dialogic Inquiry: Towards a sociocultural practice in theory of education*. Cambridge: Cambridge University Press.

Wragg, E. C., Wikely, F., Wragg, E. and Haynes, G. (1996) *Teacher Appraisal Observed*. London: Routledge.

INDEX